The Disciplinary Frame

The Disciplinary Frame

Photographic Truths and the Capture of Meaning

John Tagg

University of Minnesota Press
Minneapolis • London

The Introduction was first published in *Crossings: A Counter-Disciplinary Journal of Philosophical, Cultural, Historical, and Literary Studies* 3 (1999): 187–212. A shorter version of chapter 3 appeared as "Melancholy Realism: Walker Evans's Resistance to Meaning," *Narrative: The Journal of the Society for the Study of Narrative Literature* 11, no. 1 (January 2003): 3–77. An earlier form of chapter 5 was first published in translation as "Der Zeichenstift der Geschichte," *Fotogeschichte* 49 (Marburg: Jonas Verlag, 1993), 27–42 (translated by Sebastian Wohlfeil); it was published in English in *Fugitive Images: From Photography to Video*, ed. Patrice Petro (Bloomington and Indianapolis: Indiana University Press, 1995), 285–303. A version of chapter 6 was first published in *Art History* 15, no. 3 (September 1992): 72–94.

The poetry of the book's epigraph was originally published in Hugh MacDiarmid, *Complete Poems* (Manchester: Carcanet Press, 1993). Reprinted courtesy of Carcanet Press Limited.

Published by the University of Minnesota Press
111 Third Avenue South, Suite 290
Minneapolis, MN 55401-2520
http://www.upress.umn.edu

Library of Congress Cataloging-in-Publication Data

Tagg, John.
  The disciplinary frame : photographic truths and the capture of meaning / John Tagg.
    p. cm.
  Includes bibliographical references and index.
  ISBN 978-0-8166-4287-8 (hc : alk. paper) — ISBN 978-0-8166-4288-5 (pb : alk. paper)
  1. Photography—Philosophy. 2. Photography—History. I. Title.

  TR183.T344 2009
  779—dc22

                                                              2008039551

The University of Minnesota is an equal-opportunity educator and employer.

For Bill Tagg

The sunlicht still on me, you row'd in clood,
We look upon each ither noo like hills
Across a valley. I'm nae mair your son.
It is my mind, nae son o' yours, that looks,
And the great darkness o' your death comes up
And equals it across the way.
A livin' man upon a deid man thinks
And ony sma'er thocht's impossible.

—HUGH MACDIARMID

Contents

Illustrations

Preface

I see now, having finished this book, that, by at least one count, I have failed again—failed, that is, to produce a systematic or even integrated work. What I have written continually stops and starts again, moving off at a series of tangents on paths that might well have been pursued on their own and now might well be followed independently or out of order. Yet each of these tangents touches the space of the photographic at a glance, at a particular point, and it is at these particular points that we find ourselves engaged with the contingency and the historicity of all attempts to give photography a discursive fixity. If the scattered encounters gathered in this book fall far short of a systematic account or even a continuous narrative, I therefore accept the failure. This falling short has something purposive to say about the photographic field, just as it has something to say about problems of method. Caught in an uncertain space between the institutional monoliths of historical science and literary criticism, the concomitant advantage for the homeless offspring of art history and cultural studies is that they are free to ask again what it might mean to answer the prevailing demand to historicize and whether it is possible to find ways to work in the breach that has opened between historicity and history.

There is, even so, a kind of continuity of interest in evidence across the chapters that follow. It turns on the varied and often incompatible ways in which photographic technologies have been claimed and deployed and the ways in which the meanings of photographs have been framed and adjudicated. From the earliest pronouncements of François Arago and William Henry Fox Talbot, photographs have been attributed a remarkable status as evidence and proof. Yet this force of meaning, which has been so important to certain processes of power, has been hard to institute and secure. What makes the issue even more compelling is that the institutionalized function of the photograph as a privileged form of evidence and record has been pivotal historically not only for certain disciplinary apparatuses and agencies of social governance but also for the discipline of history itself. This complicates and perhaps undermines the task of historical writing, whose protocols of evidence and argument are also shown to turn on a kind of violence: the violence of meaning.

This is the brief of the present book and the risk it runs. The fact that it has been possible to complete it is owed, in the first place, to four people: Annabel Wharton, without whom it would not have been begun; Betty Friedlander and Grazia Tonelli, without whom it would not have been continued; and Lily Tagg, without whom there would have been no joy in finishing it. The book hardly pays the debt. And books take time to write, and time accumulates more debts. Others know this too and, without listing all their names and thus risking omissions, I can only thank those who have been more patient than the final work deserves. I must, however, name those with the University of Minnesota Press whose generous support and considerable efforts have seen this book through to its finished state: Adam Brunner, Kathy Delfosse, and Richard Morrison.

The book started life as a series of Benenson Lectures at Duke University, given at the invitation of the Department of Art and Art History. The earliest material was written while I was Ailsa Mellon Bruce Senior Fellow at the Center for Advanced Study in the Visual Arts at the National Gallery of Art in Washington, D.C. Further chapters were begun or completed during periods as a fellow of the Society for the Humanities at Cornell University and as a Clark Fellow at the Sterling and Francine Clark Art Institute in Williamstown, Massachusetts. My thanks go to the administrative and library staffs of all three centers, to all those who were fellows at the same time, and, especially, to Hank Millon, Dominick LaCapra, and Michael Ann Holly for the extraordinary collegiality fostered under their tutelage at their respective institutions. I could not have enjoyed any of these periods of extended leave without matching support from successive deans of Harpur College and from Binghamton University. I am grateful that, despite the relentless political assault on its funding base during the period I have been writing this book, this public institution somehow still refuses to be a "university in ruins."

The Violence of Meaning

It would seem there is something futile about writing about photographs, about saying what is there to be seen.

In Winfried Georg Sebald's scrupulous and disarming work *The Emigrants*, photographs appear on the pages here and there, matter-of-factly and without attribution.[1] It is unusual, perhaps, to find photographs in what one might have taken for a novel, at least since the brief rise and fall of the photographic book at the turn of the 1930s and '40s. But the photographs in Sebald's text evoke no surprise.

Someone's father is said to have driven a Dürkopp in the twenties, and we see a photograph of a car with four passengers on a cobbled street. There is an elementary school outing "to the conduit house above Hofen and the powder magazine where the Veterans' Association kept their ceremonial canon, on the hill where the stations of the cross led up to the Calvary Chapel"[2]—and there is a church spire rising from the jostling heads of little boys. We are told that the photograph that follows in the text was taken in the Bronx in March 1939: a family dinner showing relatives who had emigrated from Germany during the Weimar years. A photograph is mentioned that resembles another, clipped earlier from a Swiss magazine, and then one or other of these appears in a break between paragraphs. The pilot of a launch generously allows the narrator to take her picture, and a figure is shown in a photograph, dressed like the woman described in the text. On a walk along a New Jersey beach, Uncle Kasimir pulls out his camera and takes "this" picture of the narrator, a print of which he sends two years later, along with his gold pocket watch. On a trip to Jerusalem in 1913, Uncle Adelwarth poses in what we are told is "Arab costume,"[3] while, in Constantinople, his traveling companion secures a photographic souvenir of a dervish boy aged about twelve. And there they are—the photographs I mean. A character remembers a photograph taken by his father almost thirty years before, and he himself has a photo he took of his father on the Brauneck, newly returned from Dachau, "one of the few that have survived from those years."[4] The photographs are there, sure enough. Nothing to remark on here. Except that, as the pain of memory rises, the unaffected prose turns chilled like the stone of a monument, and a thin film passes across the images like the ghost of Vladimir Nabokov, trying to catch something in his net.

We are shown other images, too: an automatic tea-making machine; a neglected garden; a Manchester canal; derelict housing in the Hulme Estate; some indecipherable structures said to be salt-frames; a three-storied, turreted villa; the locked gates of the Jewish cemetery in Bad Kissingen. We do not know where they have come from, though, in the narrative itself, photographs keep turning up, casually yet somberly: a slide show of a trip to Crete; an album of photographs put before the storyteller, with notes in a dead man's hand; another album that had belonged to the writer's mother, come by at a propitious moment; yet another leafed through at the table, after tea with Aunt Fini. A collection of postcards carefully mounted by Uncle Adelwarth is fetched from a bedroom drawer. A framed photograph is taken down from the wall to be looked at for what may be the first time in forty years. Photographs are handled. Memories come back, like the return of a body caught in a glacier seven decades before and unexpectedly released from the ice.

Then comes a photograph that is declared to be a forgery: a newspaper clipping, tracked down in an archive, of the book-burning in Würzburg in 1933, the picture of which must have been contrived from some other gathering since the book-burning took place on the evening of May 10 when it was already dark. The suspicion is aroused that "so too everything else has been a fake, from the very start."[5] We are not sure how widely these words should be taken to apply. Other images follow until, at the last, we come to photographs by a bookkeeper named Genewein of the ghetto established in 1940 in the Polish city of Lodz. The

I often come out here, said Uncle Kasimir, it makes me feel that I am a long way away, though I never quite know from where. Then he took a camera out of his large-check jacket and took this picture, a print of which he sent me two years later, probably when he had finally shot the whole film, together with his gold pocket watch.

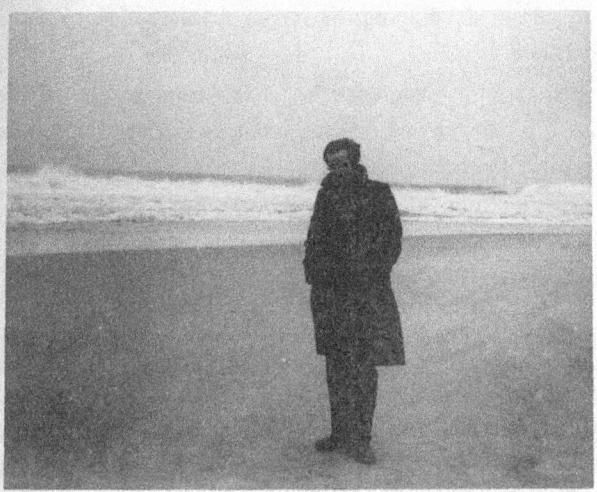

Aunt Fini was sitting in her armchair in the dark living room when I went in to her that evening. Only the glow of the street lights was on her face. The aches have eased off, she said, the pain is almost over. At first I thought I was only imagining that it was getting better, so slow was the improvement. And once I was almost without pain, I thought: if you move now, it'll start again. So I just stayed sitting here. I've been sitting here all afternoon. I couldn't say whether I mightn't have nodded off now and then. I think I was lost

Figure 1. Page from *The Emigrants,* by W. G. Sebald, trans. Michael Hulse (New York: New Directions Books, 1997). Copyright 1992 by Vito von Eichborn GmbH & Co Verlag KG; copyright 1999 by the Harvill Press. Reprinted by permission from New Directions Publishing Corporation.

photographs are, in fact, only recalled from an exhibition in Frankfurt the year before and are envisioned now projected onto flats, "which in truth did not exist,"[6] on an infinitely deep stage. In the specific image that comes to mind, there are three women:

> The light falls on them from the window in the background, so I cannot make out their eyes clearly, but I sense that all three of them are looking across at me, since I am standing on the very spot where Genewein the accountant stood with his camera. The young woman in the middle is blonde and has the air of a bride about her. The weaver to her left has inclined her head a little to one side, whilst the woman on the right is looking at me with so steady and relentless a gaze that I cannot meet it for long. I wonder what the three women's names were—Roza, Luisa and Lea, or Nona, Decuma and Morta, the daughters of the night, with spindle, scissors and thread.[7]

These are the last words in what seems to be Sebald's text, and the photograph in question does not appear. Over the page, however, there is a final image with the title "Photograph of the author by Jan Peter Tripp."[8] We have no reason to doubt it. We may make of it what we will, whatever we can bear, at the point where this imaginary is about to pass from us and is at its end. There is nothing left but seven blank pages and the final cover, on which we may read what critics have written. In one citation, Sebald's book is described as "an archive of family photos, a documentary record of German Jewish life from the late 19th Century to the late 20th."[9] This certainly throws light on the photographs. But, as Sebald writes, "There is a mist that no eye can dispel."[10]

It is not clear that Sebald writes about the photographs that appear in the pages of his book. And it is not clear that the photographs that appear are about what his writing describes. Yet is it not because these things are unclear that Sebald's "unclassifiable" book has filled its readers with the sense of being moved by something that cannot be documented, something that has remained hitherto unsayable, something that has resisted coming to light? Could it have been otherwise for the book to give witness to the unforgettable forgotten that declines to enter the tribunal of history but has not vanished into the grave?

Few have shared Sebald's scruples. His book has few companions. For the rest, meaning must be arrived at. Truth must be told. Photographs and writing must be dependable instruments. They must communicate. They must be made to do so. Though this would seem to entail that there would be something futile and something excessive about writing about photographs, about saying what is there to be seen, few have been deterred. The stakes are too high. Meaning might escape us. Repetition of what is said to be already evident is compelled. Nothing can be left unattached. The photograph must be spoken for. It must be clearly kept in place.

Now, we do indeed have something excessive and futile and all the more violent for that. And so, from Sebald's almost unbearable restraint, it is to this violence of meaning we must move.

This work is concerned with disciplinarity and discourse; that is, it is haunted by the kind of violence that surrounds the event of meaning and arrests dispute. "You have the floor, explain yourself, you are free," says Honoré Daumier's judge, leaning his thick, bare, butcher's arms on the bench and smiling down at the gagged defendant, pinned from behind by gloating learned counsel. This is the event of meaning as staged by the juridical apparatus of the State. Oh, of course, it is unjust—Daumier's graphic rendering, I mean—"hateful and poisonous," as Champfleury said, a slur on "Law, majority, force, Government."[11] It is a travesty of justice and loathing is legible in every line. Yet justice is *the issue* here, the justice of "Law, majority, force, Government," and in the midst of this abattoir of legality we see something else, other than the blood and the block and the axe. We see that for all the Justice's binding power to cut off speech, the judicial hearing will not be content with silence in court. The hearing is a summons to speech. It demands meaning. It hoards meaning. It is open to every submission and a submission it will have, up to and until the final sentence.

This is the law's charge. It is marked not merely in what Walter Benjamin has called the "law-preserving," "administrative" violence that services every court, but above all in what he calls the instigative, "lawmaking," "executive" force that violently lays down the very space of juridical reason before which we are called, to repeat its oaths, conform

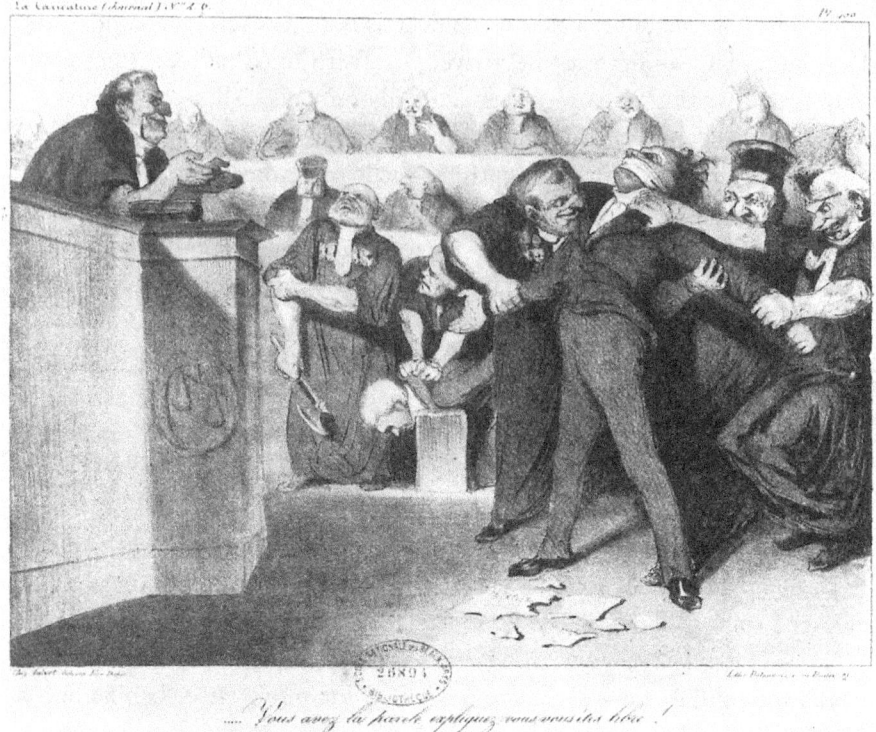

Figure 2. Honoré Daumier, "Vous avez la parole, expliquez-vous, vous êtes libre!" *La caricature*, no. 216, May 14, 1835.

to its idiom, and fall under its authority, or else be in violation.[12] But there is no tribunal before which we may appeal *this* violence. It does not confront us with an abuse of power that can be exposed and denounced. It is the threshold of the authority of the law itself, the authority that calls us to speak up and be free.

Downstairs, in the cells or perhaps in the iron-fenced courtyard, Inspector Byrnes is making a photograph. We already know the scene well, from Sir Luke Fildes and others: Seven burly screws and rozzers hold "the bashful model" down while they carry out the requirements of Parliament's 1870 Prisons Act or some such edict.[13] Of course, it is another joke, one that has survived repeated telling; an old joke, even if it is one you could not tell to Rodney King. But the punch line turns, again, on a submission and on evidence: on the violence of the encounter with the camera and on the troubling status of the new economy of photographic meanings that is not held in place without a struggle and a nervous laugh. What else is held in place is, more obviously perhaps, the "unwilling subject," for whom the making of a likeness is also an unlikely investiture: a ritual induction under the law; an endowment with a status that will bring with it its own mandates and assignments— name, rank, and number; a ceremony of investment, clothing the body with meaning, tailoring what the individual may become, investing the subject, and, in turn, drawing interest as the subject commits itself to what it must be. But this is only one of many such scenes in which, as Jacques Lacan says, we are "photo-graphed."[14] And, as we know, the "health" of society and the "health" of its members hang on the efficacy of such performances.

Again, it is not just a matter of unnecessary or excessive violence, the actions of "a few bad apples," as British chief constables like to say. Here, in this everyday scuffle, as criminality is brought to boot by the

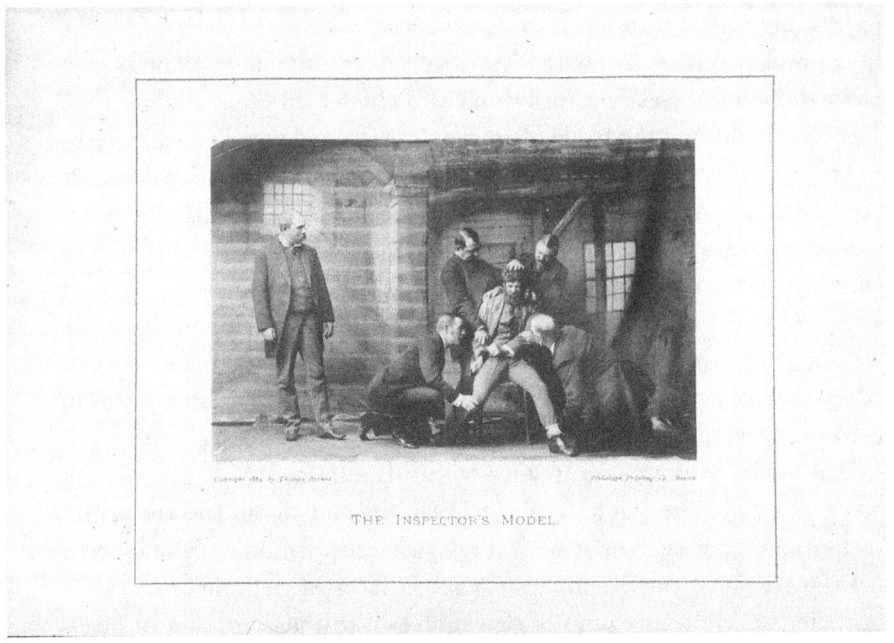

THE INSPECTOR'S MODEL.

Figure 3. Thomas Byrnes, "The Inspector's Model," from *Professional Criminals of America* (New York, 1885), between pages 52 and 53.

police, the separation of law-making and law-preserving violence is, as Benjamin himself concedes, suspended and surpassed. The police force does not just "administer" the requirements of the law. The police force embodies the force of law, the violence of whose legitimacy institutes the legitimizing violence of law enforcement. Thus, if these little scenes may be taken, in Jacques Derrida's phrase, as singularly exemplary,[15] it is not because they unveil a spectacle of coercion that usurps legal justice. It is rather because they draw out the foundational violence of the *subpoena* to appear before the law and before the camera that marks the very instance in which what *is* before the institution of the law and of photography is, *perforce*, excluded as "out of order." What engages me then is not that law and photography are duly *exposed* as the docile instruments of an exterior power but, on the contrary, that, in the performative force that animates these spectacles, the language of law and the language of photography are violently instated and, in the same instant, *instrumentalized*, cut to size and imposed as a uniform code, a universal contractual language, a means of communication that expels the remainder, yet whose mastery is always ruled out of court.[16]

So I am concerned with a violence that is brutal enough in its own way, though it leaves its imprint on the body in a different manner than fists and boots and the blade of an axe. It is the violence of an apparatus whose plurality of prohibitions, codifications, and performative demands constitutes a discursive regime whose never fully functionalized productivity is always in tension with the boundaries and limits that ensure meaning properly arrives for the subjects who are also held in place. It is a violence that acts in and across the bodies, spaces, and machines that make up the instructive tableaux with which we have begun to produce the discursive event, not only by marking it out, pinning it down, or cutting it to size but, above all, by calling it into place and exposing it, while making sure it stays within the frame. With due regard, then, to Michel Foucault's desire to keep the courtroom and the police cells of our opening scenes apart, I take what happens in each as a model of the action of the disciplines: What surfaces in the murky world of policing and in the regime of sense integral to the operation of disciplinary power also infests those other disciplines—art history securely among them—whose grasping of meaning and pasting in place of the

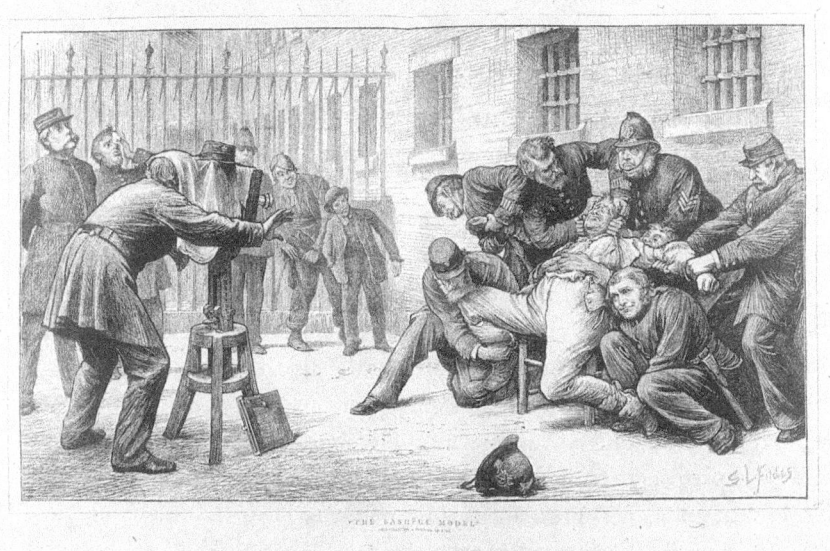

Figure 4. Sir Luke Fildes, "'The Bashful Model': Photographing a Prisoner in Gaol," *Graphic* 8, no. 206 (November 8, 1873), 440–41.

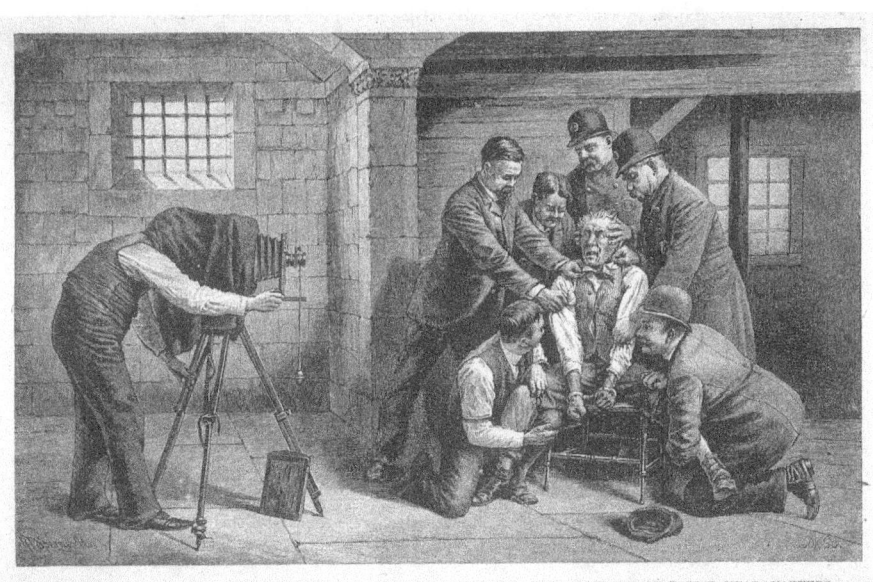

Figure 5. "An Unwilling Subject.—Photographing a Prisoner for the Rogue's Gallery at Police Headquarters," from Thomas Byrnes, Helen C. Campbell, and Thomas W. Knox, *Darkness and Daylight, or Lights and Shadows of New York Life* (Hartford, Conn.: Hartford Publishing Co., 1899).

image depend on setting in motion the entire disciplinary apparatus of cell, surveillance, document, record, case, caption, mount, frame, index, file, and archive.[17]

One might recognize here themes that have already occupied me in two previous published works. In *The Burden of Representation*, I examined the conditions under which the dangerously prolific field of photographic meanings came, in the course of the nineteenth century, to be marked out and segmented, so that a plurality of locally specified, adjacent, but contradictory *photographies* could be institutionalized—each claiming to ground its status on the fundamental character of the medium. It was, however, precisely this term, "the medium," that came under pressure. No longer could it denote an opaque material with the power to generate its own delimiting conventions, any more than it could signify a transparent vehicle—a mediating technology that might impose its own determinations but whose mechanical nature would continue to supply its epistemological guarantees. "The medium" of photography was not given and unified. It was always a local outcome, an effect of a particular closure of the discursive field, a function of a specific *apparatus* or *machine*, in the sense in which Foucault used these terms.[18] The "medium" had to be constituted and it was multiply defined.

Thus, against the notion of a continuous documentary tradition founded on the inherent properties of the camera, I argued that the function of photography as a means of surveillance, record, and evidence was the result of a more or less violent struggle—less comic than the one Inspector Byrnes shows us—to hold in place certain discursive conditions. It depended on a machinery of capture that sought to curtail the productivity of photographic meanings, exhaust their legibility, and make the camera its own, as an instrument of a new disciplinary power. What Roland Barthes called the "evidential force" of the photograph was, therefore,

> a complex historical outcome . . . exercised by photographs only within certain institutional practices and within particular historical relations, the investigation of which will take us far from an aesthetic or phenomenological context. The very idea of what constitutes evidence has

a history . . . a history which implies definite techniques and procedures, concrete institutions, and specific social relations—that is, relations of power.[19]

This was what unfolded as the "burden of representation."[20] But I no doubt should be careful here, for, to my mind, there was always an ambivalence in this title, an ambivalence that seems to have escaped those who have simply assumed that its meaning for me was quite transparent. Whatever the "burden" may be, it is not simply the load or even the charge of an apparatus that falls on some—those others, the powerless and excluded. Nor is it just an obligation or a responsibility, to stand forth, perhaps, and be representative. It is also that which is born of representation, representation's burden, precisely a *meaning*—not baggage that is carried, but the pith or the gist, which is, at the same time, archaically, what drones on in the undersong. So if the phrase counts for anything, then it is for this undecidability, its shifting between imposition and progeny, force and meaning—which is where it interested me to find photography.

It is hard for me, then, even amid the increasing violence of academic competition, to see here what is attributed to me: "a base–superstructure model of power" in which photography has no effectivity of its own but dissolves compliantly into the determining contexts of a surrounding culture whose "historical frames" are thus the true source of photographic meaning. This is a model in which photography exercises no power of its own but is, in the lurid terms of one polemic against me, merely an "instrument," a "vehicle," a "conduit," a "passage" through which those who already have "real power" violently inseminate their conceptions in those who have none—"neatly" paralleling "phallocentrism's figuring of woman as a mere passage between man's body and that of 'his' offspring, as if her materiality is of no account."[21] That is the charge. A discursive formation, however, is not a surrounding context. Nor is a frame. Instrumentalization is not a given, but a specific, unstable discursive effect. To ask for a genealogy of the photograph's "evidential force" is not, therefore, as I tried to make clear in *Grounds of Dispute*, to suggest that "photography" was the transparent reflection of a power outside itself:

It is, rather, to insist that the photograph's compelling weight was never phenomenological, but always discursive, and that the power effects of photographic evidence were *produced* by the articulation of two discursive formations [the apparatus of discipline and the apparatus of photography]. If this is to grant that the photographic always exceeded its colonization, investment and specification in institutional frameworks of use, it is not to concede any intrinsicness of "the medium." It is not to equate a discursive structure with a technology. Nor is it to posit any unity or closure to photography's discursive field. It is precisely in this sense, therefore, that I have denied that photography as such has any identity.[22]

Grounds of Dispute: Art History, Cultural Politics, and the Discursive Field therefore returned to the territory of the theories of discourse that have made it possible to think beyond sociologies of culture and to redescribe the material processes of the production and circulation of meanings and their relation to cultural technologies and to questions of power and resistance. But the book also brought together a number of essays crossing a variety of genres of critical writing and engaging the "New Art History" and the institutional constrictions of art history as a discipline. The point was to bring out that the reworking of the concepts of power and representation could not but invade the practices, protocols, and institutional frames of art history and art criticism, too, even as these "disciplines" were also being overtaken by rapid changes in the cultural economy and the cultural politics of identity. The consequences of this are not, however, solely negative and, in the face of the persistence of sociologies of knowledge and reductive rejections of theory, *Grounds of Dispute* set out to defend a notion of cultural politics founded not on "invoking the force of the literal or the grounding of critique on the terror of the real"[23] but on *dispute*: on the contestability of systems of meaning and their effects of power and subjection; on the work of deconstruction across the space of the institution; and on the necessity of political calculation, strategic choices, and a sharpening of the stakes.

The Disciplinary Frame takes up these themes once more. It looks again at the systems of discursive constraint or "technologies of power" that constitute the status of the document and record and frame the evidentiary value of the image in the varied institutions of what Foucault called "disciplinary knowledge." As we have seen, however, this leads only too predictably down into the network of passages that connect and separate the disciplinary regime of sense and the regime of the disciplines, the technologies of policing and the technologies of history, the archive of surveillance and the archive of scholarship, the rogue's gallery and the museum of art.

My point of departure, in "The One-Eyed Man and the One-Armed Man" (chapter 1), is the resumption of my analysis of instrumental photography. More broadly, I am concerned with the way the assemblage of the State in the nineteenth century, operating as what Gilles Deleuze and Félix Guattari have called an "apparatus of capture," reconstituted itself, reinscribed the social, and expanded its domain. On the one side, the State sought to accomplish this by the colonization and incorporation of the dispersed local techniques that had generated and elaborated the new discursive field of discipline.[24] Such techniques included the development and deployment of new photographic technologies, new forms of writing, and new regimes of representation within a range of supervisory and regulatory apparatuses that extended their jurisdiction into areas of social life never before subject to such interventions. What it is crucial to grasp, however, is that the institutions whose dissemination constituted the disciplinary regime could only operate, insofar as they did, when certain technologies, techniques, practices, and codes of representation had been pulled into place. Integral to the disciplinary apparatus was the production of a specific and novel economy of meaning—a regime of sense that guaranteed a new order of truth and turned on a new structure of documentation whose institutionalized effect was to reverse the political axis of representation, making it no longer a sign of power and prestige to be recorded, but a sign of subjection. It is, then, only within the closure of this discursive frame, integral to the apparatuses of discipline, that we can understand how photography—or *a* photography—could come to function as an instrument of surveillance, record, evidence, and truth.

The effect of this argument, of course, is to disrupt the liberal, reformist story of documentation, documentary, and the benevolent progress of the truth. It is not only that "documentary value" can no longer be anchored in the camera itself and its imagined access to the real, so that there can be no more talk of a continuous documentary tradition arising from the nonmanipulative use of this camera's natural properties. It is also that, if there is a link between documentation and "documentary," it comes not via the pristine camera and its transparency to good intentions but via the institutions, discourses, and systems of power that invest it and sully it, and via the discursive regimen that constitutes the document and holds it in place. Such a link is the trace not of a natural continuity or a seamless tradition but of the uneven history of photography's implication in the purposeful institutionalization of limits to meaning: limits that specify photography's singularity, at the price of multiplying and diversifying it; limits that are drawn only through a process of negotiation and conflict in which—contrary to the claims of the truth machine—nothing is guaranteed in advance.

In the mutation from "document" to "documentary," however, we are not only dealing with a new level of activity of the extended State or, rather, a new momentum within the State, at a particular moment of crisis, toward a supposedly liberal version of corporatism. We are also dealing with a public *cultural strategy* that turns on a new mode of address and capture—a rhetoric of recruitment that, in the words of its theorist, John Grierson, would instill "unity and discipline," "without forgetting the humanitarian virtues";[25] that would give the irrational public "*a pattern of thought and feeling,*"[26] inculcating "civic appreciation, civic faith and civic duty"[27] through the teaching of what Grierson called "that fourth R": "Rooted Belief."[28] The history of "documentary" is therefore the history of a specific practice of representation that has to be located in the cultural strategy of a particular mode of governance: a hybrid of discipline and spectacle, of documentation and publicity; a strategy of management of meaning and identity; a strategy of *social democracy* at a moment of deep structural crisis. It is this cultural strategy that, for all Grierson's claims about the preeminence of the "British Documentary Movement," directs us toward the period of the New Deal in the United States as the paradigmatic historical moment for the official mobilization of documentary practices across the administrative agencies of the liberal, corporate State.

Documentary rhetoric coalesced in the specific conjuncture of a liberal-democratic response to the systemic economic, political, and cultural crises that Herbert Hoover had sought to elide as symptoms of a "depression." In the midst of these crises, a decisive change in the machinery of social consent was compelled upon the liberal-democratic State. It was a change registered in the strategy of social security and social welfare but, equally, in a shift in the role, currency, and mode of address of government communications and documentation. These now began to absorb strategies, techniques, and tropes not only from cultural anthropology but also from the arenas of publicity and commercial entertainment in an effort to articulate a believable public language of truth that would restore the logics of social sense, call out to a cohesive community, and relegitimize the corporate State as its paternal representative. The appeal of documentary, as the appeal of the paternal State, as an appeal to the real and the true, is, at once, a call to order and a call to identification; a call to community, to communion, and to communication; an appeal set in motion by a novel structure of address that incites a delirium of transference and signals a new politics of the imaginary.

The question of documentary is not, then, just a question of "the classic realist text." Documentary strategies and their rhetorics of recruitment have to be mapped into a historically specific field of cultural politics—though that is not to say that this can be done without also tracing the relation of documentary to the longer histories of documentation, record keeping, and discipline; without attempting to unpack overdetermined processes of investment in pictures of misery, the power of horrors, and the pleasures of the paternalistic gaze; or without remarking what escapes, resists, or scores through the limits of the rhetoric of transparency and the regime of documentary truth.

Such a project is, thus, embedded from the start in the historicity of the particular discursive closure that framed the space of "documentary." But this does not mean that it can be counterposed to an engagement with theory. Indeed, it will not be able to begin to delineate this "historicity" unless it engages the complexities of recent theories of language, meaning, subjectivity, power, pleasure, and investment. And this may take it not only to the limits of documentary but also to what within documentary and its demand for realism, in the midst of "depression," marks the trace of an ineradicable remainder, a stumbling block, the real that is the antinomy of all verisimilitude, which Lacan calls "the impossible," which Jean-François Lyotard, like Julia Kristeva, names "The Thing," the unforgettable forgotten that does not lend itself to signification.[29]

So, contrary to the return of one ghost of the social history of art as a specter of archival positivism, "history" is no antidote to "theory." There is no elsewhere to the territory of theory. And this folds back on the enterprise of this work itself. In a sense, the objective of *The Disciplinary Frame* is clearly "historical," in that it sets out to delineate specific discursive formations or regimes of sense. First, as I have said, it looks again at the new technologies and novel economy of meaning integral to the apparatuses of discipline that turned on archives of documentation, that captured the camera, and that held in place a new order of evidence and truth. Second, it tries to distinguish the documentary rhetoric that coalesced in the specific conjuncture of a liberal-democratic response to the economic, political, and cultural crises of the 1930s. But this is where the argument turns, like the twist in a Möbius strip. To propose a "history" of documentation and "documentary" is only, in a pointed sense, to redouble the problem. The formation of history was itself inseparable from the development and institutionalization of a regime of evidence, a technology of truth, and an apparatus of documentation, with its case studies, records, files, and archives. Historical practice, too, as I argue in "The Pencil of History" (chapter 5), only secures the meaning and import of its documents, its notion of the eventhood of the event, and its protocols of evidence within a specific discursive regime and disciplinary machinery. To practice history is to practice a (documentary) discipline, here, in the "liberal democracy" of academe. And if we are going to think about the doleful conjunction of documentation, discipline, democracy, and the State, we shall have to consider what follows from the fact that we have not escaped their regime even, or least of all, here.

Further still, if what we have to confront is a field of institutionalizations across which the powers and pleasures of images have been produced and enforced, how does this square with art history's peculiar scholarly and curatorial role in relation to one privileged part of the discursive field of visual culture? Does the conception of the "politics of representation" fold back over the practices of art history, too? Do questions about regimes of power and pleasure and closures of visual meaning implicate the pristinely white expanses of the discursive space of art history? Is art history's very conception of the givenness of its object of study—its confident distinction of internal and external, text and context, image and ground, art and history—not in itself a function of the apparatus that constitutes the discursive frame and the mechanisms of capture of its disciplinary knowledge? These are the questions I ask in chapter 6, "A Discourse with Shape of Reason Missing," which, like "The Pencil of History," marks the threshold at which the investigation has to double back on the art historical enterprise itself, unsettling its truth, disturbing its pleasure and power, troubling its institutions, and "striking against the frame"—another elusive phrase, though perhaps it does not entirely preclude what one commentator read in it: a call for industrial action.[30]

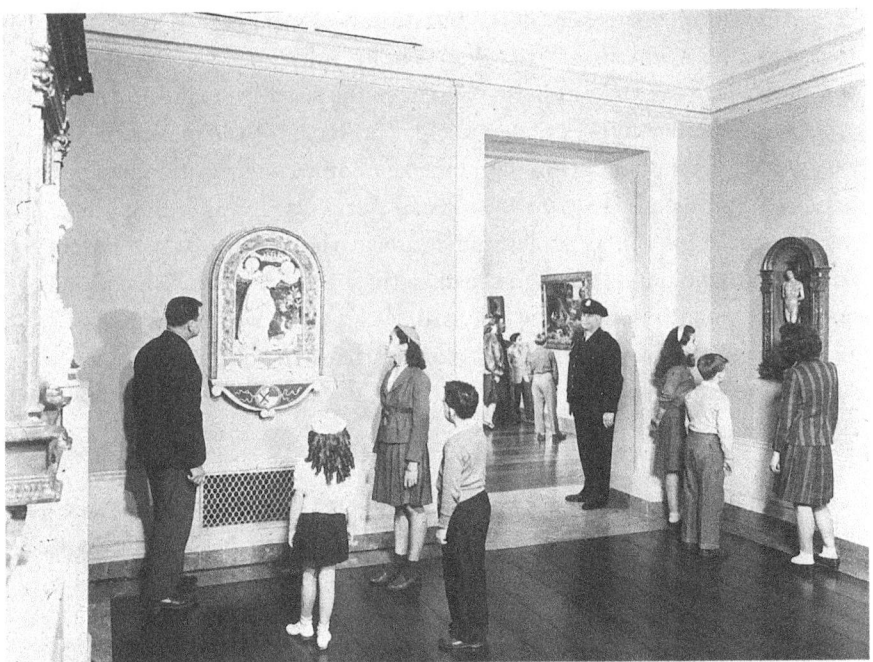

Figure 6. Visitors to the National Gallery of Art in Washington, D.C., 1947. Gallery Archives, National Gallery of Art, Washington, D.C.

We are squarely back with the rigid machineries that hold visible meaning in place. From the charge room to the gallery—there would seem to be little reason here for joy, of a Nietzschean or any other variety. And, indeed, on most days, I confess I can see in these varied mutual productions of power and meaning that capture the image only the mundane, repeated, everyday violence of the disciplinary frame as it adjudicates whether a meaning has arrived, where it ends, and what its point may be.[31] On better days, I take some pleasure in the endless failure, the falling-short, the self-defeating overobtrusiveness of the frame, for which, one might say, the picture is always too little or too large—obdurately saying less than is wanted and more than is wished. Photographs themselves, despite the pasting they receive, conduce to a similar bulimia. They bloat and starve: Against the *ecstasy* of realism is set the *poverty* of photography, always disappointing, nothing but stains; against the *probity* of realism is set photographic *excess*, always indiscriminate, always opening to chance at every stage of its processes, always out of control in its reproductive drive.

Yet if a *gap* opens here in the institution of meaning—a gap that is rent at the very center of the book, not at its outer ends—it is not a gap through which we may hope to see enter the usual figurings of resistance: the familiar figures of agency, the presence of the others of history or of a countertradition, let alone the embodiments of a teleology of negation driven by its own "historical" necessity. But is it disappointing if what steps out is something more in the shape of the Harlem zoot-suiter who bursts through the didactic "historical materialism" and documentary immiseration of Richard Wright's and Edwin Rosskam's *12 Million Black Voices*? Something more in the shape of the trio of zoot-suiters who click along the subway platform in Ralph Ellison's great novel *Invisible Man*:

> Men out of time, who would soon be gone and forgotten. . . . The stewards of something uncomfortable, burdensome, which they hated because, living outside the realm of history, there was no one to applaud their value and they themselves failed to understand it.[32]

"Running and Dodging," "rollin' and tumblin'"—this is what I make in chapter 4 of those local events of resistance that are not "in the name of" some other center, some other positivity, some repressed or excluded category that must return to found a new community, a community that will only bring with it its own exclusions and terror. The sporadic events of resistance that interest me are not "in the name of" power's supposed *other side*. They are, rather, events that make a space only in a specific conjuncture—here, at the point of disintegration of New Deal documentarism and the dominant frame of the cultural politics of transparency, even amid a nationalist mobilization for war, but before the cold hierarchies of corporate modernism have sprung up on every strategic empty block. I am using, I know, the crudest of short-hands here, but I want to foreclose the notion that, in this past moment, in this disruptive interregnum, I am looking for a paradigm of practice now. Something slipped in 1943. But the frame is adaptive, repairable, exchangeable, and we find ourselves hanging on it again. A Farm Security Administration photograph by Jack Delano of wartime women steelworkers reappears forty years later in an advertisement for "authentic" Gap jeans. Over fifty years, the zoot suit is updated, theatricalized, hung as a museum piece, and, as here, made the object of scholarly debate. Seemingly without relief, the frame casts a long shadow—and we are in it. It is not so easy to step out.

Ask the fallen heroes of modernism, if that is what they are. Chapter 3, "Melancholy Realism," ponders the nature of Walker Evans's refusals and repudiations in the mid-1930s, tracking one hard-to-read photograph of a street in Atlanta, Georgia, from file to book to museum, in an effort to gauge Evans's complex relation to the space of documentary and to assess the repeated critical readings of his work that have conflated his project with that of James Agee and have therefore seen his photographs as a limited text of the documentary "genre." Whether Evans works on the border, whether he withdraws to a cryptic melancholic space of the interior from which the present is possessable if only in displacement as the past, or whether he encloses photography in another frame are questions that plunge us back into cultural politics and the discursive field. But here, too, there waits a lure and a trap—one that is likely to be sprung on any attempt to adjudicate Evans's choices from the secure and comfortable space of the academic frame. The judgment seat of photography calls again: "You have the walls, explain yourself, you are free." The violence of the sentence is caught in the throat of art history itself. But, then again, Daumier was no more sparing of art critics than he was of judges and lawyers.

It is as well to put ourselves in the picture, especially in a work that wants to stress all that must be in place before we arrive where a certain art history would have us: *before the work*. But "before the work" is also the space of the prefatory introduction, in which it would be bad faith not to remark the undisplaceable problems of framing a work that purports to deal with the violence of the frame. The place of such remarks is part of the problem, as Agee encountered in the structure of *Let Us Now Praise Famous Men*, punctuated as it is by sessions that hover "On the Porch," by an "Intermission," and by an open, hanging "Colon."[33] But the problem is not only one of place, edge, the vestibule, the porch, the space of the supplement, and the other side of the colon. There is also the question of violence and its consequences.

Having made the stake the violence of meaning, how can I avoid reinscribing that violence here? As Alain Robbe-Grillet has written of Barthes's inaugural lecture at the Collège de France, having provoked his audience with the statement that all speech is fascist, Barthes could only go on with "a disturbing demonstration of a discourse that was not a discourse: one that destroyed in and of itself, step by step, any temptation to dogmatism." Some accused Barthes of saying nothing, of negating everything he had said. The price of declining dogmatism was, for them, too high; for what is dogmatism, Robbe-Grillet adds, "but the serene discourse of truth (complacent, solid, unequivocal)"?[34] Unequivocal, solid, grounded, squarely in place, the finality of meaning arrives. In the name of averting another terror—terror of the obduracy and unpredictability of the event of meaning, of what Foucault calls its "ponderous, awesome materiality"—in terror of "the incessant, disorderly buzzing of discourse," of "everything that could possibly be violent, discontinuous, querulous, disordered even and perilous,"[35] the guillotine falls on endless dispute. In the name of the terror of the real, there must be a cut. The guillotine must fall. The disciplines demand it. Daumier, like Karl Marx, was right: The rallying cry of the Party of Order has ever been "*Rather an end with terror than terror without an end.*"[36] Meaning must arrive. It is just violence.

CHAPTER 1

The One-Eyed Man and the One-Armed Man: Camera, Culture, and the State

> The State apparatus is thus animated by a curious rhythm, which is first of all a great mystery: that of the Binder-Gods or magic emperors, One-Eyed men emitting from their single eye signs that capture, tie knots at a distance. The jurist-kings, on the other hand, are One-Armed men who raise their single arm as an element of right and technology, the law and the tool.
>
> —GILLES DELEUZE and FÉLIX GUATTARI, *A Thousand Plateaus*

There is a dark room. A shutter opens. The room is flooded with light that threatens to bleach the interior white. Instead, it leaves a carefully patterned tracery on one wall, because, in entering the room in the only way it can, this light has been tempered, corralled, and organized, transposed from a flaring effulgence into a predictable series of rays, gathered and strung like wires or threads from the single aperture that opens to the outside. Across the darkness, the fall of light is thus graphed by the grid built into the window of the converging lens and the geometry of the walls whose rectangulate architecture orchestrates the relation of the central opening to the focal plane and to the frame marked by the boundaries of that plane's flat surface. This carefully constructed room has an old name. It is a camera. A room, but a room with a purpose: the training of light, graphing it—quite literally, *photo-graphing*, subjecting light to the punctual rule of the room's inbuilt geometrical law. The camera is, then, a place to isolate and discipline light, like a room in Jeremy Bentham's Panopticon. And, like that room in the Panopticon, the cell of the camera has its utility both as a training machine and as a device for producing and preserving text.

This text appears first where light becomes substance, as a stain in the dirt on the wall—a stain on the wall's surface without yet the power to impose distance and division. This stain, however, is already a graph that projects its cryptic structure into the eye that beholds it, capturing the palpitating organ in its depths and incarcerating it in an architecture of separation that leaves the eye hanging on an object now possessed and lost—so near and so far. Something therefore happens in this making of the photo-graph that cannot be reduced to mechanical transcription or to the workings of a kind of Morse code. The object possessed and lost, conjured up for the eye by the stain in the dirt, is an object of fantasy and desire, flickering in the imaginary and, contrary to a certain semiology of the photographic image, not so easily torn from the sight to which it appeals. For even as the calcified image is unmasked as a form of trompe l'oeil, it makes a final offer that proves so hard to refuse. It offers itself, as Lacan has observed, as an appearance "that says it is that which gives the appearance":[1] an incitement to ask and ask again what lies behind.

The photograph has us hanging. But its final offer is a dangerous one. It leads not only to the deferment of desire and the socialization of the drive—the promise and goal of the photographic system. It also threatens to double back and return us to the trauma of the splitting in which the subject of photographic seeing emerged in all its inadequacy—to the splitting choreographed by the disciplinary light machine at the

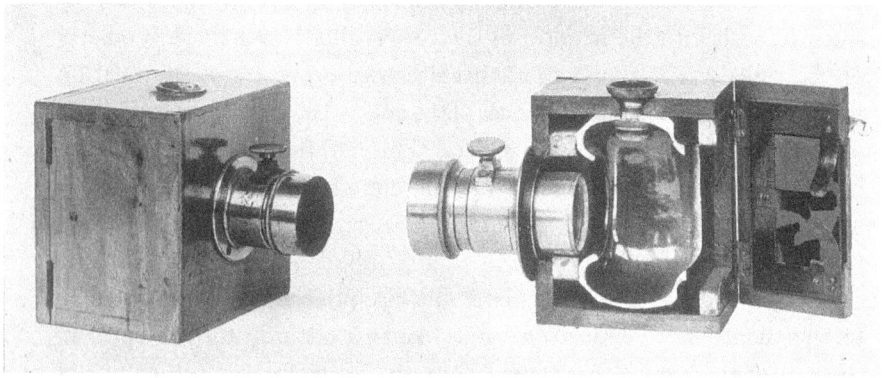

Figure 7. DuBroni wet-plate collodion camera, c. 1865. Science Museum, London.

moment of the traumatic encounter whose indelible traces still disturb the pacifying effects of all those magical devices that prolong our docile capture in the net of the image and that keep us repeating, "I know it is only an image, but all the same . . ."

Perhaps, however, the trauma can be displaced or delayed. It is, after all, rarely a matter of an image alone. With photographs, as interest palls, things are invariably arranged so that distraction is readily to hand: Read the caption; scan the layout; turn the page; move on to the next frame, the next file, the next cabinet drawer. A whole set of graphic, editorial, and verbal devices come into play, overcoding the thinness of the photograph and renewing our traffic with it, even as the image is caught up in the elaborate visual, verbal, spatial, and temporal interplay of larger machineries of staging. Where the machinery of scopic capture falters and the fetishism of the image no longer suffices, the endless substitutability of the photograph keeps the subject hanging on, suspended not just from the picture but from the circuitry of an entire apparatus: the camera, the picture, the mount, the file, the system of classification, the machinery of storage and retrieval, the unfolding space of the archive as the scene of a prolonged ritual of adjudication. The camera has always been part of a larger assemblage, like a computer wired to its peripherals. This is how its machinery of capture works. To the magical capture of the image is harnessed the mechanics of subjection of a bureaucratic apparatus. The camera, with its inefficient chemical information-storage system, comes joined to the storage and retrieval system of the filing cabinet: the One-Eyed Man and the One-Armed Man, the two modalities of power that join in the technical-machinic enslavement of the modern State.[2]

But we are moving on too quickly, and something is being missed as the photograph is cropped to fit its frame. Somewhere in the murky violence at the edge of the shadow cast by the frame, we lose our sense of the photograph as a material thing: a piece of stained paper, creasing at its corners, liable to tear and fray, picking up traces of oil and grease as it passes from hand to hand. Here, where the cut edge is shielded by the mat or the mount or falls under the protection of the frame, our attention is soon rebuffed and pulled back into the imaginary or hurried on into another space, where the photograph will come under other orders

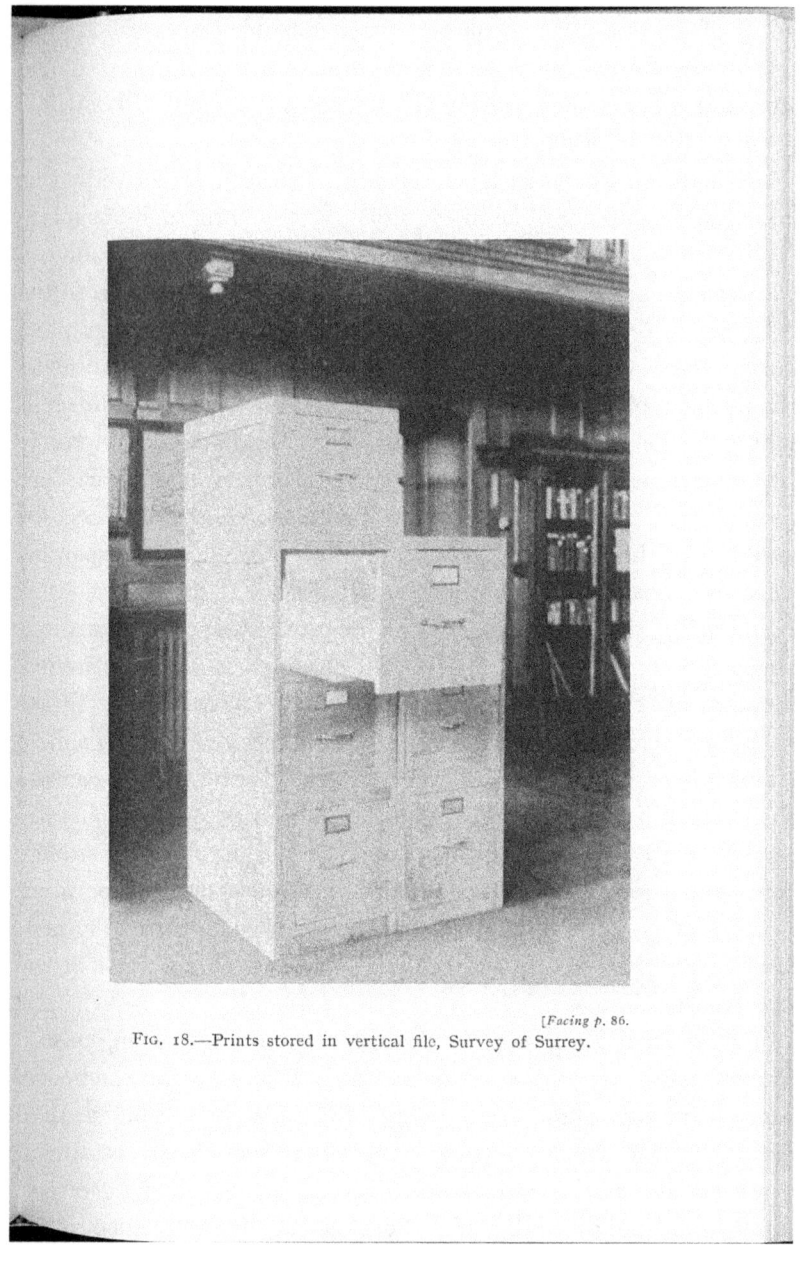

FIG. 18.—Prints stored in vertical file, Survey of Surrey.

Figure 8. "Fig. 18.—Prints stored in vertical file, Survey of Surrey," from H. D. Gower, L. Stanley Jast, and W. W. Topley, *The Camera as Historian* (London: Sampson Low, Marston, 1916), facing page 86.

and be given its rank and its status within the regimens that constitute the photographic field. Meaning prevaricates now between two worlds. Their impossible juncture is masked by the invisible thickness of the frame, for the frame is one of those great, open public secrets about which it is better to say nothing, from which it is better to avert one's eyes. This is power's persistent *alibi*. It is knowing the secret that ensures our silence. That is why a politics of exposure or unmasking is doomed to failure.

Historians of images have learned well enough how the law of the frame touches them: image or context, that is the choice. It is better to stay with the particular or get quickly lost in the cover of the background. So, oscillating around the frame, we find Alan Trachtenberg arguing in a single essay *both* that "the meaning of the photograph— what the interpreter is after—is rarely a given within the picture, but is developed in the *function* of the picture, in its particular social use by particular people," *and* that the photograph gives "immediate access to a past," as "a unique historical record, one that allows us to read, to count, even to measure what once existed."[3] It is not that either the specificity of the stain burnt into the emulsion or the particularity of the sphere of circulation, reception, and usage should be or could be avoided. But the methodological choice between the close reading of texts and the expansive reconstruction of social historical contexts begs the question of the frame as a machinery of capture and expulsion that covers the join between the image and the economy of meaning in which it comes to resonate and in which interpretation takes place.

Viewer, image, context—held together and apart, clamped in place by an apparatus less obvious than the engineering of the polished brass-and-wood devices that kept the criminal and the Bertillon-system camera operator in their respective places. Of course, they are not held there for long—not for longer than it takes. But that does not mean that, even in this instant, everything is secure. The camera is a box in Pandora's hands. The apparatus is not entirely stable and does not always work. When it does, it falls short or goes too far. And there is always the chance it will be interrupted, unsettled, undermined, sabotaged, or even smashed. But how are we to get some purchase on those disruptive events that pull the plugs and break the circuit, or that flood the channels, eroding,

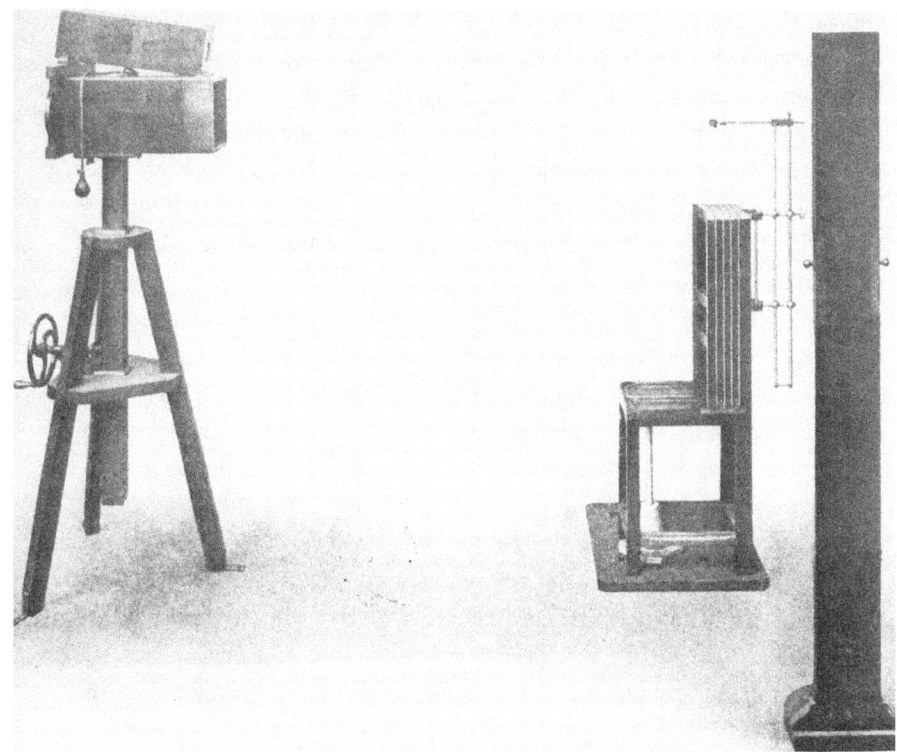

Figure 9. Apparatus for photographing prisoners. From Charlie Najman and Nicolas Tourlière, *La police des images* (Paris: Encre Editions, 1980).

evading, exceeding, or assaulting the barriers that define the limited fields of play in which the troubling mobility of images and the fluctuating attentions of viewers have come to be fixed? Do we look for resistance in the irresolvability of textual systems or in the irreducible heterogeneity of the determining context? Or must we look for vulnerabilities in the joins of the frame? How can we simultaneously account both for the assimilation of photography to a segmented and flexibly adaptive institutional order, and for those continual disturbances in the structures of this order that become particularly acute in the course of the nineteenth century with the dissemination of photography, driven as this was by intensified processes of commodification, disciplinary saturation, and archival accumulation, but also by an ambiguous popular dispersal?

These are not new questions. As I have already said, they take me back to earlier arguments that must have been ill-stated or ill-read to have been construed as they sometimes have been. Revisiting these arguments now also means returning to the vague topography that came to be so confidently colonized as "the New Art History."[4] In the mid-1970s in Britain, however, this uneven terrain seemed less like a consolidated territory than a scattering of would-be no-go areas signposted by the names of often mutually hostile journals and places: *Screen, Screen Education, Working Papers in Cultural Studies, Block*, Old Compton Street, Birmingham, Leeds, and so on. At the time, those moving in these disjointed spaces, far from art history's marbled halls, also sought to rally themselves with their own thoughts of affirmative return: to Karl Marx and to Sigmund Freud, certainly, but also to Antonio Gramsci, to Bertolt Brecht, to the Russian formalists, to Ferdinand de Saussure, and sometimes to Melanie Klein or to Simone de Beauvoir. These were returns for which the tours all departed from Paris, where the tour guides of choice were Louis Althusser, Roland Barthes, Jacques Lacan, Julia Kristeva, and, only much later in Britain, Michel Foucault, Jacques Derrida, and Luce Irigaray. There was no shortage of divergent and sometimes misdirected paths. Yet what is striking in the case of the dissenting art history of this period is that, whether for tactical reasons or not, all these different tracks came to be represented as converging somehow on the road of return to a singular site with a singular name: the social history of art.

Given its most influential evocation in 1973 in the ironic and later regretted title of the first chapter of T. J. Clark's *Image of the People*, the "social history of art" became, for a time, the name of a radical homeland, a place of secession: "the place," as Clark himself put it in 1974, "where the questions have to be asked, and where they cannot be asked in the old way."[5] What was evident from the beginning, however, was that this place of return was far from a comfortably settled landscape and its occupation would bring its own conflicts. On the one hand, the social history of art constituted a wary return to the territory of Frederick Antal, Arnold Hauser, Francis Klingender, the young Meyer Schapiro, and, less familiarly, Max Raphael, since this proving ground of early Marxist art history was seen by many as offering the only available space of resistance in the history of the discipline to formalist criticism and art historical connoisseurship. On the other hand, the social history of art as reconceived in 1973 also marked a belated attempt to encompass what were still seen in Britain as new developments in Continental theory. Conflict erupted because what came through the door with this term "theory" led to an undermining of the intellectual framework and humanist commitment of the older formation of the social history of art and even, in the end, to the erosion of *any* notion of a unifying oppositional problematic. The fleeting attempt to hold things together with hyphens (Marxism-feminism-psychoanalysis-semiotics) hardly won the defense of the new domain any more time. Though the consequence was not always welcome, then or since, it was clear that the heterogeneity of critical practices could not be bounded or constrained by a single program.

More worrying still, it also became clear—at least to some—that in pursuing the multiple avenues of poststructuralist analysis, certain directions for critical art history had entered an intellectual terrain that would sooner or later have to be recognized as entirely incompatible with any sociology or social history of art, of culture, or of knowledge. Herein lie some of the deeper conflicts and striking political realignments of the discipline in subsequent decades, one of the signposts to which was the instructive double disaster of the celebratory plenary sessions on Marxism and on deconstruction in art history at the College Art Association of America annual conference in Houston in 1988.[6] If these two panels were supposed to represent the competing options for new art histories, then what was striking and welcome was that neither of them was able to demonstrate its own internal coherence, let alone separate itself from its other and claim the day.

To recall these panels and their panelists (of whom I was one) is also, of course, to remember that—helped along by Margaret Thatcher's post-Marxist slogan "There is no society"—the "New Art History" in Britain had not only been fractured but also subject to a global redistribution, even before it had had time to think in what productive or restrictive ways it had been *British* at all. Such questioning would be left to a new wave of Black British artists, filmmakers, and critics whose presence, one may pointedly note, had hardly been allowed to trouble earlier debates in the radical history of art, even in the years immediately following the landmark publication of *The Empire Strikes Back* by the Centre for Contemporary Cultural Studies in 1982.[7]

What I deduce from these developments—from this fracturing and this dispersal—is not that there was an organizational failure or a loss of nerve, but that the recurrent concern of new art histories with the concepts of representation, production, power, pleasure, and identity could not be contained. These concepts went on generating their own unanticipated, multiplying effects, and the resultant openness came to characterize what was interesting about the field of visual culture studies, before it too passed over into the world of textbooks and readers. It was not the openness that dissipated critical momentum, as threatened in the beginning by Clark.[8] Rather, this openness functioned as the principal spoiler, undoing the various attempts that were made to totalize and reincorporate the productivity of critical art histories. The effects of renewed theoretical engagements with representation, power, identity, and difference were felt in other ways, too. The orbit of these concepts defied definition solely at the level of the methodological debate that was the obsessive concern of dissident art histories in the 1970s and early 1980s. Instead, it necessitated an inescapable folding over of the argument that, in turn, compelled recognition of the discursive and institutional structures of art history itself as mechanisms of framing and exclusion that continued to operate even in art histories of the newer sort.

I make no secret about welcoming this, just as I see it as far from a sign of weakness or disintegration that attempts to claim centrality for particular disciplinary paradigms and protocols keep on being overrun. It may well be that a sense of confrontation is harder to hang on to now than it was in the framework of 1970s notions of monolithic and counterposed disciplinary camps. Yet this in itself is not proof of co-optation. The proliferation of disputes eats away at the grounding and fabric of the disciplinary edifice, holding out the prospect that it will not simply be taken over and reoccupied but will be pierced, as the Communards pierced the besieged townhouses of Paris, so that its walls will be punched through by passageways and connecting corridors, and its spaces will be perforated, opened out, dispersed, and readapted.[9]

That is not to say, however, that it will be easy, in the present conjuncture, to separate the effects of such erosion from the impact of more sweeping yet contradictory local and global economic, political, and technological processes that, with increasing rapidity since the late 1980s, have also been overhauling the economic and cultural function of art history, just as they have overtaken the institutions of national culture on which art history as a discipline has depended since its inception. The changes reconfiguring the field of visual culture and its historical representation—through the impact of new image-handling technologies, through the pervasiveness of product placements and marketing strategies, through the conflicting demands of the international museum culture and national touristic promotions, and through the social mandates of multiculturalism and consensus—have long overlaid and confused any pressure for change emanating from the so-called New Art History. Yet the double dislocation of the traditional discipline of art history still presents an opportunity, albeit one in which, for critical interventions, an analysis of the dominant economies of images and meanings cannot be detached from a continual calculation of the politics of art historical practice itself. This is an inevitable consequence of the attempt to engage with a "politics of representation," whose implications cannot but spill over from the analysis of relations of power in visual culture to seep into the workings of the art historical apparatus itself.

The "politics of representation"—even as I write this phrase, I sense the danger of merely sounding quaint. In contrast to the institutional success of the no-longer-so-new New Art History, the concept of the "politics of representation" evokes a hastily forgotten time of uncomfortably brash and abrasive confrontations, of less-than-subtle interventions and raw counterpractices that deeply upset the carefully cultivated equilibrium of the discipline. One could point here to a whole range of local institutional challenges that marked the renewal of critical art history in the 1970s in Britain, France, Germany, Australia, and the United States. However, within the insistent concern over what was then called methodology, the various strands in the debate kept threading back to the problem of how to give an account of cultural meaning that would counter "formalism" by opening the process of signification beyond itself to a sense both of its constraints and of its effects, without, however, falling into the snares of earlier functionalist and deterministic sociologies of art. This was the context for the making of common cause under the temporary banner of the social history of art. But, as I have said, this ambivalent rallying call also harbored a conflict. For how could one develop a notion of cultural politics, in the sense of the mutual implication of *power* and *representation*, without denying *both* the absolute interiority of the image *and* the radical exteriority of socially determined meaning? Not even Althusser's enormously influential reformulation of the materiality of ideology could put off the reckoning, since his logic of overdetermination could not live long with the later return of an expressive concept of representation.[10]

The "politics of representation" thus coupled two concepts that began immediately, and interestingly, to undo each other. Clearly, the implications of this held as much significance for radical forms of post-conceptual practice as for emerging attempts at radical art history, and the importance of this relationship, at least in Britain and in Australia, should not be forgotten. In the fleetingly modish area of photography, which offered a relatively unconsolidated space adjacent to but displaced from the more solidified institutions of art and art history, debate in the 1970s turned on the search for alternative avenues of radical practice beyond the well-trodden paths of leftist documentary and reportage and outside the tramlines of realism and artifice that had dictated the parallel tracks of discourse on photography since its invention. Thus, from where I stood in the late 1970s, the remapping of the field of possibilities of contemporary "socialist" practice in photography went along with the trenchant attempt to realign the political reading of the history of the supposedly populist British documentary tradition. The year of Three Perspectives on Photography, which I cocurated at the Hayward Gallery in London in 1979, was also the year of "Power and Photography," first delivered as a lecture in a series of talks at the Institute of Contemporary Arts (ICA) in London.[11] Here, by staging a confrontation between Althusser's concept of Ideological State Apparatuses and the theories of discourse and power of Foucault, I tried to move beyond expressive models of the relationship of power and representation while relocating the debate on realism and challenging the notion of a progressive "documentary tradition" by connecting an array of nineteenth-century modes of photographic documentation to the emergence of disciplinary techniques and to a new form of the State. It was not the point of either the exhibition or the essay, however, to offer a monolithic account; rather, the intent was to *pluralize* photography, to insist on the specificity of frames of meaning and, in the words of the Hayward catalog essay, "to survey a constantly shifting ground of tactical actions: a range of incursions into the formation of dominant and dominated discourses or systems of signification; a multiplicity of points of intervention in a topography of concrete institutions and apparatuses."[12]

By contrast with this drive to pluralize and specify *photographies*, one might say that the persistent bent of photographic criticism from François Arago to Oliver Wendell Holmes and from Charles Baudelaire to Walter Benjamin had always been toward the totalization of photography, treating it as a homogeneous technology or singular medium whose meaning and historical consequences were somehow already immanent. Whether condemning photography's alleged debasing effects or eulogizing its revolutionary productive potential, photographic criticism construed photography as a singular cultural force, for good or ill. The troubling openness and heterogeneity of the field of photographic meanings were thus repressed, along with the possibility of asking how such a protean pictorial technology could have come to be absorbed and contained, structured and organized, functionalized and given meaning within an array of specific, defined, but mutually excluding discursive and institutional frames.[13] Against the totalizations of photography's critical interpretation, I therefore argued that the meaning and function of photographic practices could only be guaranteed and enforced within the insecure boundaries of the discursive frames that separated them, defined them, and stratified them. From this perspective, photography could no longer be seen as a unified medium whose status and value were inherent within it. Status, value, and meaning had to be produced—and they were produced locally and unevenly across a hierarchy of contingent and mutually defining cultural spaces in which what applied at one point might be totally at odds with what applied at another. Rather than attempting to adjudicate the essential meaning and necessary effects of photography, what we needed to do, therefore, was to map out these spaces, these jurisdictions of sense.

In relation to existing modalities of visual culture, photography's advent was as much an interruption as an extension. The tensions and disruptions generated within the discursive field by its arrival nevertheless became, in themselves, spurs to concerted efforts at recoding that sought not only to disperse the threat but also to leverage its energy in the interests of the dynamic of expansion. Already, by the mid-nineteenth century, the proliferation of photographic production was exciting anxieties about how to control and regulate the torrent of images that market forces alone would not be moved to check. On the one side, these anxieties were manifested in movements toward censorship that focused particularly on civic concern over the sheer volume of pornography in circulation scarcely ten years after Louis Daguerre's invention had been made public. On the other side, control of the flow of images involved issues of copyright law and ownership of a mechanical image that did not conform to existing definitions of intellectual property. The pressure here came, as Bernard Edelman has shown, with the second wave of industrialization of photographic production and its knock-on effects on the chemical, glass, rubber, and fine engineering industries, when the levels of investment at stake rose to formidable heights that could no longer be ignored.[14]

On another plane, the troubling productivity of photography had also somehow to be reconciled with the discursive constraints of residual, established, and emergent institutions of knowledge. More-accessible photographic technologies focused the problem, but in different ways at different points in a field that was never homogeneous or integrated. In one sector, changes in equipment and process fostered the growth of camera clubs and an institutional tussle over the relation of photography to art, while in another, the same changes facilitated an appropriation of the photographic apparatus by the institutions of disciplinarity and disciplinary knowledge. This appropriation faced, however, two kinds of difficulty, beyond the most immediate ones of an unreliable technology. First, there was the technical difficulty that everywhere afflicted the utility of photographic records: It was no use accumulating records if the storage system did not make it possible to retrieve them, cross-reference them, or compare them. In consequence, the effective incorporation of record photography in policing, medicine, psychiatry, engineering, social welfare, and the geographical survey depended on the development of a composite machine—a computer—in which the camera, with its less-than-efficient chemical coding system, was hooked up to that other great nineteenth-century machine, the upright file cabinet, which, when combined with the classificatory structure of the catalog, constituted a new information technology that would radically redirect the public and legislative functions of the archive.

The functionality of photography within this extended and professionally monitored archival machinery was still, however, liable to be undermined by the promiscuity and the dubious standing of the photograph. For the status of the photograph as record was not given or technologically guaranteed; it had to be produced. And it was only through conflict and negotiation, as well as legislation, that the status and protocols of instrumental photography came to be instituted in police practice, in law, in criminology, in psychiatric discourse, and in an extending range of disciplinary apparatuses. This securing of the local functionality of instrumental photography had, however, the additional, unforeseen consequence that the photographic field began to be drawn out as a domain of coexistent but mutually excluding and irreconcilable *photographies*. This, I will stress again, is not a sociological argument. It is not a matter of the external social contexts in which photographic technologies were mobilized, instrumentalized, evaluated, and interpreted. It is, rather, a matter of the unstable and contested discursive conditions under which the camera could be instituted as an instrument of knowledge, evidence, and record and under which the photograph could be constituted as a specific object of knowledge, an object of meaning, snugly fit and seemingly fully adequate to its frame.

In fact, of course, the image is always too big and too small for its frame, saying less than is wished for and more than is wanted. The cropping out of this excess and inadequacy in order to ensure that meaning falls readily into place is the work of what I take to be a kind of violence that is, as we have seen, brutal enough in its own ways and does not balk at leaving its marks. Yet the same process that holds photography in place must also tear it apart. The discursive framing of a plurality of photographies effectively shreds the notion of "the medium," whether conceived as an opaque material generating its own proper conventions or as a transparent vehicle mediating the efficient communication of meaning. The materiality of photographic processes is a necessary but not a sufficient condition for their designation as a medium. The medium is not something that is simply given. It has to be constituted, and it has to be instituted. And it is not instituted uniformly or homogeneously but, rather, unevenly, locally, and heterogeneously, as the property of particular institutional frames and as the effect of specific closures of the discursive field. A pluralized and unbounded terrain of mutually differentiating photographies thus begins to emerge toward the close of the nineteenth century, with each local practice claiming legitimacy from what is locally construed as proper to "the medium." Yet, clearly, these practices can no more be unified by an appeal to a common medium than can the endlessly differentiated and segmented field of writing. The fact that every photograph, like the sign, refers to every other, positively or negatively, by sympathy or exclusion, opens not on the guarantee of totality but on the undecidability of a network of cross-reference in which, as Saussure insisted, there are only differences and no positive terms, only differences and the kind of violence that insists they can be held in place. It is in this sense, therefore, that I have said that photography has no identity.

Photography has no identity, but the photograph may, for the photograph captures meaning even as the inexhaustible openness of the photographic appears to be captured and fixed by the discursive apparatus of the frame. The workings of capture, however, clearly exceed the framing of the photograph. The photographic apparatus, as I have said, is in effect a composite device in which the bureaucratic administrative technologies of the archive were coupled to the mechanics of identificatory capture built into the operating system of the picturing machine. This was the platform for the assemblage's utility to sovereignty and to the State: the camera and the filing cabinet—the One-Eyed Man and the One-Armed Man, as Gilles Deleuze and Félix Guattari describe them—conjoining magical capture and legislative subjection as the axiomatic processes of technical machinic enslavement in the modern nation-state.[15] This is where we must be careful, however, especially if we are going to invoke Foucault.

"For a long time," Foucault argued in *Discipline and Punish*,

> ordinary individuality—the everyday individuality of everybody—remained below the threshold of description. To be looked at, observed, described in detail, followed from day to day by an uninterrupted writing was a privilege. The chronicle of a man, the account of his life, his historiography,

written as he lived out his life formed part of the rituals of his power. The disciplinary methods reversed this relation, lowered the threshold of describable individuality and made of this description a means of control and a method of domination. It is no longer a monument for future memory, but a document for possible use.[16]

The very techniques of documentation and documentary accumulation and the entry of the individual into their field were locked into a history of disciplinary practice and knowledge that emerged piecemeal across the workings of new apparatuses—the police, hospitals, schools, insane asylums, prisons, departments of immigration, planning, public health and sanitation—each of which sought to exert a new and fine-grained measure of control over bodies and spaces.[17] The effectivity of these new apparatuses was thus bound up with a specific strategy of representation.

Documentation, as I have argued before, belonged to a paranoid formation for which the social was always dangerously alive with potential pathologies that threatened to overrun the social body and destroy its productivity if not constantly monitored, interpreted, and subdued.[18] This fantasy of untainted functionality and perfect monitoring was the dream of the society of security—a society whose model was the humane and scientific reformatory. Surveillance would be its apparatus of restraint; the record would be its cell; the file would be its carceral architecture. It therefore seized upon the latest technologies—photography prominent among them—though it was as suspicious of their productivity as it was of sociality itself. Rather, it sought to make these technologies servile instruments of its compulsive knowledge, driven as it was to separate, isolate, and subjugate its still troubling object, to elide the erotic character of its curiosity, and to deny the presence of desire and the exchange of pleasure. In this way, the intransigent social field was to be transformed into a series of "case studies," stripped of all interiority and scrutinized, without shame, by a regular and continuous surveillance that would entirely reverse the political axis of visibility.

This was the field of operation of discipline, whose precepts and principles were most cogently represented and generalized in Bentham's Panopticon: an architectural machinery of capture whose geometrical spatialization facilitated a continuous surveillance by orchestrating vision and delimiting lines of sight, setting up a determined play of transparencies and opacities that permitted an irreversible line of observation from its central tower while excluding any lateral communication at its periphery.[19] What the plan for the Panopticon described was an edifice of vision as yet empty of subjects. Its value seemed to lie precisely in this emptiness, which promised to make it highly adaptable as a machine for harnessing bodies and for producing compliance by self-regulation. Its emptying of specific content also emphasized its function as a model: a working model of a transparent society, a community of the consensual norm, a utilitarian utopia. The Panopticon was not, however, a purely visual apparatus. Leaving aside the question of its built-in sound tubes, it functioned not only as a technology of observation and a kind of personal trainer or exercise machine but also as a truth machine—a machine for producing documentation, an archive, a machinery of knowledge, necessarily incorporating a system of information storage and retrieval, in short, *a discourse machine.*[20]

It hardly needs adding that the Panopticon, even in its periodic and partial application as an institutional template, was never a State Apparatus in Althusser's sense of the term. For all its claim to model a utilitarian utopia, the Panopticon was an assemblage—a pragmatic adaptation of locally developed techniques and technologies. It developed not as a function of the needs of State power, as an expression of class interest, or as a reflex of an economic process but, rather, as a combination of more or less cumbersome machineries selected for the utility of their effects. The imagined elaboration and generalization of these effects then led to the projection of the idea of a systemic *panopticism*, but this never amounted to the principle of a new social totality. Panopticism never exhausted the grid of power relations in the social field, and in any case, there was always an unclosable gap between the Panopticon and panopticism. The Panopticon was a combinatory of specific technologies generating a particular physics of power and a particular regimen of knowledge. It was a material apparatus, not a totalizing concept. Moreover, where its mechanisms were put into effect, its workings were never inexorable. The bodies it harnessed could never be entirely made subject to or subdued beneath its performative demands. It was actively resisted and undermined by counterpowers, evasions, and perverse reinvestments.

It generated an excess of meanings that could not be curtailed by its technology of sense. And it continued to be cut across by desires that could not be subsumed within its utilitarian rationality.

Panopticism and disciplinarity thus do not describe a remorseless and exhaustive system, but neither are they general metaphors. They are the concerted effects of specific material apparatuses and techniques, and as such, they offer a delimited framework in which to think about the "general politics" of truth in the burgeoning archives of late nineteenth-century photographic documentation. Having put Foucault's analysis of disciplinarity into play in this way, however, the matter can hardly be left here. It cannot just be a question of trying to go beyond ingrained conceptions of the "documentary tradition" by placing photographic documents and documentation in relation to Foucault's account of the historical emergence of hospitals and prisons and their deployment of new techniques of segmentation, examination, and the case study. Engagement with Foucault means that the problem of documentation and the status of the document have to be posed at the level of discourse: at the level of those practices, institutions, and orders of meaning that— through all their incentives and exclusions, their "internal" and "external" constraints, as Foucault described them—enact the field of disciplinarity and instate the regimen of instrumental representation on which it depends and which it must set in place.[21] This is, of course, precisely what alarms those who would like to contain the effects of Foucault's writings, as if he were merely a historian of policing and prisons. But the project announced with new trenchancy in Foucault's inaugural lecture at the Collège de France breaks the bounds of the narrow history of institutions because it confronts head-on the mutual production of discourse and power.[22]

"I am supposing," Foucault declared, "that in every society the production of discourse is at once controlled, selected, organized and redistributed according to a certain number of procedures, whose role is to avert its powers and its dangers, to cope with chance events, to evade its ponderous, awesome materiality."[23] Such procedures take force in a pattern of rules of exclusion, rules of limitation, and rules of employment that have the effect of rarefaction (controlling, selecting, channeling, and curtailing the proliferation of discourse) and the effect of ordering (classifying, hierarchizing, and unifying statements), thus instituting and legitimizing those regimens that control the productivity of the events of discourse and elide their dangerous materiality as *events*. Power—the positive power to produce and incite, as much as the negative power to constrain—is thus embedded in the very grammar of the event of meaning. Understanding the relation of power to the discursive event involves, therefore, not a search for something behind it, in its origins, in its cause, or in what it supposedly "expresses," but, rather, a kind of archaeological mapping of the patterns of rules that permit the production and transformation of statements—not as evolving expressions of what Raymond Williams called the "structure of feeling" but as ensembles of discontinuous, dispersed events for which we must identify the generative and exclusionary rules of appearance and transformation.[24] Such generative rules governing what is said do not, however, constitute an abstract grammar providing the conditions of existence of all possible statements; rather, they are performative rules invested in institutions, techniques, practices, and modes of behavior that mark out the limits within which meanings are actually adduced. Within this performative arena, rules of exclusion, limitation, and employment operate, therefore, as forms of instigative violence—a violence that produces the event of meaning and impinges on the body, making it subject, constituting the subject that is subject to discourse.[25]

From its inception, the discursive event is imbricated in power and bound to the generation of power effects by the constitutive constraints that institute domains of meaning and subjection. This power is not, then, a coercive force external to discourse, but an effect of a decentered field of rules, incentives, rituals, practices, techniques, and technologies that cannot easily be located as either "external" or "internal." By the same token, as Foucault repeatedly insisted, this power is never solely negative or prohibitive but is, rather, productive—productive of objects, subjects, theoretical fields, effects of truth, and effects of power.[26] That is not at all to say, however, that this power is motivated or that discourse can be decoded as its "expression," since the discursive event is not transparent to something "behind" it, whether a determinant reality or a constitutive subject, an external power or a functionalist mandate. In place of the search for what is "expressed," Foucault offers us a new set of questions concerning the intrication of meaning and power in "procedures" that would be ill described as the workings of a code or complex of codes but that, rather, present themselves with the material force of a machinery of discursive events—that is, as a discursive regime.[27]

The term "regime" is blunt enough to convey what is at stake: power and meaning conjoined, each the incentive, support, and concerted effect of the other. Yet the concept of the discursive regime also focuses the difficulties standing in the way of all those defensive attempts to deny Foucault the title historian. For Foucault, power and discourse, in their mutual implication and, all the more, in their overcoding and attempted functionalization by the State, are constitutively marked by an a priori historicity, not in the sense of belonging to a succession or progression but in the sense of constituting a distinct occurrence or event. Historicity is scored into this event and, therefore, into the decisive mutation that the "general politics" of the discursive regime undergoes between the sixteenth and seventeenth centuries, as a consequence of the emergence of new practices, technologies, and techniques whose import is only fully grasped and harnessed at the end of the eighteenth and the beginning of the nineteenth centuries.[28] This mutation is marked in the separation between the sporadic and unresolved system of sovereign power, with its juridical theory of right and its dependence on the exemplary force of spectacle, and the new technologies of disciplinary power, focused on the surveillance of bodies, on individualization, and on the production of operationally deployable knowledge. This separation was not accomplished in a moment, but neither did it allow for any process of historical mediation, just as the "new 'economy' of power" it produced represented neither a new essential principle nor the product of a dialectical movement. On the contrary, the break was first announced in a series of discrete events, each the outcome of local discoveries in defined institutions—the army, schools, hospitals, prisons, asylums—and local tactics that were only subsequently "invested, colonized, utilized, involuted, transformed, displaced, extended, etc."[29] by more general mechanisms. These local discoveries and tactics were inscribed in architectures, in technological devices, in techniques of observation, in methods of training, and in new forms of writing. They worked in ways quite other than those of sovereign power and right, in ways responsive to local conditions and particular needs, in the absence of any general strategies to weld them together into a larger mechanism. Even when such strategies were developed and partially put in place, these local innovations retained their specific character, through all those processes by which they were appropriated, adapted, and generalized and by which their effects were linked in the play of mutual engagements that began to draw out the new "economy" of disciplinary power.

This only serves to emphasize again that disciplinary technologies, even in the forms in which they were incorporated into specific State apparatuses, remained irreducible to the workings of a centralized State machinery, let alone to an internal logic of the State. There were, moreover, tensions and conflicts that the State had to negotiate as it sought to extend its reach and consolidate disciplinarity under its domain. Discipline inverted the structures of sovereign power and, against the notion of the possessive individual on which the liberal notion of the State was founded, turned on subjection and the production of docile subjects. At the same time, the proliferation of disciplinarity across the social field undermined the division of public and private by which the liberal State claimed absolute sovereignty yet, in operation, left space for competing powers designated as belonging to civil society and, therefore, as falling outside the jurisdiction of the State. Nevertheless, the incorporation of disciplinarity, the adaptation of a wide range of disciplinary institutions, and the promulgation of a general social discipline were necessary conditions for the breakdown of laissez-faire and the expansion of the State's activity from the 1870s on. By the same token, Foucault's location of a decisive shift in the "political economy" or the "régime" of truth at this time points also to the State's drive to instate itself as a discursive horizon, in its attempt to delimit sociality in the form of a managed society.[30] The State may not be the origin of disciplinarity, but neither is it external or neutral. Rather, it takes shape in the course of the nineteenth century as a massively centralized geometry of force, aspiring to a monopoly of power that it cannot in fact realize, striving to produce a society within the constraints of its geometrical order, yet, of necessity, trafficking with powers and systems that lie outside it and may even conflict with it.

Stressing the decentered character of disciplinary power and the local emergence of disciplinary techniques is not, therefore, at odds with the proposal that, in what the West calls the modern period, there is a crucial relationship to be explored between the regime of sense—the machinery of discursive events in the delimited field of the discursive regime—and the machineries of the State. The State is a particular historical configuration that operates, in historically differentiated ways, as what Deleuze and Guattari have called a mechanism of capture and expulsion, powerfully striving to construct a systematic, unified, centered, and homogeneous territory. Yet we have also seen that the State—even the State that has incorporated within itself the techniques and technologies of social discipline—cannot unify or extend itself as it strives to do. It can never saturate the realm of discourse or the social field it produces. It can never reduce discursivity or sociality to an exhaustive functionalism, as Althusser imagined in his theory of Ideological State Apparatuses. What constricts the State, however, is not just a matter of the struggle for State power; least of all is it a matter of the State's supposed internal "checks and balances." It is, rather, that, intrinsically and extrinsically, the State, as a discursive formation, always has to operate in a field of heterogeneous machineries of force and machineries of discourse that it does not determine, that it cannot eradicate, and that it cannot subdue; machineries that it may try to reduce, subordinate, or absorb but that are always simultaneously inadequate to and in excess of its purposes, falling short and overproducing in relation to the fixity the State would give them.

The State has no transcendence beyond the violent contingency of a strategic elaboration whose effects are not those of a logic of necessity and are thus neither exhaustively predictable nor uncontested. The State may continuously elaborate its mechanics of capture, colonization, territorialization, overcoding, and appropriation, but it can never realize itself as a global principle or a totality: It can never produce the society toward which it strives; it can never call a halt to the play of power and discursivity or reduce them to its territorial principle of sovereignty. It is not, then, that the State is an instrument *of* society or even *against* society. It is rather that—as a configuration of force in a field it never saturates— the State is constantly striving to *produce* the impossible, to stabilize the field of sociality as a delimited domain, as a society. It attempts to do so, in the terminology of Deleuze and Guattari, echoing the terminology of

Lacan, by *capture*: by capturing the open and nonhomogeneous field of discursivity; by segmenting, dividing, delimiting, defining, and curtailing the endless play of possibilities; by capturing divergent technologies, practices, institutions, and economies of meaning as a regime of sense and a regime of truth; by working to reduce the technologies, practices, institutions, and economies of meaning it appropriates to functional apparatuses; by capturing the field of agents as a field of subjects; by enforcing, across the fields of discourse and subjectification, hierarchies of distinctions and boundaries of expulsion that are its indices of power; by, in the process, annulling the pull and blocking the pathways of other forces; yet without ever attaining either a functional unity or the monopoly of legitimacy and power and the absolute congruence of territory and sovereignty on which it claims to be founded.

The violent attempt by the State to fix a territory as a ground without dispute is thrown into relief by its encounter with the eruption of new technologies of meaning and power—new technologies, that is, of sense and subjection. What we see then is a flurry of activity as the technologies are annexed to existing frames, their meaning specified and their productivity curtailed—not uniformly but locally, unevenly, and discontinuously across an array of discursive spaces. What then emerges is a motley field of differences, identities, borders, and exclusions across which the potential for proliferation of the new technologies is triaged, quarantined, reduced, and displaced by the gridding of a segmented field. This exclusion of proliferation yields utility, meaning, pleasure, profit, and power—but it is never fully fixed. The instability of local frames and of the hierarchy of segregation, the countereffects of one frame on another, and the pressure of the remainder cannot be entirely erased but return to undermine the integrity of the order instituted in the discursive regimen of the State.

The problem that remains is how to think the unstable stabilizing mechanism of capture and how to understand its operation as a machinery of subjection whose goal is what Foucault himself described as a certain "interiorising."[31] This process of "interiorising" is not, however, elaborated in Foucault, who refuses recourse to a system of psychological reference points that themselves derive from the disciplinary realm. We are left, therefore, with a lacuna—a lacuna that is precisely the space explored by Slavoj Žižek through recourse to a Lacanian psychoanalysis that would seem, on the face of it, to be anathema to Foucault, as to Deleuze and Guattari. "We have to rethink the most elementary notions about national identification," Žižek has argued, "and here, psychoanalysis can be of help."[32]

> To emphasize in a "deconstructionist" mode that Nation is not a biological or a transhistorical fact but a contingent discursive construction, an overdetermined result of textual practices, is . . . misleading: such an emphasis overlooks the remainder of some real, nondiscursive kernel of enjoyment which must be present for the Nation qua discursive entity-effect to achieve its ontological consistency.[33]

The element that holds together a given community cannot merely be reduced to the point of symbolic identification. The pure discursive effect, Žižek says, does not have enough "substance" to render it compelling. What is left out of consideration, he insists, is the fantasy space within which a community organizes its "way of life," that is, its mode of enjoyment.[34] This shared relationship toward incarnated enjoyment binds the members of a community, yet is never secured. It is an enjoyment that cannot be had because the drive for fulfillment is powered by a traumatic sense of lack, in consequence of which the enjoyment that never in fact could be had always constitutes itself as "stolen."[35]

This imputation of "theft," Žižek argues, opens the way for the return of the figure of the master who claims to guarantee the stability and balance of the social fabric while attributing the lack of fulfillment to those others whose greed and excess are the cause of social antagonism. The State, as embodiment of mastery and ultimate guarantor of the social pact, thus comes to stand in for the fulfillment of order. Yet it cannot directly guarantee its subjects enjoyment of their "way of life." It can do so only indirectly, by embodying a right of return and a force of retribution against those others to whom the theft of enjoyment is attributed.[36] It is this transposition that secures the fantasy organization of desire and "gives a body to our own innermost split, to what is 'in us more than ourselves' and thus prevents us from achieving full identity with ourselves."[37] In this, the State—that paradoxical entity "which 'is' only insofar as subjects believe (in the other's belief) in its existence"[38]—enacts its magical capture.

A new set of problems has been added to the chain: interiorization, identification, the extrojection of loss, the coalescence of a community, and the relation of these processes to the formation of the State. Foucault's account of disciplinary power may stop short of engaging them but, then, Žižek's attempt to make up a lack in theories of discourse ends with "the logic of Capital" and "the form of subjectivity that corresponds to late capitalism."[39] It is doubtful that Foucault, who made his own effort to trace the emergence of a discourse of theft, would have been persuaded that this is an advance.[40] Perhaps we need to pause here in order to take stock of the question of capture and the place of the machinery somehow attached to the State that captures by constituting a space of mutual (mis)recognition.

Panoptic machines constituted one of the technologies of power and one of the arenas of tactics through which the social field was to be reconstituted within a new microphysics of power as the object of a new regime of truth and knowledge. Appropriated, combined, hybridized, and generalized, such disciplinary machines enabled the State to extend and transform its mode of operation and its practices of power, intervening at levels of resolution and regularity never before attained by State apparatuses, disciplining and subjecting the bodies of the populace, driving toward an imagined saturation of the social field that, at the same time, constantly reactivated State power by generating ever more complex and demanding "social problems." This was the regimen of surveillance and social discipline but also of social welfare. It was a regimen within which the State sought to colonize sociality and thus to *produce* a society. This does not mean, however, that disciplinarity was the expression of some will to power, that it ever attained the homogeneity it projected, or that it precluded the simultaneous mobilization of machineries of power entirely at odds with the techniques of discipline, including technologies of spectacle and sovereign power that can hardly be seen as disappearing with the fall of absolutism.

The notion of disciplinarity has thus compelled a reexamination of the growth and expansion of the State and its apparatuses, but it has also undermined existing accounts of State power and their tendency to conflate technologies of power too readily with the State. There is much here to inform an analysis of power and photography and call into question the accusations of sociologism that have been leveled against it. Yet it is also clear that the instrumentalization of photography as a means of surveillance, record, and evidence in the disciplinary institutions and new government departments of the last quarter of the nineteenth century does not exhaust the question of the encounter between the reconstituted State, technologies of documentation, and practices of photographic record. Half a century later, in the midst of the crisis of social cohesion of the 1930s, the liberal state, beset to the right and left by the competing state forms of fascism and communism, would seek to appropriate

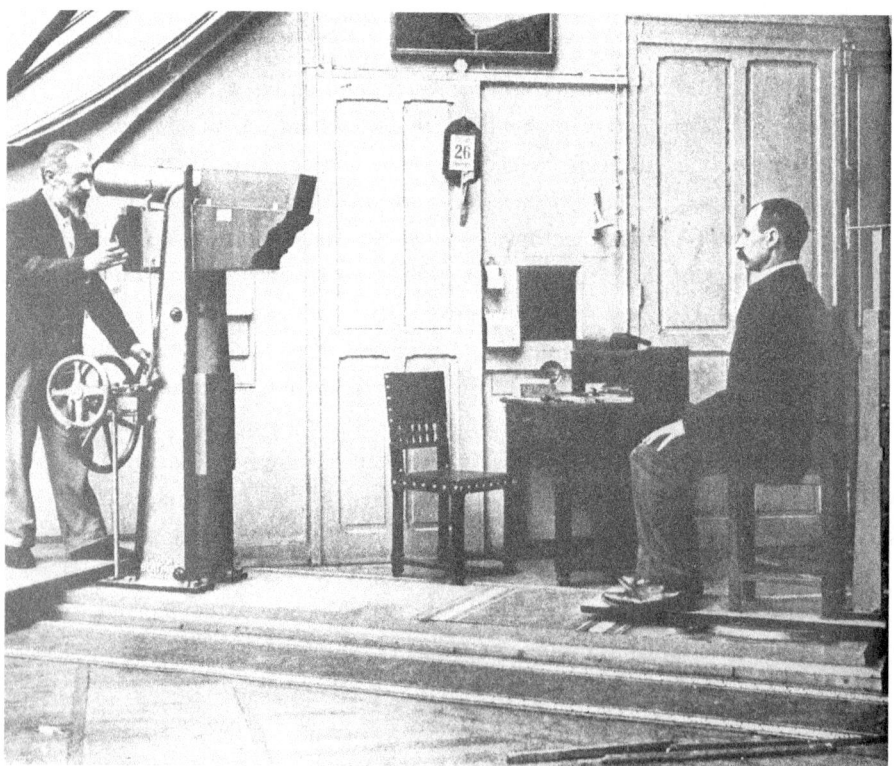

Figure 10. Alphonse Bertillon experimenting with his apparatus. From *La police des images* (Paris: Encre Editions, 1980).

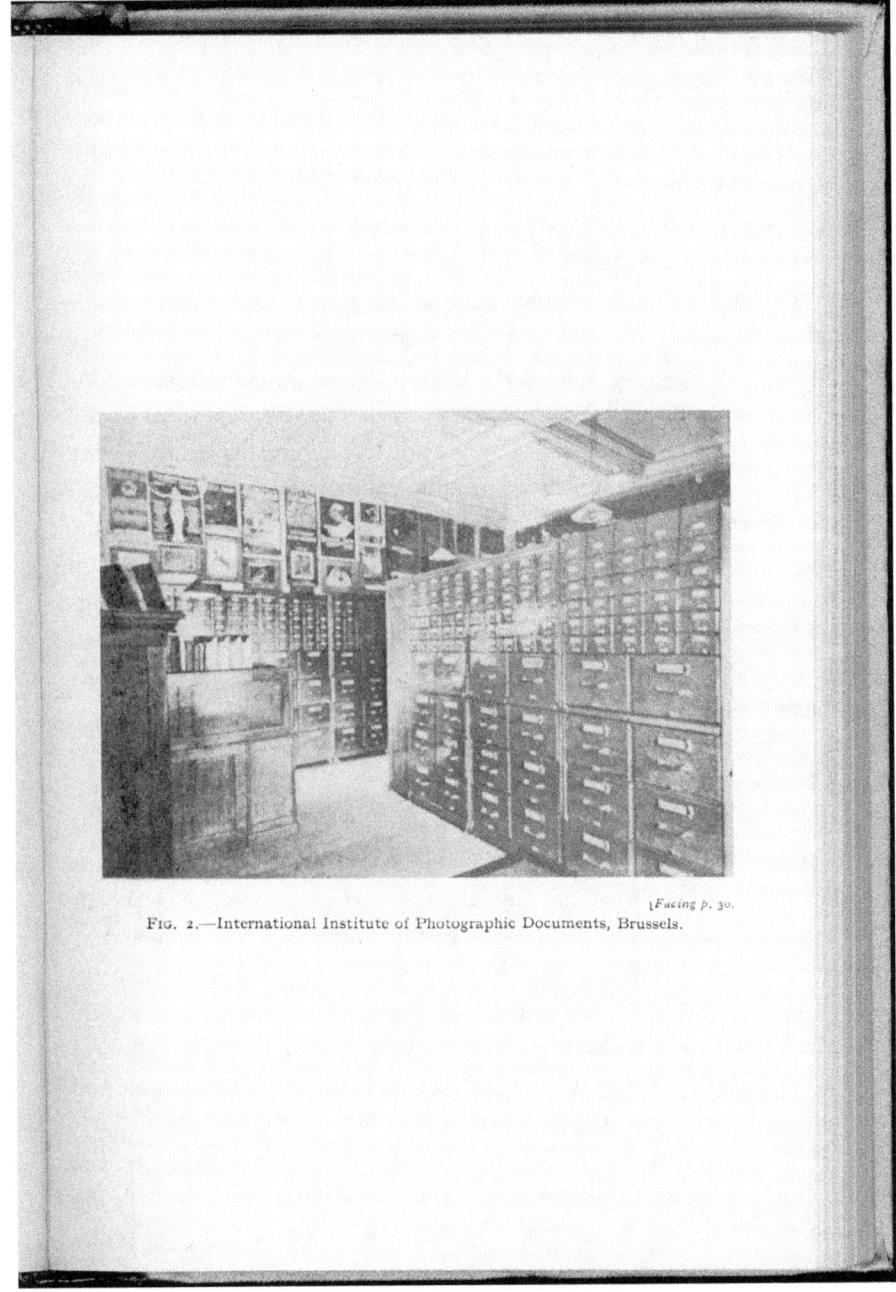

[*Facing p.* 30.

Fig. 2.—International Institute of Photographic Documents, Brussels.

Figure 11. "Fig. 2.—International Institute of Photographic Documents, Brussels," from H. D. Gower, L. Stanley Jast, and W. W. Topley, *The Camera as Historian* (London: Sampson Low, Marston, 1916), facing page 30.

photography again, as a means of public communication and popular education and, above all, as a new language of citizen formation—a spectacular rhetoric of recruitment mobilized to resecure identification with the representation of community on which the functioning of the paternalistic liberal state depended.

Here, then, we are faced with another, quite distinct intersection of new cultural technologies and the State, though, as always, these technologies remained as insecure in their instrumentalization as they were stubbornly excessive in relation to the State's efforts to harness or constrain their productivity. Hence the anxiety of state interventions in and around photography, by which I mean not just interventions that were *proscriptive*—as, for example, in censorship campaigns—but, more pointedly, interventions that were *prescriptive*, as the State sought to define and control new and restrictive statuses for photographic practices and photographic agents through the institutionalization of certain regimens of meaning but also through interventions on copyright and intellectual property law. Surveillance, disciplinary documentation, spectacle, recruitment, censorship, and copyright: What we have here, as I have argued, is an array of sometimes linked but never congruent sites that raise questions about the relation of the State to the development, deployment, framing, and enforcement of new cultural technologies and new institutions of meaning. Yet we can only make progress with these questions if we are able to find ways to think about and theorize the development and operation of cultural technologies, the structure of the State and its relation to the institutions of culture, forms of rhetoric and structures of identification, the effects on the social body of the appropriation and mobilization of new technologies and new rhetorics, and the character and locus of State power, its relation to other formations of power, and its inevitable vulnerability to resistance and simple malfunction.

How, for example, are we to understand what is specific to the State as a system of social ordering and control? What are the defining characteristics of the State that separate it from other forms of social authority and regulation? The accepted answer points to a permanent and continuous system of subjection and rule operating in a defined territory within which the State possesses a monopoly over the legitimate use of force—a monopoly articulated through codified law, legitimized through mechanisms of representation, and enacted in the State's centralized functions of legislation, administration, and enforcement. In summary, then, the State form is said to depend on the absorption and institutionalization of notions of sovereignty, territoriality, legitimacy, and representation and on the installment of specific and distinct legislative, executive, judicial, and coercive State apparatuses.

Certain complications follow, however, from this list. While it is clear that the State involves a particular polity and, in its modern forms, particular constitutional arrangements, it is not clear that legalistic definitions are sufficient to account for the constitution of the State. The question of legitimation, as I have argued earlier, presupposes a certain instigative violence and opens not only on the issue of coercive enforcement but also on the procurement of docility, if not consent. It is also clear that the question of legitimation in the modern state turns, at a number of not necessarily commensurable levels, on the process of representation. But if this process of representation is not simply transparent in its functioning, how are we to understand what is involved? Then again, if we look at the problem of territorial definition and integrality, does it not also lead to the question of what constitutes integrity and, more crucially, the sense of belonging said to be both its condition and its effect? Does not the notion of territorial belonging refer back to questions of boundary marking and the production of difference, and does it not therefore precipitate us into questions not easily contained in the structure of legal rationality: questions of nationality and nationalism and how exactly territorial boundaries come to be articulated as the bounds of national communities and national identities? In short, do not the questions of consent, belonging, and identity take us back to the intransigent problem that is the other side of sovereignty: the question of what makes a subject subject—a question that is hardly tractable solely to legalistic, constitutionalist, or even economistic analyses? And if the question is the constitution of the subject, how can this avoid taking us back to problems of meaning, language, and culture and their relation to the symbolic and imaginary registers in which human beings live what they take to be their lives?

Or again, to take another tack for the moment, if, as Stuart Hall insists, "The state is a *historical* phenomenon,"[41] how are we to pose this historicity? Does it mean that the State is a specific, located structure, differentiated from other forms of polity? Or does it have to be taken to mean that the State must be seen as the outcome of an evolutionary development in which its modern form emerges from a history of earlier state forms? Clearly, the two cannot be conflated, and indeed, the evolutionism of the one view effectively undermines the argument for specificity of the other. If the State form is a specific configuration, a specific formation, do we not have to ask how to think that specificity and its historicity? But does this mean that we have to place the form of the modern state in a line of historical development, as a synthesis, perhaps, of elements from superseded state forms? Would this not implicate us in an evolutionism that would then find it hard to grasp the discontinuity that constituted the specificity of the State form as it emerged in sixteenth-century Europe?

In Philip Bobbitt's grandiosely synthetic account, the modern state emerged where the polity of medieval Europe was weakest and had begun to come apart: among the wealthy, well-integrated, highly competitive, yet strategically vulnerable city realms of fifteenth-century Italy.[42] For Bobbitt, it was the strategic innovation of mobile artillery that left these walled cities open to military attack, but this very strategic threat animated the organization and constitutional innovation of the centralized State apparatus, with its promise to make the city and the ruler more secure.[43] This new organizational structure concentrated logistics, command, and the raising of revenue in an integrated apparatus that rested on a permanent bureaucracy, a credentialed diplomatic corps, and a standing mercenary army. At the same time, the need to confer legitimacy on this new apparatus led to the detachment of the legal and material attributes that had been the prerogatives of the prince and to their transference to the objectified structure of the State itself, which became the seat of a *ragione di stato*, a state code of behavior increasingly distinct from the moral code of the prince. As this new conception of the State coalesced, the connotations of the word "state" shifted away from the description of a state of play and toward the designation of a fixed state of affairs or structure—an index of the process by which the State would take on an autonomy and come to stand over and above the social body that had produced it.[44]

At the very foundation of the State form, therefore, as in its subsequent evolution, Bobbitt insists that "the development of constitutional forms came about in tandem with a revolution in military tactics."[45] New technologies of war required a new State apparatus in which absolute control could be concentrated, and this gave rise to a dialectic, driven by the imperative of security and a concomitant logic of negation, in which "it is the constitutional order of the State that tends to confer military advantage by achieving cohesion, continuity, and, above all, legitimacy for its strategic operations. And it is these strategic operations, through continuous innovation, that winnow out unsuccessful constitutional orders."[46] The "society of states" has thus been driven by war. Epochal wars produce fundamental challenges to existing forms of the State, compelling states to mimic or innovate around the dominant strategic and constitutional paradigms. By this means, a new dominant constitutional order and a new dominant strategic paradigm emerge with new bases of legitimacy.[47] The key to Bobbitt's narrative of the history of the State is therefore the interaction of strategic development and constitutional change in what he calls a mutually affecting "field" relation, rather than a linear causal relation.[48] Yet Bobbitt's model is still profoundly evolutionary, though, to be fair, one must say that this evolution is not clearly ameliorative, since it is driven by an escalating logic of negation, "as if the triumph of one constitutional order somehow germinates the form that will ultimately vanquish it."[49]

Bobbitt's narrative is, at least in this sense, deeply Hegelian in its structure. The thesis and antithesis of strategic innovation and constitutional change drive the evolutionary development of the State through the negation of war and the resultant constitutional settlement, with each epochal war marking a phase of transformation that will, in turn, produce the next form of the modern State. Yet even in his account of the emergence of the modern State, Bobbitt acknowledges the effects of forces not capable of being folded back into his dialectic of strategic and constitutional innovation: the development of the money economy and commodity exchange; the revolution in thought in the sixteenth century and the breakup of consensus around the medieval Church's paradigms of inquiry and practice; and the development of new techniques and technologies that produce not only a revolution in military tactics but also a new form of discipline that, in itself, constitutes a revolution in power affecting not only military training but the very techniques of subjection.[50] These divergent economies—monetary, discursive, disciplinary—are not in themselves reducible one to another, and they do not conform to the unity and coherence of Bobbitt's monocausal teleology, for which the State is the necessary goal of human history, the achievement of civilization that founds history and marks humanity's progress beyond those superseded social forms characterized by their lack of a State.

This is the nostrum of the liberal tradition: the State as the end and goal of human history, as the necessary emergence of an autonomous stratum over and above the society whose conflicts it claims to resolve. This hypostasized stratum thenceforth embodies sovereignty and claims a monopoly over legitimate violence within its defined territory, qualified only by the State's contractual relation with the individuals who constitute its subjects and by the representational functions that the State subsequently acquires. The possibility that there could be a society without a State is dealt with summarily. Such a society must be a savage chaos, a community without direction or history, a pre-historic society of scarcity clinging to the edge of survival. Yet, as the political anthropologist Pierre Clastres has insisted, the economies of power and desire central to social life cannot be reduced to the presence or absence of a State.[51]

Societies without a State, Clastres insists, are not societies of lack. Such societies enjoy an abundance sufficient to satisfy their needs. What they lack is not the means of subsistence but a surplus, and they lack this because there is no need for abundance to give place to overabundance unless there is some force to compel overproduction and to alienate labor. The absence of a State, Clastres argues, is thus not a sign of lack or underdevelopment. Societies without a State are societies of leisure, not work. It is not that they have exhausted the totality of their forces of production in the provision of minimal needs; it is, rather, that they refuse uselessness, unnecessary work, excess, and accumulation (though not necessarily exchange). They therefore take pains to exclude in advance the forms of power and inequality that would produce a State. This is not to say that they do not develop their own relations of power; rather, these relations of power operate by prestige, not authority; generosity, not greed; persuasion, not coercion. Even the development of a war machine is kept at the level of specific local skills that do not translate into political power. And whereas chieftainship may well be linked to prowess in the prosecution of war, it never develops into a force over and against the social body. Power always remains with the collectivity.

For Clastres, therefore, societies that exclude the development of a State have to be grasped in their positivity. Their definition according to what they lack is merely a function of the tyranny of the defining term— the term of difference—here dependent for its privilege on an ethnocentric universal history that sees the State as the destiny of every society.[52] Against this self-justifying evolutionism, Clastres argues that societies without a State do not represent a primitive stage of social evolution that has not yet attained the development of a State. The non-State society, he insists, has its own positive structures, social mechanisms, and modalities of social power that function as mechanisms of refusal, anticipating and precluding the development of the State. From the perspective of this society, indeed, it is the State that appears monstrous.

Even so, for all his rejection of teleological history, a form of evolutionism still insinuates itself into Clastres's critique, precisely at the point where he seeks to narrate the disjunctive development of the non-State into the State. Clearly, he cannot represent this change as economically driven, since the production of a surplus that had earlier been refused would presuppose the very force that constitutes the State. By the same token, the existence of an exploitative class structure cannot be proposed as the precondition for the emergence of the State since, for a class structure to exist, the relations of power that constitute the State would already have to be in place. There is, however, a force for change that Clastres says lies at the interface of the social and the natural. This is the dimension of demographics and population density, where involuntary shifts lead to the regionalization of the power of the chiefs, whose growing authority then, in turn, foments a reaction by prophets of a Land without Evil who preach the rejection of the society of unitary power and lead mass migrations out of the territory of the chiefs' control.[53] Paradoxically, however, it is the very power of the prophets to subordinate the multiplicity of the group to one will that marks the birth of the despotism whose inheritance is the State.[54] By this account, therefore, the society of the non-State must still be *prior to* the society of the State, even though Clastres maintains that the state revolution cannot be conflated either with an economic revolution or with the transition to urban living. Indeed, Clastres holds that "all civilized peoples were first primitives,"[55] though, by his own logic, the State must have always already been present, insofar as he describes primitive societies as societies of active refusal whose internal limit must therefore continually conjure up the State as its defining externality.

There is thus a fundamental conflict between Clastres's conception of the self-contained character of the non-State society and his insistence that it actively refuses the development of the State. On the one hand, the non-State society is homogenized as a structure that is impenetrable to any externality and from which nothing escapes. Clastres sees it as a self-contained and self-sustaining structure that, allegedly, cannot contain any relations of power as subordination (though we might well then ask how it comes to harbor both slavery and a sexual division of labor, just as we might wonder why it should ever break down). On the other hand, Clastres's notion of mechanisms of refusal necessarily implies a response to an externality against which the society of the non-State must defend itself but which cannot yet exist. Clearly, this tension between integrality and refusal also opens on the problem of the evolutionism that continues to shape Clastres's notion of the non-State society as *prior to* the society of the State. In order to be excluded or refused, the State must always already exist as an exterior. It must also be marked as an interior exterior, present as potential within the counter-State society itself. But this would undermine the temporality of Clastres's account of the emergence of the State. Indeed, the very problem of the transformation of non-State into State posed by Clastres can be seen as one generated by his formulation of the non-State society, just as his attempt to find a solution in the invocation of outside factors is driven by his conception of the non-State society as a homogeneity from which nothing escapes.

For Deleuze and Guattari, by contrast, the State does not evolve from the non-State.[56] The two social forms are radically discontinuous.[57] The society of the non-State is not a society that is not yet capable, economically or politically, of developing a State. It is, rather, a society that has developed specific mechanisms and institutions that are capable of warding off the State.[58] Yet the society of the State does not erupt when the mechanisms that ward it off collapse, as Clastres suggests. The autarky of the primitive society is nothing more than an ethnological dream since the idea of the prior existence of the society of the non-State as a society that refuses a State entails seeing it as the preemptive anticipation of what does not yet exist.[59] There must always, therefore, have been States, everywhere.[60] The relation between non-State and State must be one of complex coexistence, in which tendencies toward the State are also present within the non-State, insofar as the non-State defines itself at the threshold of the State, while the State expands itself by rendering the non-State impossible. State and non-State therefore confront each other in active tension, forever unable to eradicate the one within the other, as the State strives to render the non-State impossible yet is unable to eradicate the non-State within itself.[61]

For Deleuze and Guattari, State and non-State do not, however, exhaust the analysis of power or force in social organizations. Rather, the field of sociality is cut across by heterogeneous formations of force and their concomitant social formations.[62] To State and non-State societies, which figure in Clastres's account as counterposed and mutually exclusive forms of social organization, are added nomadic societies, urban societies, and worldwide machines or ecumenical organizations, each defining itself by its attempt to subordinate the others to its own machinic processes.[63] States elaborate their apparatuses of capture and contract. Non-State societies work to preclude the State through their mechanisms of anticipation and prevention. Nomadic bands and packs, radically external to the political sovereignty of the State, function as war machines, unbinding bonds and betraying pacts.[64] Autonomous towns and cities seek to secure their power through instruments of polarization.[65] Worldwide machines or ecumenical organizations cross over the other forms in movements of encompassment.[66] At the same time, each is entirely capable of switching over its mode of operation into that of another. Yet none is able to constitute a saturated social formation, free from disruption by the other formations.[67]

Even the State, as it strives to exert a monopoly of force and to unify itself internally, has to operate in a field it cannot exhaust or reduce to an identity through its apparatuses of capture. Within the State form itself, as we have seen, there is also heterogeneity, as the mode of capture and the character of State violence change with the State's internal development, oscillating between two archaic forms of rule: that of the charismatic despot or magician-emperor, who rules at a distance by bond, signs, and enslavement, capturing the imaginary in overcoded signs; and that of the jurist-priest, the administrator, legislator, and lawgiver, who rules by codifying the symbolic through pact, law, contract, instrumental technique, and social subjection.[68] On one side, the One-Eyed Man, on the other, the One-Armed Man: the embodiments of two forms of capture—the machinic enslavement of magical capture and the machinery of subjection and subjectification of law and the contract—both of which survive in the modern nation-state as models of realization for an axiomatic of flows combining new technical machinic enslavement with social subjection.[69]

The force of Deleuze and Guattari's argument is that it multiplies forms of power, so that it is no longer possible to see the State as a homogeneous field of power relations saturating the territory of sociality. The State has to deal with its own internal war machines—its internal exteriority—just as it has to operate in a diversified field of power vectors in which the social form of the State is in constant interaction, internally and externally, with nomadic societies, non-State societies, autonomous urban societies, and worldwide machines or ecumenical organizations. Each vector implies a different modality of rule, a different mode of operation, a different style of violence, a different way to occupy and organize space, a different structuring of work, and a different conception of knowledge. Yet none is capable of fully constituting a society.

At the same time, however, Deleuze and Guattari's taxonomy of power is not exempt from its own form of essentialism and its own guilty Hegelianism. State and war machine are consistently singled out from among the five forms of social organization and held up in contrast to each other. Set one against the other in an insistent binarism, State and war machine take on the character of expressive unities that offer inverted reflections of each other at every point: in their forms of collectivity,[70] in their conceptions of space,[71] in their conceptions of science,[72] in their conceptions and practices of architecture,[73] and in their approaches to work.[74] Why, we might ask, do the State and the war machine have to be isolated and contrasted in this way? Why does there have to be an internal coherence and even an isomorphism to each and every one of their characteristic manifestations? Why do they have to mirror each other at every point? What does it mean to say they have a pure externality in relation to each other?[75] Are State and war machine to be imagined as totalities united by machinic processes that function as essential forces or structural principles of identity? Would this not merely constitute another form of Hegelianism: counterposed totalities, each with its own center? Is it possible to differentiate forms of sociality other than as expressive wholes? Is it possible to think the mutual externality of formations of force other than in binaristic terms? Could there be more than one exterior? And must interior and exterior be thought in territorial terms? In the very terms of the model that Deleuze and Guattari offer, would territorial concepts not be one more example of State thinking—like the return of binary thought? Are the answers not crucial to how we frame the relation of power, discourse, and the State?

We live in a state of war, as Antonio Negri and Michael Hardt have been the latest to remind us, echoing Foucault, Deleuze and Guattari, and even Bobbitt.[76] The bitter contradiction in this is that the modern State claims to have emerged precisely to put an end to war—above all civil war (which is endemic everywhere now)—by securing a sovereign power that will save society by expelling conflict and strife to the borders of its territory and beyond. In effect, however, the formation of the sovereign State not only exacerbated warfare between States—as a continuation of interstate politics by other means—but also established perpetual warfare as the condition of internal peace, since the State, as embodiment of public right, predicated its status on an appropriation of lawful violence that demanded a constant state of internal war to secure its monopoly of force against all forms of transgression, secession, resistance, indifference, and dissent. In this sense, Marx's assessment of the State apparatus as a machinery of warfare is not in doubt—though the State did not generate or produce from its own trajectory the heterogeneous array of techniques and technologies that, in its promulgation of internal war, it sought to integrate into the increasingly centralized systems and institutions of surveillance, discipline, regulation, administration, and control that constituted the state of security, of which social security would prove such an essential component.[77]

As we have seen, however, the system of security depended in turn on the ability of the State to hold in place certain regimes of representation whose violence of meaning the State also sought to annex to its monopoly. Such an appropriation of the right to adjudicate meaning, to decide where and when meaning stops and starts, was a necessary support for the field of disciplinarity and its regimens of instrumental representation, documentation, and evidence, whose machinery was targeted at the body and its spaces; at their function, their reproduction, and their productivity; and at all that might go wrong. (Though this, again, is not to say that the State was the originator of or even the impetus for those locally improvised techniques and technologies of representation that the State would seek to take to itself, to normalize, to classify, and to centralize.)

Even so, the state of war on which the State was founded could not be maintained or sustained by explicit violence alone or, indeed, by the implicit violence of disciplinary training and disciplinary meaning. The risk of provoking internal discord was not the only or even the prime mover here. The development of interstate warfare and the mobilization of mass armies in the campaigns that followed the French Revolution exposed the strategic weakness of those states whose internal cohesion and defensive capability rested on coercive force and the externality of imposed institutions of rule. Hegel himself recognized as much as he fled from the battle of Jena. Military threat and the drive to modernization compelled a strategic innovation in which the State—as Foucault has shown—sought to appropriate the very discourse of those whom it had defeated: a subterranean discourse of enmity, injustice, and the perpetual war of retribution; the discourse of a subject that has positioned itself outside the history of the State as told by the State itself; the discourse of another claim to right; the discourse of an ethno-cultural people as nation, as bearer of a destiny that is not that of reason, as embodiment of the force of the body and all that flows in it and through it and from it.[78] What opened for the State, therefore, was another kind of body politics: the politics of blood and tongue—the politics of *nation* and *culture*. This was the moment when culture emerged as concept, formation, and machine. It was not the machinery of civilization and cultivation—in Germany, the machinery of all that was known in the best circles under the name of *Bildung*. It was, rather, an incorporative machinery: a machinery of capture and of identification that took power as coregent with the instruments of justice and the disciplinary regime, the One-Eyed Man and the One-Armed Man, each with its own form of violence, its own form of capture, and its own form of meaning.[79]

At the opening of the nineteenth century, the name for this machinery still retained its relative novelty and had not yet become a dead metaphor. Spelled with a *C* until the last quarter of the nineteenth century, *Cultur* had entered German only in the late seventeenth century from French, in which, at the time, the currency of the term was solely that of a noun of process and action—the culture *of* something—and not yet that of a term for a formation, state, or condition. Even at this stage, however, the metaphoricity of the word, evoking the care for and growing of plants, was already deeply inscribed, going back to the Latin root, *cultus*, the noun stemming from the verb *colere*. The meanings of *cultus* ranged from the inhabitation of a place, to care for the earth or ground and, by extension, to the care for and refinement of the person both in education and appearance—a meaning that was then extended to the adornment and ornamentation of one's body, speech, or mode of living and thence to the proper veneration of what was due to friends, to dignitaries, and to the gods.[80] The derived term *cultura* operated across a similar range of meanings, signifying the tilling or cultivation of land and the care bestowed on plants, the care or upkeep of persons, the training or improvement of mental faculties, the cultivation of acquaintances, and the observance of religious rites. What is carried within the metaphoric extension that is already marked in these root terms is, therefore, an implicit reference back to a natural and organic basis. This contrasts sharply with the root meaning of "civilization," from the linked Latin radicals: *civis*, citizen or countryman in his relation to the State; *civitas*, an organized community of citizens or State, usually a city or a city and its surrounding district; and *civilitas*, citizenship but also the science of politics. Here, the emphasis falls insistently on organized social relations and on a process of civic development in the context of city life, rather than on the organic cultivation of the individual.[81]

In German, *Cultur* had, in the beginning and even up to its usage by Immanuel Kant,[82] the sense of a process of cultivation or of becoming cultured—an inflection easily confused, therefore, with the improving process of *Zivilisation* and the educative refinement signified by the process of *Bildung*. Toward the end of the eighteenth century, however, the connotations of these clustered terms began to be differentiated again, so that *Cultur*, as a condition of life or achievement of a people, was distinguished from *Bildung*, as the process of educating and refining individuals and the attributes of the individuals so produced. The relations of *Cultur* and *Zivilisation* are harder to disentangle. Yet despite Wilhelm von Humboldt's attempt in 1836 to associate "culture" with the material control of nature by science and technology and "civilization" with the qualitative improvement of humanity,[83] it still seems that the term *Cultur* retained the distinct sense of an organic connection to an individual or people, while "civilization" connoted the articulated achievements of a social formation.

The most comprehensive account of the genealogy of "culture" and its emergence as "a technical term" in anthropology, sociology, and psychology remains that of A. L. Kroeber and Clyde Kluckhohn, who trace the emergence in English of the ethnographic concept of culture back to the publication in 1871 of E. B. Tylor's *Primitive Culture*.[84] Tylor's field-shaping publication borrowed the term so prominently flagged in its title from German—from the work of Gustav Klemm and from later nineteenth-century German discussions in which something akin to the word's modern technical meaning was already well established.[85] As early as 1843, Klemm had argued that the new task for historical studies was to focus on "what is essential in history, namely culture (*Cultur*), as it is manifest in customs, in beliefs, and in forms of government."[86] In the genealogy sketched by Kroeber and Kluckhohn, the definition of culture given here by Klemm stemmed, in turn, from a line of late eighteenth-century universal histories, most famously that of Johann Gottfried Herder, in which interest focused on "concrete fact" and on the historical variety of forms of actual human activity.[87] This particularizing and empirically descriptive historical tradition had, according to Kroeber and Kluckhohn, separated itself from "a formal philosophical current" whose prime concern was to deduce the evolution of human social forms from essential principles, in relation to which "culture was of *decreasing interest*."[88] Confident in this assertion, Kroeber and Kluckhohn thus feel able to dismiss Hegel from further discussion. With passing reference only to the posthumously published transcription of his lectures on *The Philosophy of History*, Hegel's writings are summarily shunted into a sideline as "part of the last florescence of the concept of spirit"—a grandiose deductive project that supposedly directed Hegel's thinking away from engagement with the emerging concept of *Cultur*.[89]

The difficulty here is that Kroeber and Kluckhohn are wrong in the impression they leave that Hegel never used the word *Cultur*. More broadly, the problem with their argument is that, from Johann Christoph Adelung and Johann Gottfried Herder to Gustav Klemm, the universal histories that supposedly founded the descriptive empirical tradition and gave the word *Cultur* its wider German usage were themselves as normative in their narrative framework as they were relativistic, presenting the diversity of historical forms of custom, knowledge, art, religion, and belief as developmental stages in the progress toward a higher civilization.[90] The conception of culture to which they were committed was, moreover, as organic as it was teleological—a view that they clearly shared with Hegel, who was to give it its most fully developed articulation. It was in the shadow of the works in which he did so, from the *Phenomenology of Mind* to the *Philosophy of History*, that Klemm was writing. The opposition of Spirit and culture, *Geist* and *Cultur*, on which Kroeber and Kluckhohn's notion of counterposed traditions rests, thus collapses, since Hegel's conception of Mind or Spirit was perforce an attempt to articulate that collective rationality whose progressive development finds expression in the organically integrated practices of determinate cultures. Kroeber and Kluckhohn themselves recognize this by default when they acknowledge that, in discussions in Germany after 1850, "philosophers, historians and literary men were more active and influential than anthropologists"[91] and that, for these writers, as Heinrich Rickert put it in 1898, *Geistesgeschichte* had become *Kulturgeschichte*—precisely an indication not that the opposition of Spirit and culture had been dissolved in the latter's favor but that the opposition had been a false one from the start.[92]

There is thus no escaping Hegel and, without engaging his writings, we cannot understand the emergence of *Cultur*, not only as a "technical" concept but as part of a machinery of social reform. From his days in Tübingen, Berne, and Frankfurt, Hegel had lamented what he took to be the distance of modern values from the Greek ideal of a form of life or "Spirit" capable of uniting and directing social, political, and religious conduct. In the world of classical Greece, as he imagined it, personal freedom and public morality were held in harmonious balance in the figure of the classical hero. In modern society, by contrast, the subjective will of the individual presented itself in opposition to the objective will of the State.[93] What was needed, Hegel began to argue, was a new religion that would lead to a moral and spiritual renewal and thence to social reform. Such a renewal could not come, however, either from the subjective moral regimen of the individual or from the external imposition of duties and obligations. It had to come from the individual's identification with a larger ground, unbounded by self or other: a ground on which the State could unite its citizens by giving form to a common project capable of claiming their full and uncoerced allegiance.

The immediate example before Hegel, as he arrived in Jena in 1801, was that of the overwhelming superiority of the French military, based on the French ability to mobilize unprecedented numbers of devoted conscripts whose intense identification rallied them to the cause of nation and revolution. By contrast, the army of the politically impotent Holy Roman Empire, held together solely by drill and discipline, was manifestly incapable of instilling such a sense of solidarity. The difference was telling. What it showed was that, if Germany was to become a true State, it would have to find the means to unite its people in such a way that they would come to identify with its collective sense of purpose. The question of the proper form of the German State thus converged with the question of establishing a people's religion.

In the first decade of the new century, Hegel, of course, was not alone in holding the view that the ideal of unity brought to realization in the ethical harmony of the Greek city-state had been rendered remote from contemporary life by a utilitarian culture (Hegel's term at this time was *Cultur*) that was driving the decomposition of society into a fragmented multitude of individuals, all pursuing their own immediate self-interest and competing with others rather than joining together for the common good.[94] At the same time, it seemed that the sheer size and scale of the modern State, with its increasing centralization and bureaucracy, had also undermined collective commitment, insofar as it confronted the individual as a hostile and alien force whose purpose was domination and control. The fractured and self-alienated world of modernity that had emerged from the collapse of aristocratic norms and the convulsive overthrow of established institutions thus found itself estranged from shared goals and ends and deeply torn between an arid intellectual culture divorced from all tradition and an emotionalist pietism that called for an immediate individual reckoning with God. Neither, in Hegel's mind, could ever hope to command a general allegiance, and neither would ever be in a position to generate an ethical orientation capable of restoring social cohesion.

Healing the symptomatic ruptures in modern life, Hegel argued, would demand more than could be given by the brilliant but brittle and one-sided philosophies of self-determining subjectivity, and more than could be restored in the immediacy of the natural community of blood, tradition, and faith. Only the systematic development of a socially and historically construed logic could account for the trajectory of the experience of consciousness that had produced the modern standpoint and the crisis of modern culture, and only such a philosophy could move on from there to promote the modern community's collective reflection on its ultimate purposes and ends.[95] The search for an ethical form of life more adequate to the tensions of contemporary living and more effective at binding the community at large thus became the urgent focus of Hegel's thought and writing in Jena, where he worked to transform his early ethic of love into a conception of the communality of mutually recognizing subjects as the social and historical realm of Spirit whose highest manifestation is the State.[96]

It was above all in the *Phenomenology of Spirit* of 1807 that this ethico-political project took shape, quite literally amid the upheavals that would expose the bankruptcy of the existing regime. Completing the last pages of the *Phenomenology* on the eve of the battle of Jena, in which Napoleon's army would again send the once-dominant Prussian troops into full-scale, chaotic retreat, Hegel reported seeing Napoleon himself and was confirmed in his sense of German weakness and the necessity of his argument. The historical inheritance of the State, he reasoned, was to embody the full mutuality that is the foundation of self-consciousness. Only in this way could it enact for the individual a space of recipro-cal recognition and thereby come to secure the identification of its citizens. As the willing union of rights-bearing individuals, the State would then take shape as the most developed and objective form of eth-ical freedom, held together by social and political institutions whose ethical bonds had not been determined by any single constituency.[97] Ethical freedom would thus be achieved when individuals came to find their fullest development in and through the sense of identity they shared with the whole community. True reform of the State therefore entailed an advance toward an ethical community in which the demands of absolute knowledge would be realized not as the external abstractions of skeptical reason but as the collective's internalized understanding of itself as the necessary result of humanity's own history, embodied in a way of life that could both justify its claims to allegiance and continually reinvent itself along rational lines.

Key to the argument was Hegel's deployment of the concept of *Sittlichkeit*, which narrowly signifies morality but also carries the broader connotation of the whole way of living of a person or people, founded not on imposed decrees but on what is accepted without question as the standard and foundation of action. For Hegel, this extension of mean-ing was clearly implied in the relation of *Sittlichkeit* to *Sitte*—custom or tradition—just as classical Greek *ethics* had its foundation in *ethos*: cus-tom or habit but also, by extension, the characteristic spirit of a people or community.[98] *Sittlichkeit* thus carried within it both *ethos* and *ethics*, going beyond individual morality (*Moralität*) to articulate what it was that bound the individual to the rational authority of the community as a whole. One might respond that what is glossed over here is an im-plicit circularity that threatens to expose the generally problematic place of the conventional structure of language in Hegel's system: The ethical community that secures identification presupposes the community of custom—the community of a code that must have already constituted the community as community at the level at which it operates as a commu-nity of discourse.[99] In the *Phenomenology of Spirit*, however, the form of ethical life is seen as bringing to a higher level of self-consciousness what is only habitual in the communality of custom. In this way, *Sittlichkeit* comes to fill out the space of *Cultur* in earlier texts, disclosing in its higher development what is fundamentally at stake in the general outlook or shared form of life of a people.

For the project of reform, the practice that would shape this ethical substance and secure the "immediate confiding trust of the individuals in the whole of their nation"[100] was to be education, conceived as an arena of *Bildung*, or process of self-cultivation.[101] Such a process of education could not, however, be founded on the imposition of discipline, any more than it could be driven by the competitive pursuit of individual cleverness or by the critical negativity of an abstract and skeptical rationality. For Hegel, these alienated manifestations of *Bildung* represented no advance over the blind certainties of an imposed faith that set itself against them. Disciplinary structures and the alienated worlds of codified knowledge and law only caused the communal interest to appear as an external will opposed to the individual, obscuring the original identity and unbroken continuity of consciousness. To be restored to its proper function, *Bildung* had to return "out of its confusion to itself as *Spirit*";[102] it had to be fired again in the furnace of philosophy and recast as that process of transmission and emulation through which, in the course of their self-formation, independent individuals would come to discover themselves as members of a conscious community capable of realizing the demands of rational development, actualizing an ideal of self-directed humanity, and serving as the foundation and support of a reformed and rational State.[103]

This investment in the ideal of *Bildung* was one that Hegel shared with a generation of German classical humanists who, following Johann Joachim Winckelmann, committed themselves to the emulation of a seductively idealized image of Greek ethical harmony, first as a critique of modern life and then as an instrument to reform it. Central to this cohort and to its determination to turn commitment into policy were Wilhelm von Humboldt, who laid the foundation of the university in Berlin on the principles of *Bildung* and *Wissenschaft*, and Karl Sigmund Franz vom Stein zum Altenstein, Humboldt's successor as minister for religion, education, and health, who personally solicited Hegel to accept the chair of philosophy in Berlin and who supported him because he saw Hegel's systematic philosophy as the rationalization of a reform movement whose ideals of ethical life described the framework for a modern, constitutional Prussian State that would supersede both the absolutist traditions of the ancien régime and the emotional bonds of the *Volk*.[104] In the period of post-Napoleonic Prussian reform, with the old elites discredited by a military, economic, and political crisis they had failed to forestall, neo-humanists such as Humboldt and Altenstein saw *Bildung* as the means to produce an elite stratum of self-motivating men of cultivation and learning not tied to the rule book and not bound by narrow allegiances of region or class, but wedded to the State in their mission to direct social life and shape a new German culture according to the rational precepts of universal principles.

Yet this idea of *Bildung*, which took shape in German neohumanist educational circles in the first decades of the nineteenth century, could not, in effect, remain solely a technique of the self that was the exclusive property of a social elite. Certainly, the projected program of modernization and liberal reform turned on the creation of a privileged class of civic leaders and superior public servants. But it also required a broader transformation of subjects into citizens, and this entailed the dissemination of *Bildung* and its incorporation into all aspects of social life, moving beyond the schools, gymnasia, and universities to take root in the family, as the nexus of basic training in personal mores and ethical values. Again it was Hegel's philosophy that provided the systematic framework in which this organic transformation of society could be conceived, even if, in this transformation, the very substance of *Bildung* would itself be transformed from what Ian Hunter has called "a specific caste practice of aesthetico-ethical self-cultivation" into a corrective technology of moral discipline and a machinery for shaping the proper attributes of a citizenry.[105]

Key here was the strategic space of public schooling, with its new technologies of corrective discipline layered over the developing disciplinary techniques of policing, penality, public health, poverty relief, and family reform. It was in this space that *Bildung* was annexed to a new mode of governmentality in which it was to function as the means to operationalize defined behavioral norms in a large-scale program for governing the population through moral management. As Hunter has argued in another context, what had first emerged as a minority technique of the self was thus redeployed across the morally administered environments of the social sphere, "not as the vehicle for an ideal general process of human realization . . . but as a repository of techniques for forming a special kind of person that these environments came to require."[106] Yet something crucial is missed if this process is taken solely as a means of engineering a social space in which individuals can be produced with the required normative attributes. When Hegel projected ethical self-cultivation as a model for the transformation of a populace into a citizenry for whom social norms would be present as the dictates of inner conscience, he was primarily concerned with the recruitment of a collectivity—a community or nation that could no longer be taken as a given, but that had to be restored or, in effect, reconstituted. The mechanism involved in this worked, moreover, less through the emulation of an ethical exemplar than through the propagation of a systematic logic of historical self-recollection.

Insofar as Hegel, in the *Phenomenology*, had defined his object as the experiential process (*Erfahrung*) of consciousness, he had thereby irrevocably connected consciousness to the axis of history and transformation.[107] And insofar as he had rejected the division of consciousness from a self-consciousness that depended, in turn, on a framework of mutual recognition, he had effectively made consciousness a function of changing forms of collectivity. It was this collectivity as ethical substance that was then given form in the historical manifestations of art, religion, philosophy, custom, and law, whose essential truth could only be grasped by the cultivation of a historical understanding that could recognize these forms of communal life as embodiments of the cumulative experience of consciousness. Restored in this way to the internal history of humanity's progress toward absolute knowledge, art, religion, philosophy, custom, and law then took on a special status not only as expressions of the collective community but as the very arenas in which individuals were made conscious of the bonds of trust that bound them together as a citizenry. Such arenas were, therefore, central to the ethical reshaping of the State.

When, in the 1820s in Berlin, in popular lecture series on art, religion, philosophy, and history, Hegel elaborated and narrativized ideas that went back to his Jena years, what opened up for his reform-minded adherents, as it had for the generation of Altenstein, was the prospect of a new field of policy: the field of *Culturpolitik*, in which the techniques of self-cultivation that had been the province of an elite might begin to take on a different value both as a State-mandated program for education and training and as a means of capturing a populace for the rational, reformist State.[108] If, on his arrival in Berlin, Hegel had found influential scope as philosopher and administrator for his passionate commitment to *Bildung* and to a *Bildungspolitik*, his later lectures on the history of philosophy and on the philosophy of history, religion, and art effectively worked to cohere and functionalize a set of "cultural" domains as the embodiments of a process of collective experience through which humanity, internalizing the cumulative stages of its self-realization, came to fulfill its absolute ends. For those who followed the historical exposition of his systematic logic, the way was thus prepared for the return of the concept of *Cultur*, not merely as a means to articulate the essential identity and organic totality of a range of historical practices, but also as a lever of policy under which these same areas of social practice could be instrumentalized as the forcing grounds of the ethical community and as tools of recruitment to the new nation-state.

If it was Thomas Hobbes who dreamed of sovereignty as a means to put an end to the war of all against all, and if it was Bentham who dreamed of the democracy of discipline and utility as a means to put an end to the wasteful discharges of the body, then it was Hegel who dreamed of culture as the lived union of belief of the people and the State—even if Hegel did not give this collective imaginary its name, which would have to wait for the codification of his philosophy of Spirit as a secular, historical anthropology capable of providing the theodicy of the modern nation-state. As witness to the contrast between the victorious French citizens' army and the isolated military caste of the German states, Hegel saw that cohesive sociality could not be produced or sustained solely by discipline or domination, within the dyad of master and slave, or even by a modern disciplinary training oriented to utility but imposing its benchmarks and demands from the outside. Such external forms could not secure the internalized allegiance to collective norms that the rational redirection of society required. This necessary redirection could only come about through a process of cultivation or culture capable of producing those self-directing subjects for whom the potentiality of modern freedom was embedded in a complete form of life. Culture, as *Bildung*, was therefore the necessary catalyst, but only insofar as it was not a tool but an end in itself, and only insofar as it was capable, through the training of a meritocratic cohort of teachers and civil servants, of spawning a new form of life, or *Cultur*, in which the collective recognition of shared ends and mores would be realized.

If culture in the sense of *Bildung* was the primer, then culture in the sense of *Cultur* was the effective means of capture: the sphere of realization in which a populace would be recruited as citizens of a new State that itself embodied the inherent rationality of history. *Cultur* was the apparatus that would accomplish what the Enlightenment had failed to do and that pietistic faith effectively blocked. As the very process of collective self-consciousness, it would resolve the opposition between the externality of an abstract, rational civilization, with its alienated structures of "pure culture" that devalue natural being, and the organic and indwelling, if unrationalized, culture of integration of the community of faith.[109] Culture's task was the creation of a citizenry adequate to the modern State, not by calling them out in the name of an abstract humanity and reason but by raising to consciousness a rationality supposed to be immanent within them and embodied in the continuity of indigenous custom, tradition, and belief. Where Kroeber and Kluckhohn are inadvertently right, therefore, is in stressing that the crucial period of transformation and extension of the concept of *Cultur* in Germany lay between the end of the eighteenth century and the middle of the nineteenth century, at a time when, as they tentatively suggest, the concept of culture deeply engaged the sense of disproportion between Germany's artistic and intellectual emergence and its political arrears.[110] Conceived as a means to capture a population for modernization and predicated on the reality of German underdevelopment, the concept of culture emerged in the first decades of the nineteenth century as a discursive machinery for recruitment and mobilization that would reconcile rationalization and belief while simultaneously displacing the threat of destruction and revolution. To discipline and sovereign right, we must add this third machinery—the Third Man in the room who will also soon seek to make the camera his own.

CHAPTER 2

The Plane of Decent Seeing: Documentary and the Rhetoric of Recruitment

I look to register what actually moves: what hits the spectator at the midriff: what yanks him up by the hair of the head or the plain boot-straps to the plane of decent seeing.

—JOHN GRIERSON, "What I Look For"

"One of the favored words in the photographic literature of today," wrote Edward Steichen in 1938, "is 'documentary'":

It is used with particular glibness by writers who are in the process of patting themselves on the back that they have suddenly, and without any help from Papa or Mamma, discovered photography. They proceed to dissect and analyze the various phases and branches of photography, wrap up and tie them into neat little packages that they file away into convenient pigeonholes, and the one marked "documentary" usually contains the conclusion that the beginning of photography and the end of photography is documentation, and that's that. In choosing examples to illustrate their reasoning, frequent reference has been made to pictures of vegetable fragments, egg beaters, telephone wire insulators, power line poles, etc. So as not to interfere with the logic of their arguments, they conveniently overlooked such other documents as passport photography, the "mugging" of criminals, the photographs of nuts and bolts for hardware catalogues, etc. etc.[1]

Steichen is obviously tilting at rivals—photographers, curators, critics. Yet he makes a point worth pondering, one that promises to interrupt the continuist history that in 1938 was only beginning to be constructed for a practice of photography newly categorized as "documentary."[2] In the event, it is a point that does not delay Steichen long. He is in too much of a hurry to steer the argument against the sophisticates of a new photo-criticism and toward the defense of pictures that "tell a story." But even these polemics turn out to be no more than staging posts on a path whose ultimate goal is to direct our eyes "into the faces" and into the "stories" of the men and women pictured in the photographs that surround Steichen's text—photographs drawn from just one section of a large commercial exposition, a section selected by photographers of the Historical Section of the Farm Security Administration (FSA) from that government agency's controversial archives.[3] In a sense, our path will have to follow the one laid out for us by Steichen: to Washington, D.C., and on, into the burgeoning filing cabinets of the Historical Section, on to the card-mounted, numbered, and captioned prints that fill their gray metal drawers, and onward, along the very lines of sight that Steichen is careful to prepare for our eyes, toward the "faces" and "stories" Steichen finds in what he calls "the most remarkable human documents that were ever rendered in pictures."[4] Yet if we set ourselves to follow Steichen here, it may well be only to find ourselves in a space with very different coordinates from the one he describes.

Before setting out, however, let us not be so quick to pass over those "overlooked" documents that Steichen throws down as a challenge, though only, in the end, to let them drop. These "other documents," as Steichen terms them—identity pictures, police photographs, instrumental records—will find themselves expelled from the story of concerned "documentary" because they echo with disturbing voices, voices that issue from the singular theaters of meaning in which these "other documents" were always spoken for, even while, by a kind of ventriloquism, they seemed to be made to speak for themselves. Passport offices, police charge rooms, warehouses and storerooms, archives of all kinds—such spaces of meaning, though old enough by the time Steichen was writing, marked out the sphere of operation of what had been for the nineteenth century a new order of writing and representation, a new language, that harnessed the latest imaging technologies and systems of information handling to a novel purpose: the careful scrutiny of bodies and spaces with a view to their regulation, modification, and productive application; the

COMMENTS ON FARM SECURITY ADMINISTRATION PICTURES
(Made in writing at The International Photographic Salon, Grand Central Palace, New York)

"Without a doubt the most vital and living exhibit in the whole show. Worth the forty cents if only to show photographers how to interpret our natural life."

"I know what it is. Try living in it four months and your aspect on life is soon down to zero. You don't care 'cause you've got 'nothin' anyhow. If you make a few bushels of potatoes and corn for the winter, God has been good. We fight for schools, clothes and books."

"I think that these are the best photographs I have ever seen."

"These candid photographs need no comment. The story is true, and sad and tragic."

"If the newspapers don't print these—can you get them before the public in some other manner?"

"As pictures O.K. but a false impression is given of American farm conditions. Typical of the New Deal bunk at tax payers' expense. However, F. D. R. and the whole gang is about washed up, Thank God, and a majority of Christians in the U. S. A."

"Best photography. Most living art in the show."

"Absolute proof of the great need of a continuance of the work of our administration. If this work was not to be continued, one would be tempted to curse the economic system that produced such human wreckage. For goodness sake . . . continue."

"Lousy bunch of prints. Subjects very sordid and dull for exhibition. They don't tell the story convincingly enough. Make them more sensational. P. S. More nudes."

"Now, more than ever, have I learned to realize what our West is like. I have seen it in person, but at the time was only sight-seeing."

". . . Touched me to the point where I would like to quit everything in order to help these stricken people . . ."

". . . American's who think F. S. A. waste of money should see these."

"Excellent work. Enlarge the project and take more pictures. Very fine use of public funds."

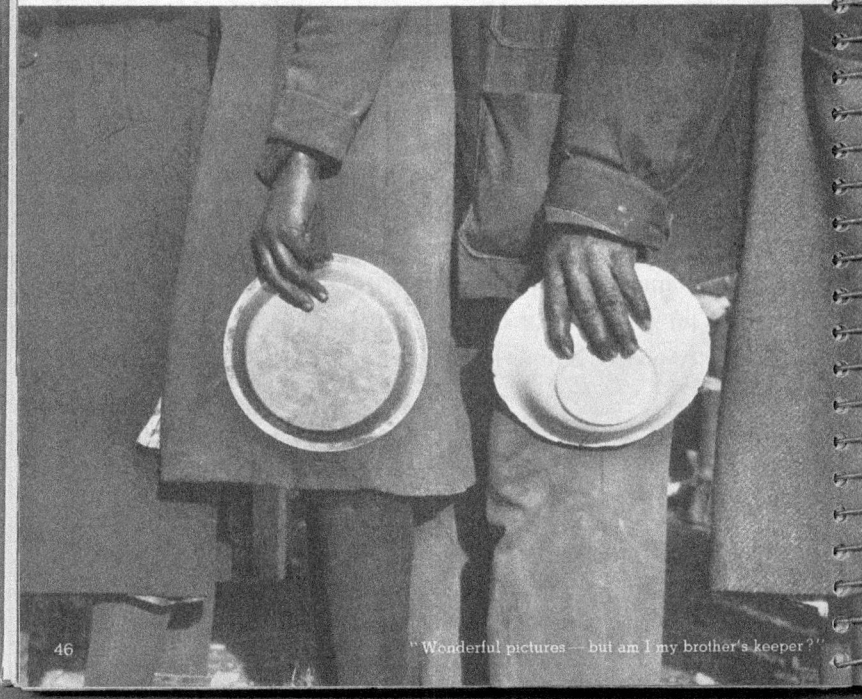

46   "Wonderful pictures—but am I my brother's keeper?"

Figure 12. Farm Security Administration photograph from Edward Steichen, "The F.S.A. Photographers," in *U.S. Camera Annual 1939*, ed. T. J. Maloney (New York: William Morrow, 1938).

accumulation, from this sustained observation, of dossiers, case studies, files, and records; the labeling, cataloging, and painstaking storage of these discriminating texts; their jealous, expert handling; and their elaboration into new systems of knowledge, new professional jurisdictions, and new institutional hierarchies. In short, these "other documents"—commonplace and trivial as they seem—bear the indelible stamp that registers their place in the annals of surveillance and record, in what Foucault has described as the archives of disciplinary power and disciplinary knowledge.

What I tried to stress in chapter 1, however, was that the techniques, technologies, and institutions whose dissemination constituted the disciplinary regime could only operate, insofar as they did, when certain codes of representation had been put in place. Integral to the disciplinary apparatus was the production of a specific and novel economy of discourse—a regime of sense that guaranteed a new order of truth and that turned on a new mode of documentation whose institutionalized effect was to reverse the political axis of representation, making it no longer a sign of power and prestige to be recorded but a sign of subjection and subordination. It is, then, within the closure of this discursive frame and its investment of the apparatuses of discipline that we have to understand how photography—or *a* photography—could come to function as an instrument of surveillance, record, evidence, and truth. The problem here for Steichen, of course, is that this is a doleful legacy to have been passed on as the inheritance of those "most remarkable human documents."

The story of "documentary," even as told by Edward Steichen, finds itself rudely interrupted. It is not only that "documentary value" can no longer be anchored in the camera itself, with its imagined access to the real, so that there can be no more talk of a continuous documentary tradition grounded on the nonmanipulative use of this camera's supposed natural properties. It is also that, if there is a link between documentation and "documentary," that link is now seen to come not via the pristine camera but via the institutions, discourses, and systems of power that invest the camera and sully it, and via the regimen that holds the document in place. What links document to "documentary" is not a natural continuity founding a seamless tradition but, rather, the uneven history of photography's implication in the purposeful institutionalization of boundaries to meaning: boundaries drawn only through a process of conflict and negotiation in which—contrary to the claims of the truth machine—nothing is guaranteed in advance; boundaries that specify photography's singularity only at the price of multiplying it and dividing it.

Needless to say, this is not the linkage that the apologists of "documentary" were seeking. It does not serve their purposes that the closeness of documentary to the document is rhetorical, institutional, and strategic rather than ontological. Nor does it serve their purposes that the history of documentary is the history of a strategy of meaning for which reality is not only a complex discursive effect but also an effect of *power* that returns its own force to the struggle to control the social field. It is not, then, just a matter of the textuality of the documentary image. Like all realist strategies, documentary seeks to construct an imaginary continuity and coherence between a subject of address and a signified real—a continuity and coherence in which not only the work of the sign but also the effects of power of a particular regimen are elided. What interests me here, therefore, as we try to follow Steichen's instruction to look into "faces" and "stories" caught in the "human documents" of the FSA, is what that look itself engages: the capture of an object for a subject and a subject for an object and the effects this capture produces in the field of sociality.

Realisms turn on the construction of an imaginary continuity and coherence between a subject of address and a signified real. The mobilization of such rhetorics of continuity and coherence has thus been most urgent and insistent at times of deep social crisis or transformation, in which conceptions of social identity and notions of reality have been rendered acutely unstable. In the face of instability, realist strategies of representation, as diverse and contentious as they may have been, have worked to retrieve certitudes of identity and reality from the turmoil of uncertainty by guaranteeing a given externality to a given internality—a given reality to a given subject.[5] What drives this strategy is, in each case, the critical conjuncture in which it is articulated as a response to particular historical demands—crisis-driven demands for common recognitions, for bedrock certainties, for uncontestable even if unpalatable truths. As a result, wherever realist strategies may have been positioned on the political spectrum and however critical of prevailing explanations and prejudices they may have been, however intent on putting authority in question, they have always sought in one way or another—even in the midst of an open conflict of realisms, as in the 1930s—to put an end to disputability and partisan sense. After all, the real is the real, and no one

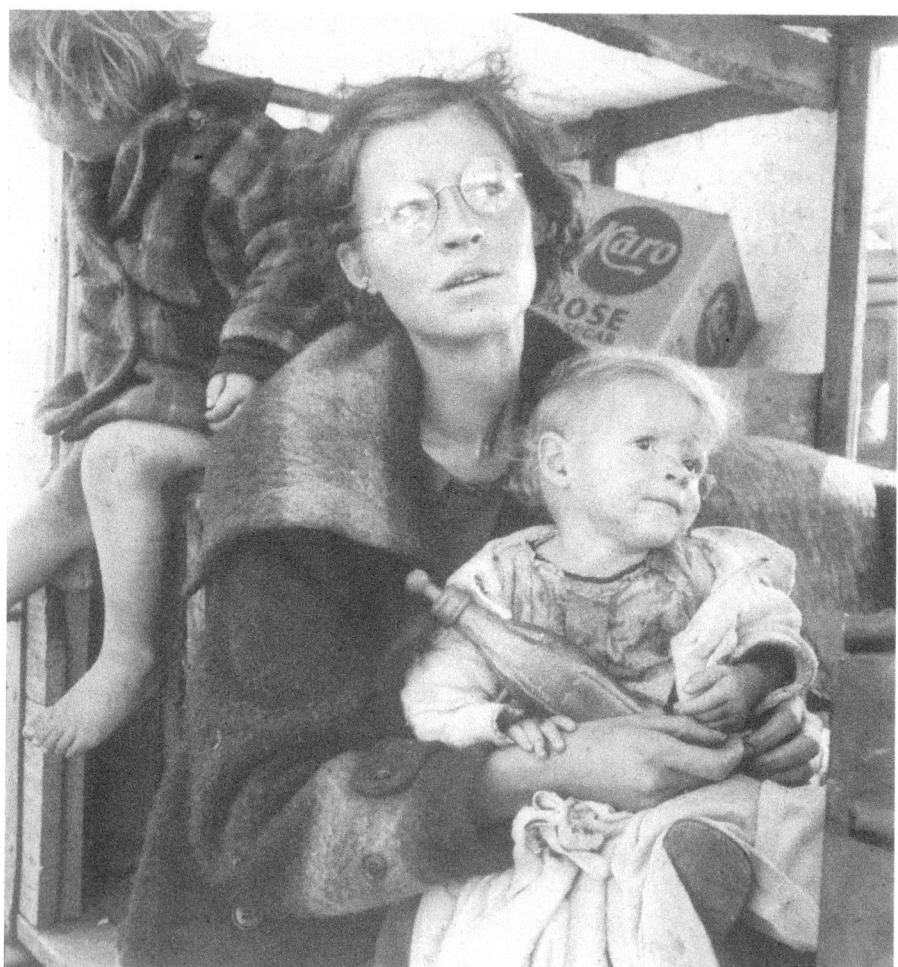

Figure 13. Dorothea Lange, "Family, one month from South Dakota, now on the road in Tulelake, Siskiyou County, California," September 1939. FSA-OWI Collection, Prints and Photographs Division, Library of Congress (LC-USF34-020992-D).

can argue with that. Realisms, by definition, claim to ground themselves on a finality that ends all dispute. Thus, they have never been able to brook the endless, open play of meaning that marks the contingency of the social and undoes all attempts to give a final fixity to social reality.

Finalities, in any case, tend to have a limited shelf life. In order to be effective, the timeless truths of realism have to be timely, since it is always within particular historical frames of discourse that effects of meaning are produced, mobilized, and enforced. Realisms are thus always specific and conjunctural: activated in specific historical frameworks, determined by specific representational resources, and effective only as specific historical rhetorics. The necessary corollary of this, however, is that they must also be plural and, in spite of or because of their individual claims, in conflict one with another. For the real is not just an effect of representation; it is also a stake in the circuits of power. In consequence, there is always a struggle of realisms, however marginalized this struggle may be at moments other than those of deep crisis, such as we had in the years of the Great Depression. Realism was a matter of contention in the 1930s precisely because the systemic collapse set off a crisis in the regime of the real—a crisis in the authority of established discursive regimens to articulate reality and to call into place the subjects of this real. This is the crisis to which documentary sought to respond.

Documentary realism is thus more than a system of coding. It is a concerted attempt to forestall a crisis in the field of meaning and the field of the subject. It works explicitly as a rhetoric of recruitment whose mobilization seeks to incorporate its targeted audience in an identification with the imaginary coherence of its system—an identification that enacts and secures a particular regime of truth, of subjectivity, and of sense, closing down the openness and disputability of reality that is so dangerously prone to erupt at times of crisis. But in documentary, the refinement of this strategy of appeal is also, as we have seen, tied in some way to the disciplinary reconstitution of the social field and to the history of a strategy of governance—a history bound up, in turn, with the configuration of the modern, interventionist State.

In the latter half of the nineteenth century, as we saw in chapter 1, the State in the core countries of capitalist development had come to annex new domains and assume new powers, increasing its responsibility for social order, social regulation, and social provision through policing, education, health, housing, water, sewage, planning, and transportation. Such extensions of state power did much to integrate the internal workings of social discipline and population management, but little to check the socially disruptive and internationally catastrophic effects of unregulated market forces, competition for global resources, and the rule of the gold standard. Undeterred, however, the growth of state power continued and even the disastrous impact of these destabilizing forces was to be leveraged in the 1930s into an occasion for the further expansion of the State and its apparatuses. The State in effect lives by crises, alternately engendering them and positing itself as the only force capable of overcoming them. Thus, in the midst of an economic collapse that seemed to threaten the very survival of liberal democracies, the ambit of state power in the United States was to be greatly expanded again through the increased interventionist role of the State in a more and more integrated economy, but also through the State's designation of a widening field of social problems across which it spread an ever more refined net of social security. In the immediate term, the reforms associated with social security may well have functioned as a means of procuring social cohesion by appropriating the ground of radical dissent. From a longer perspective, however, the system of social security worked as a system of governance by extending the State's power to objectify its populations and by setting in place those very relationships of dependency for which, ironically, the system would be criticized at the time of the breakup of welfare structures in the 1990s.[6] In the political context of a widening franchise, the system of social security responded to the need for new and effective mechanisms of incorporation, compelling the State to mobilize its populations in new ways by making itself not only an engine of census, surveillance, statistics, and administration but also an engine of publicity.

Documentary spoke to this necessity whereby state agencies sought to harness new techniques and new technologies to mold public opinion not only through the dissemination of what John Grierson described as "the information necessary to organized and harmonious living,"[7] but also, more effectively, through the inculcation of what Grierson called *"a pattern of thought and feeling."*[8] It was a pattern that did more than merely shape the reception of information in the citizen's mind. The pattern was the effective information—the linkage between the "thought and feeling" of the subject as citizen and the State. This is the space in which documentary's rhetoric of recruitment was enacted, in the guise of a program of public education in which, as Grierson insisted, it would be "the needs of the State," "the machinery by which the best interests of the people are secured," that would "come first."[9] Other advocates of civic resurgence of the time shared the conviction that the nexus of documentary, education, and emotional recruitment was crucial. For Roy Stryker, head of the Historical Section of the Resettlement Administration, later the Farm Security Administration, education was "the primary value"[10] of the Division of Information's pioneering use of photography, whose purpose was not only to "tell what a place or thing or person *looks* like" but, above all, to "tell the audience what it would *feel* like to be an actual witness to the scene."[11] Likewise, explaining the "documentary approach" in 1938, Beaumont Newhall insisted that "a seriously sociological purpose" was definitive for documentary photography, though the documentary photographer "will not photograph dispassionately; he will not simply illustrate his library notes. He will put into his camera studies something of the emotion which he feels toward the problem, for he realizes that this is the most effective way to teach the public he is addressing. After all, is not this the root-meaning of the word 'document' (*docere*, 'to teach')?"[12] Looking, feeling, teaching, a particular machinery of witness, all in the service of the State: perhaps we are not so far away from the machinery of the Panopticon as an instrument of public education as well as of punitive discipline. One is reminded of Bentham's dictum: "Preach to the eye if you want to preach effectively."[13]

Understanding the centrality of the relation of "documentary" to the State opens the way to reseeing documentary photography in its strategic moment, at a moment of crisis in which documentary's rhetoric of appeal took shape in a space of overlapping investments. One stratum was certainly the State's deployment of the disciplinary technologies, information storage systems, and instrumental knowledges that made it possible to engineer a takeoff in social administration. Overlaid on this was the State's investment of the new techniques of statistical survey and public opinion research that came to service the management of consent. Finally, there was the State's appropriation of the developing technologies and the rhetorics of mass communications that defined the emergent field of public relations. These efforts to functionalize an array of techniques and technologies converged in the mid-1930s around the drive to secure the necessary conditions for the politics and public culture of the social security State: the liberal, corporatist response to the crisis of the 1930s; a response that allowed the State a role as economic facilitator for capital, even while it repositioned the State in a resecured public culture as paternalistic mediator and guarantor of a transcendent national interest. It was a response that would also include what I will come on to call the New Deal cultural strategy—a strategy performatively enacted in the very structure of documentary.

The strategic moment is crucial. Against the continuist history of "documentary"—that word that worried Steichen, that "dread word," as Pare Lorentz called it[14]—we have to see "documentary" as a strategy and, indeed, as a term with a very particular history that cannot be extended beyond its moment or conflated retrospectively with the history of those practices of documentation and record keeping with which documentary is habitually associated and on which its status trades. This is not, of course, to say that the "prehistory" of "documentary" is not highly significant, taking us back, as it does, to the emergence of the apparatuses and institutions that set in place a new mode of discipline and governance. What we have to grasp, however, is that the specificity of "documentary" is embedded in a particular conjuncture, a specific set of institutions, and a specific discursive strategy concerned not only with representation and truth but, above all, with social reform and citizenship. It is this specificity that ties "documentary" to a particular conception of the liberal democratic state, of its relation to the individual, and of its structural problems at a time of crisis in the early 1930s.

The specificity of "documentary" and its moment has to be mapped out. At the same time, however, this mapping has also to take in the remarkable dissemination of documentary forms in the decade of the 1930s and their intentional crossing of media and genre boundaries. As the specific discourse of "documentary" began to take shape, it supported a range of hybrid practices of a diversity unfamiliar to us now. In the mid-1930s, such emergent practices may well have centered on the then new media of popular cultural consumption—photography and film—but, as William Stott has shown, they also extended across a much broader field, encompassing novels, travel guides, journalism, sociological writing, radio drama, radio reportage, didactic theater, advertising, mural painting, public sculpture, and new hybrids such as the photographic book.[15] Too much that is central is lost, however, if this is merely taken to mean that documentary constituted a new genre. As its founders recognized, documentary was, in a triple sense, a hybrid that crossed over the limits of media conventions, that crossed over the divide between the formal experimentalism of a socially isolated avant-garde and the popular appeal of a vapid commercial culture, and that crossed over the modalities of discipline and spectacle, as part of a crucial process of negotiation within the crisis-ridden structures of the capitalist state. This is not just the creation of a new genre. Looking back, Grierson would insist, "Documentary was born and nurtured on the bandwagon of uprising social democracy everywhere";[16] it was "the first and only true art form produced by social democracy."[17] The characterization of documentary's political coordinates may be questionable, but not the sense of its implication. Documentary proliferated because it was a strategy with multiple points of application, born and nurtured on the bandwagon of social security, one might say, as a machinery of capture plugged into a retooled mode of liberal democratic governance.

The sense of this historicity has been largely lost to us through a broadening of usage that has also drained documentary of the specific character of its politics of meaning.[18] In the 1930s, however, the novelty of the word and the stakes that had accrued around it were very much a matter of comment, and establishing a history of the term was important to attempts to explain it. As the American curator and librarian Beaumont Newhall recorded in 1938, the first to use "documentary" in its new sense in English had been the Scottish-born sociologist, film critic, filmmaker, and administrator John Grierson, though Grierson himself acknowledged the earlier French usage of *documentaire* to describe a more serious form of travelogue or expedition film. In France, at least, there were certainly earlier and more pertinent associations with photography and film. In Paris in 1898, for example, the expatriate Polish cinematograph entrepreneur Bolesław Matuszewski published a striking pamphlet calling for the creation of "a historical film depository" of records of spectacles and events of "documentary interest" (*d'un intérêt documentaire*) that would lay the basis for a State-sponsored library of national and public life in filmic form, to serve as an educational resource and an incontrovertible archive of historical evidence.[19] This said—and having insisted that the history of the word itself is crucial—it has to be admitted that this history has yet to be adequately traced. The circumstances of Grierson's transposition of the term into English, the development of his usage, and the passage of the word from adjective to noun are far from entirely clear, in part because, from 1946 on, the canon of Grierson's collected writings on documentary has always excluded key early essays and memoranda from the late 1920s, works in which Grierson's thinking first coalesced.

The earliest habitually recognized usage of "documentary" occurs in a February 1926 review of Robert Flaherty's filmic evocation of Polynesian life and rituals, a review written by Grierson for the *New York Sun*, for which he was serving as a stand-in film critic under the pseudonym "The Moviegoer."[20] The connotations of "documentary" in this founding text are not, at first appearance, positive. The film's "documentary value" is dismissed as "secondary" to its principal value as a beautiful work of naturalistic primitivism: "a soft breath from a sunlit island, washed by a marvelous sea, as warm as the balmy air."[21] Yet this "secondary" and even negative "documentary value" will prove to be a sleeper that will come to the fore as Grierson develops his critique of what, by 1932, he was calling Flaherty's "Neo-Rousseauism": his failure to develop "a form adequate to the more immediate material of the modern world."[22] Three years earlier, however, writing in the British periodical the *Clarion*, Grierson had already begun to contrast a cinema that "has, for the sake of an easy romance, gone primitive" with what he variously called a "cinema of the actual," an "actualist cinema," or "Natural cinema":[23] a cinema "of things and men as they in all dramatic reality are, with the world living and moving as in truth it does."[24] The critique of Flaherty and the counterposed theory of an "actualist cinema" that was to take on the name "documentary" were certainly in place, therefore, well before 1932, the year in which Grierson wrote "First Principles of Documentary," the earliest essay in the 1946 collected writings that specifically uses the term "documentary"—"a clumsy description"—in laying out the precepts for a new kind of film practice.[25]

In actual fact, the positive revaluing of "documentary" and its separation from the example of Flaherty were thought through at an even earlier date, in articles published in the United States in 1926 in *Motion Picture News* and in reports written for the Empire Marketing Board in 1927, on Grierson's return to England. The precise trajectory of the term "documentary" in Grierson's writings, and its definitive displacement of alternative names in the network of distinctions and oppositions that structure his argument, has yet to be exactly plotted, however. Nevertheless, we can see that the name is far from transparent: In the moment of its emergence, its connotations are complex and thickened by the accumulative layers of an elaborate and eclectic argument. It is to gain some access to this argument—to understand something of the load that the term "documentary" was expected to bear—that we have to go back at this point to consider Grierson's career and his intellectual formation prior to 1932 and the "First Principles of Documentary."

Grierson was born in 1898, in the northeast of Scotland, of schoolteacher parents who brought him up in a highly disciplined tradition of Christian reformism that was both Calvinist and utopian socialist. He was educated at Stirling High School and, with a break for war service in the Royal Naval Volunteer Reserve, at Glasgow University, where, as a liberal arts and philosophy student, he was further immersed in the influential if unlikely concoction of Hegelian Calvinism that represented the principal avenue for attempts by the philosophy faculty to reconcile religious morality with scientific knowledge and political reformism.[26] Hegelian Calvinism turned on a heavily moral conception of social obligation that subordinated individuality to the social body of a community conceived as a collective subject whose organic ideals were given expression in the form of the State. It was this conception of the social subject and the State that prompted the rejection of laissez-faire liberalism—a rejection founded on a strongly corporatist and utopian Christian basis that was clearly a far cry from the contemporary revolutionary socialism of Red Clydeside and John MacLean.

From Glasgow University, Grierson went directly in 1923 to an appointment as assistant registrar at Armstrong College of the University of Durham at Newcastle upon Tyne, where he established the academic connections that were to bring him a Rockefeller fellowship to carry out social science research in the United States. The topic of Grierson's research was to be "immigration and its effects upon the social problems of the USA" and, to pursue it, he went first, in 1924, to Chicago, then a vibrant center of immigration and cultural diversity but also the home of the University of Chicago, where the faculty in sociology and political science had established themselves as leaders in the field of public opinion research. Chicago sociology was heavily empirical, quantitative, and behaviorist, and its research on public opinion turned on the pessimistic, conservative view that a mass democratic system could never be an effective form of government because the limitations of direct experience and subjective judgment meant that a public not given to rational calculation could never be adequately informed, rendering any notion of popular democracy unscientific and inoperable.

Grierson appeared to accept this diagnosis, even though he was markedly opposed to the Chicago school's methodology, its social outlook, and its technocratic conclusions. It was in an effort to find a way out of this conflict that he began to look beyond the failures of the educational system, toward the dramatic and emotional techniques by which the popular mass media—the press, the movies, radio, and advertising—had been able to engage the identification of the general population that the schools and churches had lost. What interested him was the potential these new popular media might hold for informing, directing, and integrating communities and for communicating the corporate character of communal life. As a result, Grierson changed his research topic to "public opinion, social psychology and newspaper psychology" and set about trying to produce an idealist social democratic response to the political views of Chicago sociology. Of particular importance to the direction of his research was Walter Lippmann, the political scientist and influential editor of the "yellow press" *New York World*, whose pessimistic rejection of democracy Grierson repudiated but whose arguments he absorbed. It was Lippmann, too, who was instrumental in directing Grierson away from newspapers and toward popular cinema and specifically

Hollywood's audience reaction records as an important means to analyze the effects of mass communications on public sentiment and the formation of public opinion.[27]

In 1925 and early 1926, Grierson undertook a tour of some twenty-five cities across the United States, talking to local newspaper editors and reporters, but then began to concentrate his research on box office and audience response records in Hollywood. At the same time, he started writing for U.S. newspapers on issues of immigration, on how best to integrate new populations, and on the role to be played in this by the mass media. Capitalizing on his new film contacts, he also began publishing film criticism as a stand-in critic for the *New York Sun*. And it was between these areas of engagement that he started to develop his theory of what he later called the "directive use" of film,[28] as a means to equip a disoriented public with what it needed to take its bearings in a complex, information-saturated world, not through rational explanation but through a dramatic language that would inculcate an identification with the State and with the responsibilities of citizenship.[29] This is the discursive context for the emergence of Grierson's theory of "documentary" and his advocacy of publicly sponsored documentary films. Though associated now with the years of economic depression and heightened social conflict, the conceptual framework for Grierson's arguments was laid down at this time in the mid-1920s in seven articles he published in *Motion Picture News* between November 20 and December 18, 1926, in which he discussed the crisis in the consumption-driven film industry, its inability to experiment, the need to develop new kinds of inspirational film, and the means to overcome obstacles in the way of a socially purposive, epic, and naturalist cinema.[30]

The chance for Grierson to develop his theories in a practical way came in 1927 on his return to London, where he talked himself into a job with the Empire Marketing Board, the largest governmental publicity organization in Britain, set up after the failure of tariff reform with the purpose of securing Britain's food supply and advancing trade in the British Empire, needless to say, without questioning the character of British imperialism. Since the government was disallowed from supporting particular companies, the Empire Marketing Board came, of necessity, to concentrate on disseminating a broad, unifying representation of the empire as "a society for mutual help"[31]—a practical, cooperative venture of mutually concerned individuals around the world, by this account not unlike Grierson's idealist notion of the subsuming of worthy and committed individuals in the social community. This, then, was the conduit through which Grierson's theory of the educational value of dramatized factual films entered public service—a paradoxical context, perhaps, for the emergence of government-sponsored documentary, though, in fact, the promulgation of a paternalistic view of the role of individuals within the collective remained a fundamental thematic structure of documentary.

In 1927, Grierson was commissioned to produce a series of reports on film production for the Empire Marketing Board Film Committee.[32] The first of these he presented in April, in two parts: "Cinema and the Public—An Account of Audience Reactions and of the Conditions of Popular Appeal in the Cinema" and "English Cinema Production and the Naturalistic Tradition." Like his earlier articles for *Motion Picture News*, Grierson's lengthy memoranda proceeded from the view that public demand was determinant of effectivity and that socially purposive films, just like commercial films, had to engage public identification. Thus, public service films would need to be naturalistic, familiar, and positive but, at the same time, dramatic and emotive if they were to be capable of directing the popular imagination to optimistic images of the social world, to positive models for social action, and to a recognition of the interdependence of individual and collective. From these premises, Grierson envisaged two possible ways forward: the theatrical distribution of popular feature genres, such as the western, remade in nonindividualistic ways emphasizing the struggle to build social institutions, and the more economically viable option of producing publicly financed, naturalistic, yet cinematically dramatic nonfiction shorts to direct opinion formation and to promote identification with the common interests of the social whole, as represented by the State. A second report, "Further Notes on Cinema Production," filed in July 1927, argued that, with public sponsorship, such shorts would not have to make the compromises demanded for distribution through mainstream channels but could be circulated through a network of nontheatrical outlets such as church halls and society meetings, avoiding problems of pricing and profit margins and thereby also making it possible to create a new public for the new cinema. It was this second option that came to provide the route for documentary, giving the practice its economic structure, its aesthetic philosophy, and its political goals.

In 1928, Grierson was appointed assistant films officer to the Empire Marketing Board. In this capacity, he not only dominated the board's publicity plans but also put himself in the position to direct his own films, most notably *The Drifters*, a dramatic vision of the elemental confrontation of man, nature, and the demands of the market in the North Sea fishing industry. In subsequent years, from 1930 until its abolition in 1933, Grierson went on to supervise the Empire Marketing Board Film Unit while continuing to elaborate in his writings the precepts and protocols of the new form of practice. Perhaps, though, this is enough to establish something of the institutional, political, and discursive frame in which the term "documentary" was first fused as the name of a new kind of practice: not a practice of instrumental realism but, rather, a practice grounded on a belief in the ready capacity of the camera to produce naturalistic representations that promoted identification, a practice that focused on the everyday and the spontaneous but that conceived the real in a philosophical sense as an underlying form beyond appearance, and a practice that insisted on revelation and emotion as the only effective basis for communication of this essential truth to an irrational public. Such a practice was populist, but hardly democratic. Framed by an elitist view of the management of communications and an idealist view of collective social institutions, documentary harnessed itself to the service of a State that needed to shape public opinion just as it needed to manage its population through its techniques of social governance. In this field of social technologies, documentary's function was the procurement of identification in order to produce citizens inculcated with a sense of responsibility appropriate to their role in the collective whole. For Grierson, this was the central purpose: the production of civic subjects adequate to their representation in the State.

The everyday, the real, naturalism, emotionality, identification, service, citizenship, corporatism, the State: This is a very particular discursive chain, anchoring a very particular practice that is no longer something that can be readily generalized or something, perhaps, that is still so familiar. Even this truncated account of Grierson's career and intellectual formation brings out the extraordinarily eclectic mixture of Calvinism, Hegelianism, positivist sociology, public relations, and mass-communications theory that made up the theoretical equipment of the man who coined the term "documentary" in English, a man who was also typical of the reform-minded technocrats who populated the new state agencies, as the State, in the 1930s, took on new interventionist roles in the attempt to save an economic and political order from collapse.

Grierson's coinage of the term "documentary" was deeply embedded in a particular conception not only of the appeal of naturalist or realist representation and narration, but also of society as an ideal, interdependent community. It was this idealist conception that shaped Grierson's notion of the State as the representation of common interests and a common morality and framed his vision of the role of the mass media in the training of citizens for modern democracy through a new form of public discourse. Within this discursive knot, the rhetoric of documentary took shape—as a form of emotional dramatization rather than epistemological transparency, and as a rhetoric in which signs of the everyday operated as levers of identification with the collectivity and with the imagined poetry of the collaborative processes of industrial work and industrial technology. The rhetoric of documentary appeal was therefore inseparable from its form of address: a machinery of witness and identification founded on the familiar, on emotional incorporation, and on what Grierson called "Rooted Belief."[33] It is this apparatus of capture that is fundamental to the institutional incorporation and imagined functionality of documentary practices within the agencies of the State, where the State is conceived as the unified and unifying representation of communal interests.

The name for "capture" in Grierson's writing is "education." Whether polemicizing the early ideas of documentary or looking back on the first years of film production in an attempt to synthesize an administrative theory, Grierson insisted again and again that what drove the documentary movement was not an attachment to the aesthetics of film but a commitment to education.[34] This was not, however, a commitment to "the old liberal individualist and rational theory on which so much of our educational planning is based."[35] It was a commitment to a conception of education that had been entirely recast under pressure from the imperatives of the new mass society, whose citizens had proved damagingly ill equipped to play their role in governance. In this context, education had to become "activist or it is nothing."[36] "It is not a time for contemplation and contemplative form," Grierson declared, "but a time for action and *activist forms*."[37] The tasks of modern government and citizenship demanded education be reconceived as "an active constructive system in the maintenance of democracy,"[38] "a social instrument,"[39] "an instrument of state"[40] with its "part to play in fulfilling the democratic idea."[41] This meant that education had to get away from "the servile accumulation of fact"[42] and see its primary tasks as "bridging the gap between the citizen and the community"[43] and bringing alive "to the citizen the world in which his citizenship lay"[44] by dramatizing "the materials of citizenship"[45] and inculcating "patterns of civic appreciation, civic faith and civic duty."[46] Reenvisioned in this way, education held "the key to the mobilization of men's minds."[47]

Even so, an instrumentalized education system could only achieve its civic ends insofar as it could be made to remember what Grierson called "the part of democratic education which the educators forgot."[48] What this meant was that educators needed to learn from the methods by which the market-driven mass media had "taken charge of men's minds":[49] They needed to abandon the "intellectualist approach"[50] and embrace "the new dramatic methods of appeal":[51]

> We shall have to learn and speak a new language. . . . the way of information will not serve; it is too discursive. And the way of rational explanation will not serve, because it misses the corporate life we are dealing with. The new language of apprehension which must communicate the corporate nature of the community life must in fact be something more in the nature of a dramatic language than a rational one.[52]

The outmoded rationalist methods of education had to be discarded, Grierson argued, in favor of a new approach whose purpose would be not to analyze but to show.[53] The aim of this approach would not be to promote knowledge, literacy, or rational judgment but, rather, would be to excite feeling, "crystallize the emotions," and direct loyalties.[54] Its method would lie not in the presentation of facts but, rather, in reaching for "the story"[55] capable of communicating "a pattern of faith"[56] and of installing that "Rooted Belief,"[57] which alone can provide the "moral imperative" men crave in times of crisis,[58] at those periods in history "when the whole basis of truth is reexamined."[59]

What must be rebuilt, Grierson insisted, is the "Belief" that will found an order of truth but that will also lead to action. What is needed, therefore, is not knowledge but "a leadership of the imagination"[60] that will determine the "patterns of thought and feeling which will guide the citizen in his citizenship," while giving "far less opportunity for the promiscuous exercise of mental and emotional interests."[61] It is here that the "directive,"[62] as opposed to the reflective, use of film makes its entry. Educators have failed in their "duty" and lost their "opportunity," Grierson declared, not only because they have neglected to see education as "related to an active and participant citizenship" but also because "education has not known how to absorb the vast and complex materials of civic observation and action today."[63] Here, documentary film offered "a kind of educational shorthand,"[64] "a shorthand method for world observation,"[65] a "shorthand method of dramatization"[66] promoting "quick and immediate comprehension"[67] "for the sake of quick decision and common action."[68]

For Grierson, the "directive use" of new educational media rested on "two essential factors": "the observation of the ordinary or the actual, and the discovery within the actual of the patterns which gave it significance for civic education."[69] It was, therefore, more than just a matter of turning the everyday into a new kind of text, for this, in itself, would be little better than a return to "the servile accumulation of fact."[70] It was only by drawing out the "basic dramatic patterns"[71] of complex social relations that documentary films could furnish citizens with "a pattern of thought and feeling"[72] that would give them, in turn, "a grip on reality,"[73] "a true sense of their living relationship to events,"[74] "a sense of the corporate and a sense of growth."[75] Documentary—"the language of the corporate mind"[76]—shortcut the all-but-impossible task of universal education for democratic citizenship in the complex modern state, not by teaching people to know, but by teaching them "to feel."[77] "The decent intention"[78] was only the beginning. What mattered most was what

Grierson had looked for in cinema from his earliest years as a film critic: "what actually moves: what hits the spectator at the midriff: what yanks him up by the hair of the head or the plain boot-straps to the plane of decent seeing."[79] What documentary offered in place of knowledge was "an emotional map."[80] It was only by such means that it was able to conjure up "the images that direct men's vision and determine their loyalties,"[81] crystallizing sentiments and loyalties in forms that were useful to the State and conducive to corporate action.[82] In short, documentary provided "the imaginative training for modern citizenship"[83] in "a world where only the corporate and the co-operative will matter."[84]

This is what constitutes "documentary's primary service to the state,"[85] just as the State is, in turn, documentary's logical sponsor.[86] The State needs the powers of documentary, and documentary serves the power of the State. The relationship is fundamental and inescapable. The State, Grierson asserted, represents the logical outcome of the increasing integration of the industrial economy and the centralization of finance and technocratic initiative.[87] The State is the agency of "common unified planning"[88] and "that measure of social control"[89] that "social justice and the complexity of the modern world demand."[90] Its watchwords are "Discipline, Unity, Coordination, Total Effort, Planning":[91] words that need to be dramatized "so that they become loyalties and take leadership of the Will."[92] This might sound "totalitarian," Grierson conceded, but "You can be 'totalitarian' for evil and you can also be 'totalitarian' for good."[93] This good—"the common good"[94]—is embodied in the State: "For Europe, the state has from the first represented the positive and creative force of the community, operating as a whole to positive ends."[95] "The State is the machinery by which the best interests of the people are secured. Since the needs of the State come first, understanding of these needs comes first in education."[96]

A conception of education as the production of citizens adequate to the needs of the State and caught in a desire for the State as their own self-completion might seem to verge on the function of propaganda. This did not trouble Grierson. We should realize, he replied, that such "government information services are natural and necessary to modern government."[97] Indeed, propaganda is a "more urgent necessity"[98] for democracies, where persuasion has taken the place of compulsion.

Against the mental and emotional confusion that undoes the individual's "faith in the whole,"[99] propaganda is "an essential function of the State,"[100] as it has been wherever nations have tried "to plan their society to an end."[101] "The possibility of abuse does not mean that proper uses cannot be allowed."[102] In fact, propaganda has "developed hand in hand with the responsibilities of the state and has grown in direct proportion to the use of the state as a creative instrument of the community, operating as a whole to definite purposes."[103] Propaganda is "part of that process of persuasion or education which is the tap-root of the democratic idea."[104] And in the end, Grierson concluded:

> This is not an educational matter at all: it is a political matter. In other words, the key to education in the modern complex world no longer lies in what we have known as education but in what we have known as propaganda. By the same token, propaganda, so far from being the denial of the democratic principle of education, becomes the necessary instrument for its practical fulfillment. Everything else is incidental.[105]

Propaganda is "education in a world where the state is the instrument of the public's enterprise."[106] Herein lies the "secret of the relationship between propaganda and education in the future": in the dramatic and interpretative "technique" that makes it possible to "translate the materials of citizenship into terms which are capable of being grasped and which are inducive of action."[107] This is the source of the documentary idea. Exposed to the analyses of political science, the function of education gives place to the "directive use" of "the brilliant new instruments of dramatization and enlightenment":[108] newspapers, radio, film, and photography.

The insistent force of Grierson's advocacy, his determination to make his argument add up, is plain enough, and it puts us on distinct and unfamiliar ground. Documentary is not documentation. While documentary practice may have traded rhetorically with the quasi-scientific techniques of nineteenth-century documentation, it no longer functioned as a jealously guarded technical discourse produced by experts for experts. While the authority of documentary may have played on the evidential status of the document, its truth claims rested on a populist rhetoric—

an emotionalized drama of witness—that worked to wed its audiences to its realism, its viewers to its look, sealing them into its system of enacted truth. The place into which the identifying viewer was to be called, however, was not only that of a subject of performative meaning. It was above all that of a subject of the State: a civic subject of liberal democracy whose conscription was all the more urgent in the midst of the crises of the 1930s in which documentary's strategy of recruitment was fused.

Even so, what is striking about our earlier review of Grierson's career is that it makes clear that the discourse of documentary, which we so much associate with the 1930s, was in formation as early as 1926 and 1927—before the Crash of 1929 and the ensuing "Depression." The same lesson might be drawn from the early career of Roy Stryker, under the influence of the modern management theories of Rexford Tugwell in the Economics Department of Columbia University.[109] Documentary was the product not of the collapse of speculative capital and a crisis-driven urge to tell the unpalatable truth but of the continuing problematics of governance, at the point of intersection of political and economic science, educational theory, pedagogical practice, and the nascent field of communications. The collapse, however, gave impetus and focus to the application of the new theories and new technologies of public opinion management by exposing the instability of the structures of social cohesion and by opening new avenues to public sponsorship—limited though it was—around the edges of belated and often piecemeal State programs.

Nevertheless, rattled government structures in the besieged liberal democracies of the 1930s would respond differently to a crisis that marked not just the collapse of national economies and the international system of finance, not even just the chronic undermining of the institutions of political consensus, but also the deep fracturing of those shared structures of meaning, identity, and belief that frame the imaginary cohesiveness of social life.[110] Britain went over to a National Government that was the continuation of Conservative rule by another name. Little credence attaches to Grierson's suggestion that it represented "a Tory regime gradually going Socialist."[111] Socialism, in any case, was hardly the issue for documentary, and it can be argued at least as plausibly that it was only in the United States, with the pressure of new forms of mass action and organization forcing the hand of Roosevelt's first two administrations, that a cultural and communications strategy would be mobilized by agencies of the central government as a concerted part of a program of State expansion and crisis management that needed to rebuild the mechanisms of social identification. It is not incidental that Grierson's crystallization of the theory and practice of documentary itself began, under the influence of American political science and public relations, with his research into the operations of the mass media and the problematics of citizenship in an increasingly corporate American society. And when the crisis came, for all the pioneering role of Grierson's British documentary movement, it would be the America of the New Deal that would become the effective homeland of documentary. In Britain, by contrast, the documentary project would remain relatively peripheral to the policies of a Tory-dominated government throughout the 1930s, as Grierson, in effect, conceded in his claim that it was documentary that educated the British public, that made social democracy "emotionally real,"[112] and that prepared the way for the Labour government of 1945. But by 1945, the cultural politics of "documentary" were dead. The moment of "documentary" was over.

This is only to reiterate, however, that it did have a moment. And perhaps we are beginning to thicken our sense of what it means to say that documentary realism was a conjuncturally specific strategy: a strategy conceptualized in a framework of social governance that turned on the management of public opinion but that was only fully mobilized in the context of a corporate liberal response to a crisis with whose displacement documentary was also to pass away. We may also be beginning to have at least some sight of why, without denying the innovatory role of Grierson or his activities at the British Empire Marketing Board, one might insist that it was above all the context of the Roosevelt administration's New Deal that would prove crucial. Yet this argument for the strategic specificity of documentary has other consequences, too. However familiar the photographs of the Resettlement Administration and the Farm Security Administration may have become as part of "American Memory,"[113] a sense of the historicity of documentary discourse may leave us less able to insert ourselves in their form of address and less willing simply to follow the directions laid out so insistently by Steichen for our look.

"Have a look," Steichen urged readers of the *U.S. Camera Annual* in 1938:

> Have a look at the three figures with hoes. . . . Then look at the picture of
> the nervous looking parlor organ out in the stubble of what once was a
> corn field. . . . "Now step up folks, and look this way!" Have a look into
> the faces of the men and women in these pages. Listen to the story they
> tell and they will leave with you a feeling of a living experience you won't
> forget. . . . If you are the kind of rugged individualist who likes to say "Am
> I my brother's keeper?", don't look at these pictures—they may change
> your mind.[114]

This look, which Steichen repeatedly invokes and which the photographs
from the FSA Historical Section are said to invite, is offered as something immediately available and naturally assumed. Yet it is clear that in
being invited to take up this look, we are being asked to take on more
than just a viewing point made ready for us by the perspective of the camera. More than this, certainly, though the viewpoint may well be where
our entrapment starts and where it may be hardest to resist the lure of
the invitation, now or in 1938. We are back with the machinery of capture that is documentary's "primary service to the state." But how does
this capture work? And what is it that is captured?

The picture, Lacan tells us, is a trap.[115] It captures and it tames
the viewer's gaze.[116] It gives the voracious eye something to feed on but
invites the viewer to whom it is presented to lay down and abandon their
gaze, "as one lays down one's weapons."[117] Like animal mimicry, void of
any instigative intersubjectivity, the picture is a lure, a function whose
exercise grasps the viewer and into which the subject is inserted.[118] At the
same time, it is also an incitement, an "appearance that says it is that
which gives the appearance," driving the viewer to pursue what is behind
it, to hang on the question of the thing "beyond appearance."[119]

The picture solicits the eye as a palpitating organ with an endless
appetite for the iridescent, flaring, flickering, flaming, scorching light
that flows into it, spilling around the ocular bowl, staining the retinal
surface, burning, and compelling the eye to defend itself—contracting
the iris, blinking and screwing up the eyelids.[120] For this eye, there is no
distance between the stimulus and the stimulated organ. It pulses to an

optical sensation unstructured by any relation of subject to object. Vision is a sensation that diffuses within, percolating into and locating the body. Vision is a bodily event, a touching of the eye's surface that spreads out across the retina and is absorbed into its layers, not a cognitive event pinpointed by a geometry of converging light rays strung taught like a construction of wires or threads whose spatialization of the optical field would be graspable even by the blind.[121] A light ruled out as lines of sight is not what the optical organ seeks. The light it craves is pulsatile and dazzling.[122] It paints something in the eye's depths—"something that is not simply a constructed relation, the object on which the philosopher lingers—but something that is an impression, the shimmering of a surface that is not, in advance, situated . . . in its distance."[123] The eye is not, then, an organ whose operation can be described by that philosophical invention, the punctual eye—alibi of a punctual consciousness that is itself a sort of geometral point, a point of perspective already at a distance from its objects. What we have in this philosophical construction is a description not of the organ of vision but, rather, of a certain concerted effect: an effect of "the fatal function" the eye carries within it "of being in itself endowed . . . with a power to separate."[124]

Like the philosopher's model, the pictorial system of central vanishing point perspective, with its attendant machines, works within this function of separation. The central vanishing point construction—the system the camera was built to reproduce—projects a spatialized relation of eye to external world by plotting, through a rectangulated geometrical grid, notional lines of sight spatially connecting three-dimensional objects to a posited point of vision. The relationships graphed across the intersecting grid are then intelligible from, and only from, the single, central point in relation to which they were generated: a point that is simultaneously the projected viewing point and a virtual vanishing point—the furthest point of concentration and geometrical convergence of externalized visual space. Central vanishing point perspective thus conjures up a world of sight that is both objectively external and, at the same time, "given" to a singular, subjective point of view. A visual field structured like this is also, however, reversible: The perspectival viewer may command a singular vision of the world ordered for sight, but the externalized world looks back from all sides, from a multitude of potential points unattainable to the subject of representation's eye.[125] From this reversed perspective, the subject is itself put in the picture, seeing from one point but seen from an infinite number.[126] The viewing subject is thus caught in a pulsating space, on the surface of a membrane of vision that is pulled inside out and right side out again, like the finger of a glove[127] or like an elongated soap bubble stretched back and forth on each side of a wire ring. The wire ring is what we might attend to here, for the geometral look and the gaze outside are only held in place, together and apart, by the geometrically gridded frame. The subject's visual centrality and command of a visually rational world are had at the price of submission to the gaze of the gridded frame that calls the punctual subject into place. The subject may enjoy its sense of visual command, but it is the subject itself that is "caught, manipulated, captured, in the field of vision,"[128] that is "literally called into the picture, and represented here as caught."[129]

By the same token, the captured subject may be summarily expelled. In Lacan's much-quoted example of pictorial entrapment, the viewer's enjoyment of the confident bulk of the enlightened protagonists in Hans Holbein's *Ambassadors*, well satisfied as they are to display their scientific apparatuses for reducing the visual-spatial world to quantifiable calculation, is interrupted by the intrusion of a smear on the visual field—an oblique footnote to rationalist vision, the force of whose looming, eyeless death's-head thrusts the viewing subject aside, back into the abyss of its contingency, at the very moment that the vainglorious ambassadors—like Rosencrantz and Guildenstern—disappear from the stage and are obliterated from sight.[130] The subject of representation can only see the picture from one position. But, from one position, the picture cannot be seen. The perspective grid is turned against the subject, who cannot be in more than one place and therefore cannot command the picture. The fullness of vision enjoyed by the subject is shot, its object is lost, and the subject itself is exposed in its irremediable inadequacy and, as such, is annihilated. To what, then, is the eye of the fallen subject, torn from perspective's rational world of sense, thrown back in this rude ejection? To the traumas of bodily vision; to the eye's dangerously insatiable appetite for light, for light as irradiation, for light that destroys sight. Against this, the socialization of the drive by the system of central vanishing point perspective seeks to elide both the materiality of light and the materiality of the eye as organ. "What is at issue in geometral perspective is simply the mapping of space, not sight."[131] What engages vision escapes.

Throughout his discussion of the eye and the gaze, light and line, anamorphosis and the picture, what is fundamental to Lacan's analysis is his intransigent opposition to rationalist and phenomenological notions of "visual centring"[132] and "that form of vision that is satisfied with itself in imagining itself as consciousness,"[133] encountering the external world through the perception of appearances. Vision is, rather, the site of a trauma induced by an unwelcome encounter with the real, from which the subject emerges, compelled to repetition by a failure of memory. The effect is to leave the subject hanging, in an ambivalent relation of distance and desire, pleasure and anxiety, expulsion and loss that fills the space the trauma has opened between an inner self and an outer world that this inner self can henceforth only possess in separation.[134] The subject emerges in the field of vision, as Lacan says, only at the price of a "self-mutilation"[135] as a result of which the subject is suspended, depending from its separated object, caught in a flux of desire and inadequacy in which the subject seeks to displace the trauma of an encounter and separation that it cannot consciously remember. This is how the eye is driven desperate. And, as Lacan remarks, "It is to this register of the eye as made desperate by the gaze that we must go if we are to grasp the taming, civilizing and fascinating power of the function of the picture."[136]

In common with the philosopher's wire construction, Albrecht Dürer's *lucinda*, and the perspective frame, the camera offers a vision the blind can understand.[137] The camera is a device for disciplining and delineating light. Modeled after the principle of earlier Renaissance picturing machines, it graphs the iridescent flood of luminescence by gathering it to a central monocular lens set perpendicular to a rectangular, framed focal plane defined by the camera's internal architecture. Ushered through the aperture into this darkened space, the light then produces an image, as it has been contrived to do, according to the codes of the camera's inflexible, built-in operating system, registering it as a stain[138] etched into the dirt of the phototropic emulsion. It is then this stain, this "small dirty deposit,"[139] that captivates us. As the image itself was burned in by a scorching light incarcerated in the geometrical prison of the camera, so, in turn, the stain captures our ever-eager eye in the linear cage of its perspective grid. It is this imaginary capture that harnesses the body to the prosthetic machine and violently ensures that, as FSA photographer Arthur Rothstein once wrote, "the lens of the camera is, in effect, the eye of the person looking at the print,"[140] inscribing vision for the viewer around a single, central viewing point marked at the point of convergence of the geometrical orthogonals that structure the perspective of the image. This viewing point constitutes the place of intelligibility of the photograph, the place from which alone the "message" in the stain is legible, just as it simultaneously inscribes for the subject of this viewing point a spatial world posited as external, behind the picture plane, and, indeed, behind what is recognized as a representation, an "appearance that says it is that which gives the appearance."[141]

What, then, are the consequences of this geometral inscription for the viewer? The viewer's eye is captured and surrenders to a Cyclopean vision that functions as the operation of a disembodied punctual eye and that serves as the alibi for the space of cognition of a punctual subject. And yet the same movement that captures the subject as an interiority of consciousness separates it from an externalized world now set apart as giving itself to be seen, but also as, at once, an infinite elsewhere from which the subject, in turn, cannot shield itself from being seen.[142] This is the space of the gaze imagined by the subject at the horizon of the field of the Other.[143] And, Lacan says, "From the moment that this gaze appears, the subject tries to adapt himself to it, he becomes that punctiform object, that point of vanishing being with which the subject confuses his own failure."[144] Vacillating between the subject of the eye and the object of the gaze, "the being breaks up, in an extraordinary way, between its being and its semblance, between itself and that paper tiger it shows to the other."[145] This is the split in which the drive of desire is manifested at the level of the scopic field:[146]

> This is the function that is found at the heart of the institution of the subject in the visible. What determines me, at the most profound level, in the visible, is the gaze that is outside. It is through the gaze that I enter light and it is from the gaze that I receive its effects. Hence it comes about that the gaze is the instrument through which light is embodied and through

which—if you will allow me to use a word, as I often do, in a fragmented form—I am *photo-graphed*.[147]

Light and line; eye and gaze; drive and desire. The photo-graph, after Lacan, has been bent in two, around a kind of hinge. In capturing its scene, it captures the viewer as a subject whose eye has been tamed and who has surrendered to the gaze. But to what does the subject surrender in surrendering to the gaze that is "at the heart of the institution of the subject"? To the system of representation, certainly: to photography as all-seeing, as conceived, for example, by those who launched *Life* magazine in 1936 and who saw in photography a means to harness that urge "to see, and to be shown," "to see and to take pleasure in seeing," which "is now the will and expectancy of half mankind."[148] But with the consumption of photographs put into circulation in ever-greater numbers in the mid-1930s by the rotogravure press, we are also dealing with what Lacan calls the "social function,"[149] in which the audiences of images are given over communally to the "gaze behind," "*le regard là-derrière*."[150] What is this "gaze behind," of which, Lacan says, there have been many and which was always there? It is something that seeks to impose itself but of which the subject is not completely aware, something that is "hypnotic" and, indeed, operates the subject "by remote control."[151] It is always a particular institution of desire. For *Life*, it is a certain economy of spectacle. For "documentary," it is a certain collective regimen embodied in the social democratic State that calls the civic subject into place and holds it there, "voluntarily," by force of "Rooted Belief." More particularly, for the film and photographic agencies of the Roosevelt administration, giving to be seen the "forgotten man," making visible the "invisible third of the nation," the "gaze behind" is the paternalistic gaze of the New Deal state—the fulcrum of a machinery of capture that has so little to do with the poor and dispossessed, those *objects* of documentary, and so much more to do with the recruitment of *subjects* as citizens, called to witness, called to reality and coherence, precisely at a time when the established regimes of sense and sociality were profoundly threatened by a crisis that was never solely political or economic.[152]

This is documentary's simple demand—that we look: "Look at the picture." "Look into the faces." It is not just Steichen voicing this demand;

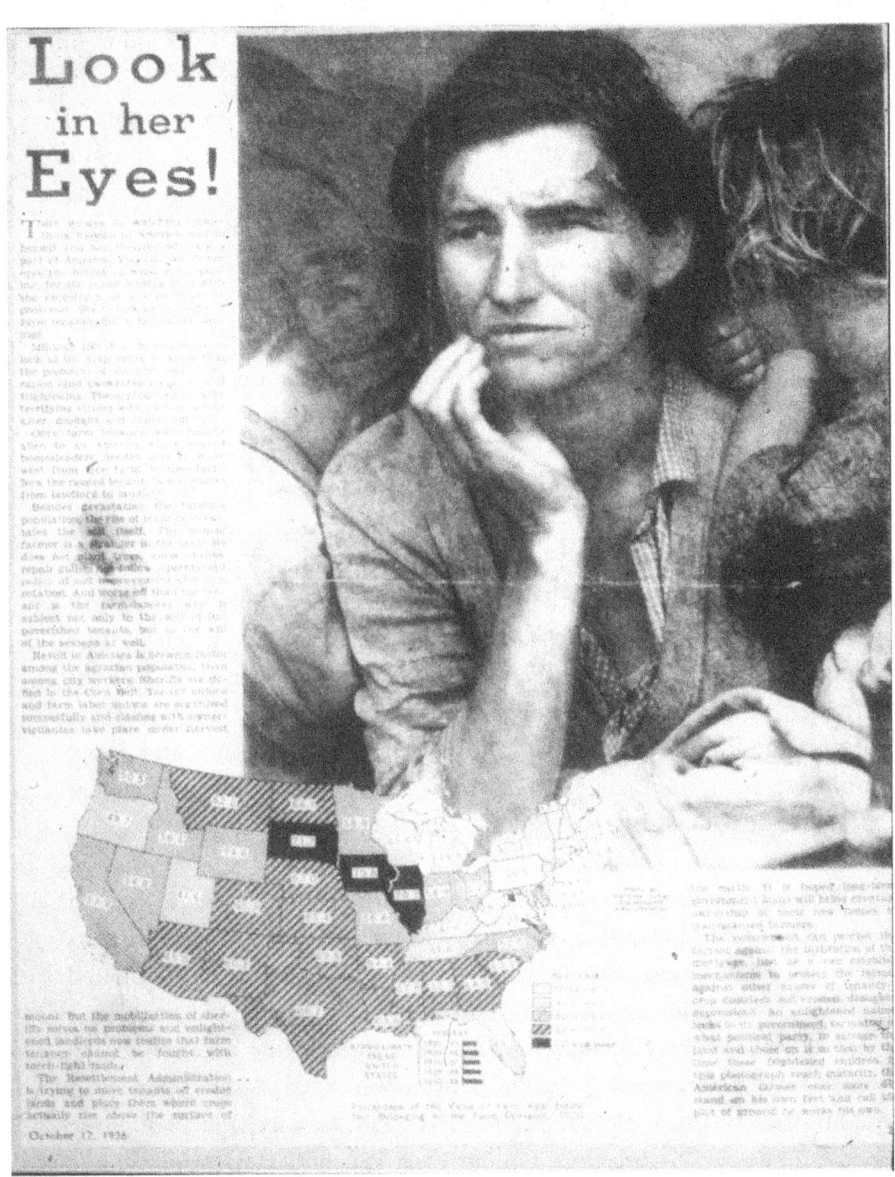

Figure 14. "Look in her Eyes!" *Midweek Pictorial*, October 14, 1936.

he only echoes an entire machinery—the machinery not just of an encroaching apparatus of commentary but, above all, of the staging of the photographic event itself. "Look in her Eyes!" orders the headline in the *Midweek Pictorial,* falling almost in the line of vision of the "Migrant Mother"—Dorothea Lange's too easily appropriated photograph of Florence Thompson in a camp for migrant farm laborers in Nipomo, California, on a rainy March day in 1936. "This woman is watching something happen to America and to herself and her children who are a part of America. You can see in her eyes the horror of what is happening."[153] Look! And look at her look. What could be simpler, more purely voluntary, further from propaganda? Yet if we follow Steichen's directions, we will know where we are and be lost. We must, therefore, in sense that is not merely metaphoric, tear these pictures from our eyes and return them to the look whose vision is not ours and is not simply given for us to see. One might say that, feeling again the pull of the sightless skull in Holbein's painting, we have to address these photographs obliquely, as if no longer from in front, from the viewing point, the point of identification, but from the side: to see, then, not "faces" and "stories" but the anamorphic machinery of the image that sets the viewer and the real in place. For as we try, as it were, to move around, out of the picture's aim, out of its sights, its "shoot,"[154] we confront the machinery of staging, a machinery of staging that is, in turn, mounted in a more extensive apparatus, which I take to be the apparatus of a particular strategy: the cultural strategy of the New Deal State.

Whether we understand the economic collapse that followed the Crash of 1929 as a unique and extraordinary event or as the predictable outcome of stagnation-inducing forces endemic to a corporate-dominated system has obvious consequences for our assessment of the needs and limitations of government action and, thus, for the view we are likely to take of the public spending policies promoted by successive Roosevelt administrations after 1933. Even more than forty years after Paul Baran and Paul Sweezy wrote their famous essay on the American economic and social order, there is still force enough in their arguments to make a powerful case for the view that the Great Depression of the 1930s was symptomatic of the "stagnationist tendencies inherent in monopoly capitalism," operating in the absence of major external stimuli to the absorption of surplus.[155] Applying their model of the increasing surplus capacity generated by the growth of corporate monopoly to an analysis of historical fluctuations in economic indicators across a period from 1929 to 1939, Baran and Sweezy present a lucid picture both of the structural crisis faced by the New Deal—37 percent of productive capacity idle in 1931, rising to 58 percent in 1932; 18 percent unemployment in 1931, growing to 25 percent by 1933—and of the political and economic barriers it encountered to effective reform and to government-led attempts to reverse the causes of the economic slump. Whatever we make of this argument, however, it is equally clear that an analysis of economic structures and their internal constraints does not exhaust the problem and that a larger sense of the character of the social collapse facing the United States at the beginning of the 1930s cannot simply be derived from the failure of economic institutions and processes, whether we view this failure as inherent in the structure of corporate monopoly or not.

The crisis of the 1930s was threatening precisely to the degree that it was simultaneously an economic, political, and cultural crisis: a crisis of overproduction, of overcapacity, and of inadequate outlets for investment-seeking surplus, no doubt; a crisis of economic management and of the credibility of political institutions, certainly; but also, and inseparably, a crisis of established frameworks of sense and social identity, whose impending collapse threatened to destabilize the social field as constituted by the discourses and institutions of liberal democracy. This was not, therefore, a breakdown that was first and foremost economic but whose effects subsequently rolled over the other institutions of society. What made the situation critical was its overdetermination as a crisis of belief, authority, and sense. Indeed, it was this overdetermined character of the impending social catastrophe that drove the second round of reform measures into which a hesitant and even reluctant Roosevelt administration was pushed in 1935.

This Second New Deal, enacted in the Emergency Relief Appropriations Act and Roosevelt's five "must" laws on social security, labor relations, and financial reform, represented not only a vastly expanded plan for public investment and public works and a restabilizing program of mass relief but also a cultural and political mobilization that sought to resecure social authority, belief in the reformability of the capitalist system through state regulation, and identification with a cohesive national culture. This is a crucial point. It has been argued that the programs promoted by the New Deal never contained any effective measures to redistribute wealth or power or to deal with the persistent problems of poverty and racism. It has also been said that they never effectively sought to redress the structural problems in the economy, being intended only to tide the system over by promoting rationalized planning, by strengthening corporate structures, and by developing a new, mediatory, and interventionist role for the State. Despite conservative opposition, the economic measures of the New Deal, it has been suggested, were primarily geared to creating the centralized planning mechanisms that would rationalize competition, coordinate national employment programs, and incorporate organized labor so as to displace the threat of more-radical demands arising from widespread social misery.[156] Indeed, whatever one's view, it has to be conceded that, until the outbreak of the Second World War at least, the New Deal's vision of public spending was always constrained, if not by the limits of the monopoly capitalist system then certainly by the political institutions that, after the collapse of the famous Roosevelt alliance, operated to displace any consensus for government-led reform and, by 1938, had reached a deadlock that effectively barred further measures, even while the effects of deep-seated economic depression persisted. But why, we might ask, if the New Deal was an economic failure, was the country not pulled yet further apart?

If New Deal economic measures demonstrably failed to reverse the stagnation-inducing forces that drove the economy into depression, then the New Deal must have negotiated its perceived success at other levels. Here, I would argue, the checking of the social crisis of the first half of the decade points toward the broad cultural and political dimensions of the Roosevelt administration's program and their role in a new mode of governance that operated through mechanisms of social security.[157] As we have seen, in the crisis of the 1930s, it was not only economic institutions that faced collapse, nor even just the machinery of social administration; it was also the sense of national unity and cohesion, the legitimacy of political institutions, the credibility of official pronouncements and media representations, the belief in shared values—in short, the very underpinnings of deference and power in society. Widespread deprivation and despair sent seismic shock waves through the geology of the social imaginary, fracturing the sedimented layers of social identification and subjection. Conditions seemed too acute for discredited forms of explanation and the failing institutions of self-recognition. With other political solutions and competing ways of making sense of the crisis beckoning to the right and to the left, the country was pushed toward what Stuart Hall, in his analysis of the contemporary conjuncture in Britain in the 1930s, has described as a crisis of the "social logics" by which a socially effective reality is signified.[158] The United States, too, had entered one of those moments when these logics begin to collapse inwardly and to be usurped by contending logics, contending systems of sense. The danger was that, if ignored, this process of erosion would precipitate a collapse that could no longer be contained. Government was compelled to respond, as mass action against the hesitancy of the First New Deal showed. It had to address and displace more-radical articulations of the deepening social calamity. It had to reinvent a believable sense of national community and civic identity, even if it could not or would not address the structural causes of social disintegration. It had to overcome public distrust and disenchantment and meet the demand for guarantees of authenticity and truth in its public pronouncements, even in the face of unimaginable events. And it had to negotiate consent to a further extension of the State into the sphere of social governance while representing its interventions as those of a paternal body mediating between conflicting interests to secure the national interest and the general good.

It is arguable, then, that the New Deal's effectivity lay, in significant part, in its muddled actions to avert the disintegrative effects of crisis and to rebuild national unity and cohesion. Even if its social measures were not the agency of any major redistribution of wealth or power, they were a means of stabilizing confidence, incorporating threatening social movements, and rebuilding consensus. Even the economic measures themselves were intended to have cultural effects—rebuilding communities and restoring belief in market institutions and in the efficacy of government. But in addition, we have to see the New Deal—and especially the Second New Deal of 1935—as involving, in the broadest sense, a *cultural* as well as a political and economic strategy: that is, a concerted attempt to restore belief in a common language of experience and in the legitimizing unities of nation, people, and culture, each of which had been made vulnerable by the crisis of authority and the crisis of identity that marked the moment of social collapse.

Questions of social consensus, national cohesion, the displacement of radical explanations, and the restoration of a sense that policy could be grounded on shared recognitions of authentic experience take us far beyond the domain of economic policy narrowly conceived. We might also remember that it was often the cultural agencies and the cultural initiatives that, as conspicuous signs of a supposed New Deal "socialism," drew most attention from hostile conservatives and convinced New Dealers alike. But in a more critical sense, too, these cultural projects were not as peripheral as they have often seemed in general historical accounts,

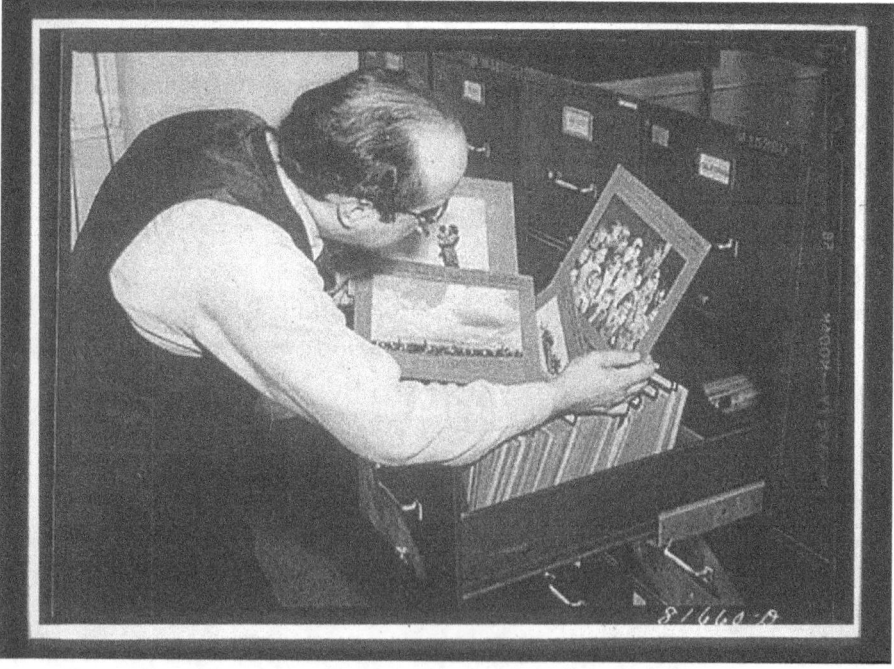

Figure 15. John Collier, "Washington, D.C.: Preparing the defense bond sales photomural," 1941. FSA-OWI Collection, Prints and Photographs Division, Library of Congress (LC-USF34-081660-D).

for what we begin to see emerging within them are the outlines of a strategy: the *cultural strategy* of the New Deal State.

As early as 1936, Holger Cahill, the pragmatic and populist national director of the Federal Art Project, which had been set up under the major agency of the Second New Deal, the Works Progress Administration (WPA), had argued for a program that would do more than merely promote cautious public commissions and provide temporary security for unemployed artists and cultural workers, as earlier Civil Works Administration and Treasury Art Programs had done. While the working rationale of the Federal Art Project was that it functioned as a work-relief and skill-preservation program, comparable to WPA interventions in other sectors of the economy, Cahill envisioned a more ambitious and far-reaching initiative that would reverse "a cultural erosion far more serious than the erosion of the Dust Bowl"[159] by promoting "a sound general movement," by inculcating in project artists "a sense of an active participation in the life and thought and movement of their own time," and, in an echo of Grierson's rhetoric, by fostering a "new concept of social loyalty and responsibility."[160] Under Cahill's direction, the Federal Art Project thus set itself the goal of building a "usable" national cultural tradition that would rest on a social and geographical redistribution of cultural activities, that would break down the institutional separation of fine and applied arts, and that would integrate art into "the very stuff and texture of human experience"[161]—not merely as a decorative accompaniment but as the very fabric of social cohesion and as the medium of social communication, social change, and what Cahill called "the expression of those qualitative unities which make the pattern of American culture."[162] If not exactly the "cultural revolution" hailed by Archibald MacLeish,[163] this was still little short of a vision of a government-led reconstruction of the infrastructure of a socially divisive, market-driven pattern of cultural production, in the name of a new national community no longer divided by the conflicts and contradictions of capitalist development. Whatever the obstacles blocking its realization, the aim was national reconciliation through reform of the cultural economy and through the "naturalization of art in all our communities"[164]—though this is not to suggest that it was ever intended that the project should unleash forces capable of disrupting what an intransigent Stuart Davis, as a project artist and the former president of the Artists' Union, kept calling the "monopoly in culture."[165]

What Cahill's administrative vision for the Federal Art Project shows is that, to grasp the most ambitious goals of the cultural programs of the New Deal, we have to think beyond the preservation of skills through work relief and beyond the sustaining of the art market in a period of economic collapse. We have rather to think about the projected role of cultural initiatives in affirming a national sense of purpose by articulating values that could be presented as shared and by calling out a new civic subject whose identity would be the reflection of a devolved and popular national culture. Of course, such a program, never fully thought through in itself, was bound to prove politically contentious. In any case, it was hedged about and constantly constrained by the obstacles that boxed in the entire New Deal. Starved of funds, hampered by local officials, and attacked by threatened private interests and a vociferous political opposition, the Federal Art Project was never effectively able to restructure cultural frameworks and, because it remained heavily centralized and bureaucratized, it failed to build a durable local consensus. Yet at a time of instability, public works of art, community art centers, art education classes, graphic design projects, and circulating exhibitions sponsored by the project gave the new direction in government a distinct visibility at the local level and had effects: devolving a sense of connection, giving some substance to the rhetoric of national community, and going some way to reforge that chain of identifications on which consent to the extension of the activist State depended.

Such social effects did not change the unemployment figures, but they were not negligible in localities where government had come to seem so remote and faith in the ability of government to act effectively, at any level, had fallen to such a low ebb. Nevertheless, if we are going to pursue the idea of a New Deal cultural strategy further, we will have to go beyond the nationalist and populist sentiments of well-meaning murals, historical epics, and regionalist celebrations to see something larger at stake: to see how the very institutions of a shared cultural language had to be recast if belief in official representations and a community of interests was to be restored while avoiding accusations of propaganda. It is in this larger frame that we have to think again about the relation of the

New Deal to the promotion of new documentary rhetorics in photography, film, literature, theater, painting, and music. And this, in turn, makes it necessary to take a broader view of New Deal cultural initiatives—one that does not adhere to institutional divisions but that tries to connect the federal arts projects to the mobilization of new forms of writing and image making in New Deal agencies seemingly far from the domain of art.

The crisis to which the New Deal cultural strategy responded was not just a crisis of culture with a capital *C*. It was, as I have argued, a crisis of shared systems of understanding, of the codes that constitute the community of sense: a crisis of the very language of reality. It had taken a profound social dislocation to compel the State to become active in new ways and at the root of this dislocation was a crisis of representation that propelled a search for new rhetorics of the real, for new techniques, institutions, and logics of signification. The reformist program of State intervention thus crucially came to involve a cultural mobilization that sought to define and fix the meaning of the crisis, as part of the incorporative strategy of restoring national unity and consent through identification with the State as the representative of the national interest. The attempt to accomplish this called for the development, expansion, and consolidation of new agencies, for new techniques of administrative intervention and social governance, and for new rhetorics of actuality, which together would give the State new and powerful means of communicating "social problems," of making the crisis visible in a particular way, of calling a national audience into place, and of shaping public opinion.

Across the alphabet soup of New Deal agencies and revamped government departments—the Federal Emergency Relief Administration, the Civil Works Administration, the Public Works Administration, the WPA National Research Project, the National Youth Administration, the Civilian Conservation Corps, the Department of the Interior, the Department of Agriculture, the Soil Conservation Service, the Tennessee Valley Authority, the Rural Electrification Administration, and, most famously, the Resettlement Administration and the Farm Security Administration (FSA)[166]—a new task began to be set that was not just one of recording public works or of generating publicity. Least of all was it a matter of propaganda, which, at a time of profound distrust of government purposes, would have run entirely counter to the political effects that were being sought. The problem lay at a less explicit and more structural level, demanding the invention of new languages of reality to combat the crisis of representation, the development of effective forms of communication to procure recognition and consent, and the mobilization of new technologies of truth capable of recruiting those they addressed to an identification with the New Deal vision and the stewardship of the corporate State as a benevolent force for rationalized planning, centralized coordination, and social welfare, safeguarding the interests of the nation as a whole. It was this attempt to articulate a new and believable official language with the power to make sense of a shattering reality and to shore up the legitimacy and credibility of state-led solutions that framed the emergence and promotion of those pressing rhetorics of appeal that took the name "documentary."

The development of documentary rhetoric and the deployment of documentary techniques were thus tied in a fundamental way to the crisis-driven strategy of the liberal democratic state in its attempt to rebuild a cohesive national audience, to retrieve the sense of a shared national experience, and to reestablish the common ground of national interest. The chain of connection here, however, did not primarily run through documentary's relation to those earlier practices of documentation that had reconstituted the social domain as a field of problems defined and acted on by agencies for which the techniques and technologies of documentation were, at once and inseparably, mechanisms of population control. While documentary still bore the marks of a disciplinary strategy of representation that mapped the social body as an object of surveillance, documentary rhetoric charted a decisive shift away from the technicism and professionalized address of earlier documentation, toward the structures of appeal that were integral to its machinery of capture. As we have already seen, the very connotations of the term "documentary," coined by Grierson in 1926, soon moved away from associations with factuality, scientific objectivity, neutral observation, and information and came to center on the notion of a form of communication that would shape public opinion through emotional appeal and the recruitment of popular identification. Within documentary practices themselves, this registered in a rhetorical shift from technicized protocols, instrumental realism, and isolated case studies toward emotive realism, identificatory drama, and a moving theater of bodies in space.

More profoundly, however, the shift involved more than just the working of a rhetorical code. Identificatory drama gestured to something else. The reality of documentary was a coded reality, but a coded reality *for* someone—for a viewer, for a subject. As Arthur Rothstein recognized, the documentary photographer was forced "to become not only a cameraman but a scenarist, dramatist, and director as well," deploying "a highly developed dramatic perception" toward "not only the influencing of the subject before the camera, but also the influencing of the person looking at the finished print."[167] "The photographer who consciously uses principles of direction in his work," Rothstein observed, "exercises great power over the person looking at the pictures."[168] This power was pivotal and around it turned the engineering of the viewer into a particular confrontation. The task for the photographers of the Historical Section of the Resettlement Administration was not just to bring before the public the facts of rural poverty and what section head Roy Stryker called "the appalling waste of lives and land that was threatening, in some areas of the United States, to create a class of American peasants."[169] "The task," Stryker reported to his superiors, "has been to confront the people with each other, the urban with the rural, the inhabitants of one section with those of other sections of the country, in order to promote a wider and more sympathetic understanding of one for another."[170] Central to the function of the photographs in Stryker's files was a theater of the imaginary in which "the populace confronts itself in these pictures."[171]

This was the core of the pioneering "technique," and it was this that justified the place of "still photography" in an emergency agency for which, as Stryker saw very clearly, "immediate action was imperative, and to act at all effectively the cooperation of the public had to be assured."[172] The problem was "too large for ready solution,"[173] and there was little time. Urgency demanded "the creation of an educational program that would begin to make itself felt in the passing of months rather than years."[174] It meant that the message would have to be "soundly based on reality,"[175] but this, in itself, was not enough. "Cooperation" had to be assured, and the mechanism for securing it was the staging of a confrontation that would lead to a recognition and profoundly affect the viewer's sense of self. This is what was engineered in the structure of address of the documentary photograph: the rhetoric of appeal of documentary photography activated the machinery of capture of the camera to orchestrate a confrontation—perhaps one could say an encounter, an unwelcome encounter, no doubt—that would appear in "American memory" as a moment of recognition and identification. The viewer was caught in an act of recognition that ignited the photograph's reality effect and opened a luminous space of separation and identification. It was not an identification with the abject object—the alibi of documentary's "decent intention." It was, rather, an identification with something more fascinating, directed at that object and returned through it: the lucid logic of a graphic light; the captivation of the geometral look, the look of the concerned camera, itself the vehicle of a gaze behind; the gaze behind of the paternal State at and through its subjects; a transcendent gaze whose subject is the viewer, caught in a glare from which the photograph is the viewer's only shield.

We are returned, then, to the imaginary field of the New Deal State and to a cultural strategy enacted in the structure of documentary itself:

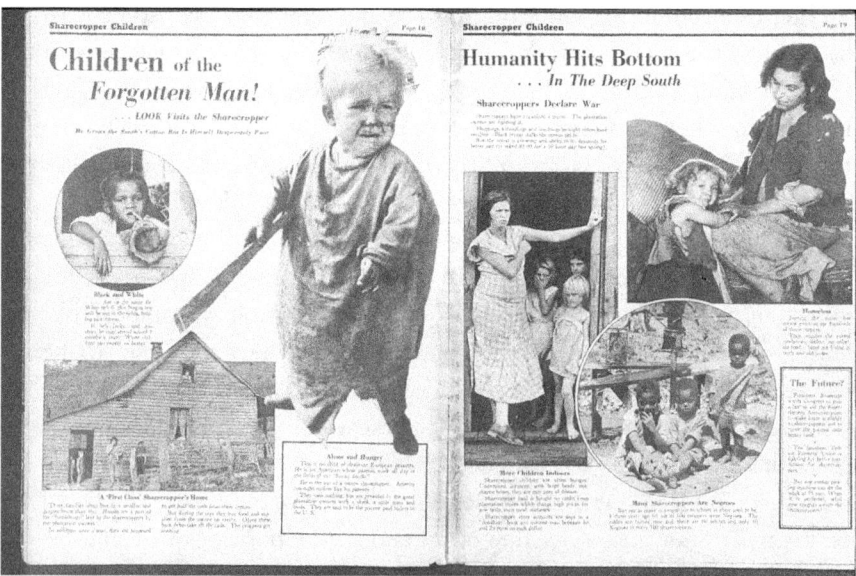

Figure 16. "Children of the *Forgotten Man!" Look,* March 1937, 18–19.

in its dramatization of witness, in the very visibility it gave to crisis, and in the relations of viewing to which it recruited its subjects. To be captured by this machinery was to be captured in the imaginary of the benevolent, impartial, paternal State, but to be captured in the act of compassionate looking: an act of decency and the act of a citizen, a civic subject called to duty. For all Grierson's readiness to concede the point, to be captured in this way was not to be caught as the victim of propaganda. It was, rather, to have reality restored; to be immersed again in transparency, communication, community; to become a full citizen and find one's place at the precise moment that the authority of the State was incorporated and, in a sense, disappeared. As Judith Butler has observed, "The process of forming the subject is a process of rendering the terrorizing power of the state invisible—and effective—as the ideality of conscience."[176] This was the political stake of documentary in its moment. This was "the photographer's moral burden":[177] the joining of "the dignity of fact," "the integrity of truth,"[178] and "the innate decency of the ordinary"[179] to the direction of conscience and "the crystallizing of new loyalties."[180] To feel the moral imperative to look headlong at catastrophe and to meet the eye of the forgotten who look straight back was to bear witness to the truth of citizenship and to renew again the ethical contract between the citizen and the State as the form of our collective participation in that truth. From crisis came the renewal of the corporate community. If only it worked, at least for a time.

Such was the New Deal strategy of crisis management, enlisting identificatory realism in the service of state intervention in order to implicate the viewer in the politics of truth of the administration and in the very perspective of the paternal State—the triumph of its gaze over the eye. To be implicated here was to be caught in a particular closure of sense and in the reality and the relations of subjection it produced: its exteriority and its interiority; its setting in place of a subject for an object and an object for a subject. To be implicated here was, then, to be caught inside a closing down of the disputability of the real, as part of the displacement and incorporation of dissent. Yet the ending of dispute and the disappearance of dissent did not apparently happen by force— beyond the force of recognition. For to be implicated here was, above all, to be caught in a delirium of transference through which desire was foreclosed and the community "reconstituted" within what the philosopher Jean-François Lyotard has called "the imaginary of management."[181] It was not, therefore, only a rhetoric that was at stake. It was, rather, a *cultural-political strategy*—a strategy of governance, a politics of representation, an instrumentalization, as always, of "culture" itself as what is essential to politics. This takes us a long way from notions of a progressive documentary tradition or of the democratization of visual culture. If documentary documents anything, it is only a certain strategy of power and desire. If documentary captures anything, it is only a certain subject—subject to that strategy of power and to that strategy of desire: the subject of documentary—hit at the midriff and yanked up to the plane of decent seeing.

CHAPTER 3

Melancholy Realism:
Walker Evans's Resistance to Meaning

"It is characteristic of philosophical writing," wrote Walter Benjamin, in the opening sentence of a book he was misled enough to hope would bring him academic preferment, "that it must continually confront the question of representation."[1] We might equally substitute "historical" here for the adjective "philosophical," though no doubt it will be insisted that this view is itself dated. Be that as it may, "the question of representation" survives both the 1920s and the 1970s, if not as the slogan of a particular project then as the marker of what, like some colonial administrator, Paul de Man once called "local difficulties"[2]—local difficulties, one might add, that are only too apt to turn into awkward *events*, the events of representation that compel a shift, as de Man put it, "from historical definition to the problematics of reading."[3] The difficulty, then, is how to get a handle on these events, even while we also have to worry about how they handle us—their subjects, that is, even those who cannot reconcile themselves to being in their grip.

What concerns me here is the character of the photographic event: not just the production of meaning at a specific moment, in a specific cultural field, but above all the relation the photograph is driven to establish to meaning and to the subject it captures. The moment is that of the Second New Deal in the United States—precisely a moment at which new technologies of photomechanical reproduction enabled a further quantum leap in the proliferation and social dispersion of photographic images, crossing a threshold that marked the emergence of a new economy: visual,

social, and political. The status of photography in this economy constituted a particular knot, threading together those dreams of transparency,
efficiency, and accelerated exchange that marked the instrumentalization
of photographic meaning, in social administration as in commercialized
communications, in the documentary archive as in the photojournalistic
picture file. The social saturation of the New Deal and the market saturation of the New Media: What space for response did they allow, other
than seduction, immersion, and subjection? What recourse remained to
the subject in the face of their new calls to emergence? What prospects
might there be for resisting or evading their new machineries and their
demands for the efficient delivery and receipt of meaning? This is the
problem of Walker Evans with his camera in the mid-1930s—the problem
of the character of his stubborn refusals, his perennial lassitude, boredom,
and inertia, his "negative personal magnetism," and what Lincoln Kirstein
irritably called "the skimmed decadence of so much of his work."[4]

Before we can approach this tangle of issues, however, we must
understand something of the economy of meaning in which Evans had
to find a way to use his camera. Where to begin? At the barbershop, perhaps, with Roland Barthes. But, there, we may find ourselves out of luck,
at least as regards our choice of magazine.[5]

Laying hands on a copy of the February 15 issue of *Life*, with its frame-
filling face of Japanese premier General Senjuro Hayashi, was surprisingly
difficult in the winter of 1937. Surprising, because more than 650,000
copies had been produced. But this was nowhere near enough to meet
demand.

When *Life* had been in the planning stage in August 1936, a modest circulation of 200,000 had been projected for the new picture magazine.[6] By the time of its first issue on November 23, 1936, however, it
already had 235,000 charter subscriptions and the print order had been
raised to 466,000, with more than 200,000 copies earmarked for newsstands.[7] At ten cents each, these sold out on the first day and dealers
pleaded to increase their orders by as much as five times. For the more
than three hundred advertisers who had committed to *Life* before the
date of the first issue, this was a windfall. It delivered them an expanding
national audience, while their contracts guaranteed them fixed space rates

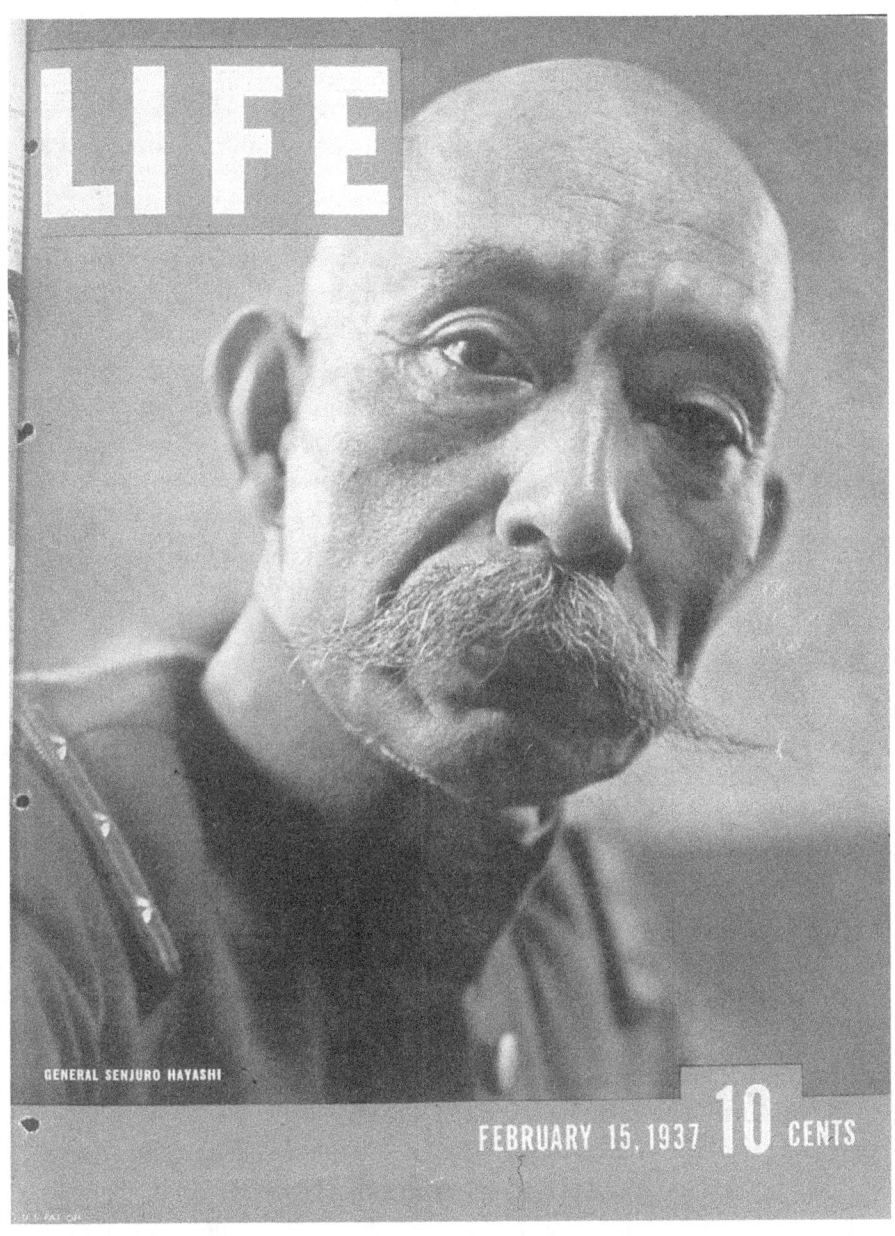

LIFE

GENERAL SENJURO HAYASHI

FEBRUARY 15, 1937 **10** CENTS

Figure 17. Cover of *Life*, February 15, 1937.

for a year at $1,500 per page, $800 per half page, or $2,500 for a page of inside color. When *Life*'s circulation jumped far beyond its quarter million guarantee and kept on climbing, its budget projections were exposed as a disastrous miscalculation. With its low cover price, the magazine, which by design depended on advertising fees for running costs and any profit, lost more than $5 million in its first year.[8]

The loss did not slow momentum. An extraordinary market had opened in the pages of the magazine. With each issue, production numbers were increased, breaking 650,000 in January 1937 and one million before April. It was still not sufficient. Circulation research on a targeted town in Massachusetts suggested that, nationally, five or six million copies might have been sold.[9] This was, however, far beyond the capacity of the improvised rotary presses at Donnelley's in Chicago, on which the technologically innovative magazine was being printed. Presses ran day and night in these early months, only clearing one issue in order to begin printing the next. Still the complaints poured in, inflamed by the widely held suspicion that the shortage was being manipulated to force readers to subscribe and to compel dealers to take more copies of *Life*'s sister magazine, *Time*. *Life*'s circulation manager responded defensively, telling Time Incorporated employees in December 1936 that

> The demand for *Life* is without precedent in publishing history. If we could supply the copies, the dollar volume of our newsstand sales this month would be greater than the dollar volume of sales of any other magazine in the world.[10]

So it was that a copy of *Life* in the winter of 1937 remained a prized possession, the object of competition at barbershops and cocktail parties, as at newsstands. Frustrated vendors resorted to displaying dismembered copies in their shop windows in order to preserve the goodwill of their customers.[11] In such ways, the actual readership of *Life* far exceeded the plain circulation figures. In fact, by April 1938, when circulation had reached two million, George Gallup's American Institute of Public Opinion was to estimate that upwards of seventeen million adults saw that month's first issue, suggesting a "pass along readership" of more than eight adults per copy.[12] It would have been hard indeed to dispute the boasting of proprietor Henry Luce when, in April 1937, barely five months after the first issue, he told a meeting of the American Association of Advertising Agencies, "Evidently, it is what the public wants more than it has ever wanted any product of ink and paper."[13]

Nothing but ink and paper *Life* may have been, but the level of demand it excited was extraordinary, even granting that it had been painstakingly designed and promoted to have this effect. What was it that drove this demand, or shall we say desire? Novelty, of course, and the established promotional machine of Time Incorporated. But also the seduction of production values: abundant photographs, satisfying paper quality, big format, engagingly varied typography, a dramatic yet open and modern-feeling layout and design, all made possible by a technological leap involving the production of coated paper in rolls for printing at speed on rotary presses that "flash dried" the printed ink. Then there was the new content package, planned like the evening's viewing of a later network television age: news, features, sports, gossip, celebrity biographies, entertainment, modest titillation, spectacle—"equal parts," as Bernard DeVoto suggested in 1938, "of the decapitated Chinaman, the flogged Negro, the surgically explored peritoneum, and the rapidly slipping chemise."[14] The tone was equally variable, at turns urgent, solemn, comic, crass, or cute. From the beginning, going beyond *Time*'s middlebrow digest and even beyond the dramatizations of the *March of Time* newsreel, *Life* was planned to take a broad perspective in tackling its subjects, to be, in Henry Luce's words, "simple and naive," "partly for people who find it too hard going to read *Time every week cover to cover*."[15]

Seeing the magazine quite consciously as a calculated step down from *Time*, Luce's particular ambition for *Life* was that it should be "the best magazine for look-through purposes" or, on second thoughts, remembering *Esquire*, "the damnedest best non-pornographic look-through magazine in the United States."[16] What bound the mix, therefore, was a new mode of address. As Daniel Longwell, *Life*'s first picture editor and office manager, argued early on: "the quick nervousness of pictures is a new language."[17] His views were echoed by Luce's team, who saw "pictorial journalism" as "a new language, difficult, as yet unmastered, but incredibly powerful and strangely universal."[18] In the drive to harness that power for profit, the claim to universality would become commonplace;

the strangeness would be forgotten. Longwell's earlier assessment was nearer the mark. The "pictorial journalism" of *Life* was an enervating language that excited an irresistible drive to look, to possess in the stains of ink on paper all that belonged to the Imaginary, all that was given to sight and, now, had to be seen.

This was the core of Henry Luce's idea. As he famously remarked, "Today I may not be in a mood nor feel the need to read the finest article about the Prime Minister. But I will stop to watch him take off his shoe."[19] Or, as his editorial team put it, "Fortunately perhaps for the race, all standards of news-value yield before the imperious desire to see, and see again, the female form divine."[20] The Prime Minister's shoe, the "female form divine": The object changes, but the "imperious," overriding compulsion to see, this scopic drive attributed to all, without difference, is the primary process in the reader's identification with the picture magazine. "The appeal of pictures is universal," declared an advertisement for *Life* in the December 1936 issue of *Fortune* magazine: "Pictures answer the Great Inquisitiveness which is born in a living animal, part of its lust for life."[21] We look and look, searching for our object. The only competitor to "the female form divine" is, tellingly, the face:

> Farmer faces, mining faces, faces of rugged individualists, Harlem faces, hopeful faces, tired old faces, smart night club faces—faces from Tennessee and Texas, faces from New England and the Pacific Coast—the faces of the U.S.[22]

From the beginning of *Life*, these faces stare out, page after page. The reader searches them for recognition, hanging on their gaze, wanting, as *Life* photographer Margaret Bourke-White would say: "Not just the unusual or striking face, but *the* face that would speak out the message from the printed page."[23] An object for a subject and a subject for an object, joined by "the message": *Life* is a mirror and a window, a screen and a frame. In its pages, readers cannot but find themselves looking and looking.

This is what the first prospectus for a picture magazine then called *Dime* says in mid-1936:

The basic premise [of publication] is that people like to look. They like to look at everything including themselves in the mirror. They also like to look at pictures, and especially in these swift-changing days they like to look at pictures which show them what is going on in America and in the world.[24]

This is how *Life* would finally declare itself:

To see life; to see the world; to eyewitness great events; to watch the faces of the poor and the gestures of the proud; to see strange things— machines, armies, multitudes, shadows in the jungle and on the moon; to see man's work—his paintings, towers and discoveries; to see things thousands of miles away, things hidden behind walls and within rooms, things dangerous to come to; the women that men love and many children; to see and to take pleasure in seeing; to see and be amazed; to see and be instructed.

Thus to see, and to be shown, is now the will and new expectancy of half mankind.

To see, and to show, is the mission now undertaken by a new kind of publication.[25]

The lure is the incitement of the drive—the drive driven desperate. Everything that can be seen is put before us, "half mankind." What cannot be shown and seen is unimportant, though it goes on as before. Government, bureaucracy, policing, surveillance, intelligence, the circuits of capital, the violence of exchange—all this means nothing, except insofar as it is accumulated and commodified as spectacle, the scopic harnessed to consummativity, calling into place a new field of subjects, overcoding the program of social life.[26] Such patterns of investment may be overly familiar now, but the lust for *Life* marked a quantum leap. It registered the emergence of a new polity, a new economy, a new pattern of imaginary recruitment, a change in the very unseen structures of identification and consent—in short, a retooling of the social Imaginary that enabled the cycles of the social economy to enter a new phase.

A new economy? Hard, perhaps, to see this in the pages of a ten-cent magazine. Yet these pages are screens and their images points of condensation and capture in which a certain compelling force makes its subject arrive. For Luce's enterprise, *Life* called into existence a new national market. For advertisers, it delivered a national consumership. For readers, *Life* was a conduit to an imaginary integration that was national in horizon yet founded on fantasized interactions and relations whose locus was the individual, for whom this fantasized field increasingly served as compensation for a displaced, divided, and hollowed-out social life. But I am getting, perhaps, too far from my theme.

February 15, 1937. Volume 2, number 7, page 9. The header tells us this is "LIFE." Immediately below, spread almost across the entire page like a banner headline, "WORLD'S HIGHEST STANDARD OF LIVING," edged in patriotic stripes running nearly parallel to the top of the page and decorated at the margins with white stars. A thin black wedge to the upper right is warning this is no headline. Below it, what looks like a cable connection crosses "LIVING" and obliterates a star. Then comes the giant, foreshortened family—if such it is—faces pressed against the windscreen of a car, the driver's knuckles bulging through the glass, only the family dog escaping the crush through the open side window. The dog is also the only one without perfect teeth, at least as far as we can see, but its eyes are as button bright as all the others' and set on the road ahead. *"There's no way like the American Way"* floats in cursive over the hood of the car, before a suggested landscape, like the vision of St. Paul.

The atmosphere is certainly that of a kind of ecstasy. The overwhelming general impression is of a spotless health and happiness in which everything is new, everything is moving forward—moving obliquely toward the right, which is where the huge yet toylike car will come into collision first with some sort of barrier and then with a rather less fortunate, strung-out group of people who are all Black, unlike the shiny occupants of the looming car, and who, though far from shabby, do not seem so newly pressed. Radiant sunshine falls on the figures in the car, but those in the line cast no shadows. They are caught in a general gloom. Only one of them, a man in a leather helmet, looks back and sees what is coming their way. Another man, further down the line, glances behind, to our left, beyond the frame. Five others look right at us, or to where the camera once was. The remainder stare blankly ahead, over to the right,

LIFE

VOL. 2 NO. 7

FEB. 15, 1937

WORLD'S HIGHEST STANDARD OF LIVING

There's no way like the American Way

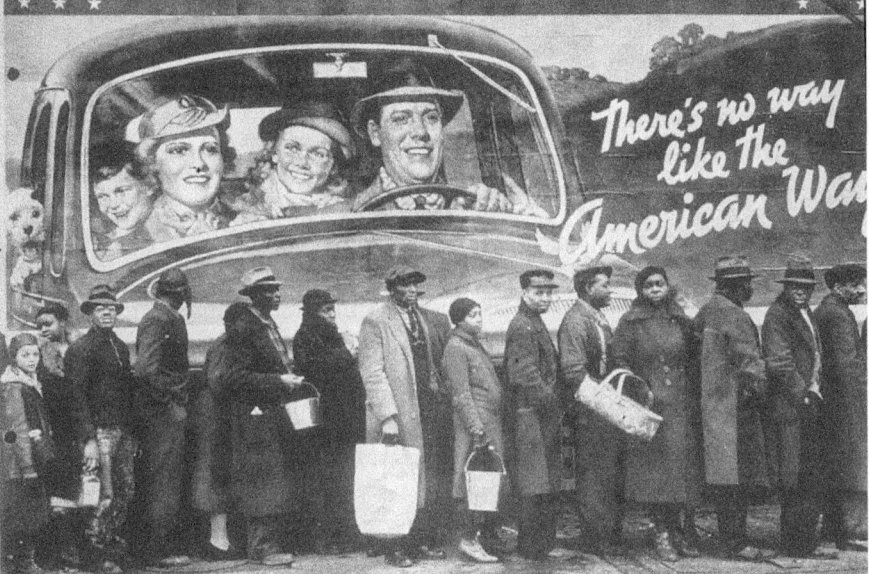

THE FLOOD LEAVES ITS VICTIMS ON THE BREAD LINE

FOOT by foot the Ohio Valley reappeared, as the Great Flood passed on down the Mississippi. Impatient refugees waded back to homes still sloshing in water. Cleanup crews worked day and night to remove the debris which made a ghastly mess of every street. Throughout the floodlands there were some 400 dead, but except for pneumonia and influenza there was little sickness, no epidemics.

The one flood problem which did not abate was that of relief. The water had cut off not only shelter but food and income. Lines formed outside each overworked relief agency. People came with baskets, bags, pails, or merely empty hands and hungry stomachs. Some of them, residents of the completely inundated Negro quarter of Louisville, appear in the picture above. They are inching past a sign erected

before the flood as part of a propaganda campaign of the National Association of Manufacturers. For the time being the Red Cross was bearing the brunt of relief. But soon most of the cost of relief and rehabilitation would shift back to the Government. It was going to take a lot of money to restore the American standard of living in the cities and towns of the Ohio Valley.

Page 9 LIFE Feb. 15

Figure 18. "The Flood Leaves Its Victims on the Bread Line," *Life,* February 15, 1937, 9.

but apparently not at the future toward which the car rushes on. There is also a ghost, behind the line and directly in the path of the automobile grill, though not quite in either space. Below comes the sidewalk, littered and stained, though it is hard to be certain about this. Beneath the sidewalk, the white page and the black headline: "THE FLOOD LEAVES ITS VICTIMS ON THE BREAD LINE."

For those who have seen the two preceding issues, the story has been well prepared, with extensive agency photographs, maps, and pages of explanation: "Floods Drive 288,000 People from Their Homes," declared *Life* on February 1;[27] "America's Worst Flood Makes Nearly a Million Refugees," it announced on February 8.[28] "Louisville got the worst of it," its report went on, "with three quarters of the city under water."[29] The inundation had caused more damage in monetary terms than any previous flood in the nation's history. In its wake had come disease, fire, looting, martial law, and an overwhelming refugee problem: almost a million homeless along the Ohio and Mississippi rivers, filling armories, barracks, tent cities, boxcars, stations, and warehouses. The real visual drama of this catastrophe—ruptured levees, flooded fields, rooftops, wreckage, cutoff cities seen from the air, evacuations, refugees—is in these earlier editions. Yet even coming late, when the story if not the flood was receding, the lead page of the February 15 issue presented readers with a striking graphic layout and image—strong enough, indeed, to survive the visual chaos and contradictory message of the facing page: a photo-strip advertisement for Heinz Aristocrat tomato products from "The Good Green Earth" of Bowling Green, Ohio. Anchored by the headline and the brief captioning text, the message on the editorial page is trenchant and abrupt. The "Great Flood" had passed on down the Ohio Valley into the Mississippi, leaving debris, "ghastly mess," and four hundred dead: "It was going to take a lot of money to restore the American standard of living in the cities and towns of the Ohio Valley."[30]

The February 15 issue of *Life* has an undeniably forceful and sardonic opening—if opening it is, after six and a half pages of advertising for cars, cruises, fruit juice, and leather goods and a two-and-a-half-page feature, "Speaking of Pictures," on the antics of nature photographer William Lovell Finley. Margaret Bourke-White's photograph on page 9 turns, of course, on the ironies of such juxtapositions. In the magazine

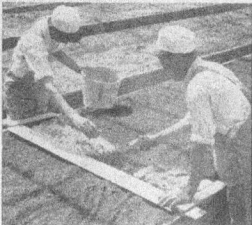 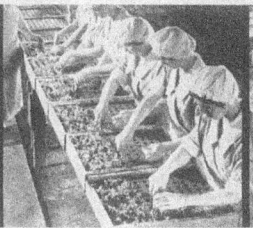 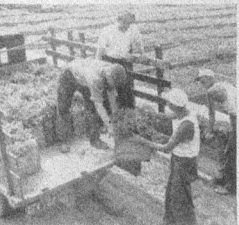
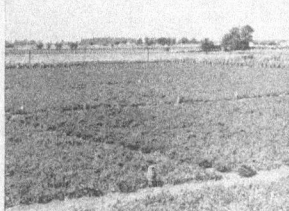 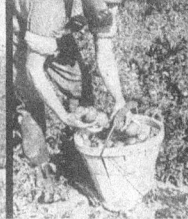 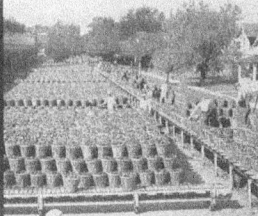
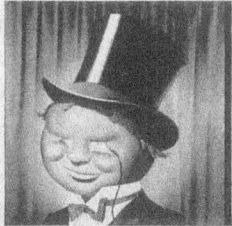 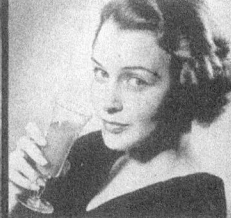 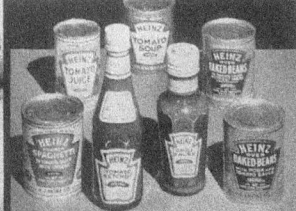
Figure 19. "The Good Green Earth," advertisement for Heinz Products, *Life*, February 15, 1937, 8.

itself, however, these jarring contiguities are to be passed over smoothly, without notice and without interruption. The convention of the separation of powers is strictly maintained, even though the picture-magazine format grew out of graphic advertising and even though advertising designers—not least for Heinz, Plymouth cars, and Goodrich Silvertown Tires, in this very same issue—had already responded to the pages of *Life* by seeking to absorb their novel rhetoric and narrative style.[31] Such mutuality makes clear-cut distinctions between editorial and advertising potentially tricky, on both sides. But that is not the convention.

Officially, then, the photograph in which I am interested, by a commercial photographer who saw the light, may fall on page 9, but it marks the proper beginning of the issue. There is plenty more to come: not the aerial photographs of drowned farmlands, broken levees, submerged railroad yards, and marooned towns that had filled seventeen pages in the issue of the week before but, rather, how the staff of the Louisville *Courier-Journal* and the Louisville *Times* got out a joint edition by lamplight; how God has provided a relief station at St. Paul's Episcopal Church; how the "swank" clubhouse at Churchill Downs has become temporary home to African American flood refugees; how five hundred other "Negroes," prisoners from Shelby County Penal Farm near Memphis, have gone to work in chain gangs to repair the levees. And, beyond this, turning the page, we see how a tiger turned on its trainer; how twenty-two-year-old Charlie Johns has married Eunice Winstead, his third-grade Tennessee neighbor; how the Women's Emergency Brigade vandalized the Chevrolet plant in Flint, Michigan; how this caused the upper stratum of Chrysler management to miss the "South Seas" party at the Book-Cadillac Hotel in Detroit; how the president, Andrew Mellon, and Jean Harlow have fared in Washington; how a wife should undress for her husband; how Spanish fascist bombers took out a munitions train from the air. Then, too, there is the Oxford Group at Malvern, Cuban cockfighting, the Japanese emperor's palace, the duke of Norfolk's wedding—plenty more. The heterogeneity and indeed the bathos of these successive topics and genres might prove disorienting, even to a reader driven along by "the imperious desire to see." But there remains at least the remnant of a conventional journalistic architecture here: Page 9 is the "Big News-Picture Story of the Week," as Henry

Luce defined it in his repeated attempts to anatomize *Life*.[32] "The Lead," Luce wrote, thinking back on the first twelve issues of *Life*, "is what the Prospectus calls 'The Big News-Picture Story of the Week.' The Inauguration, the Sit-down Strike, the Sand-hog Murder, and above all the Flood proved that there is such a thing."[33]

The Big News-Picture Story. The photograph fills almost three-fifths of the page. With only slight cropping on either side, it is, in turn, filled to its own frame—in its upper three-fifths by the poster image and in the lower two-fifths by the figures standing in line. All points of reference external to the confrontation of these two worlds are excluded. The poster is not shown as a billboard or located in a landscape. The queue has no discernible end in view and, in fact, no end in the picture at all. On the left, it runs into the gutter. On the right, it bleeds from the page. Without referring to the headline below, the line seems pointless and, in this, quite at odds with the ecstatic determination of the family above, as it moves on joyously to an end we also cannot see, across the line of standing

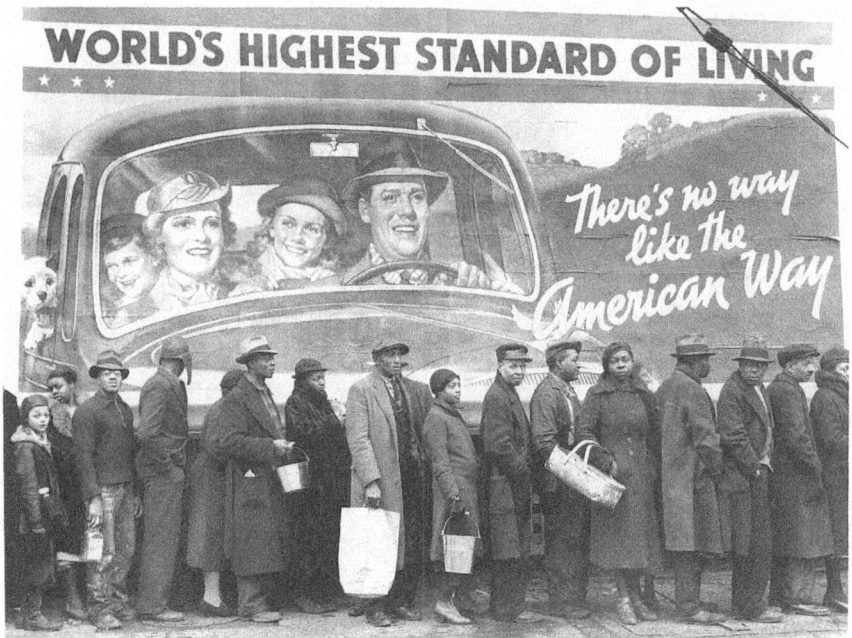

Figure 20. "When the Flood Receded, Louisville, Kentucky," February 1937. Photograph by Margaret Bourke-White/Time Life Pictures/Getty Images.

figures, along the "American Way" whose name fills a space on the right but, in illusion, hovers before the hood of the car, above its winged figure, beckoning onward. This way is "American"—that great amorphous, irresolvable signifier of a settler community, floating untroubled, here, by the violence of its forgetting. The car rushes along it, along a way not taken by those who shuffle across the vehicle's path, who seem—all but one—to have turned their backs on it and now, effectively, to stand in the way, soon, perhaps, to be knocked down like skittles, swept aside by sheer speed, washed away by the river of progress of which they have fallen foul.

The photographer, Margaret Bourke-White, has chosen her perspective carefully to give us precisely this. Typically, she spared herself no risk and others no inconvenience to get the shot she wanted. She had made her name "riding jackknife bridges, crawling over skyscrapers and pushing her lenses into white hot steel mills for just the right shots."[34] To photograph the Supreme Court, also for the February 15 issue of *Life*, she set up her camera tripod in the perfect spot, which happened to be the middle of street. With her remarkable concentration and oblivious disregard of other people, she gave no thought to fouling up traffic for blocks.[35] For Bourke-White, the viewpoint and the choice of lens were, along with the manipulation of lighting, fundamental to the didactic structure of the image—to the message—though the physical positioning of the camera certainly also signaled the heroics of what Luce liked to call the "crack photographer," the shaping of whose persona was, for Bourke-White, a second, parallel work hardly separable from the photographic work itself.

If the construction of this persona was a way in which Bourke-White negotiated the anxieties of insertion into a particular field of subjectivities, then it also had commercial value, as she realized early on, and it equally suited the economy of the new magazine. From the very beginning, the antics of the "crack photographer" were central to the glamour and modernity of *Life*.[36] The photographers were the stars. The writers carried their bags and heavy equipment and, in Bourke-White's case, reputedly did her laundry.[37] Bourke-White was always the exception among exceptions. At *Life*, she had her own staff and an enclosed office, to go with her $12,000 a year starting salary. It was a price the magazine was willing to pay, and not just as a cost of doing business, since the salary, the pose, the clothes, the travel, and the life were integral to the package being sold, in which "Margaret Bourke-White makes a picture" was always part of the performative meaning of the image and in which an essential part of the story would always be an account of her pains to meet the challenge of her assignment.[38]

The drama here was classic fare. Bourke-White's biographer tells us that managing editor John Shaw Billings gave her one hour's notice to leave on assignment.[39] Bourke-White herself was happy to embellish the tale:

> I caught the last plane to Louisville, then hitchhiked my way from the mud-swamped airport to the town. To accomplish the last stretch of this journey, I thumbed rides in rowboats and once on a large raft. These makeshift craft were bringing food packages and bottles of clean drinking water to marooned families and seeking out survivors. Working from the rowboats gave me good opportunities to record acts of mercy as they occurred.[40]

Stories like this accumulated. They were part of an expected performance and, issue by issue, over the weeks, the photographs plotted its succeeding acts. This was part of their aura, though that is not at all to say that the photographs are autobiographical. It is rather to say that, at a level of contrived connotation, Bourke-White's photographs arrived like postcards home from the airplane-hopping career of the woman *U.S. Camera* called "the most famous on-the-spot reporter the world over"—famous enough for her name to be a public byword; famous enough in the late 1930s for her own face to have become familiar in magazine advertisements for air travel, California wine, telephones, and Camel cigarettes; famous enough by the 1940s to qualify for the title "Topflight Famous American Woman."[41]

Yet in the magazine spread, the photograph is anonymous. The photographer's name does not appear until the contents page, all but lost in a column of narrow type with page numbers and names, in this issue on page 64, as always, at the back. The camera's viewpoint is, therefore, only belatedly personified. On the lead page, its first function is as the architecture of a statement: an editorial message that may be signed but that is still as efficient, professional, and anonymous as the house-style prose of the text below. The viewpoint invests the grammar of the message and its effects are dispersed across the image, in which the orchestration of space, laterally and in depth, produces a friezelike layering of shallow planes that work against any privileging of the center. The viewpoint is purely a matter of structure: the trace of a maneuver necessary to engender a particular coding effect. And this is part of the image's oddly detached effect. The viewpoint is not a subjective, located space. Nor is it the point of insertion of the viewer into a rhetorical immediacy: the point of capture by the rhetoric of recruitment that characterized the new language of "documentary." This is not a "documentary" image. It does not demand the enactment of the viewpoint as a psychic space, a point of identification at which the viewer is interpellated into the dramaturgy of the image and compelled to "the plane of decent seeing."[42] Nor is this an eyewitness account. It is not written in the first person, though that does not preclude a tone of "commitment."

What is distinctive about Bourke-White's photograph is not that it inscribes an act of seeing but that it constructs a legible message: a pictorial summation from which the arbitrariness of chance and the excess of particularity that afflict photography are strangely drained. The viewpoint is a function of composition, and the composition is painstaking and precise. The unusual choice of camera is crucial here. While the still relatively new small-format, 35 mm cameras predominated in *Life*'s original photography department and while, in the newspaper world, photographers almost invariably carried heavy 4 × 5 Speed Graphics, with fixed flash attachments, Bourke-White preferred the image quality of her 4 × 5 wooden Soho reflex camera and her 3¼ × 4¼ Linhof, with multiple, synchronized flash extensions. Bourke-White's method of working, with big camera, battery of lights, and long poses, precluded intimacy but placed the whole mis-en-scène under her firm directorial control. Erskine Caldwell said of working with her in 1936, the year before the Louisville flood, that

> She was in charge of everything, manipulating people and telling them where to sit and where to look and what not. She was very adept at being able to direct people. She was almost like a motion picture director.[43]

In Louisville, seen through the screen of her Linhof camera, the dour light from the rain-filled sky flattened Bourke-White's subject in a way that worked with her use of a long-focal-length lens, telescoping optical space, pushing the line back against the billboard, heightening both their proximity and their contrast.[44] More often, however, Bourke-White was unprepared to work with available illumination. She sought greater plasticity and contrast, thinking of photography as sculpting with light, using multiple artificial light sources set out in series, at a variety of angles, and synchronized with a remote shutter release.[45] This gave her photographs—even those taken in Buchenwald on the day of the liberation of the death camp—a melodramatic theatricality and a strange sheen, not unlike the high polish on the family in the car speeding along the American Way. The technical aspects of photography were not, however, what dominated Bourke-White's choices. Having set up her camera precisely, her method was to take the same picture, or a minutely adjusted variant, over and over, so that she could be sure of a correct exposure. As she told Ansel Adams, "I just set the shutter at 1/200th of a second, take a picture with every stop I have. I'm bound to get something."[46]

Composed in this way, the photograph as printed, almost full frame, has, for all its sorry subject, the polished inevitability and urbane wit of *Life's* smooth corporate writing.[47] Its meaning is explicit. With controlled and self-confident panache, it says what it has to say, undistracted by the irreducible richness of its anecdotal content: the way different men and women wear their hats; the ways they stand and what they do with their hands; their individual choices of shoes; the decision whether to turn up a coat collar or not; the preference for basket, galvanized bucket, or paper bag—not likely, one would think, to prove equally serviceable to every end. It is not that such incidentals are negligible to the image, to the extent that they give the "bread line" a lived particularity excluded from the untarnished ego ideals above. What matters, however, is the contrast, the overarching polarity that every local detail has to serve, as concrete particulars are obliged to express the underlying movement of the Hegelian dialectic. Economy, force, and aptness of argument are the prime rule. The argument works by binary opposition, its empirical richness only the cumulative elaboration of an essential internal principle.

This is not, after all, an informative image. It does not give us cues to where we are. It does not tell us why the line has formed. It does not show us the causes of the glazed, bemused, or resigned expressions. It does not allow us to see why only African Americans queue here, why or whether they are the sole "victims," where the White folks form their line, or whether we would be right to surmise that White folks all ride in cars. The photograph does not answer questions such as these. It is not that kind of journalism. Nor does it do what Edwin Locke and Walker Evans, on a short leash from their government boss Roy Stryker, were dispatched to do at exactly this time, accumulating entries for the photographic file, some way downriver in Forrest City, Arkansas, on the floodplain south of the confluence of the Mississippi and Ohio rivers. For Bourke-White, the meaning of the flood was clear: It was, as she wrote, "another bitter chapter in the bleak drama of waste of our American earth."[48] And when it came to making the photograph, Bourke-White had the same summarizing intentions. *Life*'s "Big News-Picture Story of the Week" was not a cumulative record that risked the awkward, the fugitive, and the fragmentary. It was a condensed visual headline. And it was Bourke-White's skill in writing in headlines that shaped the internal economy of meaning in this image, anchored by the headline "THE FLOOD LEAVES ITS VICTIMS ON THE BREAD LINE."[49]

"The American Way" and the path of "The Flood." The "World's Highest Standard Of Living" and "The Bread Line." Consumers and "Victims." Living and lost. Above and below. Movement toward us and movement to the margin. Speed and stagnation. Ecstasy and apathy. White and Black. American and something else. One antithesis overlays another. The accumulation of connotations condenses in a single trope. This is the rhetorical gambit of the image. This is the nexus of irony that, for Bourke-White, spoke what she saw. Photographers believe they find their tropes in the world. That is what makes them insist these tropes are real. For Bourke-White it was straightforward:

> There was the irony of the relief line standing against the incongruous background of an NAM [National Association of Manufacturers] poster showing a contented family complete with cherubic children, dog and car, its printed message proclaiming, "There's no way like the American Way."[50]

"There was the irony . . ." What Bourke-White did with her large-format camera was driven by her determination to fix this rhetorical structure, which she took herself merely to have discovered, yet whose organization into an effective picture involved a process she thought of as symbolization.[51] Where Bourke-White positioned herself put distance and externality over proximity and intimacy, while the long focal length of her lens flattened the queuing figures and collapsed the uncertain space between the billboard and the line, just as the unknown billboard designer had compressed the foreshortened space in the fictive car. It is as if the line of figures has been pasted on the bottom of the billboard, the whole being flattened like a poster, exposing—yet repeating—the spatial deception in the poster itself. This is, however, where the rhetoric of irony begins to turn and the tropic structure of the image begins to efface itself. The symbolic momentum gathered by the car is thrown into reverse. It is the line that now stands out as the rhetorical platform of the picture, a truth that cannot be ignored, the embodiment of a passive need that calls forth government action. Those who seemed to be the fall guys of a cruel joke made behind their backs now rise up as a concrete reality against which the joke falls flat. They are the Real that measures representation, the Real that marks its final frame.

The rhetoric of the image cashes out in a decisive way. The wrinkled, puckered surface of the poster shows itself, paper thin, easily, we now see, peeled away. The world of the billboard is the world of illusion, held up by its superstructure over the social reality at its base. To use again a favorite term of Birmingham cultural studies in the 1970s, the meaning of the fictive scene is "cashed out" in the real social relations beneath it. The poster is nothing but a representation, demonstrably inadequate to the reality of the "Bread Line." This is the bad faith of representation: Representation is tendentious, motivated, trompe l'oeil. Reality, outside all interest, present to itself, is given, unmediated, without re-presentation, to the unfooled eye. We see the truth now. The careful rhetorical construction of the image has brought us to this point. Representation, which seemed to be put at issue in the photograph, is only being *cited*, only being quoted in the image; but what falls outside all quotation marks is the Real itself.[52] It is this to which the photograph claims to give us access. And this is its authorization. The image makes a play with representation only to release itself from representation's limits, placing itself outside citation on a ground beyond dispute.

There is a striking economy here. The message of the photograph is succinct—succinct enough to be read at a glance, undelayed by ambiguities or uncertainties. But the message of the photograph, unlike the message of the billboard, is the message of the Real itself, given to us to see, even before our eyes drop to the bottom of the page and we read:

> The one flood problem which did not abate was that of relief. The water had cut off not only shelter but food and income. Lines formed outside each overworked relief agency. People came with baskets, bags, pails, or merely empty hands and hungry stomachs. Some of them, residents of the completely inundated Negro quarter of Louisville, appear in the picture above. They are inching past a sign erected before the flood as part of a propaganda campaign of the National Association of Manufacturers.[53]

Everything is accounted for in this economy. Meaning always balances out on the bottom line. The argument may be rhetorical, but the argument ends with the Real, and you can't argue with that. It is beyond dispute. As in the inveterate structure of ideology critique, the photograph finally exempts itself from the charge it levels against representation. Representation is "propaganda," betraying interests. The denotative force of the photograph puts before us the reality in which these interests are formed and the reality against which representation can be judged. The photograph itself, therefore, is put beyond adjudication. No need for representation when absolute reality already assumes the force of law.

One has to say it is impressively done. Only a day after the image was published, Beaumont Newhall was writing to Bourke-White for permission to include it in the Museum of Modern Art's exhibition Photography, 1839–1937.[54] Bourke-White's photograph of the Louisville flood is, indeed, exemplary, watertight. Nothing leaks. There is no remainder. Always granting, of course, that we do not get distracted by the cable wire that marks the corner like a dog-eared fold. The cable pulls at the inevitable force of the frame, marking the arbitrariness of the cut of the camera's field of view and the cut of the cropping knife. The wire is like a hair on the negative: By rights, it should not be there, but it cannot be blown away. Then there is the line of figures: the idiosyncrasy of their clothes, their gestures, their facial expressions, their choices of footwear, the things they carry and have seen fit to bring with them on the line. None of this detail quite plays its allotted role. It is not wholly subsumable within the rhetorical function the line must perform as mirror to the other world of the billboard Imaginary. It is not wholly absorbable into the structure of binary difference. Even ignoring the ghost, with its spectral witness to the mark of time on the materiality of the photograph, there is too much left over that does not disappear.

In the background, too, the billboard itself has a thickness at odds with its paper-thin function. Reduced to the role of fall guy, of comic stooge, the poster looming over the figures in the foreground has taken on for later audiences the status of a generic kitsch object, laughable in intent and weakened in effect. It stands for the cynical corporate jingoism and the naively patriotic public culture of a superseded time, gone the way of Ozzie and Harriet. In 1937, however, it meant both more and less than this—something charged with specific resonance, topical controversy, and an identifiable stamp. *Life*'s editorial writers were themselves quick enough to name it and separate themselves from its taint: It is "a sign erected before the flood as part of a propaganda campaign of the National Association of Manufacturers." Yet this caption launches more boats than it can keep afloat. We are not told what the National Association of Manufacturers is or why it would engage in "a propaganda campaign" at this time. Propaganda for what? Directed at whom? How much did *Life*'s writers feel they could assume? How much were readers already cued to supply?

The poster has, in fact, no signature, other than that of the graphic artist, which Bourke-White's photograph does not show. Yet as they appeared on the streets of American towns and cities in December 1936 and in the early months of 1937, billboards such as the one in Louisville were recognizable enough.[55] They caught the eye not only of Bourke-White but also of government photographers Ed Locke, Arthur Rothstein, and Dorothea Lange, who logged them for the Resettlement Administration file in Memphis, Tennessee, in Kingwood, West Virginia, in Birmingham, Alabama, and along U.S. Highway 99 in California.[56] The billboard campaign, lasting three months and encompassing three different designs posted at sixty thousand sites across the country, was something new, something to remark, even in the turbulent and inventive political landscape of the second Roosevelt administration.[57] Its sloganizing fed into the rising drone of political noise that marked this moment of conflict, the turning point for New Deal reformism, in which new media and new techniques of public communications began to rework the political process. At the level of content, however, the message, if not the smooth delivery, was more familiar—as was the voice, whether identified on the billboards or not. Controversy over the political activities of the National Association of Manufacturers already had a history, but it was gathering to a head again at this time in 1937, when, under force of subpoena, full-time officials and elected officers of the association were called to hearings in Congress, before a Senate subcommittee investigating violations of the right to free speech and assembly and interference with the right of labor to organize and bargain collectively.[58]

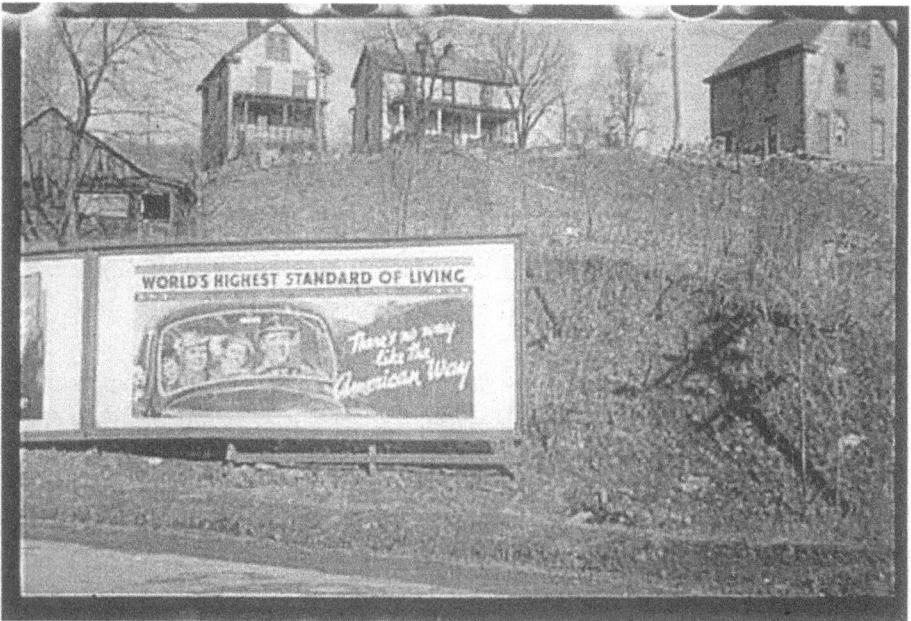

Figure 21. Edwin Locke, "Road sign near Kingwood, West Virginia," February 1937. FSA-OWI Collection, Prints and Photographs Division, Library of Congress (LC-USF33-004228-M3).

The National Association of Manufacturers, "a mutual and cooperative organization of American manufacturers in the United States,"
had been formed at a gathering of industrialists in Cincinnati, Ohio,
on January 22, 1895, at a time when the organizational and legislative
successes of craft unions were pushing manufacturers to go beyond
existing trade organizations, to organize themselves across industries
and on a national scale.[59] What spurred action in 1895 was the backlash
from the wave of violently suppressed "anarchistic strikes" that accompanied the severe economic slump of 1894. In the struggle to shape
public opinion, the National Association of Manufacturers emerged as
what one historian has called "a permanent propaganda association,"
advocating for the interests of industrialists, mobilizing for control of
the legislative agenda, and vehemently attacking the rise of unionism.[60]
In its publications, the National Association of Manufacturers condemned the American Federation of Labor as "un-American, illegal
and indecent."[61] Its president railed that "The American Federation
of Labor is engaged in an open warfare against Jesus Christ and his
cause."[62] So determined in the early 1900s was the association's opposition to legislation favored by the American Federation that its political
and legislative maneuvering came under investigation by committees of
the Sixty-third Congress. It was not to be the last time it would come
under congressional scrutiny.

By the mid-1930s, the prime targets of the National Association of
Manufacturers had changed: Now the object of its wrath was no longer
the American Federation of Labor but, rather, the regulatory agencies
of the New Deal, on the one side, and, on the other, John Lewis's Committee for Industrial Organization, armed with its new weapon of the
"sit-down strike." Nineteen thirty-seven was the year in which conflict
between all three parties erupted into the news.[63] The National Association of Manufacturers then had 4,500 members, representing companies employing between a third and a half of all manufacturing workers
in the United States.[64] The association was, however, dominated by a
core of around two hundred large firms and corporations that contributed
49 percent of the organization's total income and controlled its board
of directors.[65] The same companies bound the National Association of
Manufacturers closely to affiliated organizations, such as the National

Metal Trades Association, that actively promoted company unions, anti-labor espionage, strike breaking, tear gas, and other "instrumentalities of industrial warfare," as Senator Robert La Follette Jr. (D–Wisc.) was to call them.[66] Such policies brought the National Association of Manufacturers into headlong conflict with the extension of union activity stimulated by the National Industrial Recovery Act of 1933 and given new protections by the National Labor Relations Act of 1935. The National Association of Manufacturers condemned the work of the National Labor Relations Board and was one of the "most active" elements in the movement to discredit the National Labor Relations Act, arguing that it was unconstitutional and hostile to the welfare of industry and, even after its passage, inciting companies to defy it.[67]

Yet, in the words of one of its own earlier general managers, the National Association of Manufacturers was "not primarily a labor-busting organization."[68] The definition of its general objects and purposes given in its constitution had committed it, from the beginning, to "the education of the public in the principles of individual liberty and ownership of property."[69] By the mid-1930s, however, in the face of government intervention and "the growing menace of industrial disputes," "the cultivation of public understanding" had taken on a new prominence, even as the tactics of "industrial warfare" showed signs of antagonizing public opinion.[70] "Now, more than ever before," the association came to realize, "strikes are being won or lost in the newspapers and over the radio."[71] A 1933 policy review by the National Association of Manufacturers' Law Department gave early warning, arguing that

> The problem of public relations must have an active consideration that the Association has never been able to give it. The public does not understand industry, largely because industry itself has made no real effort to tell its story; to show the people of this country that our high living standards have arisen almost altogether from the civilization which industrial activity has set up. On the other hand, selfish groups, including labor, the socialistic-minded and the radical, have constantly and continuously misrepresented industry to the people, with the result that there is a general misinformation of our industrial economy, which is highly destructive in its effect.[72]

Writing with admirable candor in September 1937, the head of the National Association of Manufacturers' "field force" put it more succinctly: "The hazard facing industrialists is the newly realized political power of the masses. Unless their thinking is directed toward sane and established measures, we are definitely headed for adversity."[73]

The solution, modeled on new practices of corporate public relations, was a "Nation-wide educational movement" that would cover "every known channel of reaching the public—press, radio, industrial management, stockholders, employees, industry, farmers, and other groups."[74] Accordingly, in February 1934, a National Industrial Information Committee was set up to raise special funds for "an educational program" prepared by a Public Relations Committee, under the guidance of a publicity director.[75] In December 1935, the affiliated National Industrial Committee, housed in the National Association of Manufacturers headquarters in New York, was also reorganized, primarily to promote its Public Information Program more effectively. The National Industrial Committee itself went back to 1907, having been organized as the means of extending the reach of the National Association of Manufacturers to forty thousand additional companies. By 1935, the National Industrial Committee linked the National Association of Manufacturers to thirty-three state industrial associations, eighty-five industrial employment relations organizations, and seventy-eight national manufacturing trade associations.[76] With this extended network as its base, the annual income of the National Association of Manufacturers Public Information Program grew from nothing in 1933, to over a hundred thousand dollars in 1935, to half a million dollars in 1936, to three-quarters of a million dollars in 1937—fully half the total income of the association as a whole, though this was only seed money for the actual publicity campaigns.[77]

The 1937 report *Industry Must Speak!* published by the National Industrial Information Committee outlined what "public information" and an expanded "educational program" entailed: press bulletins to daily newspapers, syndicated newspaper columns, news stories, news-clipping services, cartoons and comic strips, newspaper advertising, outdoor advertising, radio features, radio dramas, motion picture shorts and newsreels, foreign language transcriptions, public speeches, newsletters, direct mailings, employee contacts, bulletin-board posters, circular letters, pamphlets, and publications.[78] The campaign to present "industry as a courageous, progressive force" was to embrace "practically every known medium."[79] Rarely, however, was the National Association of Manufacturers' authorship of its publicity materials identified to target audiences. The tactic was to work through local businesses and "civic organizations," who would sponsor local campaigns using the association's materials. In April 1937, for example, the National Association of Manufacturers commissioned a series of thirteen "Harmony ads" designed by the advertising agency of MacDonald-Cook, under the slogan "Prosperity Dwells Where Harmony Reigns." The National Association then promoted these ready-made advertisements to local business leaders as "the means of organizing a community against labor agitators before they get in their work."[80] When they appeared in local newspapers, however, as they did in 367 cities across the country, their message carried only the endorsement of the civic organizations and "citizens committees" that underwrote the publication costs and used the advertisements to raise local donations in support of their antilabor vigilante activities.[81]

The billboard campaign that appeared on the streets of Louisville and other American cities in December 1936 and the early months of 1937 was, therefore, only part of a broader, concerted program to shape public opinion and to mobilize "merchants, professional men, farmers, white-collar workers, and other groups which are known as the Public" as "a third party" in the sharpened struggle with labor.[82] The aim of the outdoor advertising strategy was to proclaim "on the billboards of the nation that 'There Is No Way Like the American Way' with its 'World's Highest Standard of Living,' 'World's Shortest Working Hours,' 'World's Highest Wages.'"[83] The unifying slogan derived from the first of a series of broad themes conceived in 1934 and outlined originally in eight free booklets published under the rubric of the "You and Industry Series."[84] The theme was "The American Way—An explanation of how our system operates," part of what the National Association of Manufacturers saw as "a constructive, affirmative story of industry."[85] In all, the billboard campaign cost $53,461.97 to prepare, but it would have cost almost one and a quarter million dollars if billboard space had not been furnished free by outdoor advertising companies contacted through the General Outdoor Advertising Association.[86] Nothing on

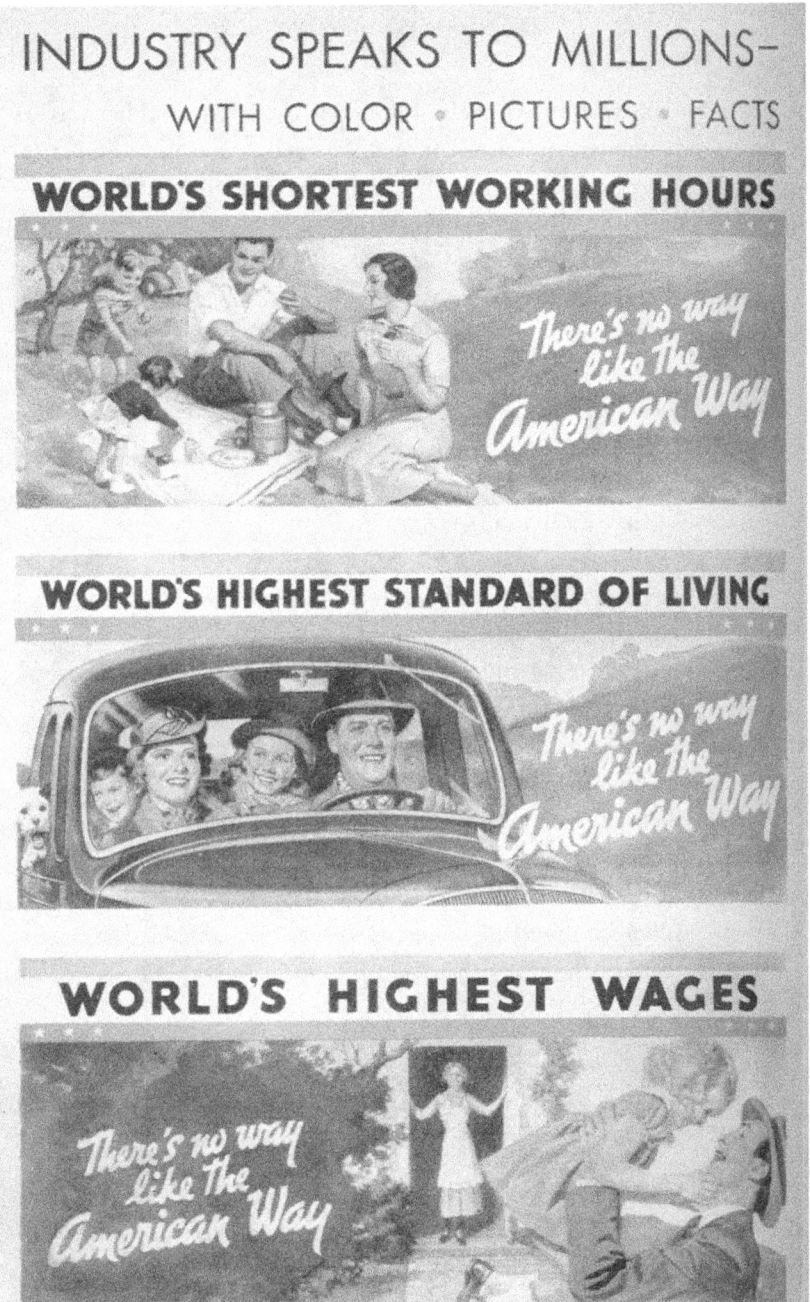

Figure 22. Leaflet of National Association of Manufacturers of the United States of America, *Along the Highways of America,* describing the outdoor campaign "There's No Way like the American Way," 1937.

the posters identified either the publisher or the sponsor. That was, as we have seen, standard practice for the National Association of Manufacturers, but, pressed on the point by the Senate subcommittee, the association's executive vice president blustered:

> They were upon the American Way, and the conditions that surround our industrial life, because we felt it was important that the American people commence to have some full appreciation of the industrial system as presented from the manufacturer's standpoint, and there we were presenting the American Way as being superior to any other industrial system in the rest of the world, and did not necessarily think at that time that it was necessary to identify a "hurrah for America."[87]

The distribution for this "hurrah for America," as for the "Harmony ads," was certainly widespread and general. As Ernest T. Weir, chairman of the National Industrial Information Committee, boasted:

> Industry's first outdoor campaign shows the happy America which industry helped to create . . . reaching every class and group through 60,000 billboard advertisements placed throughout the country . . . blazing the trail in placing facts about industrial progress and achievements before the public with pictures and color.
>
> Millions will see it . . . millions will read it . . . telling and repeating to millions the truth that "There's No Way Like The American Way."[88]

Yet the National Association of Manufacturers also pointedly concentrated its publicity campaigns on the sites of protracted strikes and coordinated strike-breaking interventions, and on localities torn by civic strife spilling over from the industrial arena. This is what brought officers and officials before La Follette's Senate subcommittee investigation of violations of free speech and the rights of labor. Monroe, Flint, and Lansing, Michigan; the Mahoning Valley, Ohio; Johnstown, Pennsylvania; Tonawanda, New York: These were the place-names that filled the pages of the association's publications and then echoed back through the hearing room. Yet the civil conflicts born of ecological disaster down the Ohio and Mississippi valleys and across the dust-choked farmlands of the Great Plains posed as much of a threat to national cohesion and were not without their own relation to the drives of industrialization. Flood, dereliction, and sit-down strikes jostled together on the pages of *Life* in the winter and early spring of 1937. There was a reason for the National Association of Manufacturers to be there, incognito, in Louisville, Kentucky. There was a relationship to be brought out, just as *Life* had cause enough to think about the role of mass-produced images in the new economy of publicity and public opinion formation that had reinvested corporate affairs and the political field in the United States in the mid-1930s. Bringing out such linkages was not the magazine's purpose, of course, any more than it was the purpose of Bourke-White's photograph. Her headline picture depended on this topicality, this tacit sense of suspended connections; it was part of the photograph's currency in February 1937. Yet Bourke-White's strategy worked to reorganize the unruly dissemination of photographic meaning into an immediately readable message whose rhetorical condensation and graphic simplification would absorb particularities and take on the quality of a symbol. In the process, other stories were lost, even to readers in 1937, but the thickness of meaning could not be entirely flattened out.

This is not all, perhaps, that shows itself and cannot be closed off by the finality of a reading imposed by the dialectic of the manifest message. Since we have begun to confront the *overdetermination* of meaning in the photograph, here is the story of a dream: Written in characteristic style, it comes from Bourke-White's autobiography, *Portrait of Myself*, published in 1963. In this stylized narrative, itself strikingly subject to processes of displacement and condensation, the dream is placed sometime in the first half of 1936, though this is not entirely clear in the compressed narrative time that moves very rapidly from five days in 1934, in which Bourke-White flew from the Dakotas to the Texas panhandle photographing the drought for *Fortune* magazine, to the "miracle" in which she would happen to hear about Erskine Caldwell's project to collaborate with a photographer on an authentic book about people and conditions in the South.[89] The dream falls, in this carefully plotted account, "a week or two" before the miraculous event and is offered as final explanation of Bourke-White's rising determination to repudiate her lucrative career as an advertising photographer, whose staple accounts in the early 1930s were Buick cars and Goodyear tires.[90]

Set aside from "real life," like propaganda, advertising marked what had to be repudiated but could not be escaped.[91] In a convenient distinction, Bourke-White would later insist that her work in the field of advertising gave her "practice in precision," but that her "style" and, "even more importantly," her "convictions" were formed in her experience photographing the heavy industries of Cleveland and the Midwest.[92] In March 1936, however, Bourke-White wrote to Erskine Caldwell that

> I have felt keenly for some time that I was turning my camera too often to advertising subjects and too little in the direction of something that might have some social significance.[93]

In the search for "social significance," however, Bourke-White's "unreal" past was apt to stage unexpected returns. In her autobiography, again, Bourke-White writes of traveling with Caldwell in the summer of 1936:

> As we penetrated the more destitute regions of the South, I was struck by the frequent reminders I found of the advertising world I thought I had left behind. Here the people really used the ads. They plastered them directly on their houses to keep the wind out. Some sharecropper shacks were wrapped so snugly in huge billboard posters advertising magic painkillers and Buttercup Snuff that the home itself disappeared from sight. The effect was bizarre.
>
> And inside, the effect was equally unexpected. The walls from floor to ceiling were papered in old newspapers and colorful advertising pages torn from magazines. Very practical, Erskine explained to me. Good as insulation against either heat or chill, and it's clean and can be replaced for next to nothing. I had the uneasy feeling that if I explored around enough, I would find advertisements I had done myself.[94]

Guilt and unease. The bizarre disappearance of the home. The reappearance of what had been left behind. They suggest a rather different relationship between advertising and the real than that to which we are

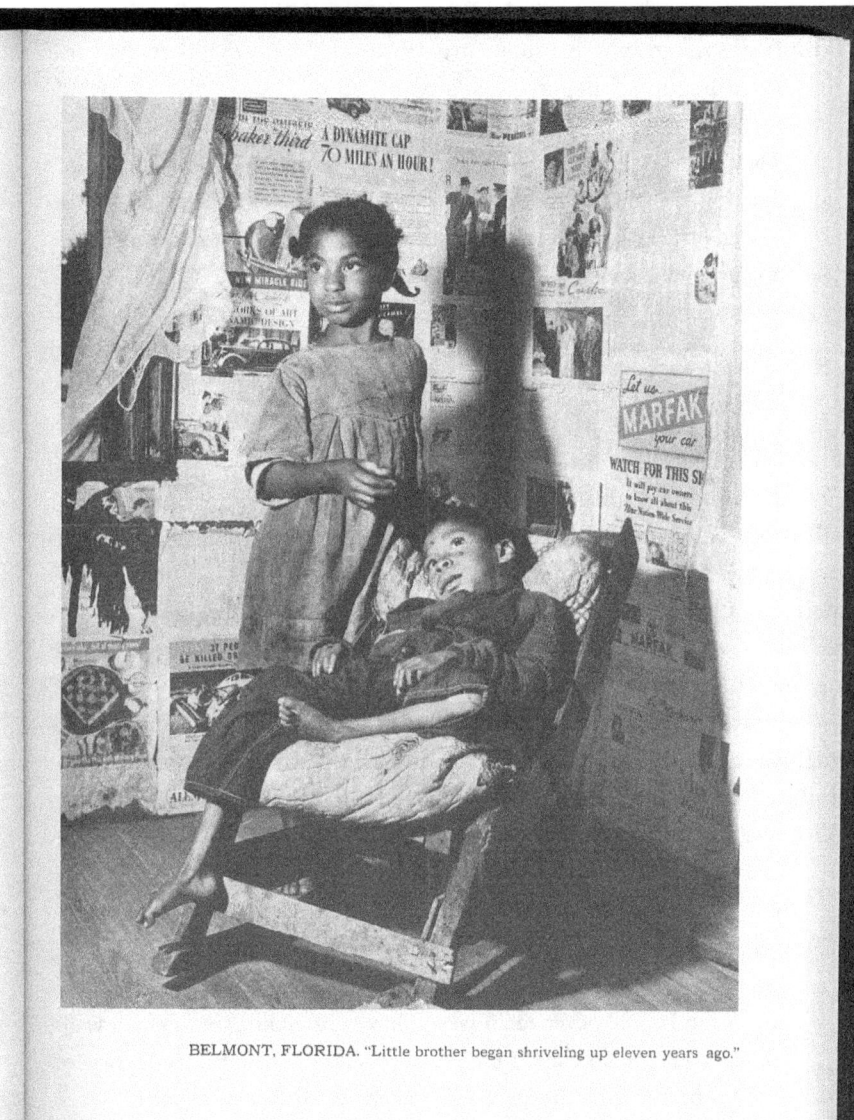

BELMONT, FLORIDA. "Little brother began shriveling up eleven years ago."

Figure 23. Margaret Bourke-White, "Belmont, Florida. 'Little brother began shriveling up eleven years ago,'" from Erskine Caldwell and Margaret Bourke-White, *You Have Seen Their Faces* (New York: Modern Age Books, 1937). Courtesy of the estate of Margaret Bourke-White.

asked to cling in the midst of the Louisville flood. The recoil in Bourke-White's autobiography is immediate, however. She remembers "a little girl named Begonia." Begonia had a twin sister:

> They went to school on alternate days, so as to share their single non-descript coat and their one pair of shoes. And here, right behind Begonia's wistful little face as she told me this, was this spectacular and improbable background showing all the world's goods. Begonia and her sister could look their walls over and find a complete range of shoes, jackets and coats. But never would they find that real coat and real pair of shoes which would take the second twin to school.[95]

The real is secured again in the foreground, as an antidote to the "spectacular and improbable background." But the real is also an enigma that will never be found, however much the sisters give themselves over to looking and to the world of magazines. On the one hand, the real settles the issue. On the other, it will never resolve the troubling narrative of doubling, separation, and loss that cannot restore the missing twin, the missing coat, and the missing pair of shoes.

I have not forgotten the dream. In *Portrait of Myself*, the encounter with the twin follows the repudiation of the world of advertising precipitated by the dream that ruptures the "circle of madness." Bourke-White writes:

> The circle of madness was closing on itself. Rubber was chasing rubber around in a vacuum. I longed to see the real world which lay beyond the real tire, where things did not have to look convincing, they just had to be true. I felt I could never again face a shiny automobile stuffed with vapid smiles. Never again could I build and rebuild the road that led nowhere.
>
> Then I had a dream. I still remember the mood of terror. Great unfriendly shapes were rushing toward me, threatening to crush me down. As they drew closer, I recognized them as the Buick cars I had been photographing. They were moving toward me in a menacing zigzag course, their giant hoods raised in jagged alarming shapes as though determined to swallow me. Run as fast as I could, I could not escape them. As they moved faster, I began to stumble, and as they towered over me, pushing

me down, I woke up to find that I had fallen out of bed and was writhing on the floor with my back strained.[96]

It may be remarked that the narrative in which the dream has its function and the reported dream itself turn on images, tropes, and compressions of space that echo those of the Louisville photograph of 1937: the counterposing of "the real world" and the world of appearance; the "shiny automobile stuffed with vapid smiles"; the road to nowhere; the giant hood, towering above, moving inexorably forward, pushing down, crushing. This repetition alone would be of interest, irrespective of whether one thought one was dealing with the work of a dream in 1936 or the work of a text in 1963. In the story of Bourke-White's life as she wished it to be told in the late 1950s, the episode of the nightmare is contrived as a turning point. The retelling of the dream alleged to have disturbed her sleep almost exactly a year before the Louisville photograph was made invests the figure of the advancing car with portentous personal meaning, not untypical of the operation of dream images in the genre of life stories to which Bourke-White's autobiography conforms. Such investment of meaning, whether consciously wrought or unbidden, must certainly complicate the question of what we are to read in the 1937 photograph. At the same time, the lurid imagery and melodramatic hyperbole of the written account, even if expected of the genre, still register at a less calculated level as excessive in relation to their narrative function, speaking more than may be intended of paranoid fantasies of prostration, engulfment, suffocation, and engorgement.

Whether dream or not, the excess of Bourke-White's story has meaning. It has meaning, no doubt, for the motivation of so driven a woman as Margaret Bourke-White, though psychobiography is not my purpose here. Biographical speculation may well be beyond the pale and beside the point. That does not mean, however, that the tropological activity of the texts in play—dream, autobiography, photograph—can be conveniently closed to the uncertain reaches that have opened up. The least we might say for the photograph is that, once such relays of meaning come to animate the image, there is no ready way to exclude them. Or, to put it another way, there is inescapably an unexcludable excess of meaning in the photograph that does not lend itself to didactic reduction, to functionalism, or to efficient communication, even in an image such as this, in which semiotic economy and discursive frame work to curtail meaning as exhaustively determined and complete. The economy of accomplished meaning is in doubt, even in Bourke-White's practice of engaged journalism, in which the message must always arrive.

As I have said, it was not only photojournalists who, in the early months of 1937, found themselves in the floodplain of the Ohio and Mississippi rivers. Photographers and filmmakers working for the government were also dispatched to record the disaster and the relief effort and to send back images that might be useful to various forms of governmental, interagency, and public advocacy. Carl Mydans had been in Louisville in March of the previous year, photographing the flooded streets for the Historical Section of the Division of Information of the Resettlement Administration.[97] In 1937, it was Walker Evans and Edwin Locke who were sent out from the Historical Section's Washington office on a "quick trip to flood," this time headed further downriver, to the point where the Ohio and the Mississippi rivers flowed together, pouring out their flood waters into the valley bottom south of Cairo, Illinois.[98]

This was no freewheeling assignment. The photographers were to link up in Memphis, Tennessee, with Pare Lorentz and Willard Van Dyke, who were gathering dramatic footage for Lorentz's didactic documentary film *The River*. They were also to record the catastrophic effect of land mismanagement in the upper valleys and the short-term emergency response by governmental and local agencies to the resultant inundation of the floodplain. Evans was characteristically relieved to be out of Washington and away from routine jobs, but with his reputation for low production and a way of working intractable to direction, he may also have guessed he was being given a final chance by the cash-strapped Historical Section, for which he worked as "Information Specialist" at a salary of $3,000 a year.[99] Clearly, Evans was meant to be under the watchful eye of Locke, who duly reported back to Roy Stryker, office chief of the Resettlement Administration's photographic record and publicity arm.[100] For his part, while maintaining friendly terms, Evans thought Locke on assignment looked like "a communist commisar in the Winter Palace."[101] Certainly, there is pomposity and condescension in

Locke's letters to Stryker. "I had a job annoying Walker out of his lassitude," Locke would write from Memphis on February 4, "but today in Forrest City, Arkansas, he worked as I am sure he never has before."[102]

Forrest City was the destination. Having left Washington at three o'clock on the afternoon of January 30, Locke and Evans had driven west, through Lexington, Knoxville, and Savannah, Tennessee, arriving in Memphis around one o'clock on Tuesday, February 2. The following day, they moved on by train to Forrest City, Arkansas, photographing waterlogged farmlands, stranded farmhouses, and the frightening rush of the swollen river on either side of the raised railroad tracks.[103] Over the next five days, despite Locke's comment, the two worked hard to document the broken flood defenses, the ruined homes, the refugees, and the relief response. But they also could not avoid recording what *Life* would not name: forced Black labor on the levees, segregated breadlines, and the racially separated camps for victims of the flood. This was far from Evans's first assignment in the South, but what he saw across the wall of segregation still drew him in.[104]

After his first full day working in Forrest City, Evans noted in his small, red-leather engagement book:

> To white refugee camps in the morning, a sunny day. Refugees being brought in, tents set up in a lot near high school, by CCC [Civilian Conservation Corps] men. This is all in charge of Red Cross who want us to be sure to include their insignia in pictures. Careful not to do this. People seem thoroughly depressed, mostly worries about future. We did a good deal of work and got tired. Negro camp at other end of town much larger, much more interesting. Negroes *really* deflated, more so than I've ever seen them. I tried a few shots with synchronized flash inside the large compress where the sick were lying in an assortment of fancy iron beds (their own?). Felt completely ill-mannered but wanted at the same time to make just these pictures.[105]

Ill-mannered or not, he was back the next day and, in fact, it was in these camps for African American flood refugees that Evans would make the only images he would later choose to publish and reuse from what has been judged a failed assignment.[106]

One of these images was a photograph taken with flash and a four-by-five view camera almost at eye level with a young African American woman, seemingly one of the sick in assorted iron bedsteads in the over-crowded cotton compress building in Forrest City. Evans appears to have held the negative back from the Resettlement Administration file and, in 1938, he included a print from it in the monograph that accompanied his Museum of Modern Art solo exhibition—an exhibition in

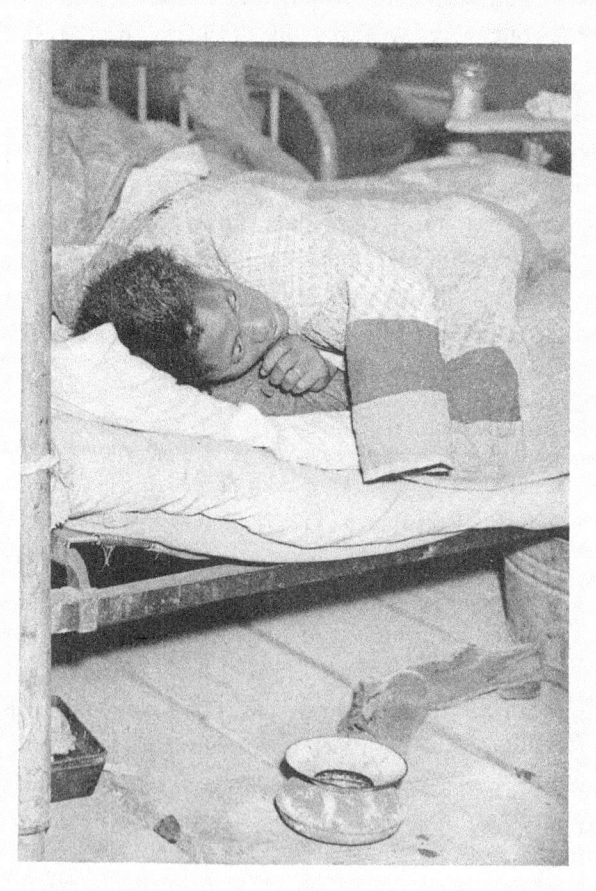

Figure 24. Walker Evans, "Arkansas Flood Refugee, 1937," from *American Photographs* (New York: Museum of Modern Art, 1938), plate 44. RA/FSA original photograph.

which he hung two different images from the Forrest City series of Black refugees in the segregated relief station.[107] In the book *American Photographs*, "Arkansas Flood Refugee, 1937" appears in Part One as plate 44, uncaptioned on the page, falling between the uninviting boardinghouse bed of Evans's friend John Cheever and White working-class residents relaxing outside their house in Ossining, New York.[108] Documentary continuities of time and place are entirely dispensed with. The sequencing makes the refugee image all the more enigmatic, no longer segregated, but also kept from too easy a juxtaposition with the detail from a "Minstrel Showbill" discovered on a wall in Alabama in the summer of 1936, which is placed here as plate 42, following and echoing an image of White entertainment in Coney Island. The conclusive meanings characteristic of journalistic contrasts are thus withheld. The relationships of image to image are not those of thesis and antithesis but of rhyme, repetition, discrepancy, and reversal.[109] No image finally adjudicates any other. The order is deliberate, but the process of reading is not curtailed in advance.

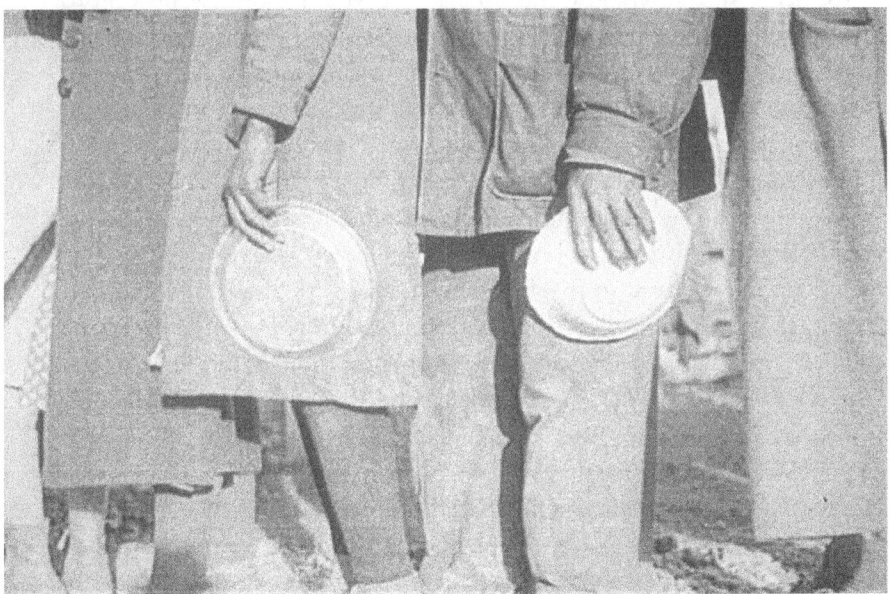

Figure 25. Walker Evans, "Negroes in the line up for food at mealtime in the camp for flood refugees, Forrest City, Arkansas," February 1937. FSA-OWI Collection, Prints and Photographs Division, Library of Congress (LC-USF33-009217-M3).

A second image from Forrest City, Arkansas, that would also find its way into publication shows a segregated breadline, not unlike the one Margaret Bourke-White saw in Louisville at around the same time. This photograph belongs to an extended series of 35 mm exposures made in the Black refugee camp with a Leica, all on the same day.[110] Tightly cropped by the handheld camera, it frames a woman's hand holding a tin plate and a man's hand holding a broken china bowl. The figures are cut off at the forearms and ankles. The dishes stand out against the dark clothing. Without comparison with other frames on the same roll of film, it is hard to grasp the context: No spatial setting is given, no wider explanatory frame, no supporting ground, not even feet or heads or faces.[111] By Evans's standards of emotional distance, however, the photograph might still seem vulnerable to being taken for an image of outrage or pity and, indeed, it appears it was.

In late April 1938, Evans's photograph was among eighty-one prints selected and arranged by Arthur Rothstein and Russell Lee for a major Historical Section exhibit at the First International Photographic Exposition, at the Grand Central Palace in New York.[112] Evans went to the show and wrote to Stryker, "the whole thing is so commercial it made me sick."[113] This was somewhat less than tactful, since Stryker regarded the exhibit as a coup, boasting that "Even Steichen went to the show in a perfunctory manner and got a surprise when he ran into our section."[114] It was, indeed, Edward Steichen who, that same year, would edit a selection of Farm Security Administration photographs from the Grand Central Palace exhibition for publication in *U.S. Camera Annual 1939*.[115] The selection included two of Evans's small-format Arkansas flood pictures, together with another by Edwin Locke, though the anonymity of the "F.S.A." photographs and the style of presentation were not designed to please Evans. Stryker, on the other hand, was in rapture and bought up several copies of the annual to pass on to Department of Agriculture administrators.[116] He was all the more pleased in that, introducing the forty-one selected photographs, Steichen was insistent that it was the collective achievement of Stryker's photographers as a group that had to be celebrated. Even so, Steichen conceded, "For sheer story telling impact, the picture of the hands with the plates on page 46 . . . would be hard to beat."[117] This also seems to have been the view of Richard Wright and Edwin Rosskam, who, in 1941, would put Evans's breadline picture on the dustcover of their sweeping, rhetorical photo-documentary book, *12 Million Black Voices*. For all the complexity of his record of Black living conditions in the South, it would be one of only two photographs by Evans in the entire publication.[118]

Granting these tributes to its "sheer story telling impact," the Arkansas image is hardly demonstrative. In contrast to Margaret Bourke-White's headline picture of the Louisville flood, it has no polemic, though one might obviously be supplied. Nor does it make an emotional appeal to the viewer through an imaginary dramatization of the act of looking. It may be informative, but not in the way of a government report. The focus of its attention seems to be on the smallest differences of gesture and anatomy affecting the ways the two hands hold the two utensils. To make the image, Evans must have been embarrassingly close, squatting down in the mud, hardly himself a confidence-inspiring spectacle. No wonder he wrote that he "felt completely ill-mannered" in his urgent drive "to make just these pictures."[119]

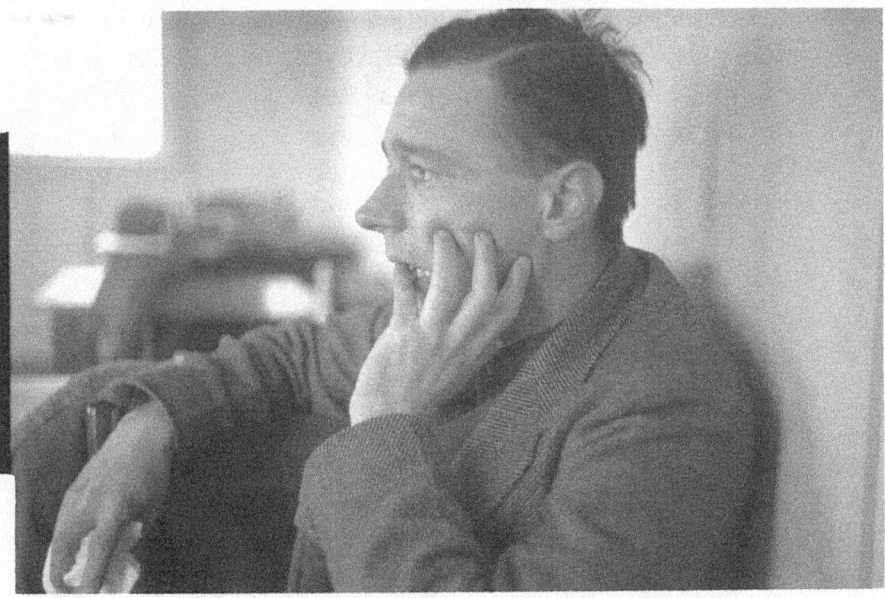

Figure 26. Edwin Locke, "Walker Evans, profile, hand up to face, Forrest City, Arkansas," February 1937. FSA-OWI Collection, Prints and Photographs Division, Library of Congress (LC-USF33-004225-M4).

On the morning of February 9, however, all photographic activity in and around Forrest City was cut short when Evans woke with influenza. Sickness and fever kept him in bed until the fourteenth and work could not begin again until the seventeenth, two days after Margaret Bourke-White's flood photograph had appeared as the lead in that week's issue of *Life*. By then the assignment was, to all intents and purposes, over. On Saturday, February 20, Evans and Locke scrapped plans to go on to Paducah and Louisville, Kentucky, and started back, driving through Tennessee and Virginia, stopping by the roadside in Kingwood, West Virginia, while Locke photographed another of the National Association of Manufacturers billboards that had first caught his eye in Memphis.[120] By 6:00 p.m. on Thursday, February 25, Evans and Locke were in Washington, where, less than a month later, Evans would lunch with Roy Stryker and have an "extraordinary conversation."[121] Newly transferred to the Department of Agriculture and no longer independent, the Resettlement Administration had fallen under heavy congressional scrutiny. Its chief administrator, Rexford Tugwell, had resigned a month after the 1936 election and, with the programs he championed in doubt, the Division of Information's budget had been cut. On March 23, Evans would receive his final dismissal notice. No more biweekly checks for $120. His work for the government was over.[122]

On the other hand, the work of his negatives was not. With the exception of those promised first to *Fortune* for the story "Three Tenant Farmers" that turned into the book *Let Us Now Praise Famous Men*, all Evans's work in the picture file of the Resettlement Administration, later the Farm Security Administration, was government property, available for circulation without his further consent. This is what happened, for example, to a large-format photograph Evans had made in Atlanta in 1936. The photograph, captioned "Houses in Atlanta," appeared without Evans's foreknowledge in the 1938 photo-documentary book *Land of the Free*, published with Stryker's blessing by the poet Archibald MacLeish.[123]

MacLeish was a figure of national stature: a Pulitzer Prize–winning poet, editor at *Fortune*, and occasional writer for *Life*, with connections in the Roosevelt administration and the backing of a major publishing house. His goal, as in earlier experiments with a dance drama and radio play, was to find ways to shape opinion through the direct and public use of poetry, hybridizing his writing with forms drawn from mass media, such as the newsreel and the short documentary film. For his part, Stryker knew that he needed to have his files put to work in a public way in order to justify his hard-pressed budget. He was, therefore, more than eager to cooperate with MacLeish's proposal to compose a poetic photographic book using the Historical Section's collection. In fact, Stryker took it upon himself to pull an initial set of five hundred photographs to start MacLeish off, and he wrote enthusiastically to section photographer Russell Lee that the book would contain "a series of pictures which will portray the people left behind after the empire builders have taken the forests, the ore, and the top soil."[124]

MacLeish began work with Stryker's initial selection in July and August 1937, editing, sequencing, developing new orders for agency

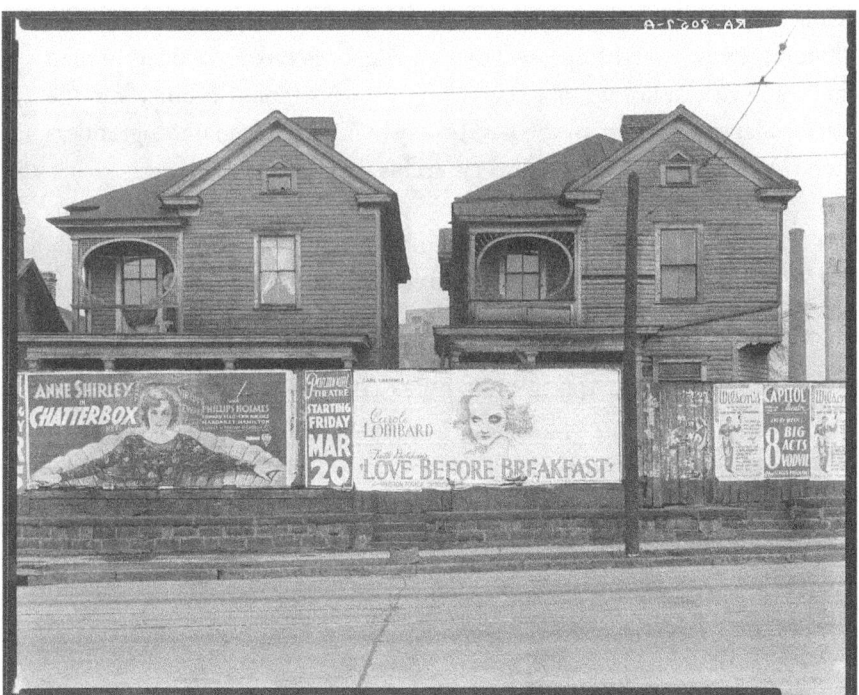

Figure 27. Walker Evans, "Frame houses and a billboard," March 1936. FSA-OWI Collection, Prints and Photographs Division, Library of Congress (LC-USF342-008057-A).

photographers, and writing his poetic "accompaniment," like the sound-track to one of Pare Lorentz's documentary movies, trying, as he put it, to give the photographs "a theme, a running, continuing sort of choral voice."[125] Like the "Voice of God" commentary in *The Plow That Broke the Plains* and *The River*, the "choral voice" of MacLeish's *Land of the Free* is sonorous, grandiloquent, affectedly populist, mixing Southern Agrarian themes of the betrayal of Eden with quasi-Marxist themes of capitalist exploitation in a way that seemed convincing at the time to so many East Coast intellectuals, including Evans's friend Lincoln Kirstein. Delivered in high oratorical style in the first person plural, MacLeish's verse rises to anger but has little depth as an indictment of the American system, never descending to the level of specific institutions or concrete alternatives. Its preference—part Popular Front, part frontier myth—is for larger histrionic gestures and the overarching rhetoric of an imaginary collectivity that transcends private interests and rises above the violence of the class struggle. On this would-be epic plane, MacLeish's "Sound Track" sought to give voice to the faces of the "eroded human beings" in the photographs, conjuring up a metaphoric unity for the images far removed from the day-to-day concerns of the photographers and the metonymic realism of their archival project.[126]

Evans's photograph did not yield easily to this enveloping context. His measured view of an empty street in downtown Atlanta was especially oddly placed in MacLeish's troubled meditation on rural decay, the collapse of the land, and the loss of the promise of plenty that asked if "the liberty's back of us," now the "Land's gone," "Or if there's liberty a man can mean that's / Men: not land."[127] Bled to the edge of the page and with no identifying caption, "Houses in Atlanta" falls about halfway through MacLeish's orchestration of image and text, next to page 43, opposite the line "And we're not telling them: not from our own front doors." "We're not telling them" marks the breakdown of what "we've been telling ourselves" for "a hundred and fifty years" about liberty, self-evident truths, and being American.[128] It is one of a series of repeated refrains—"we can't say," "we don't know," "we aren't sure," "we get wondering"—that turn, on the very last page, into "We're asking."[129] It is not clear on page 43 who "we're not telling" or, indeed, whose front doors these are, since they are not visible and, in any case, may be unreachable. It is also uncertain what meaning there might be for a radicalized agrarianism in boarded-up Victorian houses in the heart of Atlanta.

The sequence only adds to the puzzle. Evans's urban street scene is preceded by a view of a "bleeding hillside" in a Virginia valley, eroding away one hour after rain, and is followed by an image of wind-stripped, hardpan land in Alabama with a seemingly abandoned farmhouse.[130] The continuity of context is far from clear. What it is that the photographs bear witness to is not readily discernible. MacLeish's "chorus" goes on gesturing and declaiming, but the action itself is hard to follow, even though MacLeish maintained that it was *the photographs*, "the power and the stubborn inward livingness of these vivid American documents," that carried the narrative, only "illustrated by a poem."[131] The intransigent particularities of the photographs have, of course, been stitched up. Bound into MacLeish's book, the photographs are over-ruled by a uniform graphic code, subsumed by sequence, and interpellated by a text that calls them into the epic space of the collective subject as it emerges into its historical consciousness—unless, that is, they prove intractable. Evans's photograph is more "stubborn" than most. As the thick black graphic line and the voice-over of the "Sound Track" move resolutely on, "trying to find words for the purgatory of the Depression, for the American hopes and expectations and what had happened to them,"[132] it seems to be left stranded. Sprung from worn-out fields, bracketed by rural decay, it goes on standing in another semantic space, unassimilable and unreadable.

This tear in MacLeish's book did not seem to worry its readers. Published in April 1938 by Harcourt, Brace and Company, *Land of the Free* was never a best seller, but it did receive heavy coverage in the press, and not just in the small magazines. The *New York Herald-Tribune* hailed it as "a document of real social significance."[133] The *New York Times* saw it as a "Poem for Our Day . . . a grim and beautiful book, a masterpiece of collaboration."[134] Evans was less taken. A couple of months after publication, he sent Roy Stryker a note with a clipping from a book-trade pamphlet reproducing, without acknowledgment, a plate from *Land of the Free*: Evans's own 1936 photograph of the elaborately carved wooden porch of a boarding house on Fourth Avenue in Birmingham, Alabama. Evans insisted that he was sending the cutting to Stryker only "as an

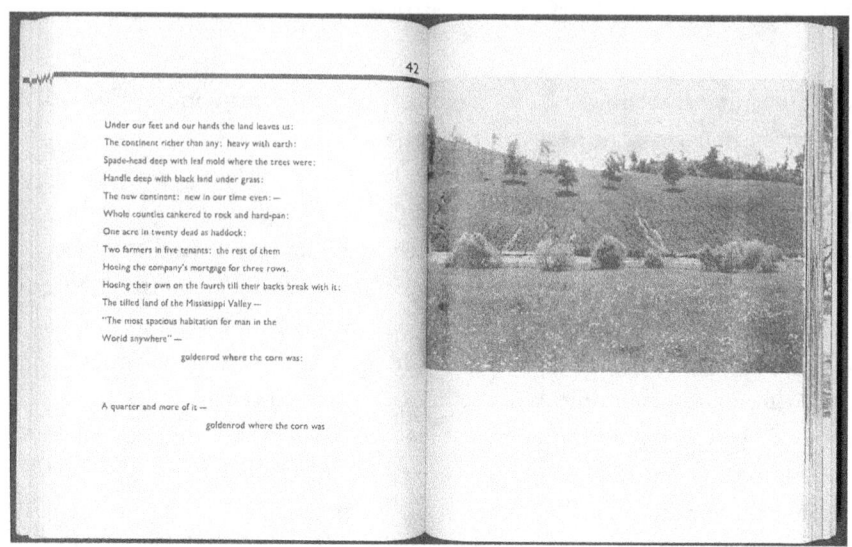

Figure 28. Archibald MacLeish, *Land of the Free* (New York: Harcourt, Brace, 1938), 42 and facing. Photograph for Tennessee Valley Authority. Text copyright 1938 and renewed 1966 by Archibald MacLeish. Reprinted by permission of Houghton Mifflin Company. All rights reserved.

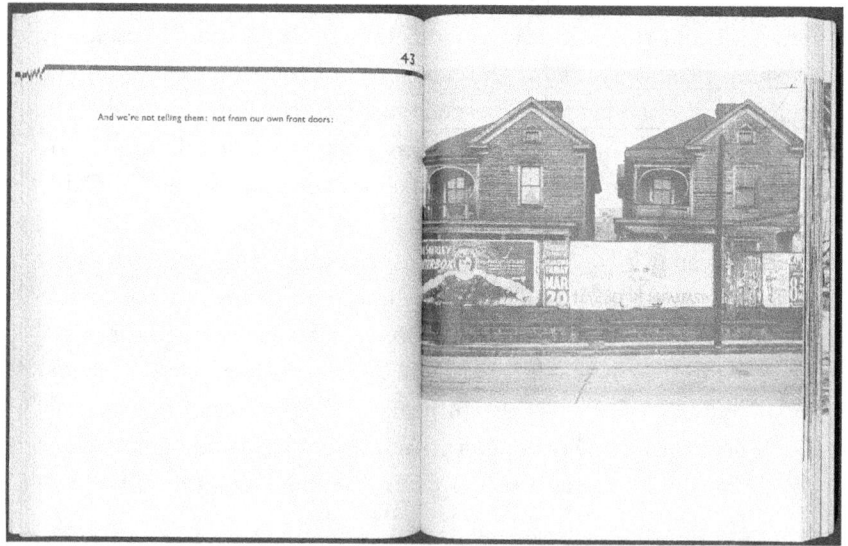

Figure 29. Archibald MacLeish, *Land of the Free* (New York: Harcourt, Brace, 1938), 43 and facing. Photograph by Walker Evans for Resettlement Administration. Text copyright 1938 and renewed 1966 by Archibald MacLeish. Reprinted by permission of Houghton Mifflin Company. All rights reserved.

item of mild interest and amusement, not as a howl of pain." But the clipping was annotated with the one word: "Gawd!"[135]

Evans, of course, had understood from the start the risks he was taking for his work by entering government employment. At one level, he seemed to think he could deal with these risks by maintaining a contempt for bureaucracy and by continuing to operate behind the back of officialdom. He made duplicate negatives and additional prints and held them back for his own use, just as he padded his often-thin file submissions with work made before his official employment, for purposes other than those of government record and publicity. His distrust and self-interest did not stop here. From the outset, he had worried about interference and the taint of association that government work might bring. In 1935, still in negotiations over various possible government jobs, defensive and self-protective as ever, he tried to clarify issues in his own mind, scribbling down lists headed "Want," "Will give," and then, on a second sheet of paper, in an accusatory tone:

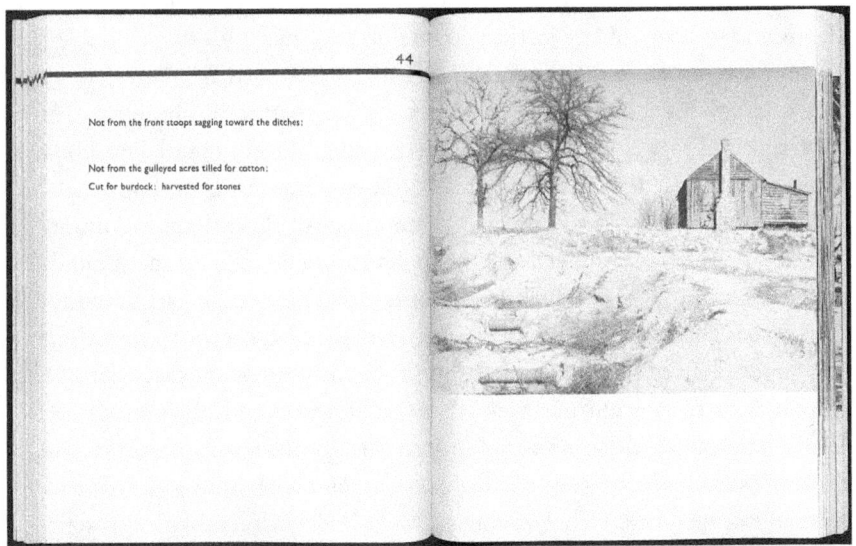

Figure 30. Archibald MacLeish, *Land of the Free* (New York: Harcourt, Brace, 1938), 44 and facing. Photograph by Arthur Rothstein for Resettlement Administration. Text copyright 1938 and renewed 1966 by Archibald MacLeish. Reprinted by permission of Houghton Mifflin Company. All rights reserved.

never under any circumstances asked to do anything more than these things. Mean never make photographic statements for the government [or do photographic chores for gov. or anyone in gov. no matter how powerful, (inserted)]—this is pure record not propaganda. The value and if you like, even the propaganda value for the government lies in the record itself which in the long run will prove an intelligent and farsighted thing to have done. NO POLITICS whatever.[136]

In equal measures intransigent and naive, Evans's notes start in mid-breath: an unattached adverb; verbs with no clear subject, unqualified, undecidable in tense or person, with no identifiable addressee. "Want," "Will give," "asked," "mean": These are the fragments of a speech he cannot own, into which he cannot quite insert himself. Without doubt, something has to be defended and protected. But even to speak about this "pure" thing, in itself, proves impossible.

Evans would still be at it more than a year after his summary dismissal from government service, even while preparing for his exhibition and major publication with the Museum of Modern Art in New York. At one moment, he would be jotting down notes for his "file on STRYKER."[137] At another moment, he would be writing a letter to Stryker that he might later think better of sending, on "the matter of the extent of my freedom in th[e] choice of pictures for this Museum book," "a book about and by me" that the museum "is to bring . . . out as an example of the work of an artist" and in which the number of Resettlement Administration pictures reproduced "has been determined solely on the grounds of my opinion of their worth as pictures."[138] The book clearly focused Evans's anxieties, especially as Stryker would not hesitate to point out that "about half of the photographs in the book are from negatives in the Department of Agriculture files."[139] Even the preparation of a belated formal contract had Evans scribbling notes, speaking of himself in the third person, insisting that the book appeared "without a hint of commercial compromise," that it was he who had "installed the [present] style of government still photography," and that he had "retired from the government" "because of the readiness of the bureaus in Washington to play with and cater to commercial interests and to aim at [immediate] publicity [more] than at [straight] historical recording."[140]

Evans's anxiousness returned as he sketched a "PLAN or ARRANGE-
MENT OF MUSEUM BOOK." His first thought was that he wanted it recorded
on the inside front flap of the dustcover that he had worked "more or less
independently" since 1928 and that he himself had "arranged and divided
and ordered" the selection of photographs "made by him from this ten
years' work."[141] As his thinking developed, he made notes for "PEOPLE BY
PHOTOGRAPHY," "a book of pictures without captions," on the back of
what seems to be an old photographic mount, and still felt the need to
write down that "this work is arranged in seriousness not journalism
or not a trick."[142] Then he began painfully drafting, annotating, amend-
ing, and redrafting an explanatory "NOTE."[143] He wanted to draw a clear
line between the compromised commercialism of contemporary photojournalism and the picture selection in his book. His aim, he said, was "to
sketch an important, correct, but commonly corrupted use of the camera."[144] The pictorial journalism of the period, he argued, was too corrupt
to produce, other than by accident, "records which will become valuable
in themselves," images capable of revealing "the movements and changes
or, again, the conflicts which in passing become the body of the history of
civilizations."[145] Turning, "perhaps sick," from this commercialism, with
its parade of pictures of "prominent people," Evans asked his reader to

> think of the general run of the social mill: [these (deleted)] anonymous
> people who come and go in the cities and who move on the land. It is on
> what they look like now; what is in thier [*sic*] faces and in the windows and
> the streets beside and around them; what they are wearing and what they
> are riding in, and on how they are gesturing, that we need to concentrate,
> consciously, with the camera.[146]

Evans's "NOTE" would not be published; nor would any of the tortured versions of his "Acknowledgments," which had said too much
about a history of intellectual and emotional debts. As it appeared in
1938, *American Photographs* was emptied of all direct captions and almost
all words of Evans's own, leaving the images facing bare white pages,
cleansed of everything but the plate numbers, with brief titles consigned
to pages at the end of each of the two parts. The acknowledgments had
contracted to two sentences, unsigned, recognizing permissions from

the Farm Security Administration, Harper and Brothers, and the editors of *The Hound and Horn*. A further blank page had the inscription "J. S. N."[147] Then came a page with the single heading: "PART ONE." Nothing else was to intervene between the reader and the photographs. Yet something still remained of what Evans had wanted to say in his defensiveness. It survived in traces in Lincoln Kirstein's afterword and in what Frances Collins excerpted from Kirstein's commentary for the jacket text. It also survived, in greatly shrunken form, in a curt and impersonal sentence added to the acknowledgments:

> The responsibility for the selection of the pictures used in this book has rested with the author, and the choice has been determined by his opinion: therefore they are presented without sponsorship or connection with the policies, aesthetic or political, of any of the institutions, publications or government agencies for which some of the work has been done.[148]

The sentence marked what still rankled. It was the stunted heir to all the notes, the unsent letter, the drafting and redrafting, the curdled prose. Masked as restraint and good taste, it was the strangulated sound of words that seemed to have to be cut off in the throat. Prevented from speaking and compelled to speak, Evans seemed to want to disown all debts, to disallow all frames of meaning, all the nets in which his work might be caught, even, or especially, those that had prompted and occasioned the photographic acts whose results made up the corpus of the book. Everything had to be purged from the space of the "pure record." Yet the photograph cannot stand alone, in its own discursive space; it must enter circulation, pass from hand to hand, in some form. The medium of this pure circulation was the book. Not the photo-book as Archibald MacLeish conceived it: a filmic blending of words and pictures. Not the photo-documentary book that had become something of a publishing fashion since the appearance of Margaret Bourke-White's and Erskine Caldwell's *You Have Seen Their Faces* in 1937 and that critics were then claiming as a new medium.[149] It was to be a new kind of photographic book; a book for which there was no real precedent in photographic publishing, severe and restrained from the first, bound in "Bible cloth," with no image on the cover.[150]

Still, the book did carry the imprimatur of the Museum of Modern Art. The museum had supported Evans's work since 1933 with exhibitions and commissions. It seemed to be the one institution with whose policies, "aesthetic or political," Evans was not unwilling to be associated, even if he thought little of its director, Alfred H. Barr, and had open contempt for its "so called curator of photography," Beaumont Newhall.[151] This exemption of the museum, despite distaste for its social aspect, is odd. Certainly, the museum conferred status, and Evans wanted it seen that the museum was bringing out *American Photographs* "as an example of the work of an artist."[152] Yet Evans also defined his notion of "pure record" as "non-artistic" photography, as distinct from "romantic art-photography" and New Vision experimentalism as it was from the commercial corruption of photojournalism and the "advertising values" of photography's "Chrysler period."[153] It is not clear, therefore, how he could blind himself to the framing machinery of the museum and the way it worked to establish his reputation, establish the terms of an appropriate critical discourse, and establish a space of difference for his work. "There's the problem," Evans would later say of his connection with the Museum of Modern Art. "How do you get around Establishment when something is establishing you?"[154]

One must be cautious here, however, in judging Evans's incorporation of the museum as a condition of his work. It is tempting, for example, to see the monochrome space that opens in the pages of *American Photographs* as a replication of the white cube of the modernist museum: a contrived space of erasure that is the condition for the apparent self-presentation of art. Yet such a space, extending and purifying the function of the frame, did not exist for photography at this time. *American Photographs* took shape precisely at the time when the Museum of Modern Art's new international-style building at 11 West Fifty-third Street was under construction. The exhibition took place in a temporary space in an underground concourse of the Rockefeller Center, at 14 West Forty-ninth Street. There, at the last possible moment, Evans rejected the installation ideas of the museum's staff and set about hanging his prints himself, showing some with mats, in frames and under glass, others matted but mounted under glass without frames, and still others mounted on cardboard cropped to the edges and glued directly on the wall. There were also great discrepancies in print size: Some were overscale, others comparatively small; occasionally they were hung two or three deep, but always on or around a continuous horizontal line that gave continuity to the erratic clustering of thematically related images without softening the sudden contrasts of format and presentation.

Beaumont Newhall called the installation "exacting," "simple and straightforward—and daring."[155] Certainly, there was nothing about it to suggest an attitude of preciousness. Evans did not fetishize his negatives or prints. In later life, he said, "I would cut any number of inches off my frames in order to get a better picture."[156] His was not a pristine minimalism, as it has retrospectively appeared. We must be careful, therefore, about what we deduce from the luxurious austerity of *American Photographs*. Yet its spare lines still marked a tension. On the one hand, the design of the book constructed an ideal, Evans might have said "pure," space under the shelter of the museum. Here, it is hard to avoid seeing at work the bad faith that allowed Evans to designate the museum a nonsite from which he could then declaim the freedom of his work from contamination by the aesthetic or political policies of any of institution.[157] On the other hand, the sparseness of his book was also the product of an active negation. Just as the photographs themselves emerged through what they precluded, so the book defined itself by what it excluded. Tom Mabry was quick to grasp Evans's strategy and wrote to Lincoln Kirstein that when writing his essay for the book, "I should think that you might want to define as simply and clearly as possible the difference between Walker's work and the majority of photographers both 'documentary' and 'lyric.'"[158] In particular, a line had to be drawn between Evans's vision and "the canonization of the commonplace that documentary photography has turned into."[159] Mabry's examples here were Margaret Bourke-White, *Life*'s photographers, and a good many of those who worked for the Federal Art Project.

American Photographs was therefore, in part, Evans's corrective to the photojournalism of *Life* and a judgment on books such as MacLeish's *Land of the Free*. Ironically, however, when the book came out on September 27, 1938, it was the poet who had the first, if not the last, word. Sealing the book was a contrasting yellow paper book-band quoting a testimony from MacLeish:

Walker Evans' remarkable work suggests that great photography may translate objects into meaning. These American photographs are not Sandburg—no photographs could be—but they do much more than record one area of American experience. They make it speak.[160]

Translating objects into meaning. This, of course, was the problem: the problem of meaning. But it is meaning that seems to be strangely withheld in Evans's work.

Here is that street in Atlanta again, now titled "Houses and Billboards in Atlanta, 1936." It occurs as plate 47 in the first part of the book, which Kirstein advised "might be labeled 'People by Photography'" and in which, he said, "we have an aspect of America for which it would be difficult to claim too much."[161] The Atlanta photograph comes after "People in Summer, New York State Town, 1930" and "Birmingham Boarding House, 1936," which also appeared in *Land of the Free*. It is followed by two photographs of "South Street, New York" from 1932 that Evans privately distinguished as "Trio" and "Close up, unbuttoned."[162] The last picture in the sequence, closing Part One, is "Louisiana Plantation House, 1935." Then come the titles. The reader should know from the dustcover and from the concluding paragraph of Kirstein's essay that "The photographs are arranged to be seen in their given sequence." The difficulty is in saying what the sequence discloses.

The houses with their balconies overlooking the street follow images of life around the doorstep and on the porch, ambiguous spaces between sidewalk and interior where the public and private meet and become confused. Then comes the collapse of the private onto the street: the homeless men in lower Manhattan reading, sitting, sleeping on cardboard on shallow workshop steps. And finally, the collapse of an entire social world: the decayed plantation house and the massive fallen shade tree, "cumulative emblem" of "a doomed civilization" Alan Trachtenberg calls it,[163] rhyming with the prostrate bulk of the sleeping vagrant who fills his niche like a tomb figure, his fly undone. It is a somber procession, building to an emotional crescendo. Yet at the same time, following a sequence of four telescopically compressed frontal images, the space in the view of the plantation house and dead tree tilts and pulls back, letting us see sky and sunlight. The didacticism of the sequence and the

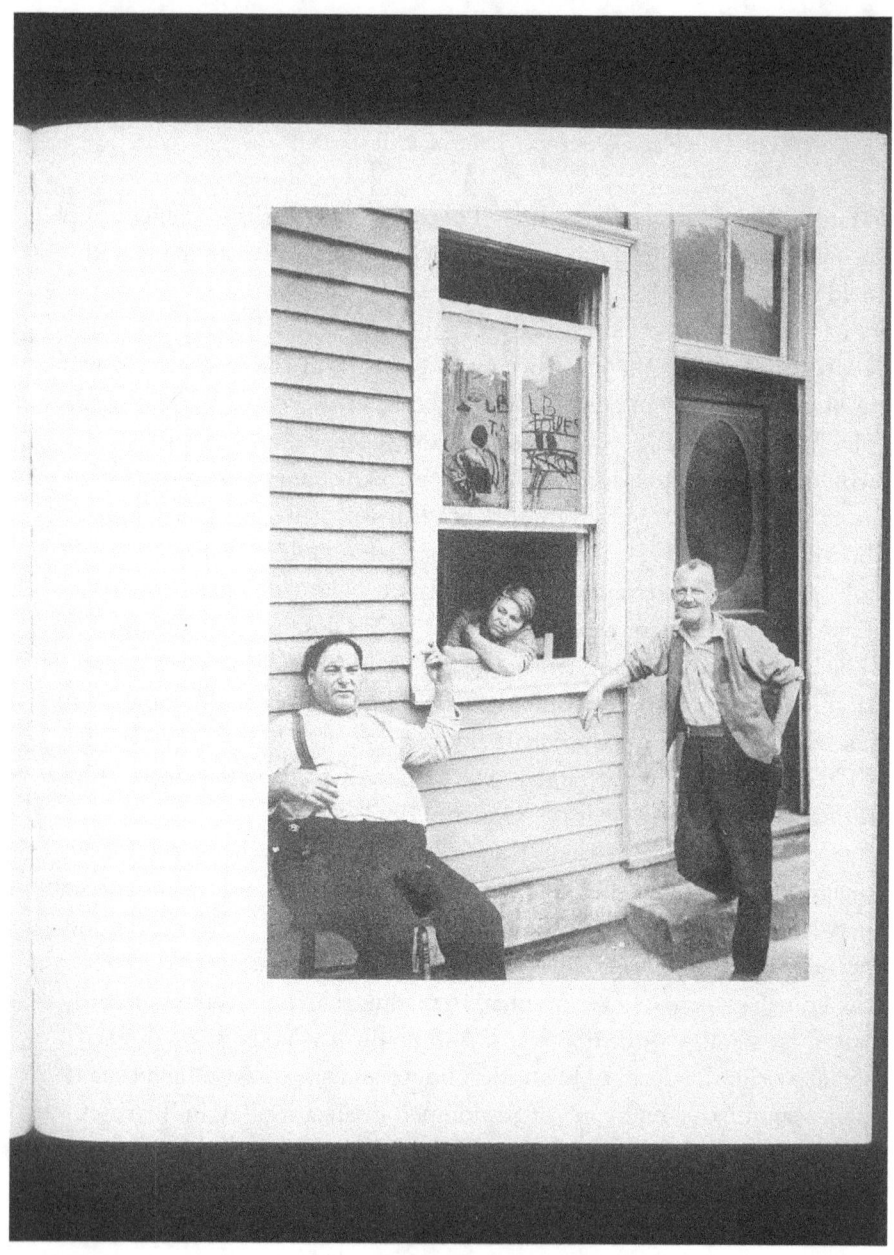

Figure 31. Walker Evans, "People in Summer, New York State Town, 1930," from *American Photographs* (New York: Museum of Modern Art, 1938), plate 45. Courtesy of the Walker Evans Archive at the Metropolitan Museum of Art.

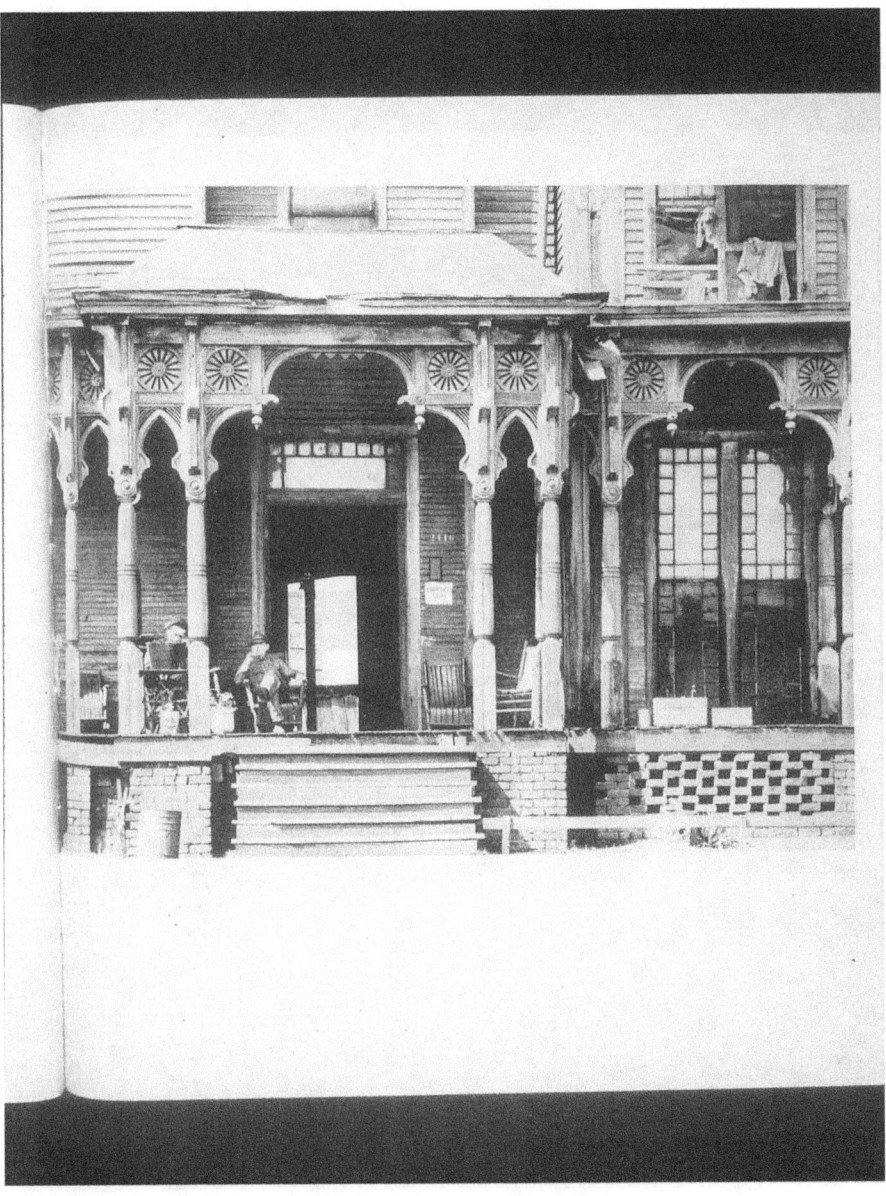

Figure 32. Walker Evans, "Birmingham Boarding House, 1936," from *American Photographs* (New York: Museum of Modern Art, 1938), plate 46. RA/FSA original photograph.

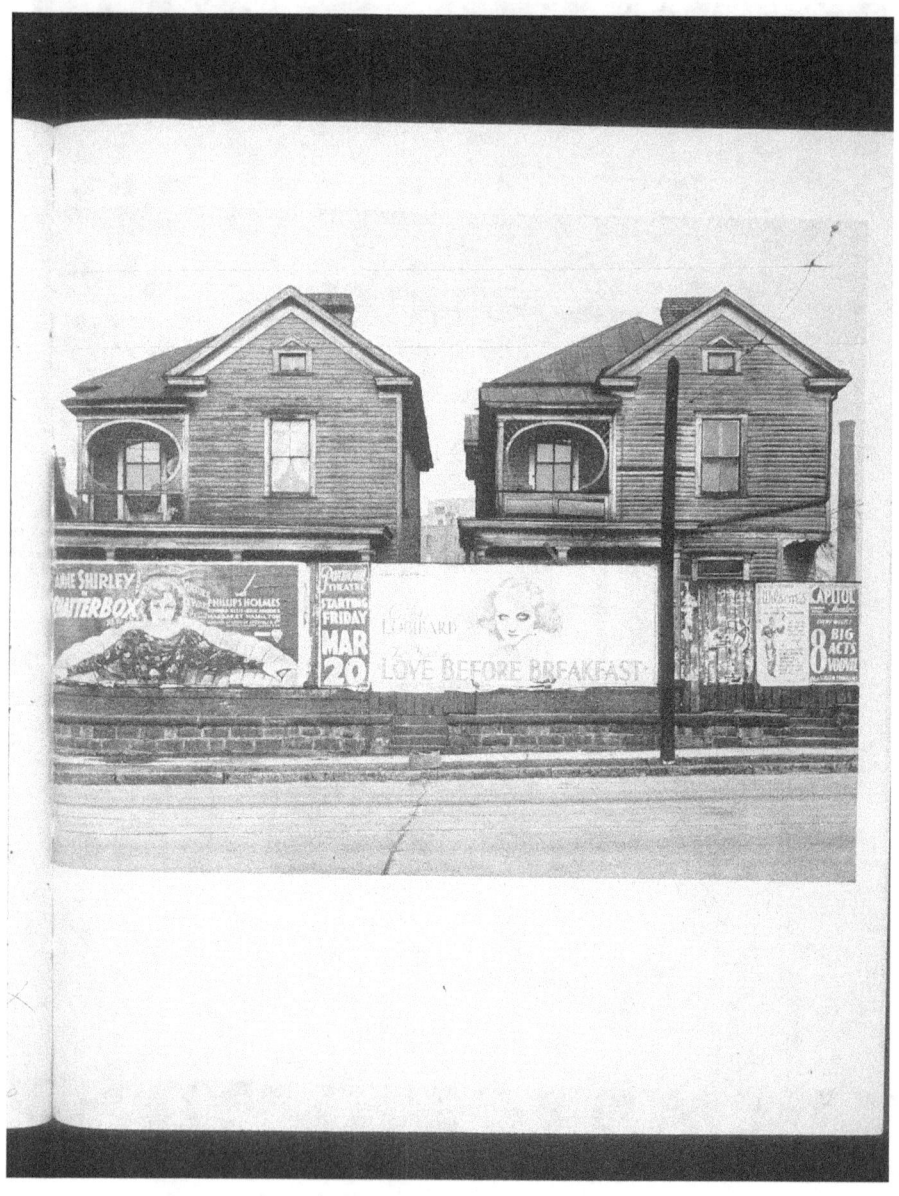

Figure 33. Walker Evans, "Houses and Billboards in Atlanta, 1936," from *American Photographs* (New York: Museum of Modern Art, 1938), plate 47. RA/FSA original photograph.

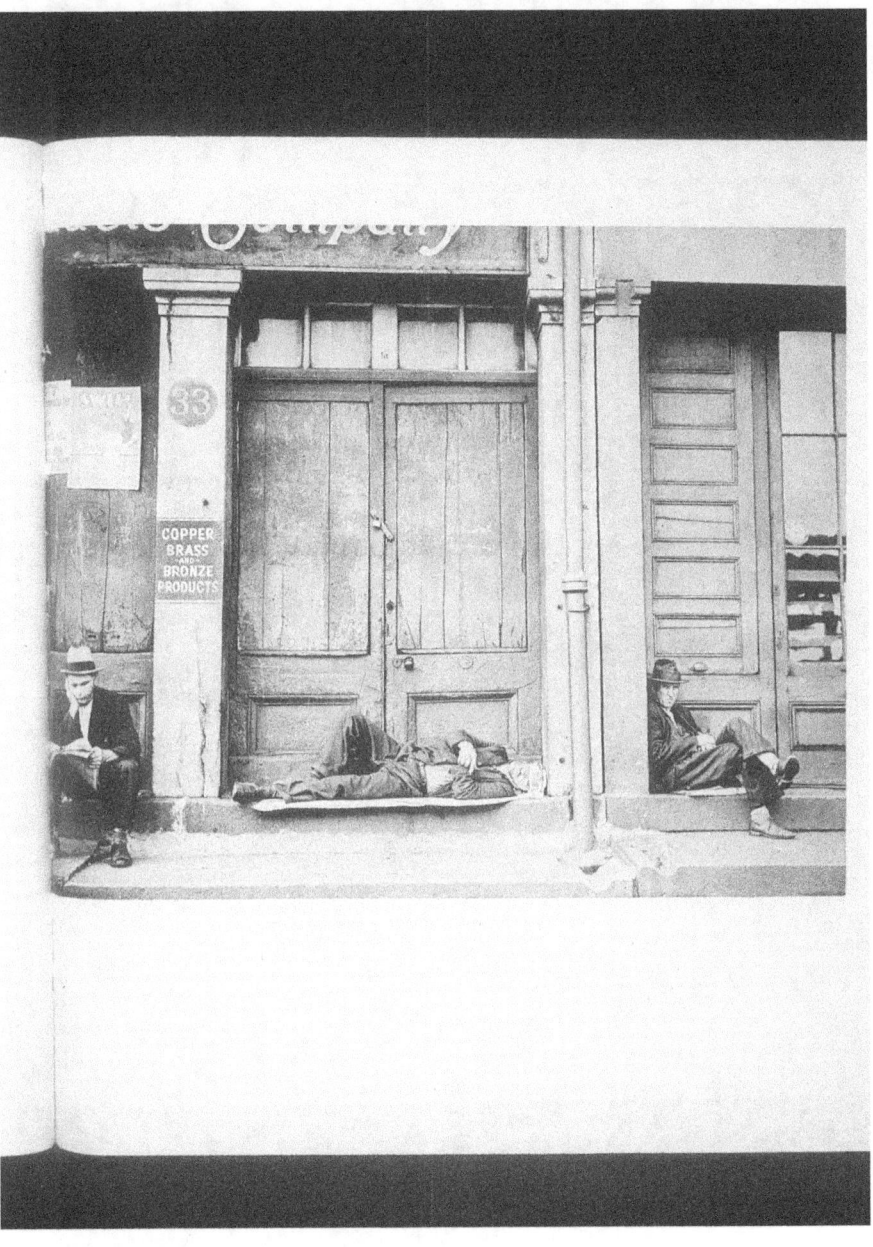

Figure 34. Walker Evans, "South Street, New York, 1932," from *American Photographs* (New York: Museum of Modern Art, 1938), plate 48. Courtesy of the Walker Evans Archive at the Metropolitan Museum of Art.

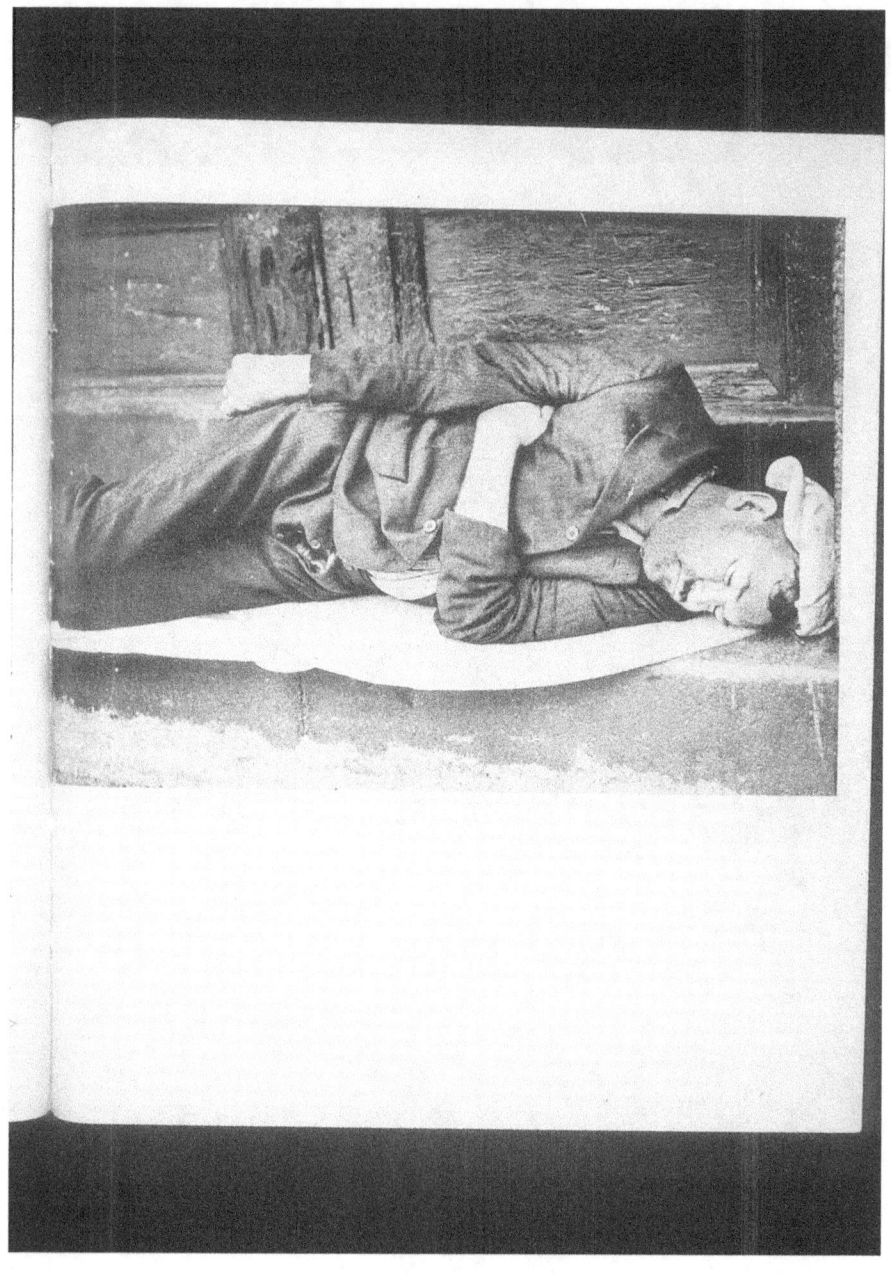

Figure 35. Walker Evans, "South Street, New York, 1932," from *American Photographs* (New York: Museum of Modern Art, 1938), plate 49. Courtesy of the Walker Evans Archive at the Metropolitan Museum of Art.

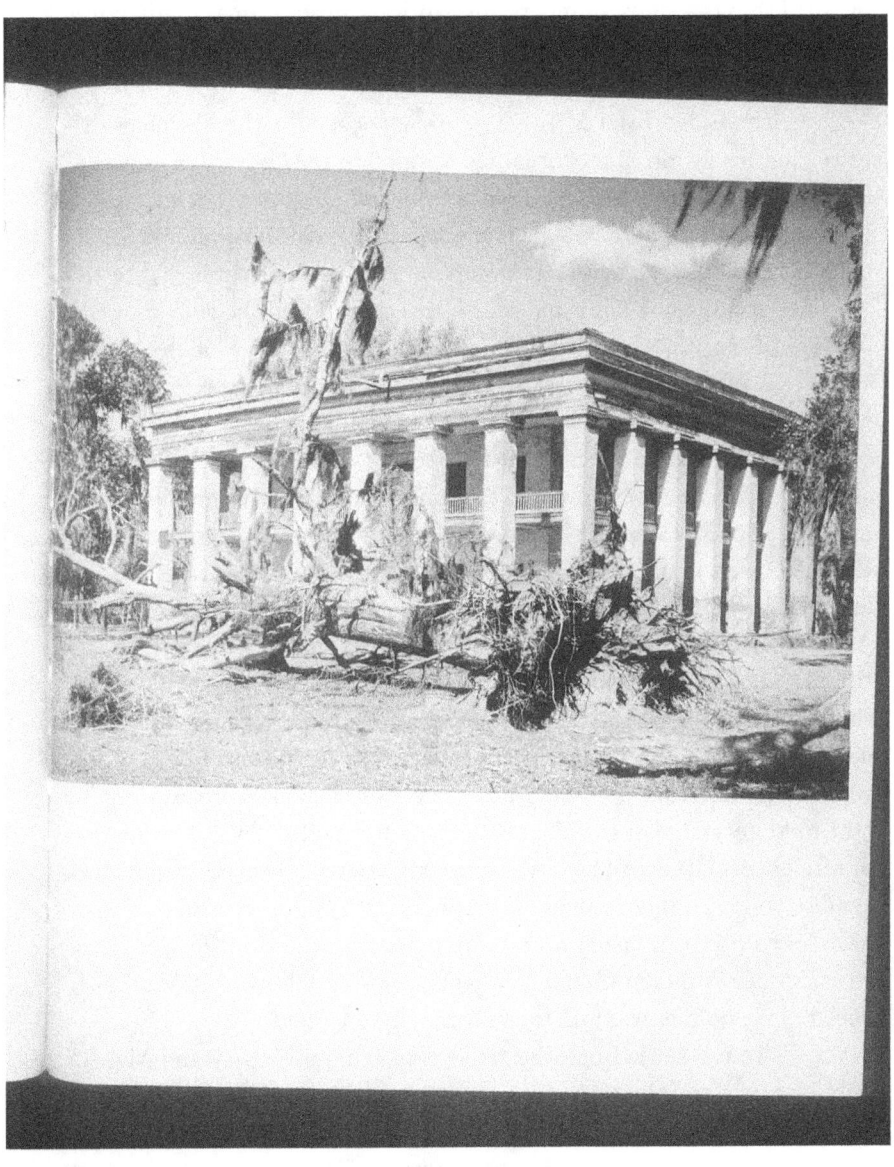

Figure 36. Walker Evans, "Louisiana Plantation House, 1935," from *American Photographs*. (New York: Museum of Modern Art, 1938), plate 50. RA/FSA original photograph.

weight of visual metaphor are tempered, just as the pace with which image follows image is likely to be changed by the fact that we get distracted by small things—signs, numbers, inscriptions, litter, stains, architectural details and moldings, carved and chalked graffiti, typography, words: "LB LOVES," "Furnished Rooms," "VODVIL," "SWIM."

With all due respect to Kirstein's advocacy for the Hegelian dialectic and his vision of an "ordained design" in the "poetry of contrast" in and across Evans's pictures, it is not beyond all doubt that we are following a narrative here.[164] Nor is it entirely certain that we are looking at "records of the age before an imminent collapse": pictures that testify "to the symptoms of waste and selfishness that caused the ruin" but that "salvage whatever was splendid for the future reference of the survivors."[165] Evans, it has to be said, liked what Kirstein wrote.[166] Frances Collins, too, found the contrast between what is and what *could be* "one of the most shattering things in the book": "it's insisted on: you're not allowed to forget it for a minute."[167] Contemporary reviewers all the way up to Eleanor Roosevelt also seemed to agree there was a message here.[168] Edward Alden Jewell in the *New York Times* saw "a true portrait of America."[169] The *Washington Daily News*, reproducing "Houses and Billboards, Atlanta" under the headline "This, Our Native Land: America, the Beautiful," called Evans's book "our truest composite portrait of the face of this country."[170] Carl Van Vechten in the Sunday *New York Herald Tribune* declared that "if all America except Evans' photographs were razed they would tell our story."[171] *New Masses* reviewer David Wolff was cut by "the merciless edge of truth" in Evans's photographs, "by a combination of reticence, delicacy and a bitter surgical honesty" that set Evans's work against those commercial photographers on assignment for *Life* who have "corrupted our taste into a desire for hasty titillation."[172] And in the *New Republic*, William Carlos Williams, echoing fellow poet MacLeish, declared, "The pictures talk to us. And they say plenty."[173]

There is a sense in all the reviews of Kirstein's essay and Mabry's publicity materials being to hand, as necessary cribs. But the orchestration of Evans's reception did not always work. The *Washington Post* saw "a parade of dreary, drab and depressing scenes."[174] The *San Francisco News* thought Evans's book "unnecessary and cruel."[175] The *New York Times Book Review* critic looked at what Kirstein hailed as "the physiognomy of a nation" and saw "bumps, warts, boils, and blackheads."[176] Privately, the photographer Ansel Adams was apoplectic, writing to Edward Weston that "Walker Evans' book gave me a hernia" and to Georgia O'Keeffe that it was "atrocious": "mixed social meaning, documentation, esthetics, sophistication (emotional slumming), etc."[177] Pare Lorentz, typically, felt that the pictures "should have been captioned."[178] Even the reviewers who did not choke on Kirstein's vision of the book as a "monument to our moment"[179] found it less easy to say what precisely it was that Evans's book said when it spoke. As Mabry, thinking to clarify matters, wrote in *Harper's Bazaar*: "Perhaps one clue to Evans's work is that his photographs are not symbols for something else; they are what they mean."[180] It was a typically skillful negotiation on Evans's behalf but, beyond the negation, it offered only tautology.

The critics' solution to this dilemma was to mimic the book. In place of a paraphrased message, what we get is a reiteration—a catalog: "a mass of motor derelicts, a cluttered slum, a row of ramshackle huts, a small town main street eye-sore, the grimace of a jig-saw boarding house in ruins";[181] "two sullen boys with 'sez-you' expressions, a moronic youth and his girl in a parked roadster, and Mr. Evans's row of drab, depressing houses, as well as his squalid interiors";[182] or, more sympathetically,

> the used cars abandoned on a field; a confused and helpless back room, revealed through an open door; the tires, tubes and spare parts displayed on the front of a garage; and the magic advertising words, the names, the signs, ubiquitous, ugly, meaningless, and powerful.[183]

This is what, in a memorable phrase, the leftist critic David Wolff called "a certain hideous miscellaneousness of American life."[184] The miscellaneous, however, has no general category. It can only be enumerated, inventoried, logged on a list, a "list that has been prepared," as William Carlos Williams remarked of *American Photographs*,[185] but a list nonetheless.

Evans was an inveterate list maker. In 1934, characteristically drafting an unfinished letter to Ernestine Evans, then an editor at Lippincott, about his ideas for photographic "picture books," Evans confided, "American city is what I'm after . . . keeping things typical":

People, all classes, surrounded by bunches of the new down-and-out.
Automobiles and the automobile landscape.

Architecture, American urban taste, commerce, small scale, large
scale, the city street atmosphere, the street smell, the hateful stuff, women's
clubs, fake culture, bad education, religion in decay.

The movies.

Evidence of what the people of the city read, eat, see for amusement, do for relaxation and do not get it.

Sex.

Advertising

A lot else, you see what I mean.[186]

Written well before Roy Stryker's "shooting scripts" for his imagined
"pictorial encyclopedia of American agriculture," Evans's list is a manifesto for *American Photographs*.[187] Architecture, smell, "hateful stuff,"
misogyny, decay, movies, frustration, sex, advertising: It is also a provisional inventory of the street view of houses and billboards in Atlanta.

Four years later, gathering his thoughts for the rushed exhibition
and publication with the Museum of Modern Art, Evans would be writing lists again, jotting the columns down hastily on odd sheets of paper:

Rivera
Paintings
Architecture
Housing
Slums
Greek Revival Architecture
Portraits
People
Shops
Street
New York
New Orleans
Cuba
Americana
Victorian Architecture

Interiors
Abstract.[188]

And again:

SHOW IDEAS
small defined sections
    people
    faces
    architecture
repetitions
small pictures
large pictures.[189]

Lists of subjects, lists of categories, lists of possible titles, lists of prints needed from Washington. Later, there will be lists of invitees, lists of those to receive exhibition notices or complimentary copies of the book, lists of the final titles. Lists are not prose: They are free from the demands of structure, coherence, and grammatical agreement that made writing for Evans such a painful process of drafting, erasure, interpolation, and revision. The list is epigraphic. It does not require to be expanded or explained. It has sequence but without finality, at least potentially retaining its mobility. The list asks to be rearranged. Like the file, it is open to reordering, insertions, recategorization, and regrouping. The list allowed Evans to handle ideas in words the way he handled his negatives, or the postcards he collected from the age of ten and methodically organized with card dividers: "Flatiron," "State Capitols," "Summer Hotels," "Persons," "Factories," "Automobiles," "Street Scenes."[190]

The list is the genre of the collector. Categories can be shuffled and reconfigured like postcards in a shoe box. For Evans, as for Roland Barthes, the pleasure of this sorting and re-sorting pointed to a solution to the problem of making a book, in whose rigid form the binding sequence might be undone by a provisionality that allowed the reader to imagine the book unmade and remade again. *American Photographs* retains the feel of having been made in this way, in spite of Lincoln Kirstein's theories and his help in untying the knots and getting it right.[191] Kirstein saw the photographic book on the model of film, in which he believed Evans might "achieve his ultimate lyricism," though, in several actual attempts, this never proved the case.[192] The structure of film, for Kirstein, the student of Sergey Eisenstein's epics, was in turn determined by montage, "elevating the casual, the everyday and the literal into specific, permanent symbols," just as the contrast of opposites in Evans's photographs, "looked at in sequence," could be seen to "elevate fortuitous accidents of juxtaposition into ordained design," turning "accidental conjunctions" into "serious symbols allied in disparate chaos."[193] This is Kirstein's view. The model of the list and the card-file index opens other possibilities, less committed to narrative convergence and the cumulative symbolic effect of juxtapositions. *American Photographs* belongs to such a model, "arranged and divided and ordered" by Evans, as part of the collector's compulsion and unending pleasure. Perhaps that is why attempts, at the time and since, to literalize a narrative in the sequence have always seemed overwrought.[194]

The list, like the file, evokes the archive—another series into which the photograph might be inserted, quite different from the book and the film. Yet the list differs from the archive in that it does not demand consistency. Its typologies are not bound to follow a general rule. The list is the archive without the law and without the public function.[195] And it was the civic function that Evans balked at. Nevertheless, we cannot neglect the fact that a complicated relation to the archive hung over all of Evans's photographic work. Indeed, as Roy Stryker was not prepared to forget and as Pare Lorentz repeated in print, "about half of the photographs" in *American Photographs* were "from negatives in the Department of Agriculture files"—or, as Lorentz chose to put it, "almost half were taken at the instigation of Professor Stryker of the Farm Security Administration and were paid for by the U.S. Government."[196]

In actually preparing the plates for the book, Evans seems to have had his own prints to work from, since he wrote to Stryker more than once that he did not have time to come to Washington.[197] Tom Mabry also turned down Stryker's offer of help with printing, telling him that the publication schedule made it necessary to use the prints that Evans already had in New York.[198] On the other hand, a one-page manuscript in Evans's hand, apparently from this time, contains a list of numbers bracketed together as "flood leica shots of mine, want prints," and a list of titles also seeming to describe prints Evans needed from the file.[199] The list includes "Atlanta billboards," indicating how Evans remembered the image and suggesting he needed at least an additional print as he began to prepare his work for the museum. Perhaps this explains why, as time ran out, the photograph appeared in the book but not in the exhibition.

Whatever the circumstance, the negative—or negatives—remained in Washington, where they had quite another place in the system of the file. Here, mounted on eleven-by-fourteen-inch blue gray board and filed between thick, color-coded card dividers, the print from Evans's plate fell under "E," the "South-East Region," where it was further classified

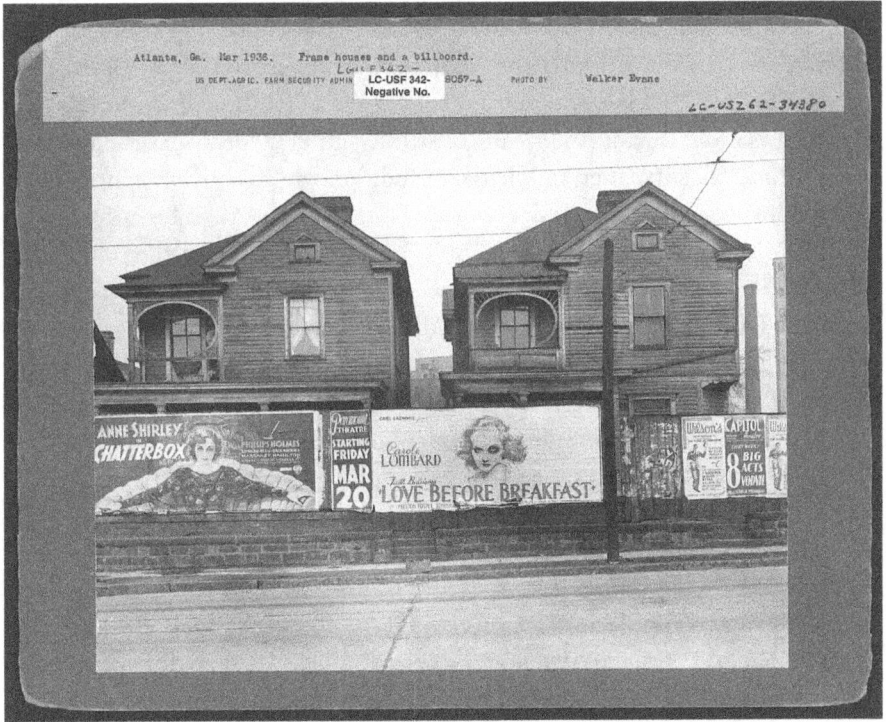

Figure 37. Walker Evans, "Atlanta, Ga. Mar 1936. Frame houses and a billboard." Department of Agriculture, Resettlement Administration/Farm Security Administration, file card. FSA-OWI Collection, Prints and Photographs Division, Library of Congress (LC-USF-342-8057-A).

as belonging neither to "Streets" nor to the categories "2563 Abandoned Buildings" or "631 Advertising," but to "213 Buildings," under the broader class "2 CITIES," itself part of "2—278 Cities and towns—as background." We should remember, of course, that this geographical and subject-based system was a later solution to the problem of storage and retrieval of somewhere around 107,000 photographs, though the place of the print in the "classified file" tells us not a little about the priorities of one nearly contemporary reading of Evans's photograph. The systematic subject classification under which Evans's image was subsumed was developed by Paul Vanderbilt only after his hiring by Stryker in 1942.[200] Earlier, prints and negatives seem to have been filed state by state, according to assignment, in the sequences developed by the photographers on location, following the dozens of shooting scripts and hundreds of memos sent to them by Roy Stryker outlining thematic directions for their work in the field. This story-driven arrangement allowed for Stryker's larger ambition to compile a "pictorial encyclopaedia" of a passing way of American life, while simultaneously catering to the outlook of newspaper and magazine editors whose cooperation was needed if the publicity goals of the New Deal agency were to be fulfilled in "bringing the facts before the public" in order to recruit their consent.[201] Even so, Stryker's didactic concern with the series did not easily survive picture editors' concern to find individual images to fit a given layout style and story line.

To what series Evans's Atlanta image might be allotted is precisely the problem. In reorganizing the files, Paul Vanderbilt took the view that Evans's work "was never quite divorced from an instinctive cynicism or even the hatreds inherent in his personal philosophy" and thus did not fit the agency's programs.[202] Stryker would not have gone so far, though he knew that Evans had little respect for his instructions. In any case, the "nice big order" Stryker sent to Evans "on the ground" in Vicksburg, Mississippi, in February 1936 does not mention Atlanta.[203] Neither does Evans's earlier "Outline Memorandum" for his projected eight-week automobile trip to the states of the Southeast. This only says, "Cross Georgia and Alabama, rural subjects."[204] We have, of course, the file caption, typewritten, cut out and pasted on the mounting card. It reads, "Atlanta, Ga. Mar 1936. Frame houses and a billboard. LC-USF-342-8057-A.

Walker Evans." The back of the card is marked "Resettlement Administration" and stamped with the classification "E 213" and the lot number 1538. The stamps are Vanderbilt's later additions. The title, different from that in *Land of the Free* and different from others Evans would ascribe, is hardly accurate as a description, even if it does go back to 1936, though, again, it suggests what it was thought important to see, in short, what at the time the picture was presumed to be about.

On the surface, this was not a mystery. As we have seen, the picture was prominent enough in the file for Stryker to pull it for MacLeish's book, just as Evans was to include it in the book version of *American Photographs*. The print had also been memorized by John Vachon, who joined the Historical Section in the summer of 1936 as "assistant messenger" and general helper but who soon became the primary custodian of the picture file. Though not officially classified as a photographer until 1941, Vachon was allowed by Stryker, after 1937, to take on a limited number of field assignments. His photographic education had been the file, and he later confessed to walking around "looking for Walker Evans' pictures."[205] From Dubuque, Iowa, he wrote enthusiastically to Stryker: "There are 4 Walker Evans type RR Stations in town."[206] And in 1938, passing through Atlanta, where he knew so well a certain house Evans had photographed, he recalled, "I walked all over town looking for it, and when I had found the real thing, . . . it was like a historic find."[207] Vachon's image, too, a duplicate of a duplicate, joined the file, under the same classification, though now captioned "Atlanta, Ga. May 1938. Houses and advertisements."[208] The incorporation of the homage in the agency archive is instructive, especially since it is offered to a man who had been fired. Clearly Vachon's response also says much about the power of Evans's work to make over the world as photogenic in its own terms. The act of replication is telling, too, driven as it may have been by something provoking in Evans's photograph itself. But the doubling of the image in the file is also uncanny.

What Vachon's reproduction brings out is that, in a sense, the file is filled with duplicates. This was itself an Evans theme and, indeed, duplication is a veritable mania in the picture that fascinated Vachon: two houses, duplicates without an original, two balconies, two billboards, two eyes, two eyes twice over, doubled doubles, duplicated in the posters duplicated by the photographic negative and again by the print that is duplicated by Vachon. Vachon's return to the scene confirms only that it is not there. This place in Atlanta, the site that had to be visited and revisited but that is now gone, was already a site of duplication—a duplication that in turn incited a gesture that set off a chain implicating the very internal processes of photographic meaning in and after the act of exposure with the camera, so that Evans's image becomes, in a certain light, a photograph about a relation to photography as a process of duplication and to meaning as postponement in repetition without a source.[209]

This is not to suggest that Evans's picture was puzzling to a degree that excited concern or critical comment. In Congress and in the press, other images from the Resettlement Administration file would be held

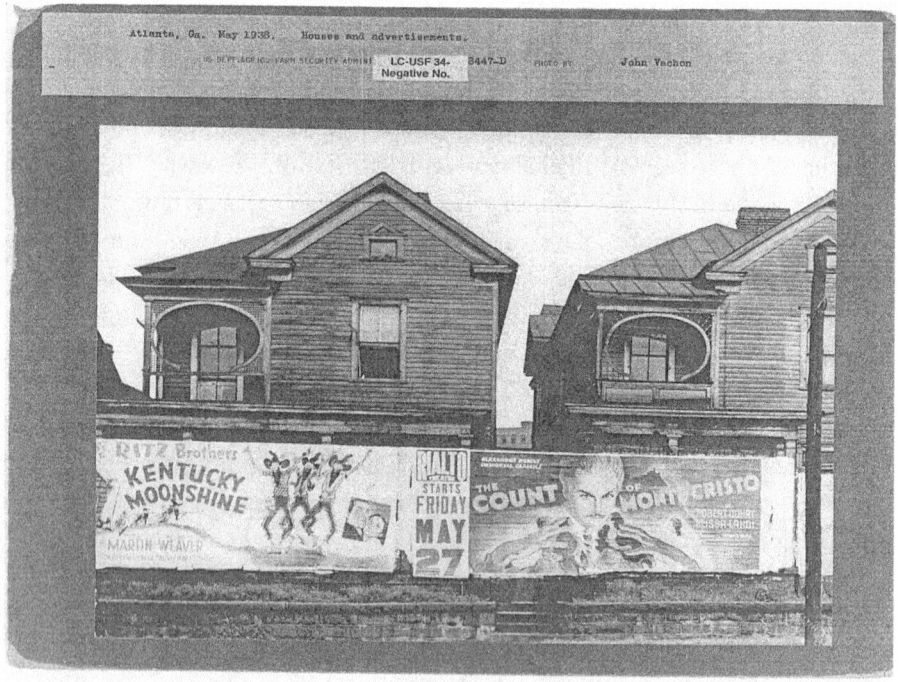

Figure 38. John Vachon, "Atlanta, Ga. May 1938. Houses and advertisements." Department of Agriculture, Resettlement Administration/Farm Security Administration, file card. FSA-OWI Collection, Prints and Photographs Division, Library of Congress (LC-USF-34-8447-D).

aloft as proof of the dangers of government run amok, wasting public money, interfering where it ought not be concerned, engaging in absurdities to justify a gross and parasitic bureaucracy. *Love before Breakfast* did not arouse such passions. This does little, however, to allay the uncertainty of the image or resolve what use it might have had in a government agency archive. Perhaps we can make more headway starting elsewhere.

The photograph was made in Atlanta on Friday, March 20, 1936, somewhere near the city's business district, probably within a few blocks' walk of the Kimball House, the landmark hotel where Evans and his unofficial assistant, Peter Sekaer, were staying.[210] When Evans arrived in Atlanta on March 12, he was working his way back from New Orleans, on the second leg of a long trip through the South for the Historical Section that had begun on November 24, 1935.[211] After recall to Washington on January 11, 1936, Evans had been sent south again by Stryker on Saturday, February 8, to pick up his car in Gulfport, Mississippi, then head down the coast to New Orleans and on northward to Vicksburg, Mississippi, the old Confederate linchpin that once held together the eastern and western territories of the Confederacy. After dropping out of sight in Vicksburg for more than two weeks, Evans had been once again rousted up by Stryker to head north to Tupelo, Mississippi, for an emergency publicity job, then back south and east to Birmingham, Alabama, and on eastward via Atlanta to Monticello, Georgia, en route for Waycross and for St. Marys at the furthermost southeastern corner of the state.[212] From here, Evans was to begin the return trip up the coast to Savannah, then on through South Carolina to Washington, D.C., via Virginia, but cutting out a planned excursion to West Virginia.[213]

Evans was known to abhor the agency jobs that Stryker's long lists of instructions pressed on him. He had no more sympathy for the increased levels of production that Stryker urged him to meet by shooting more rolls of film with his Leica. Nevertheless, after Vicksburg, Evans largely stuck to his task, following both the itinerary and the assignment schedule Stryker had laid out for him. The route to Atlanta led on from the industrial landscapes of Birmingham. Evans and Sekaer arrived on March 12, a Thursday, but Evans had to catch a plane back to Birmingham on March 14 to meet Ernestine Evans and complete certain routine assignments. It is not clear that Ernestine Evans ever turned up.[214] In any case, Evans was back in Atlanta by the sixteenth, staying till March 21, when he left by car for Monticello. On the day before he departed, he made this photograph, on the date, in fact, that appears on the billboard itself, the shutter opening exactly as prescribed.

Earlier in the city, Evans and Sekaer had set about photographing segregated African American housing, as they had in New Orleans, Vicksburg, and Tupelo. In Atlanta, Evans recorded the dilapidated wooden row houses with their ramshackle fenced yards that lined the dirt alleys leading off the city roads, behind the homes of White people. But he also pictured life on the porch, and the interior of a thriving Black barbershop, moving the barbers out of the frame of his view camera and taking care not to include the customers who appear in Sekaer's small-format shot.[215] Evans also found other things to his liking in the area: the Cherokee Parts Store and Garage on Marietta Street, around the corner from his hotel; E. J. Foy Used Tires, with its display of elaborately painted spare-tire covers and his own self-portrait reflected in the workshop window; a painted butcher's sign, like the one that had attracted his attention in Mississippi earlier the same month; and the gesturing statue of Populist senator Thomas E. Watson, in front of the columns of the state capitol building.[216]

Atlanta was the largest city in which Evans would work on this entire sweep of the South. Yet, judging by the small number of negatives produced during his eight-day stay, it seemed to offer him relatively little of what he was seeking. Evans had been in Atlanta once before, in February of the previous year, on his way through Georgia from Savannah, traveling with Gifford Cochran and his butler, James, on a commission from Cochran to photograph Greek Revival architecture in the South. Evans did not then make any known photographs in the city, though this was understandable given his particular interests on that trip. Atlanta had suffered badly in 1864 in General Sherman's last campaign of the Civil War, as presidential electioneering inflamed demands for speedy results. Bombardments of the city and the siege of Confederate fortifications from July to August had left Atlanta almost in ruins. Of the buildings that remained, most were blown up in the Confederate retreat, were demolished by Union Army engineers laying out new defenses, or were burned and blasted by Sherman's army as it pressed on from Atlanta to the sea. Evans was familiar with this history from his acquisition of the ten volumes of Francis Trevelyan Miller's *Photographic History of the Civil War*, which served him as a model of an elegiac "photographic evidence" and mapped out an iconography of the southern town, fallen into ruins.[217] In Sherman's wake, there was little architecture of an earlier period that might interest him in the Georgia capital. Little of the Victorian era had survived either, at least in the downtown area around Five Points, the new hub northwest of the old city center that was now boxed in by concrete and steel office blocks. As the contemporary WPA state guide conceded, unlike most southern cities, Atlanta had "no old houses and few old families"; the railroad-driven boom that had begun under Reconstruction had left Atlanta "few classic Columns but many smokestacks."[218]

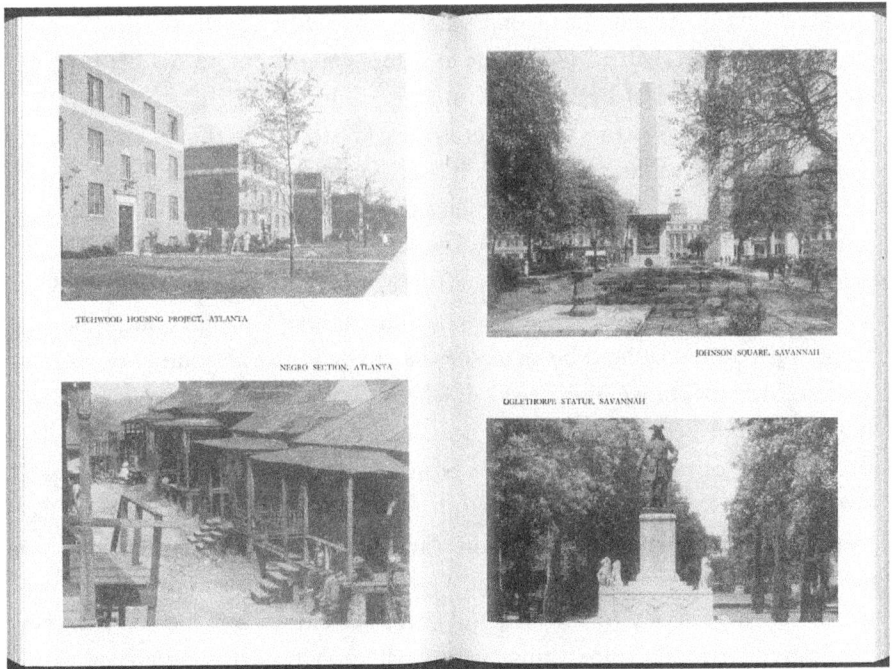

Figure 39. Page from Works Progress Administration, Federal Writers Program, *Georgia: The WPA Guide to Its Towns and Countryside* (Athens: University of Georgia Press, 1940). Walker Evans's "Negro Section, Atlanta," is at lower left.

Then Evans came across these two artisanal houses, if that is in fact what he saw first. The age of the buildings would have attracted him, as well as their variations on a common pattern-book style. The juxtaposition of vernacular houses and mass-produced billboards was also something Evans had attuned himself to notice; it was one of his trademark finds. In New Orleans, earlier on his trip, he had stopped to photograph a Black family house in the Greek Revival style next to a poster advertising Heinz tomato ketchup. At a later date, on the outskirts of the factory district, he had carefully framed a billboard against a scruffy industrial background so that all one sees is "Defective Vision."[219] There were also other billboards and movie posters along the way from New Orleans through Mississippi and Alabama.[220] So, here in Atlanta, he set up his tripod and eight-by-ten Deardorff camera, probably on the sidewalk opposite, if not in the middle of the street as the picture invites us to think, and made two exposures: one, without filter, at f/22 for one twenty-fifth of a second; the second, again without filter, at the same aperture but for one-tenth of a second. On a duplicated form headed, "Photographer's Record of Legends," Evans jotted down: "20th," "Atlanta," "houses and movie posters ('Love before breakfast')."[221] So the movie title did catch his eye. The photograph itself, however, takes more reading.

The flat light and dense print make this a day of breathless grayness, without shadow and unwarmed by the sun. The conditions, however, offered certain advantages where making the picture was concerned. Flat light makes a flat space that seems so evident, at first, but turns out to be troublingly unreadable. The space of the street is already odd enough. The steps from the sidewalk lead nowhere. They no longer access the houses behind because they have been boarded up in a way that also provides the opportunity for those posting billboards, who have quite recently pasted advertisements onto the wooden planks above the two-tiered brick-and-stone walls. Whether this means that the houses themselves are boarded up too is not at all easy to tell. There seem to be signs of life on the balcony to the left, and there are curtains at the window. Compared to what Evans shows us elsewhere at this time in Atlanta, in the back alleys south of Decatur Street, these houses seem habitable enough. They do not seem to be scheduled for demolition, as so many others in the downtown area were, "to make way for apartments, filling stations, chain stores, and open-air eating places."[222] Certainly, as we know from John Vachon's reenactment of Evans's photograph, they will still be standing two years hence, much the same, though *Chatterbox* and *Love before Breakfast* will have given place to *Kentucky Moonshine* and *The Count of Monte Cristo*.[223]

If the houses are lived in, however, there would seem to be no means of entry; at least, we are shown none. Because of our viewpoint, we also cannot be sure of the depth of the buildings or of what lies beyond. The height of the fence blocks our view and cuts off any horizon. How far it is to the blocklike building or the chimney stack to the right remains a matter of conjecture. Moreover, these puzzling arrangements are made no more legible by what is done with the camera. A hasty scanning sees the billboards in front and the houses behind, the reverse of the relation of breadline to billboard that presented Margaret Bourke-White with her "ironical" juxtaposition. But how much space, if any, is there between the temporary-looking billboards and the house fronts? How far do the porches project from the buildings' walls? How deep are the steps from the sidewalk? How much of a ledge is there where the first wall creates a platform for the second? Any calculations we might make are fraught by the compressing effect of the telephoto lens, no doubt the longest of the two components of the Zeiss Protar triple convertible lens that Evans used with the Deardorff view camera, giving an angle of vision markedly narrower than the forty-five degrees that are taken as "normal."[224] Recourse to his longest focal length lens typified Evans's large-format work at this time. It was a deliberate choice. As Jerry Thompson has remarked, the world to which Evans's lens opens is a particular world: "The world compacted, held at arm's length, flattened to be read like a page of literature, full of irony and delicate meaning."[225]

The choice of lens, the corrective adjustments: these things overcoded the entire surface of the image, as it once appeared, upside down on the ground glass screen before Evans's eyes. At the same time, certain contrivances of composition have also made our task all the harder. The difficulties seem to reach a pitch along certain confounding rift lines. Take the utility pole, which just happens to be there but which, like the factory chimney, comes in handy as a device, holding in place the grid on which the photographic frame is built. The pole, however, proves rather slippery—at least as slippery as the word "frame" in the previous sentence. If one follows the pole up with one's eye, it begins, on its left-hand side, to duplicate the edge of the Carole Lombard poster, already emphasized by what seems to be a graphic line that has, however, no parallel on the left. The pole, here, does not quite coincide with the poster edge: There is an uncertain gap and, as one moves up, more parallel lines appear to the left that seem to denote wood planking—the planking, perhaps, of the billboard support itself. But if one follows the top edge of this planking left, it disappears *behind* the capital of a square wooden pillar supporting the house porch. It does so, moreover, at around the point that a diagonally attached piece of wood passes *in front* of the pillar, intersecting the boarding on which the poster is mounted. Whether this piece of wood actually touches the entablature of the porch or the planking proves surprisingly difficult to determine. If it did—if, say, it touched them both—then that would mean that the billboards were not some unspecified distance in front of the houses but were battened to the pillars of the porches—pillars that, if only we could see them, would be grounded on the brick plinth, so that the houses would rise directly from the street, without any setback, at least until that cutout corner on the right-hand house front veers away.

This surprising conclusion seems to be confirmed by the fact that the feet of the pillars do, indeed, appear to break through the tattered lower edges of the posters, which were still relatively new, remember. Even so, a consistent correspondence between protruding base and requisite pillar is not always to be found. One extra base unfortunately appears in the middle of the billboard on the left. This is worrying, but already enough has been done to unsettle that initial assessment of the space in which the houses form a backdrop. The billboards and facades no longer have a foreground–background relation, and this is a change that does not leave the question of meaning in the picture untouched. From this point of view, the new proposal is rather unwelcome, though there does not seem to be sufficient evidence to settle it absolutely at this point. Let us try the pole's other side.

The right edge, as it appears, threatens to lead us into even greater difficulties. Where it crosses the upper brick wall, we enter a very uncertain zone. Perhaps the vertical post that the pole now seems to abut is seated on brickwork that is not a low wall but, rather, the foundation of the porch. The pole, however, gets in the way of settling this matter with any certainty. Moving up, to escape this problem, we find the edge of the pole begins to echo a series of four vertical lines that parallel but run beyond a further series to the right, where the intervals are larger and where surely we are dealing with the planking that provides the posters' support. The more closely packed lines, by contrast, seem to describe the edge and vertical grooving of a squared porch pillar, as becomes somewhat clearer further up. But how the pillar so neatly fills the available slot in the fence, where exactly one runs into the other, and in what plane pillar, plank, and post may be said to lie are all questions that remain hard to answer with any sense of definitiveness. And the further up we go, the more likely we are to be set off at right angles, with the result that we have to worry about the conjunctions of capital and board, window and fencing, shadow and stain, poster and porch roof.

The whole matter is disturbingly undecidable and, since the relation of posters to houses has been taken by critics to be the crux of meaning in the photograph, we seem to be in larger trouble. It is as if we were at one of those junctions in a text where, de Man says, the cognitive and the performative functions do not flow smoothly into each other, along the lines of a common grammar, but disconnect along a threshold of unreadability, without erasing earlier readings but without being able to resolve them, either.[226] The pole cum compositional device has brought us nothing but trouble. And doubt is contagious. Now we can no longer be certain about that object nearest to us, joined to our space by a wayward line. It is an object that might stand for the place of the camera or of the viewer reiterated in the space of the picture, in the street. Is it, by its placement on the sidewalk, a severed trash can? Or is it an upturned tin bath, having lost its bottom; the inverted double of the one on the left-hand balcony whose bottom, alas, we cannot see? But what would a bath be doing in the street? What would it say for domestic life in the houses beyond? And what sort of figure can it cut for the viewer now?

These are peculiarly enervating questions. They take us rather far from the felicitous decodings we have been offered. In contrast to Bourke-White's Louisville image, in Evans's photograph it proves surprisingly difficult to settle with any certainty the exact spatial relation of billboards and houses. Even at this level, it is not at all clear that they are physically separated or can be visually held apart as a prerequisite for some broader separation and contrast, say, of the world of representation and its refutation in the real. An additional problem here would be that the buildings themselves are part of an architectural discourse, are representations, one might say, or at least constitute a vernacular language of pattern-book architectural elements, spatial articulations, decorative emblems, and so on. As pattern-book structures, they are a bricolage of quotations and citations. As "homes," as public representations of domestic life, of the private domain, or of individual taste—representations elaborated in conventional rituals of practice and use—the buildings further enmesh us in a text that the photograph does not effectively equip us to unravel. As metaphors—"sullen houses blind and deaf to the comedy they enact against the seductive billboards they cannot see"; "aging houses plastered with ads for a pair of coming attractions . . . themselves become 'painted ladies,' unwitting victims of the Depression"—they take us even further, at least if we are prepared to follow the interpretations of the critics.[227] Representations and representations of representations. But what of the world with which the houses are to be contrasted? What of the posters? Surely, here, we are dealing with things reliably held in place, framed for us to see, here on this street in Atlanta—but also simultaneously on thousands of other streets across America?

The mass-produced billboards for national advertising campaigns already mark a tear in the presupposed unities of photographic place and time. On the left is an advertisement for *Chatterbox*, an RKO-Radio production, directed by George Nichols Jr. and based on a play by David Carb, in which a naive, stage-struck chatterbox, Jenny Yates from rural Vermont, played by Anne Shirley, runs away from her grandfather's farm and is discovered by a cynical producer (played by Eric Rhodes) who casts her as Alice Murgatroyd in a parody Broadway revival of *Virtue's Reward*—the very play and the very part in which Jenny's now-deceased mother had made her name on the stage.[228] Even as knowing kitsch, the play proves a flop and Jenny's dreams collapse, though, in her disappointment, she finds unexpected consolation in handsome aspiring artist Philip Greene (played by Phillips Holmes), who is charmed by her innocence and has come to love her as she really is. Not quite up to the standards of its Restoration prototypes, *Chatterbox* is, then, the story of an ingenue up from the country and at the mercy of the venal city. The poster shows Anne Shirley, formerly known as Dawn O'Day, who changed her name after playing the lead in the 1934 film *Anne of Green Gables*. Anne Shirley is seen as Jenny Yates playing the role of Alice Murgatroyd—all of these names fictitious, referencing only the layering of representations. Rather incongruously, behind the couch on which the actresses sit are the lights of Broadway, evoking Evans's New York here on an unknown street in downtown Atlanta but also seeming to cite "Broadway Composition," an untypical "New Vision" composite image that Evans published a number of times between 1930 and 1931, notably on the cover of *Advertising and Selling*.[229]

Next to *Chatterbox*, starting today, all across America, is *Love before Breakfast*, a 1936 Universal production, directed by Walter Lang, from a book by Faith Baldwin with the rather less promising title of *Spinster Dinner*.[230] The film is a pioneer screwball comedy, worked on uncredited by Preston Sturges, in which, in the year she was nominated for an Oscar, Hollywood's highest-paid actress, Carole Lombard, is the center of cinematic attention as fey and fickle Park Avenue beauty Kay Colby,

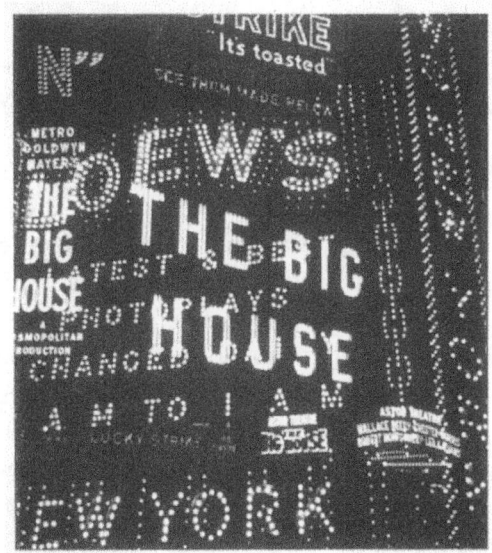

Figure 40. Walker Evans, "Broadway Composition," 1930, from the cover of *Advertising and Selling*, June 24, 1931. Courtesy of the Walker Evans Archive at the Metropolitan Museum of Art.

unable to decide between the dubious attractions of Cesar Romero playing Bill Wadsworth and rich oil tycoon Scott Miller, played by Preston
Foster. The black eye is what everyone sees. Kay gets it in reel two, in
a nightclub fight, landed in the dark by her frustrated suitor Scott as
he tries to protect her from the unwanted attentions of a college foot-
ball team. The black eye is the signature of the screwball comedy, a
metonymy for Kay and Scott's knockabout relationship, and a metaphor
for Carole Lombard's feisty screen persona. It is also, strangely, the sign
and reenactment of what must not be seen: the actress's damaged face,
badly scarred on the same left side in a 1926 automobile collision and
painfully rebuilt by early plastic surgery. Hiding what is no longer there,
the sign repeats a trauma that has been repressed, just as the photograph
will in turn. Captioned by the title of the film, which has no apparent
relation to the plot, the black eye continues to bloom with meaning: It
is a trope for Evans's own troubled love life, a social comment on the
black eye dealt by the Depression to the houses behind, a graffito put
there by the photographer himself—all this in the imagination of the
picture's readers.[231]

A film of a book, signed by a black eye that is makeup covering
the damaged face of an actress who always plays herself before her part.
A film of a play in which an actress, playing an earlier character, acts an
actress acting a repetition of her mother's signature role. The posters
and the films they advertise, by chance perhaps, compound the problem
of the houses, the billboards, and the street, the problem of the photographic event, in downtown Atlanta, "starting Friday Mar 20": the problem of representation to infinity that is the problem of representation
as such—representation for which there is no final frame of the real
made present for us in the photograph. Representation, then, as Derrida
would say, "in the abyss of presence," not an accident of presence, for
"the desire of presence is, on the contrary, born from the abyss (the
indefinite multiplication) of representation, from the representation of
representation, etc."[232]

The distance from Louisville to Atlanta proves surprisingly great.
For the photography of Margaret Bourke-White, the world itself is rhetorical: It is not merely intelligible, but constituted as a series of messages
whose tropes are present in the world. The message of the world—"the

real world"—captured by Bourke-White decodes all other messages, of which it is both the condition and the measure of truth. For Evans, by contrast, the intelligible world is a world of representation, and the proliferation of representation opens on the abyss of the real. The camera, as instrument of "pure record," is a portal to a world that has no message, that is addressed to no one, and that is seen not as "present" but, as Evans precisely put it, "as the past"—as always already lost.[233] But the camera is also a black box, a means of encrypting this encounter out of time and beyond meaning, of producing pictures as impenetrable puzzles. The camera is both crypt and encrypting machine: the tomb of the real in which the present has already passed away, and an engine of overcoding in which the unbearable encounter is buried and postponed, made bearable as the cryptic without end.

This needs unpacking. But I should say immediately that in this contrasting of Evans and Bourke-White, I do not intend to repeat what has become obligatory in the Evans literature as a means of setting off his supposed ethical superiority. The denigration of Margaret Bourke-White usually begins with scorn for her personal vanity and ends with condemnation of her luridly theatrical and manipulative photographic work. The cue here comes from Evans's friends and supporters in the 1930s, most famously James Agee, who chose to include a gushing journalistic interview with Margaret Bourke-White as an unglossed appendix to *Let Us Now Praise Famous Men*.[234] Here, preserved against the vagaries of time and fashion, Bourke-White's "superior red coat," "the reddest coat in the world," finds itself hanging next to Sadie Ricketts's flour-sack shift and George Gudger's heroic overalls. It is an image of pettiness that has been reworked many times, most notably, after the 1960 reissue of *Let Us Now Praise Famous Men*, by William Stott, for whom the counterposed images of Evans and Bourke-White stand for a moral contrast, grounded on irreconcilable ethics of life and practice.[235]

Bourke-White, of course, readily confessed that she "loved clothes" and "attached great importance to appropriate costumes for each many-faceted day."[236] Not at all defensive, she wrote,

> Believing as I do that getting pictures is only part of getting a picture story—a great part lies in persuading people to do things—I made a special

project of having the right wardrobe for each job. I always felt more per-
suasive in the right clothes.[237]

But in the 1950s, with the security of a photo-editor's salary from *Fortune*, Evans too showed a marked taste for Brooks Brothers jackets, Sav-
ile Row suits, and handmade shoes from Peal Company of London. It is
said that he shopped compulsively at this time, the more so when he was
without funds. It is also reported that, in 1961, he spent the best part of
his second Guggenheim Fellowship award on securing a coveted Jaguar
sedan, for which he was then eager to obtain a Blaupunkt radio, pester-
ing his publisher for the specs.[238] These are no doubt trivial and salacious
facts, and it is far from clear how they will help us think about Evans's
work. Is it not striking, then, that such facts have been given such prominence in the assessment of Margaret Bourke-White's?

A comparative reading of biographies would not readily furnish
material to shore up the critical myth of Evans's moral stature—the
record of the war years alone might be fatal enough. The ethics of picture
making, too, of which Stott, following Agee, makes so much, is also something that does not survive much scrutiny. Even on the trip to Alabama
in the summer of 1936, when Evans traveled alongside Agee and produced the signal body of work that would be made the ethical center of
the Evans canon, Evans, like Bourke-White, rearranged objects and fur-
niture in other people's houses where he was working, just as he brought
in artificial lighting and flash and did not hesitate to photograph his hosts
unawares with an angled viewfinder.[239] His relationships with those he
pictured and later published, even those with whom he stayed as a guest
in Hale County, do not appear in a complimentary light in subsequent
investigations.[240] On Bourke-White's side, it might be added that, contrary to Evans's later claims, she was not unreflective about the moral
implications of her practice. In her technical note to *You Have Seen Their
Faces*, as in her autobiography, she makes no effort to conceal her mis-
takes and is the first to raise the difficult questions of intrusion and exploitation that are only exacerbated by the technical setup demanded by
equipment at the time.[241]

The one-sided contrast of Bourke-White and Evans must therefore be approached with suspicion. Undoubtedly, there was antipathy on

Evans's side—even though, or perhaps because, he had exhibited along-side Bourke-White at the John Becker Gallery in New York as early as April 1931 and, again, at the Museum of Modern Art in 1937.[242] Bourke-White's reputation—her reputed behavior but also her success—called forth the misogyny that Evans had honed in his relations with his mother. Beyond this, Bourke-White was also required to serve as shorthand for a kind of practice against which Evans's backers, such as Agee and Mabry, sought to define a space of distinction for his work, in the face of Bourke-White's visibility, success, and critical acclaim.[243] The production of a difference was what Evans's supporters worked for, as part of a discursive strategy to institute a particular status for his work. Within that context, the ethical terms of the contrast had a function. Outside it, they are not only questionable, but also essentially beside the point. For what is at stake, and what interests me here in bringing together the two representations of representation at which we have been looking, is not a moral or ethical difference in personality or behavior but a difference in the relation to meaning—a difference whose ethical, political, and personal implications are not easy to unravel.

For Bourke-White, meaning must be delivered and the viewer must take receipt. In Evans's image, meaning is held back, seemingly less by the photographer than by the objects themselves, from which the viewer is cut off by an uncertain distance that reintroduces the presence of the lens between the eye and the scene. In the one case, meaning always arrives, guaranteed by the transparency of rhetoric and the finality of photographic truth, through which the misrepresentations of American capitalism can be confronted with the reality they occlude. In the other, we encounter an attachment to the object that does not accommodate itself to instrumental communication but is encrypted, locked away in layers of representation like an infinite series of Russian dolls. This is a melancholy realism whose appearance in the archives of a government department is a puzzle in itself. I call it melancholic and realist quite deliberately. Ideas of melancholia have had a long history in the West, but at play within them, from the beginning, have been not only questions of subjectivity but also questions of the limits of knowledge, of language, and of meaning. Perhaps pondering the structure of melancholy will lead us to think again about the character of those practices of representation that will not give way to the demand for efficient communication but resist the arrival of meaning, while mourning a real that is not given to representation. Perhaps, in the face of the regimens of meaning that speak to us and hold us to account, such practices of refusal are marks not of failure but of a certain kind of resistance, to which, amid all the recruitment calls of the 1930s, Evans's photograph bears witness as a cryptic memorial to an ineradicable remainder.

"I work rather blindly," Evans said in later life, "and I don't think an awful lot about what I am doing."[244] The remark was made extempore, almost casually, to a class of students at Harvard University two days before his death on April 10, 1975. For a photographer, it is an arresting statement. On the one hand, it may be taken as no more than an assertion of the artist's unconscious eye and its instinctive, avaricious reaction to a visual object: "Something strikes a chord in the photographer's restless eye. It's either there or it isn't," Evans told an interviewer in 1971. When "it" is there, however, this listless and unthinking receptivity becomes the conduit to a solitary kind of ecstasy that is sure of its possession of its object: "It's as though there's a wonderful secret in a certain place and I can capture it. Only I can do it at this moment, only this moment and only me."[245] On the other hand, against this apparent self-satisfaction, the *blindness* and the absence of thought signify a death that has already taken place: "the non-appearance of the author, the non-subjectivity" that Evans said he admired in Gustave Flaubert.[246] "Theorists," Evans wrote, as he prepared a maquette of a book of unposed photographic records of passengers in the subway, "claim almost everything for the camera except the *negation* that it can be made not to think and not to translate its operator's emotion."[247] The comment belongs to the late 1950s or early 1960s, but it echoes one of Evans's earliest evaluations. As he insisted in *Hound and Horn* in 1931, in a review strangely titled "The Reappearance of Photography": "America is really the natural home of photography if photography is thought of without operators."[248]

A photography that had been lost but now reappears, blindly, without thought, without operators, without author or subjectivity: odd opinions for a man who worked with such calculation and for one given "a calling card" so early in his career by the Museum of Modern Art's first solo show of a photographer.[249] Yet, in Evans's thinking, the approach toward automatism was inseparably bound up with the threshold of possibility of the "pure record." It was not, however, just a matter of technique. Distance, detachment, and negation were paradoxically a mode of being, more than a style, closer to a technique of the self—or the nonself.

Evans's melancholic "lassitude" was famous in the 1930s. Ben Shahn's gouache portrait from around 1930 describes it aptly, just as Evans's own posed photographic self-portraits of 1929 and 1935 ingrain it as a well-rehearsed performance. Evans's intimates and acquaintances spoke of it or wrote of it again and again. Ed Locke boasted of annoying Evans out of it on their trip to Forrest City in 1937, while, in his diary for 1931, Lincoln Kirstein made repeated observations on Evans's low vitality and "his disappointing fear, of his getting tired easily."[250] Working with Evans in April of the following year on a photographic record of Victorian architecture in New England, Kirstein complained that Evans was "a considerable disappointment in so much that he has to be constantly amused—he seems perennially bored—thin blooded, too easily tired."[251] Again, in June, "cleaning up" on the houses they had not managed to photograph earlier in the year, Kirstein recorded his increasing frustration with Evans: "No resilience or energy He resists one only on tiny details—how a door should be shut, etc. If ever opposed in conversation—he says 'I don't know.' Tired, inert—reminds me of a constipated and castrated bulldog—old and squatting before his time."[252] Kirstein felt, to his aggravation, that Evans exerted a "negative personal magnetism which is his only and suicidal claim on people."[253] In December 1931, seeing Evans off on his cruise to the South Seas as official photographer of the *Cressida*, Kirstein noted irritably, "Walker was as usual, nervous, jerky, devitalized and displaying ½ filament of magnetism."[254]

Caught between attraction and rejection, these were images other friends, colleagues, and lovers of this time shared and felt the need to repeat. Forty years on, Evans's friend and one-time photographic assistant, the writer John Cheever, still pictured, or remembered, Evans in the mid-1930s as an unenthusiastic and "rather put off" seducer with "an enormous cock that showed only the most fleeting signs of life."[255] Flaccid, flickering, secretive, bored, sexually passive, inaccessible—the sense that Evans was not entirely there was oddly compelling to his New York acquaintances, even as it exasperated them. For Kirstein, in particular, it seemed one with Evans's vision of social decay, disintegration, and inertia, and with "the skimmed decadence of so much of his work."[256]

This is a very foreign phrase of Kirstein's. The adjective is choice and puzzling, but the noun too is strange: It is hard now to think of "decadence" having a place in the lexicon of critical comment on Evans, except perhaps in certain hostile reviews of *American Photographs* and of his earlier show at the John Becker Gallery in 1931. Kirstein marks it, however, where an attitude becomes the work, or perhaps the other way round: where meaning marks the subject. This is the real issue with Evans's melancholy. It is not a matter of psychobiography. What it interests me to bring into play in relation to Evans are, rather, those accounts that place melancholy at the limits of sense, where melancholy figures as a marking of the vain excess and inadequacy of signification in relation to its object, against which melancholy holds to an impossible encounter with a real that is the condition of existence and failure of all systems of meaning.

For Julia Kristeva, melancholy points to the breakdown of symbolic bonds under the insistent pressure of an archaic and unsymbolizable narcissistic wound for which there can be no compensation and for which no agent can stand as referent, a wound arising from the loss of an unnamable, unseparated, elusive, and unrepresentable Thing—"the real that does not lend itself to signification."[257] For Giorgio Agamben, melancholy is a preemptive mourning for an unobtainable object—a mourning that, protecting against a loss that has not occurred, "opens a space for the existence of the unreal and marks out a scene in which the ego may enter into relation with it and attempt an appropriation such as no other possession could rival and no loss possibly threaten."[258] Even in those accounts, from Sigmund Freud's to Judith Butler's, in which melancholy figures negatively, as failure of mourning, melancholy is still connected by default to a refusal of normalcy, to a resistance to meaning that is paradoxically overinvested in speech, and to a withdrawal from identification.[259] What refusal and withdrawal seek to accomplish is the seemingly impossible task of sustaining the subject somehow outside the field of relations in which it is called into place: in a suspended relation to communication and language in which the subject refuses to accede to the chains of substitution of the symbolic; in a psychic space within psychic space from which the subject declines to reenter the specular field of the imaginary in which human subjects are called on to function.

This is what is at stake in the melancholic gesture: It opens the question of how the human subject, constituted in and through the networks of difference and exchange and the effects of power of the systems of meaning that speak it, can withdraw from an arena in which alone it exists, when there would seem to be no other place to go. What recourse is there for a subject in the face of a power that itself produces the subject—a power that is the subject's condition of existence and from which there can therefore be no liberation? As Butler has remarked, "To be dominated by a power external to oneself is a familiar and agonizing form power takes. To find, however, that what 'one' is, one's very formation as a subject, is in some sense dependent upon that very power is quite another."[260] In such a predicament, any assertion of the subject would paradoxically be no more than a repetition of that power and of the subject's subordination to it. And yet this subordination is unlivable—not because it demeans an authentic self, since the self is only produced in this subordination, but because of the anguish of the remainder: the unnamable loss that stains the subject and marks the limits and contingency of its subjection. The question, then, is whether the subject can somehow interrupt or resist this power by a kind of refusal or evasion—even though it would then seem to be refusing or evading itself, refusing or evading the production of itself, so that it must risk "illness," disfunction, blindness, or even death.

This is the path of melancholia. Melancholy marks the subject's poignant attempt to open a space in which it is somehow saved from the power that makes it possible, that it incorporates, and to which it nevertheless belongs. It cuts a path along which the subject is driven to insinuate an impossible internal distance from the very discursive frame in which it is produced as subject, by refusing to figure and work through its loss or give up its attachment to an impossible object: the unrepresentable witnessed by the subject's melancholy, which testifies not to a picture of loss that has to be brought back to mind but, rather, to the ineluctable blindness that is a constitutive condition of the subject and that always precludes the justice of its imaging. This is the photograph Evans gives us: less than we want and more than we desire, never adequate to our questions or to our demands, it hands us what we were not seeking and may have preferred to avoid. Inadequate and overwhelming thing, poor compensation, impossible testimony, it offers itself as a ruined monument to the inescapability of an unencounterable real.

CHAPTER 4

Running and Dodging, 1943:
The Breakup of the
Documentary Moment

For they were outside . . . running and dodging the forces of
history instead of making a dominating stand.

—RALPH ELLISON, *Invisible Man*

Everywhere and nowhere, the status of the photograph remains a sore
point, as tempting as it is troublesome to the scratching of the critics,
as likely to turn out a source of infection as it is to yield to the cures of
the disciplines. Too open to diagnosis and too unresponsive to remedy,
it seems to call for a stricter regimen, which is invariably what it receives
and what I am bent on avoiding.

Again and again in this book, I find myself detained by what may
be made of a photograph. But that is not the same as being arrested by
photography or trying to arrest it. The field of photography, as I have
said before, is like the little-studied field of writing, as opposed to literature, or of building, rather than architecture. And one of the things
I mean by this is that photographic practices, like practices of writing
and techniques of building, have developed in response to particular
problems at quite local and heterogeneous sites, proliferating across a
discontinuous field in which technologies, techniques, roles of agency,
and formations of knowledge have never been entirely reducible to the
forms of institutionalization that have sought to appropriate and delimit them. Photography, then, insofar as Sir John Herschel's diplomatic
coinage still has use, is a map of motley differences, identities, jurisdictions, borders, and exclusions that charts a territorial project: the marking out of a yet-to-be-occupied landscape by the closures of power and
meaning.[1]

"Power" and "meaning" are terms, of course, that art histories at the opposite ends of what used to be the spectrum have tried hard to keep apart or reduce to a hierarchy. But they are terms that are only too inclined to break rank, as a sign that they can neither be separated so easily nor be made to leave each other alone. (That is the problem both for formalisms and for sociologies of sense.) It is, then, the mutual imbrication of power and meaning that I have wanted to pursue, not only in relation to those mechanisms of capture that constitute the discursive territory of social discipline and the State, but also, as we shall see, in relation to the discipline of art history itself and its own mechanisms of arrest—its own disciplinary frame.

Yet there is something else that has already begun to disturb this project, and perhaps it is fitting that it should fall not at the margins but here, in the middle of the book—though that does not mean it will be readily held in place. On the contrary, the question that has opened between the last chapter and the present one concerns the possibility of an event of meaning that evades capture, resists incorporation, encrypts itself, or breaks the frame, disrupting the regimes of normative sense as it does the regimen of art historical explanation.

To recap: In the nineteenth century, one might say the summons to the real was served under many different letterheads, some more heavily embossed, some more ornate, and some better credentialed than others, no doubt. But the writ of realism that ran widest of all, that was least to be evaded, and that carried the heaviest sentence, came in the plainest envelope. Purposefully modest in appearance—sober, functional, standardized in format—it was a letter whose senders were sure it would always arrive at its destination. Yet it came not from the grand galleries of the academy, from the polished laboratories of the institute of science, or even from the new and resplendent establishments of commerce and entertainment, but from shabbier rooms: rooms crowded with cabinets, numbered drawers, and filing cards; rooms filled with the silence of documents and browning records that were, however, only waiting their time to speak. Here was the truth made instrumental. From such sequestered spaces was the power of the Real invoked by an apparatus of accountancy that sought to settle all claims, apportion all debts, calculate all penalties, and close the books. This is not the heroic story of Realism. Henceforth, all truths are brown—even, or especially, those in black and white. For where else but in these dismal rooms did photography consummate its celebrated liaison with the Real?

Perhaps this is too jaundiced a view to set against the picture of photography's golden age. Yet in seeking to relocate the frame of the argument about photographies and their histories, I have not been trying to replace one tarnished image by another totalizing scene.[2] What I have sought to do is, rather, to focus attention at a particular level of generality that has, nonetheless, its own historical specificity. What have interested me have been regimes of representation, orders of sense, and closures of meaning that organized the discursive field of photography in ways that seemed lucid and compelling at the time, and even seemed to have put themselves beyond the realm of dispute. Thus, I looked first at the emergence of an order of photographic documentation whose technical instrumentality and status as evidence took force only as the open field of the photographic was institutionally segmented and a specific photography was enclosed as an architecture of discipline and knowledge.[3] Second, I took a sideways look at the rhetoric of recruitment of "documentary" that sought, in a particular moment, to close the viewer within the relations of meaning and the relations of power of the liberal democratic State.[4] Once again, what was disclosed here was a *specific* photography, constituted in a strategy of sense that yielded dividends of pleasure and power only insofar as it could be held in place.

I hope it has been clear, however, that to place emphasis on the institutionalization of certain systems of discursive constraint is not at all to suggest that the fixities of meaning, whose effects I have tried to trace, were ever coherent, accomplished, stable, or secured. These systems are not machines that work smoothly and ergonomically, without wastage. There are always problems and leakages: malfunctions in the hardware, glitches in the software, an overflow of characters, spewing across the screen that cannot be reduced to sense within the system. There are always needed adjustments, upgrades, new sales pitches, and incessant negotiations. Without them the machineries of meaning would not remain effective, pertinent, desirable. But these machineries do not come with guarantees. They do not invariably work well. And, of course, they are resisted.

Resistance was, we know, another favorite theme of Foucault: "there are no relations of power without resistances," as he repeated many times.[5] But being no theoretician of Resistance any more than of Power, what he would never tell us was, resistance in the name of what? The Universal? History? Truth? Justice? Liberation? The fully human subject? The unhappy ones: the dispossessed? Nonpower? Is resistance born from an ontological opposition between power and its other side? Does resistance to power have to come from elsewhere to be authentic? Does resistance to the closures of power have to take its stand in another place, in another center, in the name of another homeland? Must it be *in the name of* something? Or are all such names, in the end, only one or another form of the many names of terror?

Let us go back, at least for a beginning, to one homeland of truth: to the territory of documentary, to the canonized space of the Resettlement Administration/Farm Security Administration photographic file,[6] and even to the places where documentary did its fieldwork. But let us find them at the moment when their coherence and security, their presence and conviction, begin to fall apart.

In 1943, the moment of social documentary—and, one might say, the moment of social democracy in the United States—was over. The convergence of conditions that had worked in the 1930s to rupture the conventions and constraints of consensual culture and open demands for new languages of reality, new guarantees of truth, and new securities of identity no longer held. The political limits of New Deal reformism had been reached well before the Depression receded as the effects of conversion for war were felt in the economy. The Popular Front and the left cultural movement had fallen apart under the weight of their internal conflicts and discrediting policy reversals, long before their remnants were to be assailed by the forces of patriotism and militarism. The cultural formations that dominated debate in the Depression years could have been seen to be fragmenting even before the dramatic changes brought by wartime mobilization robbed them of their currency and rendered them obsolete.[7] This was the threshold of a decidedly new conjuncture.

The massive economic stimulus of government war orders—at its height, exceeding by almost six times the highest level of public spending achieved in the previous eight years—amounted to a New Deal for Capital, enormously strengthening corporate interests.[8] At the same time, almost a decade of restructuring and government-sponsored regulatory reform fed into the wartime economy and the further integration of industry, finance, the military, and the State that it brought. On the other hand, the position of labor, which had been such a militant presence, politically, economically, and culturally, throughout the Depression, was effectively reduced. In spite of a wartime labor shortage and a return to nearly full employment, the growth years of the 1940s saw the working class become much more defensive and divided, further than ever from the articulation of any popular, democratic movement. This was not only due to the implosion of the rank-and-file leftism of the 1930s and to the legislative and industrial reforms that worked to incorporate organized labor and advance a bureaucratic, crypto-managerial union leadership. It was also due to changes in the character and composition of the working class itself.[9]

In the 1940s, this was a class whose primary cohesive and defensive community structures had begun to break up under the pressures of restructuring and relocation. It was a class whose pattern of life was becoming increasingly transient, volatile, and vulnerable and more and more deeply factionalized by racial, ethnic, and gender conflicts. The short-lived wave of militancy that accompanied the reconversion to peacetime production in 1946 did not signal what was to come. Working-class militancy would be largely diverted from workplace struggles by the consumerism of the postwar boom, while a consolidated but constricted trade unionism would accept its subordination to patriotism and national security in a permanent war economy.

Such processes of economic and political transformation were also accompanied by a dramatic realignment of the cultural circuits of everyday life through the concerted extension and intensification of a market-driven culture of consumption and passive media spectacles, in which, contrary to Walter Benjamin's prediction, the conditions of mass participation worked precisely to displace the collectivity of the crowd.[10] The year 1943, then, opens on a decidedly different conjuncture from that of the Second New Deal, the Popular Front, and the left cultural move-ment—one in which, by dramatic contrast, previously threatened insti-tutions and hierarchies are reconsolidated, previously destabilized social relations are resecured, and previously exploited spaces for dissent are closed down again. Yet we should beware of the pessimism and the economism of this account. For the social and economic transforma-tions, and even the commoditization of the cultural field, also opened spaces for cultural departures that were not economically contained or indeed fixed in economic class terms. And while these departures may always have been at risk both of suppression and of appropriation, they could never be entirely exhausted or absorbed.

We might look, for example, at the well-studied consequences of the wartime repositioning of women in the labor force and the effects this had on public culture and on the dominant regime of gender difference.[11] Clearly, women did not enter the workforce for the first time during the war years, whatever government information services and *March of Time* newsreels said at the time. Certainly, some women were compelled to take on previously unremunerative work outside, as well as inside, the home because family wage earners had been drafted. A smaller num-ber of middle-class women were also drawn into the labor market by patriotic appeals or by the prospect of a mobility that looked like an escape from the confines of middle-class gender roles. But for the major-ity of working-class women—especially African American and Mexican American women—war industry work offered a way out of unrelenting agricultural labor, low-paid domestic employment, and other service-sector jobs.

The increased visibility of women's workforce participation during the war years was not, therefore, just the result of a patriotic response; nor was it just a matter of women breaking free from confinement in the home. Rather, it marked a shift *within* the workforce and a weakening of the gendered hierarchies of waged work, propelled by the wartime shortage of labor. Nevertheless, it sent seismic waves not only across the gendered culture of the workplace but also across the wider economy of gender and the cultural systems of gender representations in which workplace hierarchies too are, in part, secured. In short, what was shaken

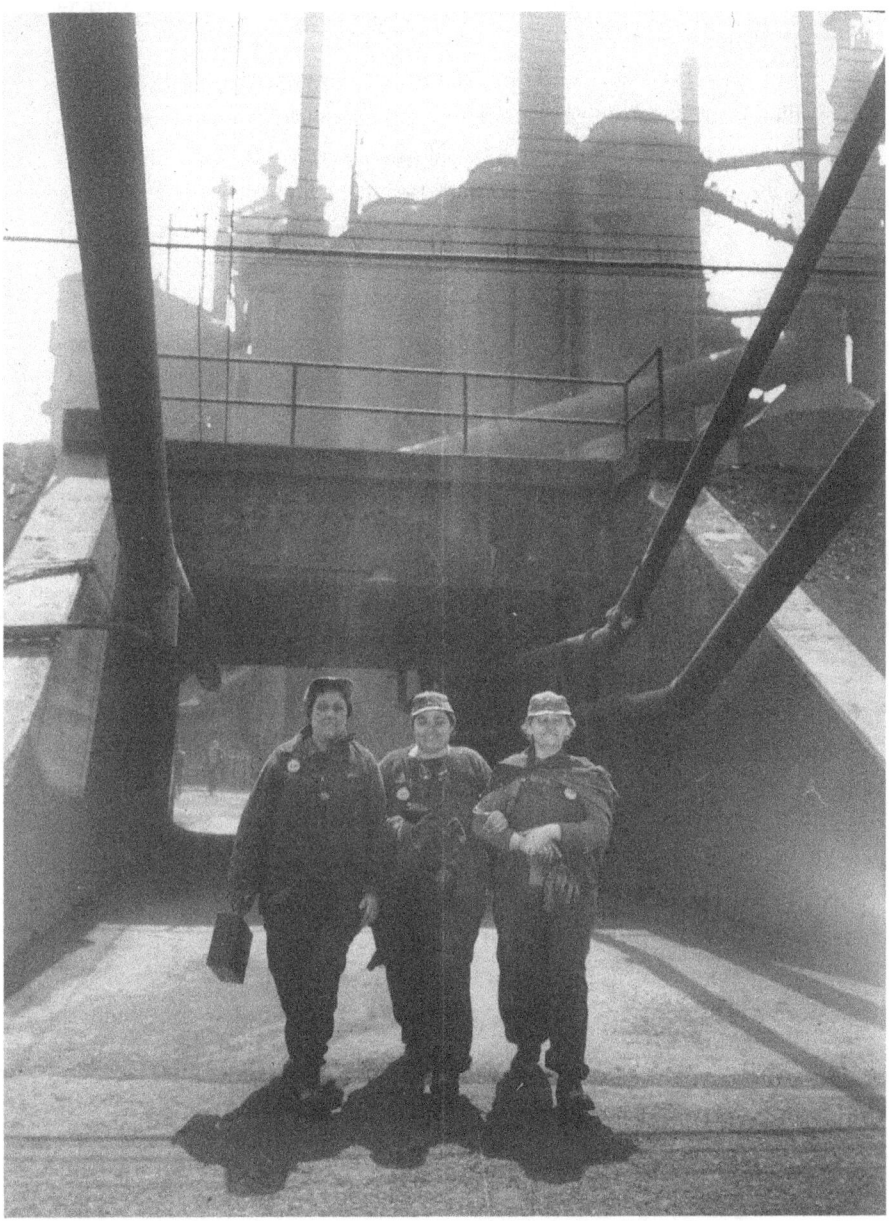

Figure 41. Marjory Collins, "Women workers leaving the Republic Steel plant. Open hearth furnaces in the background. Buffalo, New York," May 1943. FSA-OWI Collection, Prints and Photographs Division, Library of Congress (LC-USW3-025815-D).

was the security of the regime of femininity in which dominant formations of identity were fixed.

The cultural cracks and strains were evident enough, but they also compelled more-conscious attempts at cultural negotiation. Adjustments in the gender address of advertising and in the constructions of gender in official discourses and the popular media—especially in so-called women's fiction, women's magazines, soap operas, and women's films—marked an effort to contain, accommodate, and even colonize the changes that were taking place. But the changes in the meaning of gender and the unsettling of the established orders of gender identity outran such strategies of containment, just as they were registered in different ways in cultural practices that did not set out to reincorporate the shifts that were taking place back into the adaptive patterns of the dominant culture.

For example, in an area of publicly sponsored cultural production whose earlier phase in the Depression years has dominated the majority of historical studies, the drafting of men working as federal government photographers created opportunities for a small number of women, often previously employed as darkroom technicians, to pursue photographic assignments and add their negatives to those of Dorothea Lange and Marion Post Wolcott in the Farm Security Administration and the Office of War Information picture files.[12] Here, the very employment of Esther Bubley, Marjory Collins, Pauline Ehrlich, Martha McMillan Roberts, Ann Rosener, and Louise Rosskam as "documentary" photographers, functioning independently in the field, marked an immediate and typical wartime tension in what had been customarily taken for granted as the gendered limits to freedom of movement and access to public space. (As Roy Stryker, head of the FSA photography project, had earlier written to Marion Post Wolcott, outlining the terms of her employment and her initial work conditions: "There is another thing I raised with you the other day, that is the idea of your traveling in certain areas alone. . . . I do have grave doubts of the advisability of sending you, for instance, into certain sections of the South."[13] And as Post Wolcott herself wrote to Stryker, from the field, "Driving at night is definitely not a good idea for a gal alone in the South. And you know I'm no sissy. . . . If anything goes wrong you're out of luck and no one understands a girl out alone after dark.")[14]

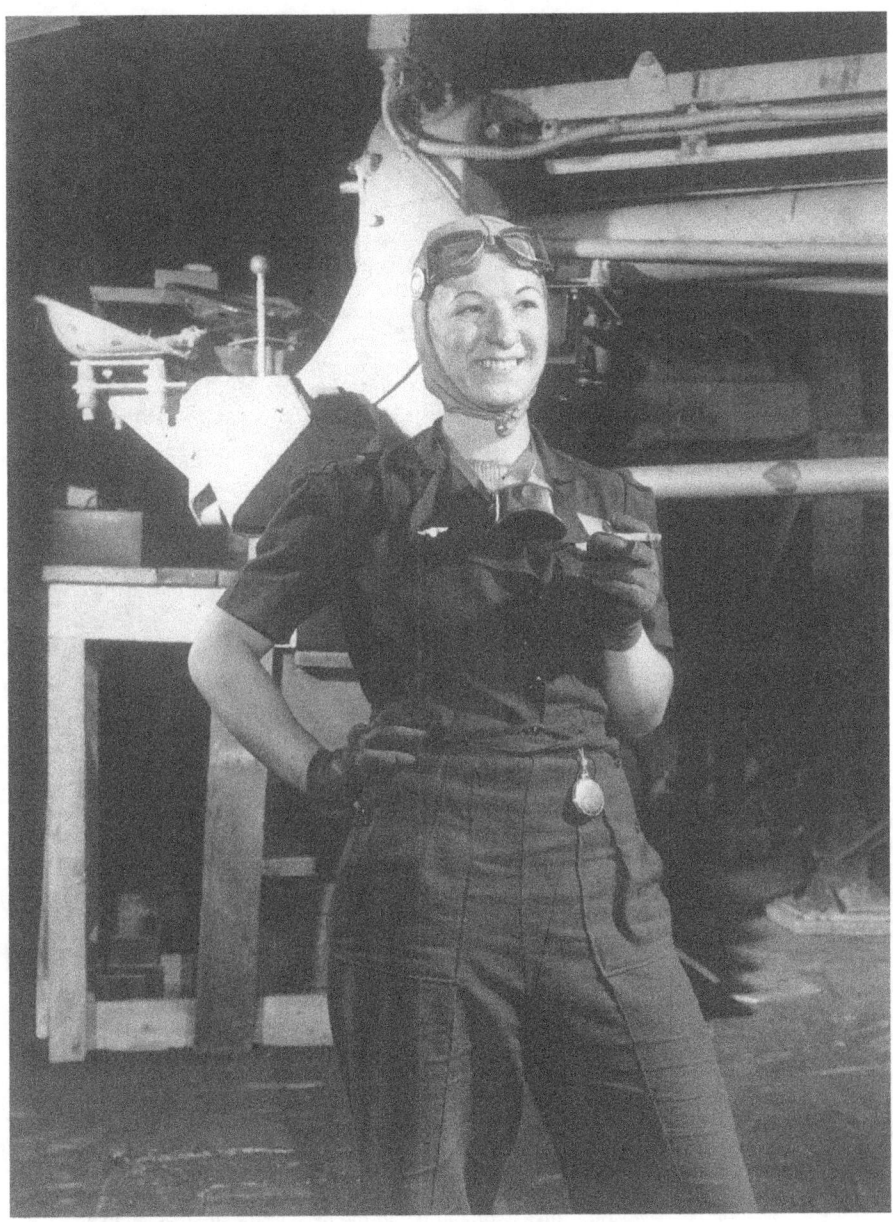

Figure 42. Marjory Collins, "Symington-Gould, sand slinger operator at rest. Notice sand on her face. Buffalo, New York," May 1943. FSA-OWI Collection, Prints and Photographs Division, Library of Congress (LC-USW3-026086-D).

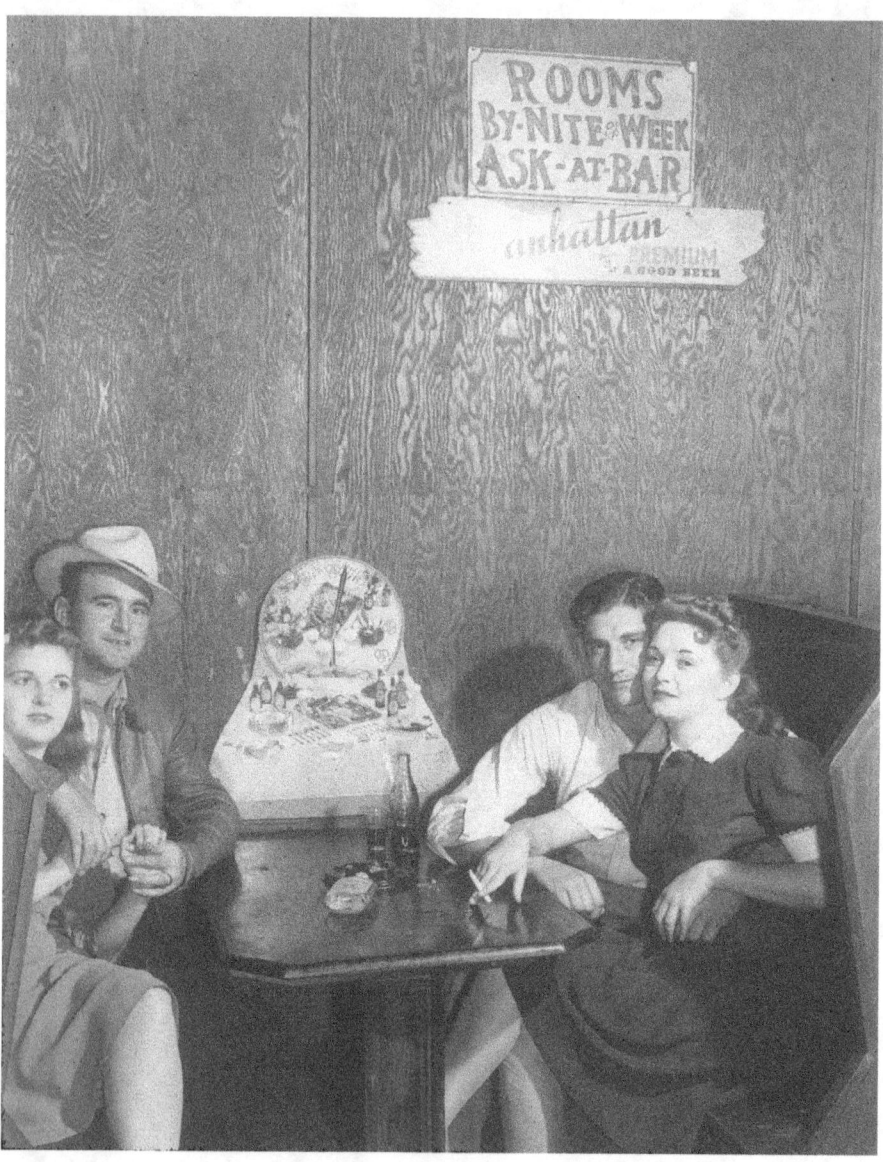

Figure 43. Marion Post Wolcott, "Juke joint and bar in the Belle Glade area, vegetable section of south Central Florida," February 1941. FSA-OWI Collection, Prints and Photographs Division, Library of Congress (LC-USF34-057094-D).

This tension, however, was also what the photographers themselves began to articulate, in images that focused on gendered structures
of space and power, on their overwriting of divisions between the public
and the domestic, and on their coding into characteristic gestures and
the bodily occupation of space. At the Symington-Gould plant in Buffalo, New York, in May 1943, Marjory Collins pictures a radiant sand
slinger operator, as dashing as a pilot, taking a break on the job and ele-
gantly posing, with one heavy-gloved hand on her hip and the other styl-
ishly holding a cigarette. But she also photographs plant worker Laura
Czaya at home, sewing, watched rather awkwardly by her serviceman husband, Frank, both framed (like the wedding picture on the wall) by the
bedroom door of the house that they share with Laura's mother, aunt,
and brother. Above the streets of downtown Baltimore, just before closing time at nine on a Thursday night, Collins again catches the shoppers
and cinemagoers—some men, but mostly women—crowding the neon-
lit commercial district. But she is also at St. Mark's Place and the Bowery
at midnight, in a different mood, on a dark and deserted corner, surprising three men standing by a car parked under a street light. In Washington, D.C., December 1943, in a cramped kitchen, Esther Bubley gets
a picture of a happy Lynn Massman, "wife of a second class petty officer
who is studying in Washington" who, herself, "does the washing every
morning," keeping an eye out for the baby straining to push up at the
edge of the kitchen table and the edge of the photograph. But Bubley
also files "Girl sitting alone in the Sea Grill, a bar and restaurant, waiting for a pickup." The woman sits at a corner table alone with a drink,
smoking, beneath the neon sign that says "on tap," backwards. We look
at her. A man looks sharply at us through the window and the Venetian
blinds, just behind her head. Bubley's file-mount caption adds dialogue
to the film-noir scene: "I come in here pretty often, sometimes alone,
mostly with another girl, we drink beer, and talk, and of course we keep
our eyes open you'd be surprised at how often nice, lonesome, soldiers
ask Sue, the waitress to introduce them to us."[15]

What we see here, too, is that attention was being turned—at least,
around the edges of workaday projects—to the effect the war was having
on the social economy of sexual difference, whose erosion was now seen
not as destructive, degrading, and *defeminizing*, as was so often the case

in the picturing of the crisis of the 1930s, but as positive and productive—as *expanding the possibilities of difference*. The transformation is strikingly marked in two images by Dorothea Lange. In 1937, photographing for the FSA in a California labor contractor's camp, near Calipatria, Lange had seen only the degradation of difference in the figure of a migrant woman from Indiana, pushed to the edge, compelled to "root, hog, or

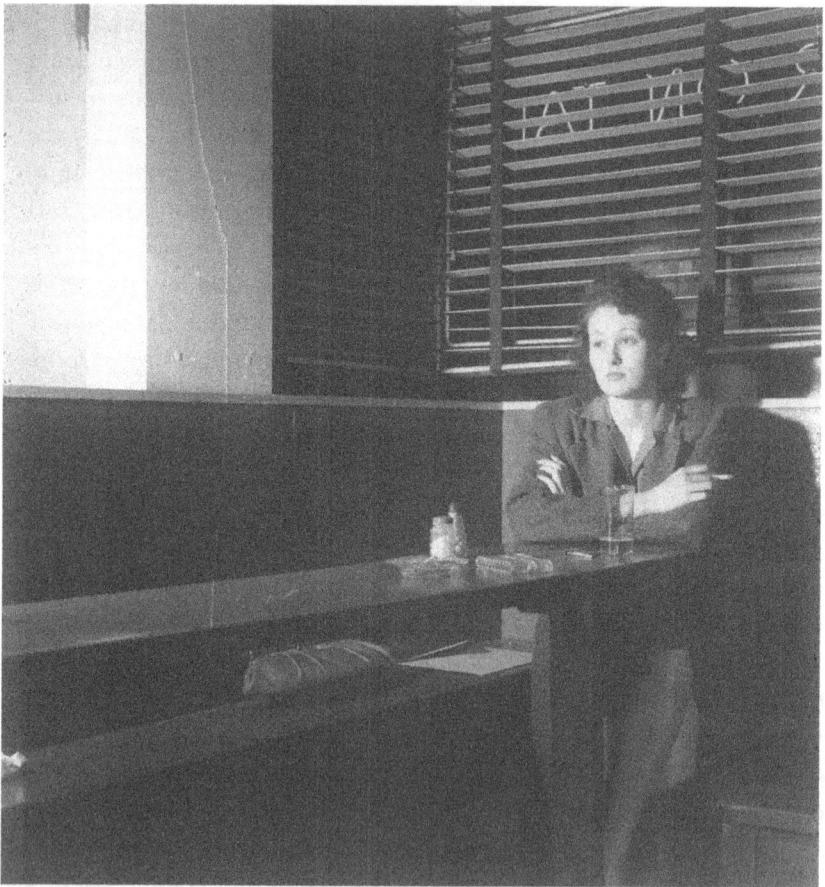

Figure 44. Esther Bubley, for the Office of War Information, "Washington, D.C.: Girl sitting alone in the Sea Grill, a bar and restaurant, waiting for a pickup. 'I come in here pretty often, sometimes alone, mostly with another girl, we drink beer, and talk, and of course we keep our eyes open you'd be surprised at how often nice, lonesome, soldiers ask Sue, the waitress to introduce them to us,'" April 1943. FSA-OWI Collection, Prints and Photographs Division, Library of Congress (LC-USW3-021005-E).

die," the very form of her body lost to work and borrowed clothes in which she would never be at home. Five years later, on a sidewalk outside a grocery in Richmond, California, what Lange encounters is the laid-back but unapologetic confidence of identity on the move, worn as a hard-earned badge by the shipyard worker shopping in her hard hat and overalls and clutching a wrapped pot of budding lilies to her side.[16]

The play of power scored into the spaces, codes, and bodily signs that were brought under scrutiny here, also, of course, implicated the spaces and codes of documentary photography itself: its gendered pleasures and meanings, its modus operandi, its habits of looking and forms of address, its ritual tropes and routine ways of positioning its subjects. Ironically enough, in the last months of Stryker's department, as the New Deal agency played out its mandate and as the Historical Section's photographers were increasingly pulled into more didactic and more explicitly directed war-service work, the FSA files began to accession uncelebrated photographs that worked away at the edges of the documentary genre, disturbing its mechanics of identification, unsettling its imbrication of vision, truth, and power. Such a project was not to be seen again, perhaps, until the feminist interventions in documentary and street photography of the 1970s and 1980s, above all in the work of Martha Rosler and Connie Hatch.[17] In 1943, it was a project that would be summarily curtailed, when the initiatives of the Work Projects Administration, the Farm Security Administration, and their photographic units were finally abolished. The moment of documentary was over.

The women photographers of the Farm Security Administration and the Office of War Information did not, of course, "return home," any more than "Rosie the Riveter" did in 1945. What they returned to was, rather, the familiar gendered hierarchy of professional employment. They continued to work as photographers, if they could—some, like Bubley, McMillan Roberts, and Rosskam, with their old FSA boss, Roy Stryker, now under the corporate patronage of Standard Oil (New Jersey).[18] But most found it difficult, if not impossible, to secure places in the professionalized fraternities of photojournalism and the military, even in the face of the fact that women photographers such as Margaret Bourke-White and Lee Miller flew harrowing missions and were among the first photographers to enter occupied Germany and confront the horror of the death camps.[19]

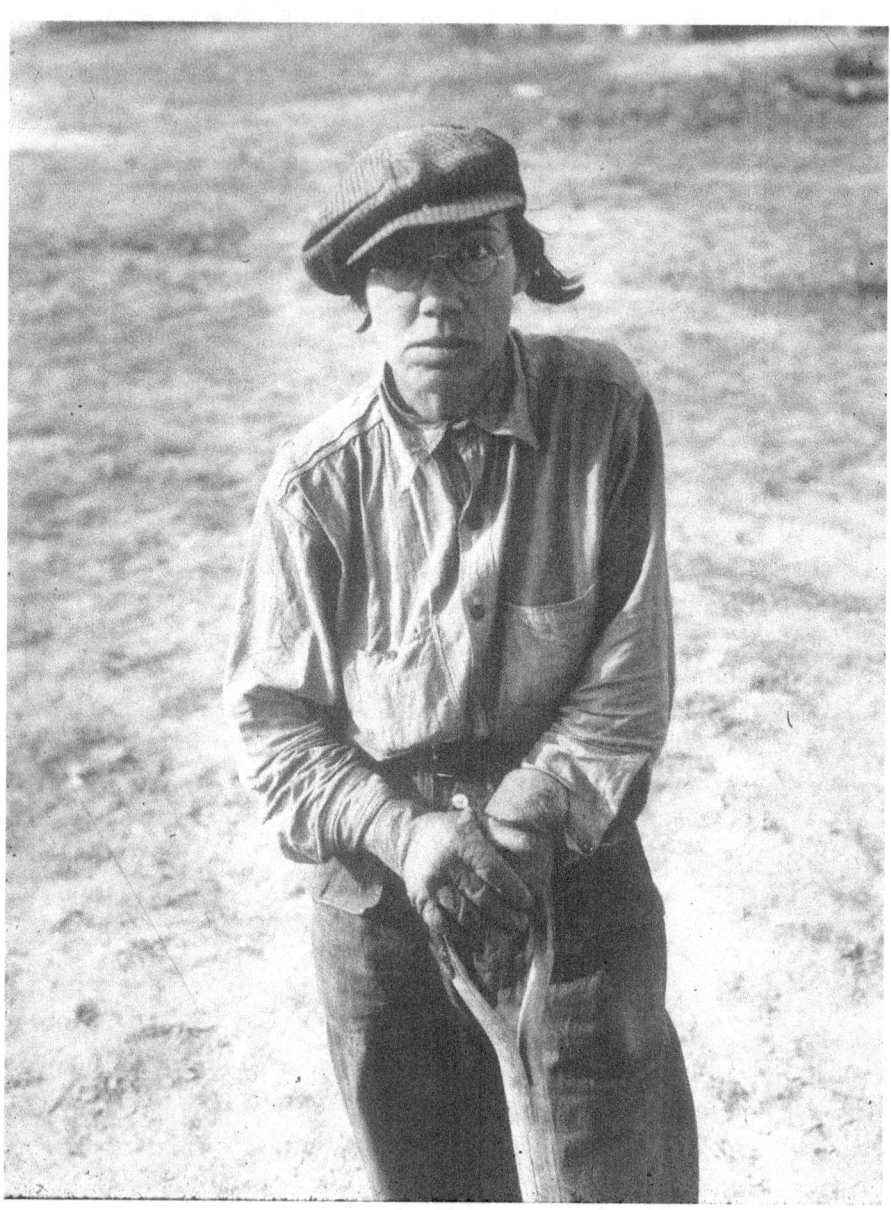

Figure 45. Dorothea Lange, "Calipatria (vicinity), California: Native of Indiana in a migratory labor contractor's camp. 'It's root, hog, or die for us folks,'" February 1937. FSA-OWI Collection, Prints and Photographs Division, Library of Congress (LC-USF34-016119-C).

The experience of women in professional photography therefore followed the pattern for other women workers who had temporarily benefited from shifting opportunities in the wartime workforce. Women workers in the war industries did not return to the home in large numbers when the enlisted men came back from war. What they largely went back to was business as usual: the prewar sexual division of labor, as marked in the socialized domestic work of the service sector and in the

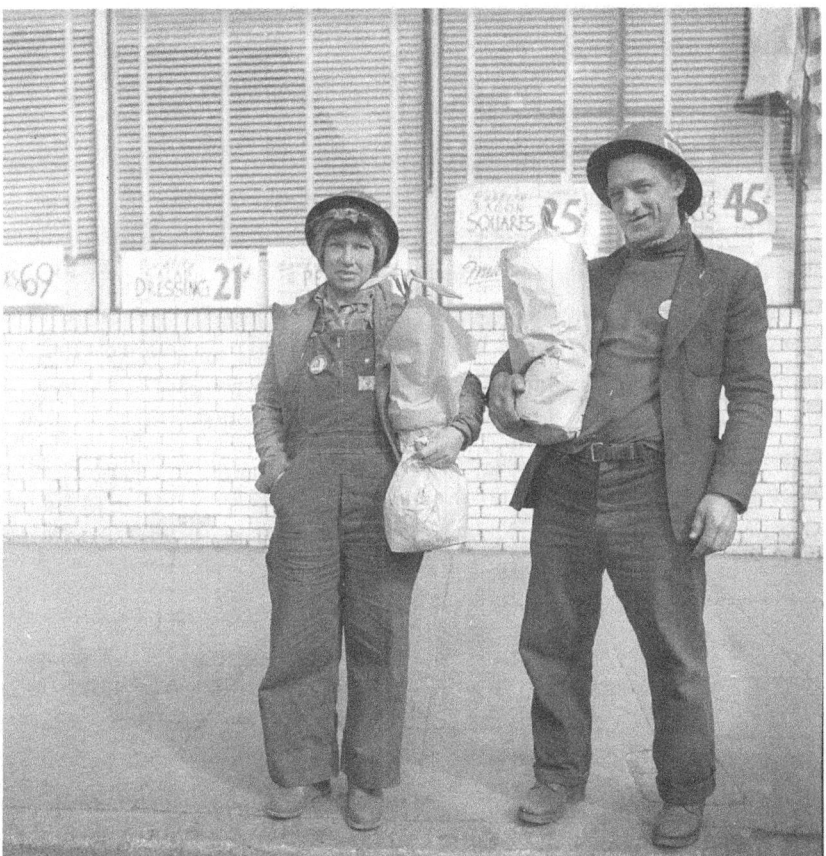

Figure 46. Dorothea Lange, "Consumers, Spring 1942." Published as "Richmond, California/1942" in Dorothea Lange and Paul Schuster Taylor, *An American Exodus: A Record of Human Erosion in the Thirties* (New Haven, Conn., and London: Yale University Press, 1969), 120. Copyright the Dorothea Lange Collection, Oakland Museum of California, City of Oakland. Gift of Paul S. Taylor.

gender hierarchy of office work. Not even the climbing postwar birth-rate, pop psychology, or the chronic lack of childcare could reverse the direction of female participation in the workforce. The removal that took place was not, therefore, of women workers but of their claims to status and of the threat their visible presence posed for the fixities of gender difference. And if this meant an economic repositioning of working women and a reclosing of the sexual politics of the workplace, then it also demanded a *cultural* displacement—a renegotiation at the level of representation, traced in advertising, popular culture, and public-service messages. After a moment of resistance, we are entering a decidedly different conjuncture.

Let us keep it at bay a while longer, however, and hang on for a moment to this unexpected image of an elated young man, immaculately dressed in a well-brushed fedora, high-collared shirt, hip-tight drape coat, and full-cut, narrow-cuffed pants, conscious of every meaning he is making on the street. The photograph was made by the unofficial Farm Security Administration photographer Louise Rosskam outside the Savoy Ballroom in Harlem, probably in 1940. It is arresting for many of the reasons I have spoken about concerning the gendered politics of space and meaning, interrupted here by Rosskam's typical determination to "catch all the peripheral stuff that was going on," "all those little moments that you don't plan."[20] But the image is also striking for what it signals and for what it does, here on the page.

The picture was selected by Edwin Rosskam, along with eighty-seven other photographs, nearly all from the files of the Farm Security Administration, for incorporation into a book layout that sought to parallel the textual flow of Richard Wright's "folk history," *12 Million Black Voices*.[21] The collaborative book was published in October 1941 and the photograph appears in Part Three, "Death on the City Pavements," in the context of an evocation of what Wright sees as an atavistic and compensatory culture of exclusion: "the surviving remnants of the culture of the South, our naïve, casual, verbal, fluid folk life."[22] But the figure from Harlem bursts out of Wright's homiletic voice-over narrative of the forced march from feudalism to urbanization, like the topical explosion of "Bombshell Values" in the store window to his right, or like the other, the white folk deny us these pursuits, and our hunger for expression finds its form in our wild, raw music, in our invention of slang that winds its way all over America. Our adoration of color goes not into murals, but into dress, into green, red, yellow, and blue clothes. When we have some money in our pockets on payday, our laughter and songs make the principal streets of our Black Belts—Lenox Avenue, Beale Street, State Street, South Street, Second Street, Auburn Avenue—famous the earth over.

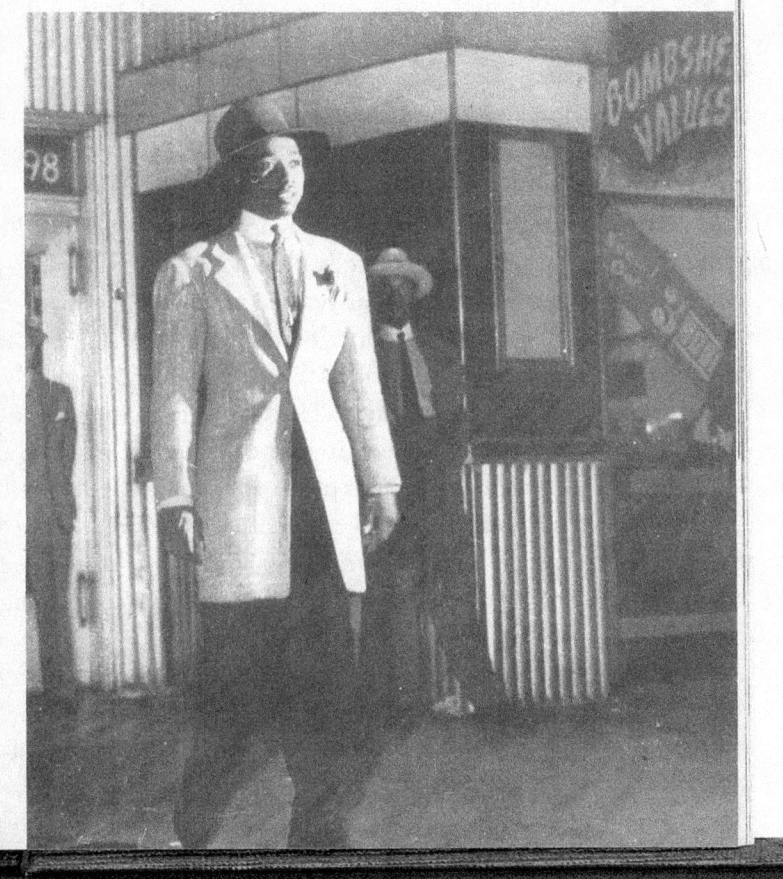

Figure 47. Louise Rosskam, "At the Savoy in Harlem, New York, N.Y.," from Richard Wright, *12 Million Black Voices: A Folk History of the Negro in the United States*, photo-direction *[sic]* by Edwin Rosskam (New York: Viking, 1941), 129. Reprinted by permission from Ani Rosskam.

three slender zoot-suiters in Ralph Ellison's *Invisible Man* who step, sway-ing stiffly, heels clicking rhythmically, out of the invisibility of the crowd in a Harlem subway and out of the design of history as conceived by the science of the Central Committee.[23] "Men of transition," Ellison calls them:[24] "men out of time," "stewards of something uncomfortable, bur-densome," "living outside the realm of history," "running and dodging the forces of history instead of making a dominating stand."[25] Here, too, just as it escapes Wright, this image evades documentary social history and the sermon on historical materialism. In its currency, in what it pic-tures, and in what it does within this text, it points to another crucial area in which the conflicting effects and uncontainable meanings of social transformations brought about by the mobilization for war upset the fix-ities of established culture and released dynamic forces that were, however, to be turned back and repressed again in the postwar reconversion.[26]

The fixing of the meaning of racial difference in the closures of the dominant culture was also to be profoundly destabilized by social dislo-cations that climbed to a peak in the war years. And the reaction was to be even more violent. The catalyst of change was the massive movement of rural populations into urban and industrialized areas—and, especially, the Great Migration of African Americans from the agricultural econo-mies of the South to the industrialized cities of the East Coast and the northern Midwest. This signaled the last phase of a profound economic transformation, but it also marked an unprecedented and unprepared-for alteration of social geography. In equal measure, however, it constituted a *cultural* event of enormous, unanticipated significance, with far-reaching implications for American culture—even though it is an event that has rarely been discussed in other than socioeconomic terms and that has never been seen in itself to fall within the horizons of histories of Amer-ican art, which have confined their attentions to more august migrants of the war years.[27]

Migrations had certainly been taking place since the beginning of the century. But they were crucially accelerated during the years of the Second World War. The figures are still staggering. After 1910, 6.5 million Black Americans moved north, but 5 million of these left after 1940.[28] Between 1940 and 1950, Mississippi alone lost one quarter of its total Black population, overwhelmingly to the cities of the north-central region, above all to Chicago.[29] Even so, the root causes of this accelerated mass migration lay in the 1930s, in the policies of the New Deal, which had otherwise offered little to African Americans in the South, studiously avoiding interference in what were described as "local" and "traditional" cultures of racial power, even in the face of swelling demands for an anti-lynching law.[30]

In 1930, 77 percent of African Americans still lived in the South; 49 percent in rural areas, eking out an existence in desperate poverty as agricultural laborers, sharecroppers, and tenant farmers, among the 8.5 million tenant families in the ten chief cotton-producing states.[31] The system of southern agriculture—dominated by the extremely labor-intensive culture of cotton—was already chronically affected by problems of underdevelopment and economic subordination to northern capital even before it was hit, in the 1920s, by a precipitous decline in prices and, in the 1930s, by an intensification of the crisis brought on by global overproduction. The bankruptcies of planters and the extreme hardship visited on tenants and sharecroppers marked the final trauma of a crop–lien system of agricultural production that could only be salvaged by fed-eral intervention. The response of the New Deal administration through the Agricultural Adjustment Acts of 1933 and 1938—was to introduce subsidies and to impose acreage limitations on cotton. But these mea-sures only worked to the advantage of large landowners, landlords, and commercial producers, who were able to use the subsidies and the profits from stabilized prices to capitalize the mechanization and land consoli-dation that changed the system of tenantry into one of large-scale, in-dustrialized agricultural capitalism. Both White and Black tenants and sharecroppers who had hung on were subsequently forced off the land in increasing numbers and were compelled either to move to the cities and towns or to become landless hired labor.[32]

Black tenant farmers and sharecroppers were hardest hit by the acreage reductions and the increasing monopolization of landholdings in the cotton states. The spread of mechanical cotton pickers and chem-ical weed-control methods removed even their remaining means of sup-port, forcing them into migration. And, since segregation and racism closed opportunities in southern towns and cities, migration northward presented itself as a last resort: They had nowhere else to go. It was not, then, the pull of high wages or the pull of life in the North but, rather, the pressures of segregation and the southern agricultural economy that pushed an evicted Black agricultural workforce to migrate to the kitchenettes of Washington, D.C., Chicago, Detroit, Cleveland, and the industrial cities of the Northeast, where they became surplus labor—a permanent, transplanted underclass.[33]

In the cities, in communities that doubled and trebled through migration in the 1940s and '50s, displaced African American workers were forced to compete for living space with a defensively solidified White working class that resented even minimal encroachments on overcrowded wartime amenities and a chronically limited public housing stock. At the same time, while Depression-era relief programs shrank, African Americans met persistent barriers of exclusion and discrimination in the expanding areas of federal employment and in government-funded war industries and training programs. As in the case of earlier New Deal programs, the Roosevelt administration's first inclination was to refuse to challenge what it called "traditional" practices and local "social patterns" or to risk upsetting southern Democrats in Congress by imposing antidiscrimination clauses in defense contracts.[34] Even after A. Philip Randolph's mobilization for an all-Black march on Washington in the summer of 1941 forced the issuing of Executive Order 8802, prohibiting discrimination in government and defense industries, an indifferent administration gave its own Fair Employment Practices Committee no effective powers of enforcement, subordinating it to manpower needs, while the U.S. Employment Service continued to accommodate "White only" requests from employers until September 1943.[35] In the armed forces, too, segregation, menial employment, and exclusion from positions of leadership remained the rule—even extending to the segregation of blood plasma for wartime combat troops.[36]

It was thus Roosevelt administration policies that both created the suddenly inflated problem of urban racial ghettos and exacerbated the racial tensions there. Even as the dangers became apparent, government remained ill prepared to meet the consequences and too concerned about unity and the war effort to care about making an issue of civil rights. For African Americans, therefore, two wars raged at the same time. As Richard Wright wrote in 1941:

life for us is daily warfare. . . . we live hard, like soldiers. We are set apart from the civilian population; our kitchenettes comprise our barracks; the color of our skins constitutes our uniforms; the streets of our cities are our trenches; a job is a pill-box to be captured and held; and the unions of white workers for a long time have formed the first line of resistance which we encounter. . . . We are always in battle, but the tidings of victory are few.[37]

Nineteen forty-three was a critical year. In June, Detroit erupted in bitter racial battles and, in August, riots swept through Harlem. Clearly, the racial divisions that White workers believed in but preferred to locate at a distance, in the South, were now exposed as a structural fact of the entire national culture.[38]

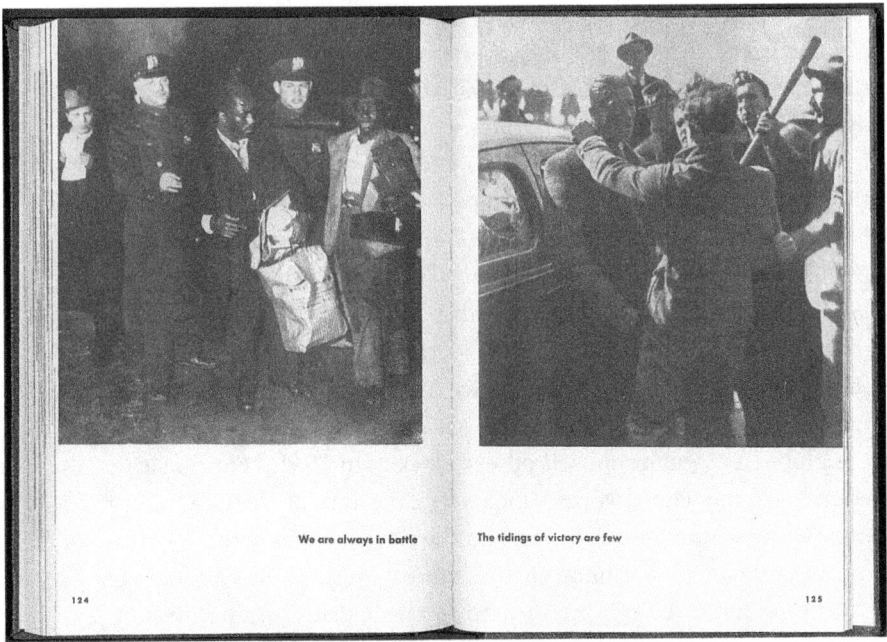

Figure 48. "Scene during Harlem Riots, New York, N.Y." and "Scene during the 'Ford Riots,' Dearborn, Michigan," from Richard Wright, *12 Million Black Voices: A Folk History of the Negro in the United States,* photo-direction *[sic]* by Edwin Rosskam (New York: Viking, 1941), 124–25.

Again, however, we should beware of the way this socioeconomic narrative, even as it runs through Wright's text, puts too negative a cast on a social transformation and the emergence of a new urban community whose cultural self-assertion was neither passive nor subordinated. What I mean is that it was out of this transplanting of an African American, southern, rural, and religious cultural pattern into the doubly diasporic urban spaces of Chicago, Detroit, and the industrial Northeast that there emerged the knowing and inventive hybrid forms of a new and distinctive cultural formation.

In the course of the Great Migration, already-elaborated African American cultural practices—practices of language, oratory, oral narration, music, dress, dance, movement, gesture, and bodily stylization—were transposed to spaces that, in themselves, were already cut across by a century's development of distinctive urban, working-class, postethnic cultures, going back at least to the Bowery Boys and Gals of New York in the 1850s.[39] In this transposition, existing cultural lines were rewritten, remixed, and reelaborated. What emerged was not a relapse into the feverish folk culture of the South, as Wright would have it, but a new urban Black cultural repertoire whose vocabularies, stylistic tropes, rhythms, and intensities were to be endlessly varied in postwar subcultures. So something else was initiated in this process, too: On the one hand, new and complex languages of difference defined a dynamic field of Black identity; on the other hand, it was also these languages—the languages of a doubly displaced and dispossessed African American working class, a so-called permanent underclass—that, as we know, largely furnished the formative structures of a postwar American popular culture that was not only distributed nationally but also exported around the globe. As Wright himself observed, even in 1941, "our music makes the feet of the whole world dance, even the feet of the children of the poor white workers who live beyond the line that marks the boundary of our lives. Where we cannot go, our tunes, songs, slang, and jokes go."[40]

One might be tempted to see in this cultural traffic nothing but a process of co-optation, incorporation, and absorption—and, undoubtedly, the expanding market for cultural consumer goods was coming to depend on a process of commodification of everyday life that reversed the earlier, downward semiotic flow of popular taste, by drawing its impetus and aura of authenticity from the inventiveness of marginalized cultures. Yet there was always a remainder in this process: an excess beyond what could be wholly appropriated or subsumed. Indeed, it was a central technique of emergent urban cultures that they consciously defined themselves in the domain of consumption, taking over commodities for unincorporated systems of meaning. And within such systems, the terms of identity were pluralized and de-essentialized: Not only was "Blackness" unfixed as a signifier that the dominant culture industries both desired and repudiated, both incorporated and expelled; but it was also a hybrid and multiply differentiated sign whose mobility destabilized the essentialist fixity on which the entire field of racial identities and racial cultures depended.[41] It is no surprise, then, that the reaction within the dominant regime of racial difference was disturbed and ambivalent, giving vent to violence and fascination in equal measure.

We see the same thing in the reaction to the unabashed culture of young urban Chicanos in wartime California. In June 1943, while Detroit burned and the relief structures of the New Deal were going up in smoke in Washington, White servicemen rolled out of the port of Los Angeles to bring the violence of their racial insecurities to the streets of downtown.[42] White men putting their hands on brown men's bodies, beating them, stripping them naked, urinating on their clothes: Repeated over several nights, it was a mundane and extraordinary performance of ambivalent, regressive rage and desire. What—we might ask—does the White man want?

A shoulder-padded, finger-length coat in an eye-catching color, with wide lapels. Draped pants with reat-pleats, ballooning to the knee then narrowing tightly at the ankle—good for wearing with a looping chain and double-soled shoes, balanced by a narrow-brimmed lid or hat. The ostensible cause of the riot was a jacket and a pair of trousers—a suit of clothes that we have met before, outside the Savoy in Harlem: the zoot suit, whose excessive rhetoric and more than ample use of cloth were read by White public culture as symptoms of a degenerate and dangerously sexualized gang culture and a slap in the face of patriotic White servicemen.[43] More accurately, the zoot suit was a performance of a racial difference that would not stay in its place.

Like the Black youth of Georgia and Harlem, with whom they exchanged style cues, the young pachucos and pachucas of East Los Angeles knew what they were putting on. Their clothes, like their hairstyles
and their dances, made meanings with their bodies. For White culture,
they made these bodies hateful and desirable. They made them visible.
And above all, they made them readable in a way that had to be denied
and recoded. This is not to suggest that there was ever a fixed and final
reading attached to the clothing, outside a specific moment, framework,
and intervention, or that the space of identity it described was ever
homogeneous or resolved. The point is that the meanings the clothes
made were *not* unreadable to the cultures they inflamed but that claimed
to find them incomprehensible. You could not miss a zoot suit in the

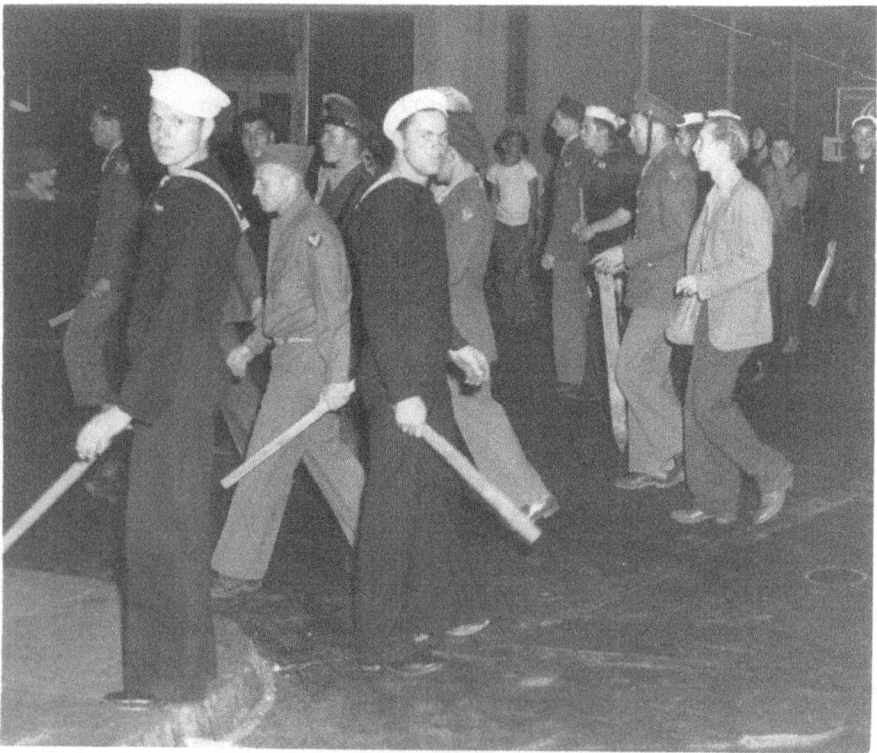

Figure 49. "U.S. armed forces personnel with wooden clubs on street during 'zoot suit'
riot, Los Angeles, CA, 1943." Library of Congress, Prints and Photographs Division,
Visual Materials from the NAACP Records (LC-USZ62-75515).

street. But not only there. It stood out in a discursive space the pachuco and pachuca extended around them: a third space, between the dualities of rural and urban, Eastside and Westside, Mexican and American, and, arguably, feminine and masculine. It was not pure negation, then, as Octavio Paz would later have it;[44] not even *mestizo*, half and half, but a greater and unbounded *mestizaje*: a new space—a new field of identity.[45]

The zoot suit was an assemblage—the product of a strategy of meaning that remained intransigent to monolingual readings. As a language of affirmation, it worked not by nostalgic return to an imaginary original authenticity but by appropriation, transgression, recombination, breaking, and restructuring the laws of grammar and usage—as in the pachucos' cross-cultural argot of *Caló* and *pochismos*, as in their stylizations of body, gesture, hair, tattoos, and dance, and as in the iconography of their *placas* that kept order in the space of the street, the barrio, and the city.[46] These were the components of a complex, hybrid culture that took over elements whose meanings had been fixed in binary oppositions—Mexican/American, brown/White, working-class/middle-class, rural/urban, traditional/modern, masculine/feminine—and remixed their connotations to shape a new urban identity that was as offensive to "Mexican" as to "American" culture.

The culture of the zooters refused subordination in the racial hierarchy of national culture and of national cultures. It was a culture neither of assimilation nor of separatism and, as such, it constituted a challenge both to the essentialism of segregation and to the homogenization of the melting pot. It was a culture that did not know its place. It wanted to be neither "inside" nor "outside"; it wanted instead to rupture their structures of otherness. It therefore outraged not only uniformed patriots and a racist press but also pillars of the community on both sides of the Mexican American border. Each side saw but refused to recognize a new, unplaceable space. Each named it delinquent, while blaming the pachuco's corruption on contamination by the other side of the border. Displaced from both, pachucos and pachucas sought to make an identity as unplaceable as the space they inhabited: the space, as Gloria Anzaldúa says, of "those who cross over."[47]

This is not, of course, to deny that pachucas and pachucos operated on historical and political grounds, that they negotiated changing

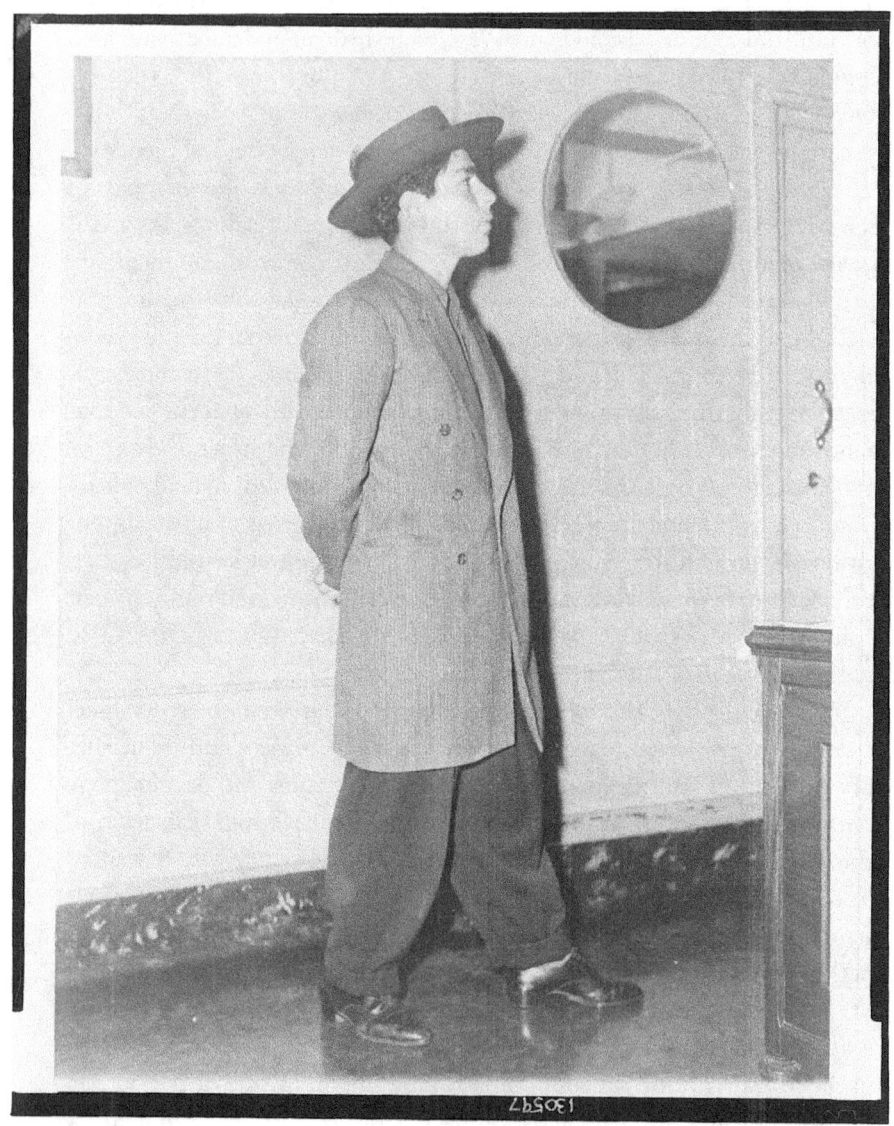

Figure 50. "Frank H. Tellez, 22, who is held on a vagrancy charge, models a zoot suit and pancake hat in a Los Angeles County jail on June 9, 1943." Photograph courtesy of AP Images/John T. Burns.

conditions of urban working-class life, family structure, and employment, or that they found their opportunity in the emerging patterns of a new cross-national and intercultural economy, as war work brought the promise of affluence, consumer credit, and changed patterns of labor and consumption. It is not to deny that they were touched by the desire for the beyond of an impossible transcendence, by that sad optimism and nostalgia for the future that is the pathos of modernism. It is to suggest that their interlingual strategy of identity and resistance was a strategy of the border and will not accommodate to the old homilies or the new historicisms.[48]

For those who wore the zoot suit, it was not a question of discovering, beneath the structures of domination, an innate individual and collective identity that could be safeguarded and cultivated until the political moment for its emergence. Pachuco culture was a survival strategy not of purity, of saying *less*, but, rather, of saying *more*, of saying too much, with the wrong accent and intonation, of mixing the metaphors, making illegal crossings, and continually transforming cultural languages so that their effects might never be wholly assimilable to an essential ethnicity, to a "social ecology" of delinquency, or to the spectacle of multiculturalism and commodified diversity.[49] Against these closures, the zoot suit offered another narration of identity: one that asserted a difference yet could not be safely absorbed into the pleasures of a global marketing culture; one that located its different voice yet would not take a stand on the unmoving ground of a defensive fundamentalism; one that spoke its location as more than local yet made no claim to universality for its viewpoint or language; one that knew the border but still crossed the line. Like the great Aztec god Xipe Totec, the zoot-suiters flayed the bodies of two cultures and renewed themselves by a change of skin.

I say this in all awareness of what was to follow, from the mass-marketed "Bold Look" of 1948 to the "updating" of the pachuco in the 1970s as hero of cultural nationalism.[50] I am aware of this history of re-tailoring but see in it no reason to think that anything had been conclusively refuted or resolved. A final truth was not hidden in the drapes like a knife, waiting to be unveiled. The meaning of the zoot suit could not be settled later, any more than, in 1943, it could be reduced to docility and definitively spoken for by contemporary police documentation and the findings of criminal psychology.[51] In the face of this bodily scrutiny and coercive reading, the resistance of the zoot suit was specific. It made the moves it had to make to cause a particular stir in a specific field of institutions, instruments, and codings that constituted the plural relations of racial power. It made its moves and it met resistance, though this did not mean it was utterly annulled. Beyond that, no one said the suit was made to last forever. And on the street, no one wants to wear a museum piece, anyway.

On the other hand, the suit had not quite become that yet. There was still good wear in the hand-me-down, and its provocations of meaning were not worn thin beyond use. Certainly, the postwar menswear industry was glad to get its hands on it. But that does not mean that a single, unambiguous construction can be put on the fact that the semiotics and the erotics of the zoot suit were to be appropriated, reduced, and formalized in a commodity sold to the very suburbs to which the White rioters of 1943 began to retreat after 1945. When it comes to meaning, does commodification always wear the trousers? Does it totally consume the play of the sign?[52] Or, alternatively, in an equally fatalistic account, does the work of the code dissipate and come to nothing? Are its threads burst apart by the obesity of simulation?[53] Was the mass-produced zoot suit simply a sellout? What else was bought in what Kobena Mercer has called these "skirmishes of appropriation and commodification played out around the semiotic economy of the ethnic signifier"?[54]

In a system of commodity production in which, *pace* Marx, coats can be and are exchanged for coats,[55] at an ever-intensified pace, the process of reproduction and absorption that drives the economy may well be a process of expropriation, disenfranchisement, and disavowal. But it is also, at once, a process that highlights the destabilizing presence of unassimilable difference in a homogenizing capitalist popular culture that is dangerously dependent on the unincorporated for its ability to grow and remain effective. The possibilities of resistance opened by the zoot suit exploited a social restructuring that had to juggle the imposition of an increasingly integrated, authoritarian order and the irreconcilable dynamic of a system of commodity production that could not expand without destabilizing itself socially and culturally through its dependence on the very proliferation of differences that it could never wholly contain.

In the midst of the political reversals of the 1940s, it was this unstable dynamic that afforded opportunities that would have been ungraspable in the agendas of 1930s forms of cultural radicalism, even had they persisted. The political calculations of the zoot suit did not, therefore, have to wait for one of those "moments of transparency" that Stuart Hall, in his classic discussion of *Picture Post*, believed to characterize "moments of revolutionary transformation or of deep crisis"—moments in which, as Hall put it, "the roots of social experience are rendered socially visible" and this "*social* transparency" is then translated into "a *visual* and *symbolic* transparency."[56] In a sense, Hall's notion of the revolutionary moment is, here, only an echo of the politics of representation of documentary itself. What the displacement of documentary in the period of great intercultural migrations shows, however, is that the rhetoric of transparency could yield nothing where what were called for were the tactics of muddy waters.[57]

CHAPTER 5

The Pencil of History:
Photography, History, Archive

> What is at issue here . . . is the violence of the archive itself, *as archive, as archival violence.*
>
> —JACQUES DERRIDA, *Archive Fever: A Freudian Impression*

Records, recruitments, riots, and resistance: The line I have drawn must seem to be one we can scarcely break off at the point I have designated "1943." The line plots a path one might well feel compelled to extend through other points—1965, 1992—that stand like names, like markers in the ground, not least in the Los Angeles we have just left. But, for now, I want to make the line of argument double back on itself, double back not only on photography but also on the question of the disciplinary mechanisms of history and art history, which I raised in the introduction and chapter 1 but have since left in suspension, as if the themes we have been discussing did not weigh upon this question too. So now I want to loop back, even at the risk of being oblique.

My chapter heading, at least, promises something with a definite point. And indeed, at the outset, I had hopes it would lead to something sharp and clearly drawn. But again, I find myself breaking off and wanting to say something before I begin. Of course, it is already too late for that. And what would it serve to say that, before beginning, I want to draw out something of the history of the remarks I am about to make, to draw back to an original context: a conference in Milwaukee whose very title, Visual Culture: Film/Photography/History, by a tempting addition of terms, seemed to project a way beyond both the daunting recent debates on "visual culture" and the internalized worlds of film and photo theory. Here "History" is set alongside "Film" and "Photography," opening "Visual Culture" with a slash to a luminous horizon in which research can free itself from narrow confinement in the claustrophobic spaces of theoretical introspection. In such an expansive light, one might do better, perhaps, than be distracted by what are little better than specks—quite marked, certainly, yet not pronounced: two dots and two dashes; unspoken codings that join the terms of the conference title as in a syllogism yet dissect them, silently dividing the rubric within itself, leaving the trace of a deep uncertainty and an unresolved incoherence.

Perhaps it is better to be distracted than to be caught. Though even before I arrived in Milwaukee, I seemed to be hooked on one particular line and what it set in place: "Photography" on one side, "History" on the other; text and context reunited, at a stroke. Yet what is going on here and now? What happens when I seek to delineate a historical setting for my remarks and say, in the process, that I have not yet crossed the line and begun? What happens when one conjoins photography and history by drawing a line between them: a line of a certain thickness, a slash that scars where the pure cut ought to have healed, a slanted conjunction that seems to have no choice but to incline to the right. I am suddenly reminded of Karl Werkmeister praising the exhaustive documentary rigor of Nazi art-world informants while insisting that Marxist art history *means* objective, documentary history, and of Thomas Crow reviewing Donald Preziosi's *Rethinking Art History* and calling contemptuously for a return from "tertiary texts" to "primary sources" and to the discipline of the archive.[1] These are positively striking conclusions for a certain kind of Marxist social history of art to have reached. They repeat the gesture of division and restoration, even as they enact a telling reconciliation with the deep-seated protocols of the academic institution of history. In all events, these gestures, too, must be in play here, if not as a context for a chapter that has not yet started, then certainly as part of its polemical field.

It is the summons to History and the appeal to "the discipline of the archive" that bring Werkmeister and Crow to mind at this point, alongside Milwaukee and the insertion of the oblique. This is an appeal that has become familiar by now in these pages as a gesture of authority, of power, secured by an entire structure of regulation. The invocation of discipline and archive takes us back to earlier arguments about instrumental discourse, the development of practices of photographic documentation, and the powers invested in them and realized through them, framed as these arguments were by questions of the "New Art History" and "the politics of representation." These were arguments, therefore, that I did not intend to leave in the nineteenth century. I also wanted them to intrude on that enduring temptation, the claim of "the Left," of "concerned documentary" and of "ideology critique" to take a stand on the Real, against the impositions of power to which the Real is always, supposedly, vulnerable.

For a telling example of this, one needs to think back no further than the time frame of the Milwaukee conference I have already invoked: April 1992—a time, it may be recalled, when the incontrovertible photographic evidence of the pinpoint bombing of Iraq in the First Gulf War was beginning to be hedged about by the belated hesitancy of the Pentagon's expert readers, and when the incontrovertible photographic evidence of the beating of Rodney King in Los Angeles County was beginning to be shown, by lawyers for the defense, to be the very model of a process of *semiosis* and a sliding of the signifier that might well take with it any jury caught in its path. At that time, between the burning of Baghdad and the burning of Los Angeles, it was only too tempting to welcome one demise of evidence and damn the other. What could be more compelling than a politics of conviction grounded on the externality of final truths to systems of power and on the inherent evidentiality of the unmanipulated photographic record? Yet the fate of the Rodney King videotape when it twice came to trial showed only that what was at stake was not evidence of reality but the reality of evidence: the institutional struggle around the production of the real and the true. The camera itself was wagered in this struggle. It could not bring the struggle to a halt. It offered no shortcut to a space beyond dispute. For the evidence of the image, there was no escaping the long trek across the more uncertain ground of the conditions of witness, the status of documentation, and the politics of disputable meanings.

A paradox is at work, of course, in all political appropriations of visual images that want, in effect, to avoid at all costs a *politics of the image*. But it is a paradox, I have tried to suggest, with definite yields, insofar as it can be institutionally contained and sustained. From the slums of Quarry Hill in late nineteenth-century Leeds to the racial ghetto of South Central Los Angeles, from the bomb sites of residential Baghdad to the pastoral spaces of Edwardian Surrey, a deep play of power is heavily staked on what, more than 150 years ago in *The Pencil of Nature*, William Henry Fox Talbot called "the mute testimony" of the photograph, with its promise of "evidence of a novel kind."[2]

What I want to suggest too, however, is that we should also not forget how much is riding on the economy of this "testimony" and all that supports it for the discipline of History. For even where they eschew any general doctrine of history, practices of historical investigation still rest their claims to truth on protocols and hierarchies of *evidence*. However pragmatic, however preoccupied with the seemingly modest questions of professional technique, such practices therefore cannot escape their own conditionality. For the court of appeal of History, as for photography, the status of evidence is always on the line. And, if recent work on photography has opened up the apparatus to expose the cliché of the evidential status of the photograph, what abyss of uncertainty opens in History through the door of a "history" of evidence or, indeed, of a "history" of the archive—the archive of history, the archive that constitutes History?

But I am getting ahead of myself. I ought to begin.

"The same century," Roland Barthes reminds us, "invented History and Photography."[3] "Invented" is a fulcrum here: These two formidable apparatuses—"History," capital *H*, and "Photography," capital *P*—these two steam-age engines of representation, are given to us as inventions, devices, machines of meaning, built in the same epoch, within the same code, in the same epistemological space, part of the engineering of the same positivist regime of sense, under the sign of the Real. Yet such a loaded reading rests too much on the coding of capitalization. It asks Barthes's twin capitals to carry a burden that is, at once, overloaded and insubstantial: a weight of meaning that is monolithic yet hollow.

As Stephen Bann has shown in *The Clothing of Clio*, the forms of nineteenth-century historical imagination—and by this he is referring only to what can be found in Germany, Britain, and France—were multiple and complex. To confine history to the professional practice of history as an academic discipline would therefore constitute an unwarranted narrowing that would fail to see the play of devices and strategies—of what Bann calls a "historical poetics"[4]—across a "vast and sprawling domain, which extends from historiography proper, through historical novels to visual art, spectacle and the historical museum."[5] Indeed, even within academic historiography, the rhetoric of historical representation was more heterodox and strategically varied than has been suggested by the reading of Leopold von Ranke's famous injunction—"to show how, essentially, things happened"—as the exhaustive program of a positivist "new history." If the demand for authenticity and authentication was persistently renewed throughout the nineteenth century, then it provoked the development of a range of quite different representational possibilities, just as later it invoked an ingeniously diverse array of responses to the equally persistent effects of doubt and irony.

So, too, with photography: What Barthes's sentence presents as a general domain was—as we have seen in earlier chapters—a field of differences elaborated over time, as a technology of sense was specified and multiplied in discursive regimes that had to be embedded, institutionalized, and enforced in processes we have hardly yet begun to understand. And if, across these diversified fields of historical representations and heterogeneous photographies, there were multiple points of contact and convergence—from the facsimile to the souvenir, from the record to the tableau—then the statuses of these hybrid historical-cum-photographic forms had to be secured in local negotiations, as the customized mechanisms of two adaptive machines were coupled and bolted together to generate new powers of meaning.

The discursive fields of history and photography are not, therefore, reducible to ponderous unities that we can wheel into action *or* into the breaker's yard, where we can flex our muscles dismantling "the nineteenth century's" baleful bequest. It is necessary to insist on this before we turn to consider the strategic attempt to embed the status of history and photography in the uncontestable denotative ground of the document and evidence. The closing of the rhetoric of historiography at the level of the fact and the closing of the meaning of the photograph at the level of its indexicality have operated in fields of historical and photographic discourse they have never saturated. Whatever their ambitions, they have remained local ploys, whose grounds have always been in dispute.

Let us head for the local, then, to see how, in particular, the line has been drawn or erased between a practice of "History" and a practice of "Photography." In 1916, in London, Messrs. H. D. Gower, L. Stanley Jast, and W. W. Topley—respectively survey secretary, former curator, and treasurer of the Photographic Survey and Record of Surrey—published what they called "a handbook to photographic record work for those who use a camera and for survey and record societies."[6] More succinctly, they titled their work *The Camera as Historian*. It is a promising starting point, though I make no "historical" claims for it. We are no longer, of course, in the century to which Barthes was referring. However, Gower, Jast, and Topley's book could certainly be read against half a century of photographic survey work in Britain, going back sporadically to the 1850s and 1860s but gathering momentum among amateur survey societies in the late 1880s.[7] Indeed, the book itself is dedicated to the late Sir

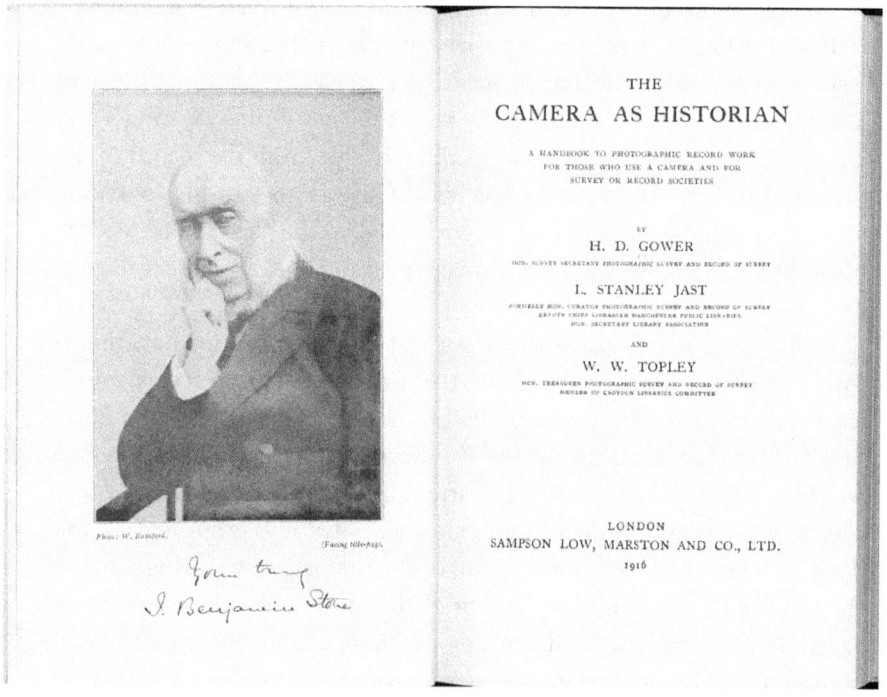

Figure 51. Photograph of Sir J. Benjamin Stone and title page of H. D. Gower, L. Stanley Jast, and W. W. Topley, *The Camera as Historian* (London: Sampson Low, Marston, 1916).

J. Benjamin Stone, M.P., founder in 1897 of the National Photographic Record Survey and, in the words of the dedication, "during his lifetime the greatest personal force in the movement for Photographic Record."[8]

The term "movement" is significant here. Yet in presenting their own work, the authors were sure: "This is the first attempt to deal with the subject in a volume."[9] Whether this claim is justifiable or not could be said to be a matter of record. The book's catalog of photographic survey and record activities—primarily in Britain, but also in Belgium, Germany, and the United States—was, however, admittedly partial and selective. Even so, Gower, Jast, and Topley had set themselves to give us something "honest" and practical and if, as a manifesto for a "movement," it was belated, then nevertheless it was a manifesto that strove to be all the more powerful for having the function of a modest and eminently practical manual that simply and without any fuss "collated" and "conserved" what common sense knew and experience had elaborated.[10]

It is, then, the banality of the text that is its interest. And this is not only a matter of its exemplary attention to the microlevel of bureaucratic technique and its unabashed resolve to speak about the smallest details of method, materials, rules, and equipment. We might, indeed, be grateful for this and hesitate to condescend toward the utter seriousness with which the authors hold their office. But the book's tone is also part of the machinery of a particular effect that goes beyond its clubbish earnestness.

The presentation of historical investigation as a modest set of techniques and protocols, calling on no general doctrine or philosophical schema, is crucial to the sense that, in the practical craft of history, theoretical decision is not in play. All we have is a practice that turns on what Lynn Hunt has called "the connoisseurship of documentary evidence,"[11] within which a certain regimen of photography can then be mobilized. Yet, as in the rules and practices of common law, which developed in parallel to the techniques of professional history, the claim to produce and evaluate evidence is a philosophically powerful one, which—as Mark Cousins has argued—profoundly privileges the notion of the event as a singular entity, present in time, whose existence it is the task of historical investigation to establish.[12] However, while legal categories and rules of evidence constitute truth as what may be argued, judged, and appealed in terms of the mode of instantiation of acknowledged law, historical practice and rules of historical verification exceed even this enforced litigation in their claim to delimit and exhaust the events of the past as having only one mode of existence.[13] In the framework of modest technique, what the eventhood of the event consists in is decided in advance, and in this decision without theory, the action of the discursive regime in which eventhood is inscribed—the regime of history—is placed beyond dispute.

This takes us back to what common sense knows: that, as the authors of *The Camera as Historian* put it, "the claim of photographic record to superiority over all other forms of graphic record is incontestable."[14] Later, we shall see that, as in other spheres of documentation, this "superiority" proves in need of the most careful protection by organizational rules and archival protocols, but it is the unquestioned point of departure. What it is taken to provide is a self-evident measure of the failures of earlier illustrations, such as those in the Pugins' *Examples of Gothic Architecture*, to accomplish the aim of displaying "every subject exactly as it exists."[15] (The echoes of Ranke's dictum in this quotation from Pugin and Pugin are pointed here and are not in themselves to be called into question.) Yet, in breaking through the limits to "absolute fidelity"[16] inherent in drafting techniques, photography is also understood to continue to capitalize on a more general power that is taken to reside in all techniques of *visualization*:

> The means whereby the past, particularly in its relation to human activities and their results, may be reconstructed and visualized, can be roughly grouped under the four headings of material objects, oral tradition, written record, and lastly, graphic record, whether pictorial or sculptural. It is no part of our purpose to belittle the value of any of the first-named tools of the historian or the scientist; but it will probably be conceded that in many respects the last named has a value greatly outweighing the others.[17]

Since the a priori aim is "visualization," one cannot help feeling that the odds were stacked against material culture, oral tradition, and written record. But this aside, we are not dealing with a new theme: It haunts the nineteenth-century historical imagination and disturbs the security of historical writing from the early years of the century. What moves the argument is a sense of loss, against which images—on condition they are also "correct representations"[18]—are attributed a capacity to arrest the decay of the present and vivify the resurrection of the past. In the words of the artist and antiquarian Charles Alfred Stothard: "To history they give a body and a substance, by placing before us those things which language is deficient in describing."[19]

Curiously enough, Stothard is describing the flattened engravings of funerary monuments that illustrate his *Monumental Effigies of Great Britain*, published in parts between 1817 and 1833, twelve years after Stothard's untimely death. We shall have to come back to this odd relation of the picture, the monument, death, and the life of the past, foreshadowing as it does the themes of Barthes's last work. But for now, let us note that the printed image excites a double desire of history: on the one hand, for the careful sifting and assembling of detailed and objective records; and, on the other, for the restoration of history as a "lived reality." Yet, in each direction, the power of the image falls flat until it is inserted in another system: on the one side, into the cross-referenced series of the file and the archive; on the other, into what Bann calls "a discourse which mimes the process of chronological sequence,"[20] that is, into a system of narration. At the same time, however, the system of the archive and the system of narration, which encompass the image and variously determine its "vivifying" effect, must also remain in some way "external" to what Gower, Jast, and Topley call the "absolute independence of each print."[21] This is because the record image's discursive value depends on its neither being seen as having its meaning in a network of differences, nor being read as having absorbed narration into itself, lest it be thought to have been contaminated by the suspect opulence and sentimental melodrama that had already eroded the documentary status of history painting.

Thus, for Gower, Jast, and Topley, narrative and archive can be treated as the purely technical issues of labeling and storage, which remain supplementary to the camera's work. It is, they tell us, "the discovery and development of photography" that "has placed in our hands a power incomparably greater than existed before of enabling the rapidly changing phases of our country and its people to be 'fixed' by means of authentic pictorial record."[22] The status of the photographic record—

the assurance of its accuracy and authenticity—is anchored in an ontology of the photographic image that, in the imaginary of history as Stephen Bann describes it at work in the nineteenth century, promises "to annihilate the gap between the model and the copy" and to realize "the Utopian possibility of a restoration of the past in the context of the present."[23] Yet, in effect, this truth function of the image evinces little confidence. As Bann again has commented: "the quest for historical realism risked becoming a vicious circle in which the period details could never be sufficiently copious, and the effect of resurrection never overwhelming enough."[24] The accumulation of detail in the print will never be enough; the accumulation of prints will never cover the field that is to be surveyed.

This fear of a lack is, however, inseparable from a horror at what may be too much. If there is always something wanting in the photographic record and the photographic archive, then there is also something more than desired, and this *excess* of photographic meaning must be brought within bounds. Here, the very want of skill of amateurs is welcomed as a relative virtue, since what is needed is a certain technical innocence, in that, we are told,

> it is often the case that the processes by which pictorial excellence are [*sic*] secured in photographic work (partial suppression of detail, double printed atmospheric effects and the like) are detrimental, if not fatal, to the production of a useful record photograph.[25]

The code for photographic excess is here the influence of a popularized pictorialism:

> Thus, to those photographers who desire to infuse individuality into their work, such processes as gum-bichromate or pigmoil will appeal, by reason of the extent to which they are amenable to modification of the image at various stages.
>
> The record worker, however, . . . will seek other qualities, and chief amongst them may be placed permanence of the image and straightforwardness of manipulation, with capacity to record detail and produce in accurate gradation a wide range of tones.[26]

Gower, Jast, and Topley's strategy therefore necessarily entails the location of the effects of pictorialism and individuality as *external* to what is *proper* to photography and to the workings of the camera. Ideally, "the camera" should be left to itself—which is why it is "the camera" that is, in effect, "the historian." Whereas, for the purposes of record, writing is dangerously liable to proliferate, "the camera," we are told, ensures that

> the photographer must keep strictly to the business in hand, which is to take something; and though to focus the mind upon an object to the exclusion of everything else even for a few moments is a difficult enough undertaking for most people in these days, the camera is fortunately unable to wander from the object upon which *it* is trained.[27]

In part, this marked concern to control photographic meaning is driven by a utilitarian ethic that dreams of greater "efficiency" and productivity in the use of the camera. This, in turn, demands that the work of amateurs be *systematically* organized:

> To the engineer it is abhorrent that any energy be allowed to run to waste.
> But in the domain of photography the amount of "horse-power running to waste" is appalling—and all for lack of a little system and co-ordination. Shall this be allowed to continue? Shall the product of countless cameras be in the future, as in the past (and in large measure to-day), a mass of comparative lumber, rapidly losing interest even for its owners, and of no public usefulness whatever? This is a question of urgency. Every year of inaction means an increase of this wastage.[28]

At the same time, however, "efficiency" is not all that is at stake. Pleasure is clearly at issue. For the amateur, record work provides a way beyond the waning of "the first flush of pleasure at the power photography places in one's hands."[29] What lies beyond is the more acceptable employment of leisure hours, in other words, a regulated economy of pleasure:

> in many cases the turning of one's energies to systematic photography will open up avenues of thought and lead to studies which will enrich life with the purer pleasures of the intellect.[30]

By contrast, unbridled or undirected pleasure is incompatible with the ethic of the archive. Out in the field, for example,

> The practice of exposing promiscuously upon any object which happens to attract attention is of far less value than that of selecting such subjects only as are of importance (from a record not an aesthetic point of view).[31]

Or again, from the point of view of the officers:

> Mere aimless wandering about and casual snap-shotting is not only poorly productive in itself, but tends to beget a slipshod attitude towards the work which it should be the aim of Survey organizers to combat, and is moreover less productive of enjoyment to the participants in the excursion than is work intelligently directed to an end of real value.[32]

So, for this end and in the end, the policing of pleasure and the themes of utility and efficiency are one. What each demands is discipline and the imposition of *systematicity*. Indeed, the very definition of the Survey is, for Gower, Jast, and Topley, "the organization of systematic photographic work."[33] But the demand for systematicness takes us back to the anxieties aroused by the truth function of the Historical Survey and Record and to a striking displacement that these anxieties provoke. While in its aspiration to comprehensiveness the archival project always fell short, its accumulative impetus threatened to overwhelm in an entirely different sense. For, as the number of photographic prints grew, it was clearly impossible to handle them or access their collective record without a system of storage—one in which "it must be possible to insert new prints at any point and to any extent"[34]—and without what the authors call a "proper *arrangement*":[35]

> not only . . . *some* arrangement, but . . . an arrangement which will serve as an efficient key to the scope and contents of the collection, not merely as it is, but as it will become.[36]

Here, the motifs of economy, efficiency, and systematicness return at a new level:

When time, labour, skill and money are to be expended in making a survey which shall do credit to the workers and benefit the present and future generations, it is worth the most careful consideration to so marshal the collection that it shall yield its information in the most direct, immediate, and specific way. This end can only be attained by a *systematic* order.[37]

To the evident enthusiasm of the authors, this question of order opens on a number of rich themes. While the meaning of the photograph can be taken as read in little more than two pages and a single strategic plate, more than a third of the book's 260 pages is given over to questions of storage, the relative merits of boxes, drawers, and vertical files, the mount and the mounting process, the masking and binding of lantern slides, the label, the "contributors' schedules,"[38] the quality of marking ink, the decimal system of classification and the subject order, the advantages of national standardization, the method of Ordnance Survey map referencing, vertical file guides and their proper use, the technical demands of the catalog and subject index, and the importance of the secretary's Register of Prints.

There is, for example, the label, without which the pictorial record—this index of truth—is said to be "useless or next to useless."[39] But the codes of the label are not self evident. The authors are insistent that

something more than a mere indication is required in a photographic record. Such matters as the nature of the process employed, the time of day when the exposure was made, the direction of the camera, and the date, above all, the date, belong to the essentials of the record, and should be supplied whenever possible. At the same time the information asked for should be limited to what is really needed to make the print intelligible. . . . An historical or antiquarian fact may add greatly to the interest of the print, but the survey label is not the place for detailed information of this kind. A reference to an account or description in some authoritative book or article is always worth making, when such information is at hand. But any source so named should be authoritative, and the references should be exact and precise.[40]

An extraordinary expenditure of commentary and moral fervor thus devolves onto this little slip: how much it should say, to whom it should speak, and to what code it should summon both object and viewer. The label must be a feat of condensation and, as in the voluminous writings of contemporary museum officials such as George Brown Goode of the Smithsonian Institution, it is believed to repay the most exacting analysis.[41] In the museum as in the archive, the label must be mastered and become the instrument of a refined and connective narrative that will "impart instruction of a definite character and in definite lines," marking out the space of the archive and the space of the exhibit for useful knowledge and expelling the wayward frivolity of mere "idle curiosity."[42]

A similar aura surrounds "the modern vertical file"—the latest information technology, that central artifact, as Allan Sekula calls it[43]— which, here, merits two full plate illustrations and a detailed description. As an instrument for organizing and handling the Survey archive,

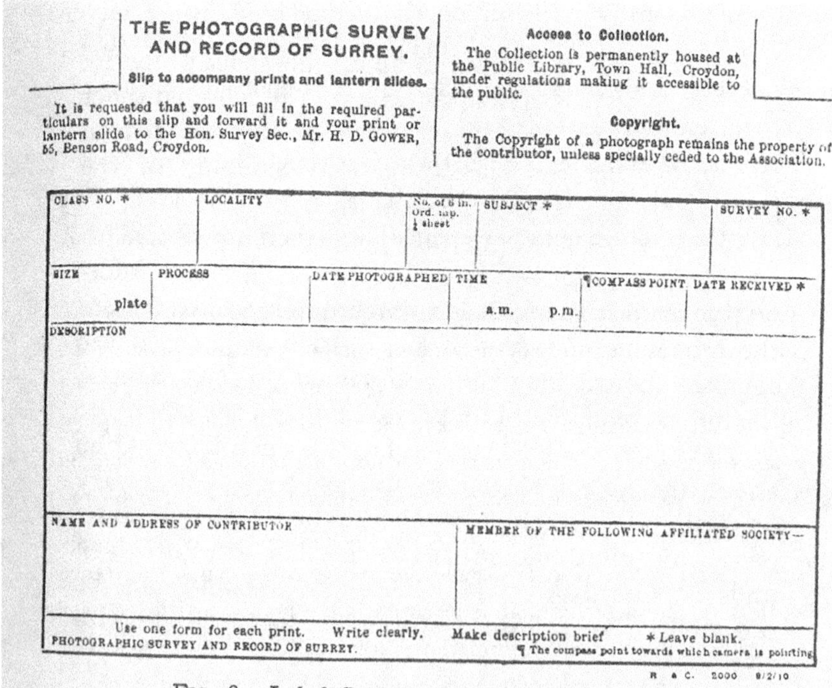

FIG. 8.—Label, Survey of Surrey. 5⅝ in. × 4⅝ in.

Figure 52. "Fig. 8.—Label, Survey of Surrey," from H. D. Gower, L. Stanley Jast, and W. W. Topley, *The Camera as Historian* (London: Sampson Low, Marston, 1916), 73.

the vertical file is said to constitute "as near an approach to the ideal as can reasonably be expected."[44] Even its cost does not weigh against it. Like the paradigm in Saussure's linguistics, it is the structure of the filing cabinet and the decimal system of classification it supports that organizes the system of substitutions and equivalences within which the photographic signs are disposed. But as in the Saussurean model, the construction of meaning across this structure of differences also radically conflicts with the notion of meaning as a fullness interior to the sign. The primacy of the camera and the indexical realism of the print are therefore displaced, suggesting that Gower, Jast, and Topley—formalists in their hearts—might better have titled their work *The Filing Cabinet as Historian.*

It could only be in the bureaucratic imagination, however, that "the modern vertical file" could be seen as functioning like an ideal language system. From Foucault, we have learned to see its ideal architecture as a disciplinary machine: an apparatus for individuation and comparative categorization; an instrument for regulating territory and knowledge, rendering them the objects of technocratic adjudication.[45] Yet, as

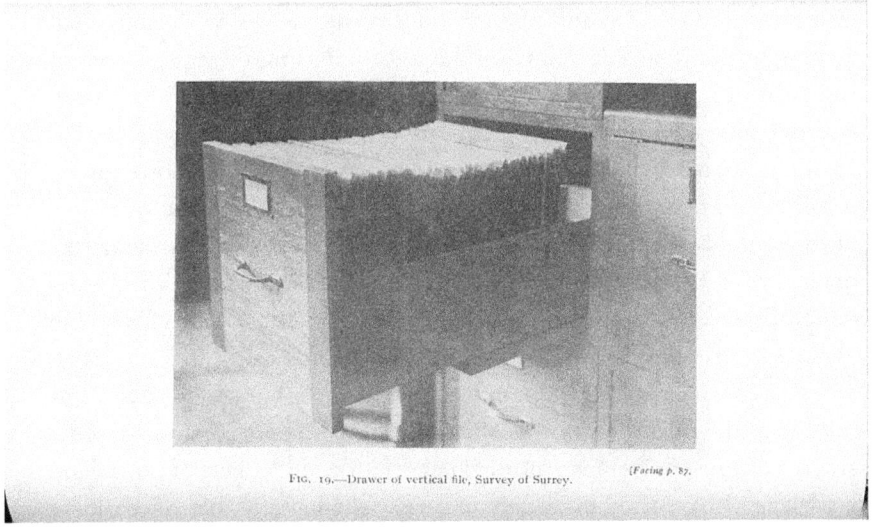

FIG. 19.—Drawer of vertical file, Survey of Surrey. [Facing p. 87.

Figure 53. "Fig. 19.—Drawer of vertical file, Survey of Surrey," from H. D. Gower, L. Stanley Jast, and W. W. Topley, *The Camera as Historian* (London: Sampson Low, Marston, 1916), facing 87.

a *technology of history*, the filing cabinet has also to accommodate two further, paradoxical, concerns: a concern for the time history takes to function and the labor it expends (which in the logic of capital amount in the end to the same thing), and a concern for the durability of history, for its duration and hardness, for the survival of history against the erosions of time. And at the point where these two concerns coincide, there is the question of the expenditure of history as a machine that is used up in the very process of the efficient production of knowledge. On the one hand, the soundly constructed cabinet is a means to prolong the shelf life of history. On the other hand, at least in the imaginary of empiricism and the economy of information handling, its rigid structure holds out the promise of closing the circuit of reading–sign–referent, which is here hardly separable from the circuit of production–consumption–profit. Already, in this cumbersome wood-and-cardboard computer, far short of the "real-time" technologies of the Cable News Network, the time of history is imagined as approaching the ideal zero time of disciplinary knowledge and the cycle of capital: "exchange in the least possible time ('real' time) for the greatest possible time ('abstract' or lost time)."[46]

These are, then, the banalities with which the model techno-historians Gower, Jast, and Topley concern themselves: with the "small techniques [as Foucault describes them] of notation, of registration, of constituting files, of arranging facts in columns and tables"[47] that are so familiar to historians; with the modest techniques of knowledge that present themselves as procedural aids but inscribe the Photographic Record and Survey in a new modality of power for which the workings of the camera give us little explanation. As Sekula has said of the development of immense police archives in the same period, for all the epistemological stakes in the optical model of the camera, it is, in effect, able to secure little on its own behalf, outside its insertion into this much more extensive, and entirely nonmimetic, clerical, bureaucratic apparatus.[48] And the operation of this apparatus has, of course, its own discursive conditions, whose institutional negotiation and effects of power and knowledge I have tried to outline in earlier chapters.[49] This—need I add again?—is not to suggest that historical record photography was the transparent reflection of a power outside itself. It is, rather, to insist that the record photograph's compelling weight was never *phenomenological*—

to use Barthes's later term—but always *discursive* and that the status of the document and the power effects of its evidence were produced only in the field of an institutional, discursive, and political articulation.

From this point of view, it would seem to be both true and untrue to say, as Jonathan Crary sometimes appears to, that photography came too late, seeming to reincarnate a model of the observer and a set of relations that had already been overthrown.[50] Within the workings of the archival apparatus, the linear, optical system of the camera obscura, with its rigid positions and inflexible distinctions of subject and object, inside and outside, could both retain its useful fixity and be articulated into a more pragmatic, adaptable system, capable of responding both to new, productive uses of bodies and spaces and to the proliferating exchange of images and signs. The look of the camera remains a crucial moment in the machinery of the archival gaze. The absolutes of realism prove readily adaptable to a new pragmatics of performance. It is this articulation that produces the evidential effect, on which certain practices not only of photography but also of history remain dependent. But let us be clear about this system and what it would mean to depart from it.

The photograph, like the name in Lyotard's sense, pins the system to the ostensible fixity of an absolute singularity. But this singularity is an empty referent answering to a name that by itself cannot be "a designator of reality."[51] For that to occur, we must situate this name "in relation to other names by means of phrases."[52] This is a process, however, that cannot be seen through to an end, because "the inflation of senses that can be attached to [the name] is not bounded by the 'real' properties of its referent."[53] The name is, therefore, as Lyotard says,

> both strongly determined in terms of its location among the networks of names and of relations between names (worlds) and feebly determined in terms of its sense by dint of the large number and of the heterogeneity of phrase universes in which it can take place as an instance.[54]

What is crucial here—not least for the regimen of the instrumental archive and the practices of history that cannot detach themselves from it—is that the phrases that come to be attached to a name (in Lyotard's words) not only describe different senses for it (this can still be debated in dialogue), and not only place the name on different instances, but . . . also obey heterogeneous regimens and/or genres.[55]

Whereas "essentialism conceives the referent of the name as if it were the referent of a definition,"[56] "the assignment of a definition . . . necessarily does wrong to the nondefinitional phrases relating to [the name], which this definition, for a while at least, disregards or betrays."[57] For lack of a common idiom, there can be no consensus on the meaning of the name—or the meaning of the photograph—historical or not. "Reality entails the differend":[58] The name does not designate "reality" so much as mark reality as the locus of radically incommensurable "differends,"[59] which summon humans "to situate themselves in unknown phrase universes."[60] To respond to this summons, the historian would have to "break with the monopoly over history granted to the cognitive regimen of phrases, and . . . venture forth by lending his or her ear to what is not presentable under the rules of knowledge."[61] To the camera as historian, Lyotard would have this reply: "Reality is not a matter of the absolute eyewitness, but a matter of the future."[62]

This might give us pause. But it is not quite the place at which we can stop. There is still the quotation from Roland Barthes with which I began but whose argument I have avoided confronting directly. Perhaps this argument is not what we expect.

"The same century invented History and Photography." Yet for the Roland Barthes of *Camera Lucida*, this is "a paradox."[63] "History is a memory fabricated according to positive formulas, a pure intellectual discourse which abolishes mythic Time."[64] Photography, however, is not an intellectual datum. It is "a certain but fugitive testimony":[65] "in Photography I can never deny that *the thing has been there*";[66] "every photograph is a certificate of presence";[67] photography "*authenticates* the existence of a certain being";[68] "it does not invent; it is authentication itself."[69]

History, then, lacks the authentication on which it would seem to depend, though it should be noted that "History" has to figure twice in this argument—I resist the temptation to say, "the first time as tragedy, the second as farce";[70] rather, it figures once as writing and again as "the past." Barthes wants to suggest that

> Perhaps we have an invincible resistance to believing in the past, in History, except in the form of myth. The Photograph, for the first time, puts an end to this resistance: henceforth the past [Should we now say "History"?] is as certain as the present.[71]

By contrast, "no writing can give me this certainty,"[72] because "language is, by nature, fictional."[73] The Photograph, however, "possesses an evidential force," though "its testimony bears not on the object but on time."[74] While "the photograph is literally an emanation of the referent,"[75] it is not a copy of a present reality but "an emanation of *past reality*":[76] the "pure representation" of the ostensive "*that-has-been*"[77]—which, from the beginning, has to become the truth of a human existence, a "*she-has-been*."[78]

The contrast with Barthes's 1967 essay "The Discourse of History" is immediately apparent, though in a striking continuity of the field of questions. Barthes, in 1967, seemed to celebrate openly the fact that "Historical narration is dying because the sign of History from now on is no longer the real, but the intelligible."[79] From the point of view of the structural linguistic analysis he was then practicing, the myth of the distinction of historical discourse from other forms of narration was "an *imaginary* elaboration."[80] The "objectivity" of historical discourse turns on a double suppression. In the first place, this is a suppression of the signs of the utterer—the signs of the "I" in historical discourse—whose absence marks a particular, telling form of imaginary projection: the "referential illusion," whose effects, Barthes says, are not exclusive to historical writing.[81] Such a suppression amounts to "a radical censorship of the act of uttering," which links the historian's discourse to the discourse of the schizophrenic, in that both seek to effect "a massive flowing back of discourse in the direction of the utterance and even (in the historian's case) in the direction of the referent," so that "no one is there to take responsibility for the utterance."[82]

In the second place, and as an inseparable consequence, it is the signified itself that is forced out: "As with any discourse which lays claim to 'realism,' historical discourse only admits to knowing a semantic schema

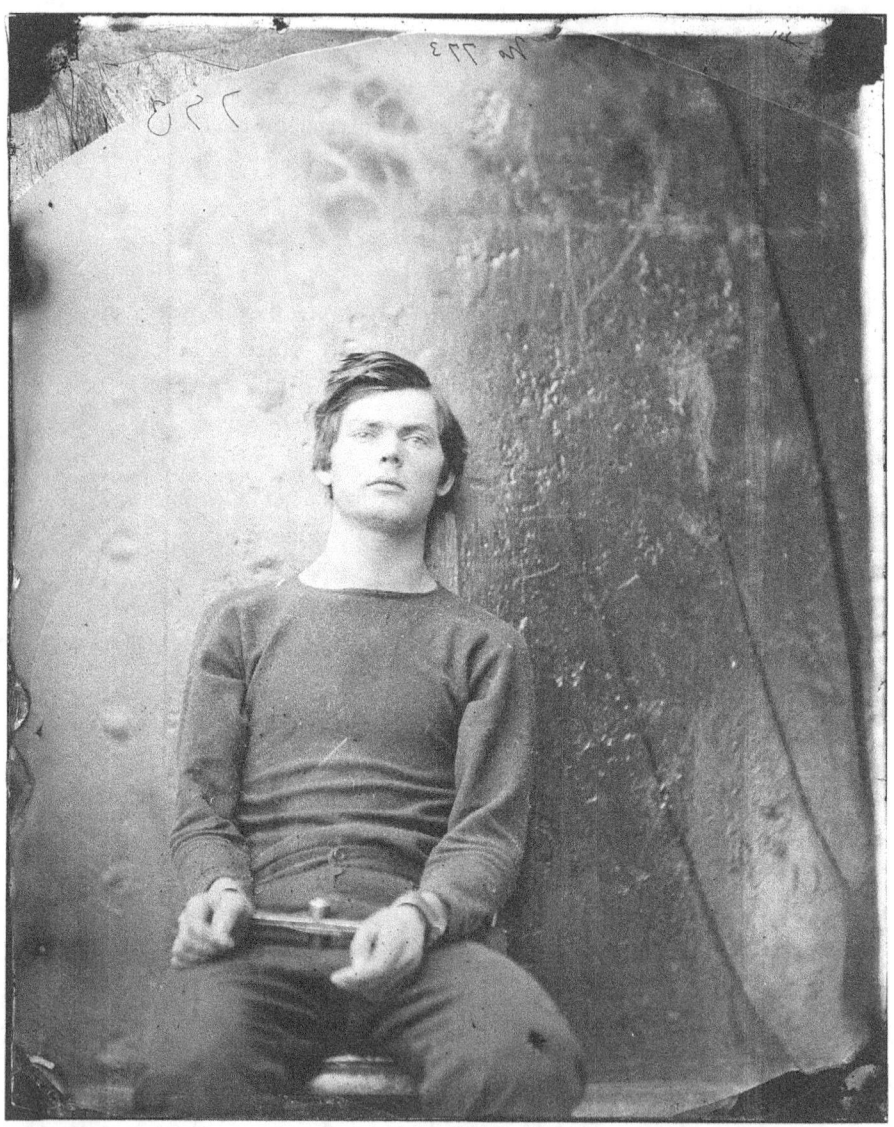

Figure 54. "'He is dead and he is going to die . . . .' Alexander Gardner: Portrait of Lewis Payne. 1865," as captioned in Roland Barthes, *Camera Lucida: Reflections on Photography* (London: Jonathan Cape, 1982), 95. Library of Congress, Prints and Photographs Division, Selected Civil War Photographs, 1861–1865 (LC-DIG-cwpb-04208).

with two terms, the referent and the signifier."[83] These are posited in a direct relation that dispenses with "the fundamental term in imaginary structures, which is the signified."[84] "In other words," Barthes writes,

> in "objective" history, the "real" is never more than an unformulated signified, sheltering behind the apparently all-powerful referent. This situation characterizes what we might call the *realistic effect*.[85]

And, from this, Barthes concludes that

> Historical discourse does not follow the real, it can do no more than signify the real, constantly repeating that *it happened*, without this assertion amounting to anything but the signified "other side" of the whole process of historical narration.[86]

Yet what is important, Barthes suggests at the end of his essay, is the prestige that has attached to this *"it happened,"* to this *"realistic effect,"* for which our culture has such an appetite, as can be seen in

> the development of specific genres like the realist novel, the private diary, documentary literature, news items, historical museums, exhibitions of old objects and especially in the massive development of photography, whose sole distinctive trait (by comparison with drawing) is precisely that it signifies that the event represented has *really* taken place.[87]

Here, we may note that, for all the footnoted reference to "Rhetoric of the Image,"[88] the *"it happened"* of the photograph is clearly marked as an effect of signification. And this is in the context of an argument in which, against the refusal to acknowledge the real as signified and in enthusiastic pursuit of the Red Guards of Mao Zedong's Cultural Revolution, Barthes seems to call for "a destruction of the real itself," which "is never more than a meaning, which can be revoked when history requires it."[89] So "history" has to make its double appearance again, even though the "destruction of the real" spells the end of the secular survival of "that very sacredness which is attached to the enigma of what has been, is no longer, and yet offers itself for reading as the present sign of a dead thing."[90]

The constant repeating of the "it happened," the "present sign of a dead thing": These return us uncomfortably to the second part of *Camera Lucida* and to "the pure representation" of "that-has-been"—the "evidential force" of the photograph. Yet we should not miss the paradoxical point that it is because of its very power as evidence that "the Photograph [and, here, Barthes is thinking of his mother] cannot be penetrated."[91] The photographic image is both full—"no room, nothing can be added to it"[92]—and finite. It offers "nothing but the *exorbitant thing*;"[93] "in it nothing can be refused or transformed."[94] This is "its unendurable plenitude."[95] The presence it discloses is entirely finished—complete and gone—and no displacement to a register of cultural meaning can allay or give voice to the "suffering" Barthes now experiences "entirely on the level of the image's finitude."[96] If the Photograph dispels disbelief and bestows a certainty on History as "the past," then it does so with the "*irony*"[97] that there is nothing to say about it, just as there is nothing to say about the flat fact of Death. If the Photograph is unarguable, like the name, it nevertheless teaches us nothing.

There is another irony to add to this. As a memorial to the past, the photograph is frangible and fleeting:

> Earlier societies managed so that memory, the substitute for life, was eternal and that at least the thing which spoke Death should itself be immortal: this was the Monument. But by making the (mortal) Photograph into the general and somehow natural witness of "what has been," modern society has renounced the Monument.[98]

It is at this point in the text that Barthes invokes the "paradox" of the nineteenth century's double legacy: its invention of History (let us say historiography) and Photography—the one fabricated, the other fugitive—together ushering in the double death of Memory, the death of the endurable, the death of the ripe, and even, eventually, the death of the astonishment of "*that-has-been*," witness to which seers into the Photograph, and even into History as Jules Michelet conceived it, love's protest against this loss.[99]

The argument begins to fold against itself, knowingly perhaps, like the fall of a shroud that hides from view yet remains translucent, as in the curtains that hang at the entrance to Barthes's book. The fugitive-ness of the photograph and the intellectual formulae of historiography have expelled redemptive ritual and displaced the continuity of memory. Yet they have also given us what remain our only fragile testimonies against the facts of Death and loss. Without being able to conceive dura-tion, however, the fullness they offer can never ripen but only be replete. It can only be the fullness of the formula and the fullness of the Photo-graph, a fullness that, like Death itself, precludes all transactions and is therefore closed to meaning: irrefutable, yet telling us nothing. The cer-tainty without meaning of "what has been" threatens to induce stupe-faction, but still its prick is felt, spurring Barthes to the revelation that "such evidence can be a sibling of madness."[100]

Madness proliferates in these texts by Barthes on History and Pho-tography. Whereas, formerly, the discourse of the historian was shunned as too close to that of the schizophrenic, now, it is the semiology and structural linguistics of the late 1960s that have been shaken off as the period of "a minor scientific delirium,"[101] while the closeness of the dis-courses of history and photography to the discourse of the psychotic is embraced as a madness, or "ecstasy,"[102] in which untamed affect (love, grief, enthusiasm, pity) is an absolute guarantee of Being.[103] In the midst of "the civilized code of perfect illusions," madness drives crazily into the piteous spectacle of the photograph and wakens there "intractable reality."[104]

"A sibling of madness": What has been taken as Barthes's belated reiteration and vindication of a realist position hardly yields evidence that would stand up in court. The evidence that is without discursive conditions is the evidence of the ecstatic, of Friedrich Nietzsche on his knees in the gutter with his arms around the neck of a dying horse. There can be little joy for leftist documentarism or social history in join-ing him there.

One could follow much more closely the vicissitudes of "History" and "Photography" in Barthes's writing: now as complicit in the imagi-nary elaboration of the realist effect; now as paradoxical inventions of the same epoch—intellectual formula set against the "message without a code"; now, again, as substitutes for memory in a society without mon-uments. But whether one reads here a continuity or a change of mind, it is clear that Barthes's final ecstatic embrace of the evidential power of the photograph is far removed from Gower, Jast, and Topley's dream of its efficient handling. This can hardly give satisfaction to "the connoisseurship of documentary evidence." But, on the question of History at least, surely Barthes's texts are more resolved: History for certain cannot claim to be a discourse without a code.[105] Yet as the analyses unfold, history keeps doubling, and the double keeps retreating, always to another space, another domain of existence, that the analyses exclude only to reinvoke.

In "The Discourse of History," Barthes frames the possibility of an analysis of the narrative structures of history only by closing those structures, thereby re-creating, from what that closure expels, an *external* space of history "in" which, as Geoff Bennington and Robert Young point out, discursive structures—and, indeed, structural analyses of history—have to work their effects.[106] So, too, in *Camera Lucida*—a book in which Barthes says his conception of photographic realism obliges him "to return to the very letter of Time"[107]—History is writing, formula, "a pure intellectual discourse." But History and Photography belong to the same century, to the same chronology, in which "the age of the Photograph" is also "the age of revolutions"[108] and in which the world of the "universalized image"[109] brings an end to belief, rendering "archaic" what Barthes lovingly treasures, leaving him to survive as one of the "last witnesses"[110] of the astonishment of a "that-has-been." History and Photography belong in history, of whose "past" existence photography offers certain evidence. And while, beyond "the civilized code of perfect illusions," the intractable evidence of photography is terrifying and ecstatic, bordering on madness, this device of madness is located within a historical frame and, like History itself, is said to have been historically invented.

So Barthes releases madness only to arrest it again. And, at this very moment, History escapes. One is reminded of Derrida's remark, in another context, that "philosophy . . . lives only by emprisoning madness," and "it is only by virtue of this oppression of madness that finite-thought, that is to say, history, can reign."[111] History, on the other hand, never does time; it is always over the wall, and it remains at large even in Barthes's most structuralist text. It makes no sense, then, to demand that history be "added" to structuralist analysis: That is only to repeat the action of the carceral logic, the logic of the limit, the logic of the frame, that constitutes inside and outside, work and context, structure and history. It makes no sense, then, to choose sides. Metaphorical or not, this penitentiary works its effects on both sides of its perimeter wall: The space of the structural interior, about which we know something from Barthes, and the space of "empiricisms of the extrinsic,"[112] about which we know something from Gower, Jast, and Topley, are kept apart only by a "thin blue line."

This is the issue: the institution in question. And, to echo Derrida again, we can only "avoid the reconstitution of a new archivism or of a new documentalism"[113] by engagement with "the problematic of the border and of framing."[114] We come back, therefore, to the obliquity of the line. And how else, outside appeals to the Real, will we ever be able to show that the police or the Pentagon have once more overstepped the mark? But there is more on the line, here. We come back not only to the mounting of the photographic record, whose evidence is always framed, but also to those convenient devices, those encompassing technologies, to which we need pay no heed but whose ruling defines the objects of art history, its fields of operation, its patterns of explanation, its endless to-and-fro of debate between the truth of history and the truth of the art itself. But this is the opening for another chapter.

CHAPTER 6

A Discourse with Shape
of Reason Missing:
Art History and the Frame

Squaring Up

"Reality," writes Lyotard, "succumbs to this reversal: It was the given described by the phrase, it became the *archive* from which are drawn *documents* or examples that validate the description."[1] It is, then, this reversal that constitutes the regime of the instrumental archive and its evidential effects—a regime that, as we have seen, implicates not only a certain practice of photography but also a practice of history. It is this regime that gives this practice of photography and this practice of history their disciplinary authority to call on the "mute testimony" of the "document." The regime is, indeed, the *condition* of this testimony, insofar as it governs the court and works to exclude what cannot be spoken within its rules of knowledge and to repress the heterogeneity of phrase regimens by the imposition of a definitive and final discursive frame.

In this sense, the instrumental regime draws a defining line around the "document," determining what is interior to it and what is exterior, what is internal evidence and what is background, what is text and what is context, what is structure and what is history. For the instrumental archive, the weighting of this ratio may be precisely fixed, but drawing the line, of course, opens endless opportunities for the to-and-fro of debate, according to whether, in marking the division, the critical edge is given to the interior or to the exterior, to what is inherent or to what is environment. Yet in the interminable advances and retreats of this methodological debate—as familiar in art history as in social science—

both sides betray a marked ambivalence and a mutual dependency, since, as we saw, structural analysis always leaves history waiting in another place, while social histories flee the interior only to take their stand elsewhere on the internal guarantees of a document.

A great deal, then, is left hanging on the frame, as a technology of discipline and a technology of history. Let us therefore try to meet it squarely.

The Image

Where to begin? Perhaps where a certain kind of art history has always asked us to begin: with *the work itself*—with the image—in this case an image of two crowds, in which I shall try to clear a space to make something visible. Or perhaps I shall only be making visible that space itself, a space that is already there. The image is John Baldessari's: a 4 foot × 2½ foot gelatin silver print made in 1984 and first published on the cover of the fall 1985 issue of *Journal*, in the context of a "Special Feature" edited by Jeremy Gilbert-Rolfe and John Johnston under the title *Multiplicity, Proliferation, Reconvention.*[2] Johnston you may know as a translator of Jean Baudrillard, Gilles Deleuze, and Michel Foucault. Gilbert-Rolfe is a painter and critical theorist who, at the time, was teaching at the California Institute of the Arts, where Baldessari had also been on the faculty since 1970.

The focus of concern in Gilbert-Rolfe's and Johnston's "Special Feature" is that play of displacement which is at work within all languages and institutional structures, continually undoing the constraints they impose against proliferation and multiplicity, displacing the bounded space of sign and system into a network of heterogeneous connections and disseminating references. We may note in passing that Gilbert-Rolfe and Johnston make a point of listing Baldessari's cover work in their table of contents and remark on it in their editorial essay, in relation to what they describe as that "multiplicity which occurs through subtraction, or more exactly, . . . the role of subtraction in the production of multiplicity."[3] They write,

> The title of the work of John Baldessari's [*sic*] reproduced here is *Two Crowds with Shape of Reason Missing* (1985), which in a sense [so they tell

us] says it all. Difference here is heightened by what is announced as a reduction of difference, the withdrawal of identity from each crowd.[4]

Clearly, we are engaging a complex theoretical apparatus and perhaps a host of associations has already begun to crowd Baldessari's image. But, for the moment, let me draw a line around this lucid thesis that the editors insert into the heart of Baldessari's picture and add only

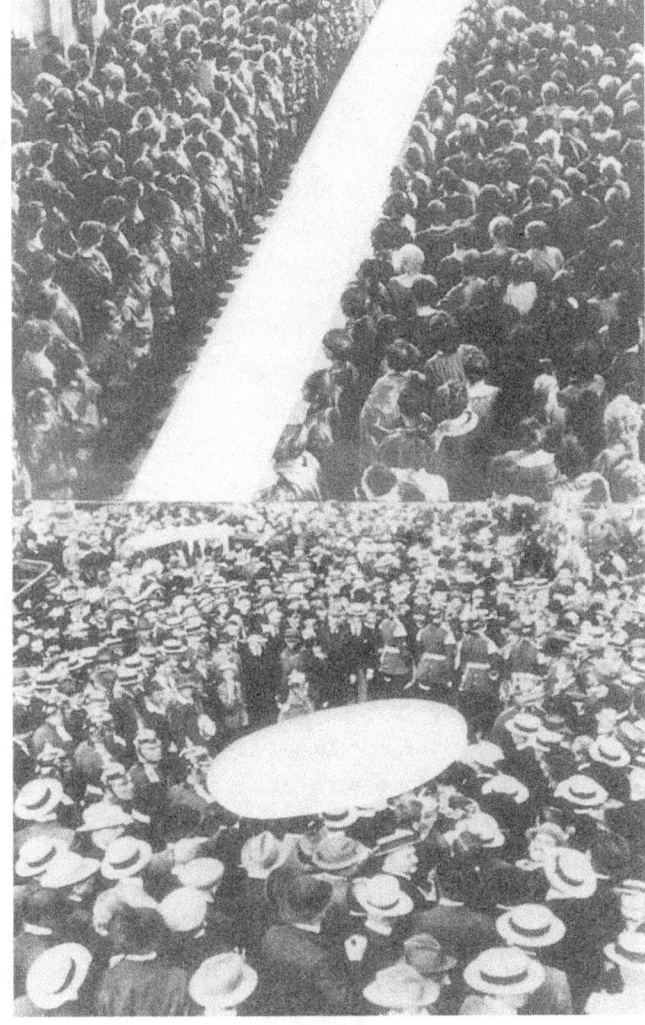

Figure 55.
John Baldessari,
"Two Crowds with
Shape of Reason
Missing," 1984.
Black-and-white
photographs
mounted on board,
48 × 30 inches.
Courtesy John
Baldessari.

that the work in fact appears twice in the *Journal* feature: first on the cover, as I have said, and then, somewhat strangely, as a "detail" placed like an illustration on the third page of an essay by Michel Feher titled "Mass, Crowd, and Pack."[5] On this page, Feher discusses Freud's concept of narcissism and its importance to the theory of the primal horde and that horde's ambivalent relation to its dominant leader. Only overleaf, not on page 47 but on page 48, does Feher go on to contrast Freud's account with what he calls "Elias Canetti's masterpiece," *Crowds and Power*, a book Baldessari is also reported to have been reading prior to 1986, perhaps as early as 1984, the year in which he made the first version of the work that the editors of "Multiplicity, Proliferation, Reconvention" have cropped and pasted into Feher's text.[6]

So Feher and Canetti can be added to the crowd. And we might go further, if we recognized the lower half of Baldessari's image as an altered version of a well-known news photograph of the proclamation of war in Berlin, on August 1, 1914. We might note that, in his chapter "The Crowd in History," Canetti, too, represents this moment:

> On the outbreak of the First World War the whole German people became one open crowd. The enthusiasm of those days has often been described. Many people in other countries had been counting on the internationalism of the Social Democrats and were astounded at their failure to act. They forgot that the Social Democrats, too, bore within them this forest-army symbol of their nation; that they themselves had belonged to the closed crowd of the army and that, whilst in it, they had been under the command and influence of a highly disciplined and immensely effective crowd crystal, the Junker and officer caste. Their membership of a political party carried very little weight in comparison with this.
>
> But those first August days of 1914 were also the days in which National Socialism was begotten. Hitler himself is our authority for this. He later described how, at the outbreak of war, he fell on his knees and thanked God. It was his decisive experience, the one moment at which he himself honestly became part of a crowd. He never forgot it and his whole subsequent career was devoted to the re-creation of this moment, but *from outside*. Germany was to be again as it was then, conscious of its military striking power and exulting and united in it.[7]

We might immediately want to ring the terms "open crowd," "closed crowd," and "crowd crystal": terms that figure importantly in Canetti's elaborate typology and collective psychology of crowd formations, terms that may, in turn, be suggestive for Baldessari's choice of images.[8] The "closed crowd," for Canetti, like the ceremonial congregation in the top half of Baldessari's picture, establishes itself by accepting its limitations, renouncing growth, and putting its stress on permanence and stability.[9] But "the open crowd"—like the crowd in Berlin, metonym for "the whole German people"—is what Canetti calls "the true crowd, the crowd abandoning itself freely to its natural urge for growth."[10] It is a crowd that wants to grow, it wants density, and it wants direction; its constant fear of disintegration means that "it will accept *any* goal" and will continue to exist "so long as it has an unattained goal."[11] Within such formations, "crowd crystals" are "the small, rigid groups of men, strictly delimited and of great constancy, which serve to precipitate crowds."[12] The uniformed soldiers visible in each frame of Baldessari's image exemplify this type of grouping, which is, Canetti tells us, "*all* limits":

> everyone belonging to it constitutes part of its boundary, whereas the closed crowd has its boundary imposed on it from outside, if only by the shape and size of the building where it meets.[13]

There is clearly space for speculation here, and Baldessari himself was to return to the same ground in the following year, extending his thoughts to a further five images, titled *Crowds with Shape of Reason Missing*, which he published in 1986, again as a contribution to a theoretical anthology: the first issue of *Zone*, edited by Michel Feher and Sanford Kwinter and devoted to the city.[14] I could go on; we are not at the end of it. Even so, let me cut off this discussion here so that we can find our way back along the route from where I began, with an image—"Two Crowds (with Shape of Reason Missing)" (with or without parentheses)—cutting it out and pasting it in place, opening in its interior the outline of an interpretation, probing its edges, even where they bleed, and giving it a frame, with all that hangs on it: the name of an artist, a title, a date, a location, a provenance of sorts, sources and influences, lines of derivation and anticipation, a whole personal history in the future anterior, as

Althusser would have said.[15] All familiar enough: habits of art history. But what this might make us think is that, if such framing marks the beginning, then it began before I started to speak and was in place or, better perhaps, described a place in which the work might find itself and be found. And if such a frame was always already there in advance, though with the shape of its reason missing, then what is ruled out is that this chapter had a proper beginning, an institution proper to itself. Let me draw a line and try to begin again.

The Frame

The crowds are everywhere, or so it seems. Filling every corner, or all but one, they press forward in rapt attention, concentrating their gaze, held back in each case only by two lines of soldiers in full ritual dress. Held back, that is, from the whiteness of a void in which each crowd's desire is projected but its reason is repressed. Now an oblique line, now an ellipse, this void is, at once, a space the crowd creates and a space on which it converges, a space to which the crowd gives meaning and a space that is its reason for being.

Even Baldessari's knife, in paring away a layer of truth in the image and cutting the sutures that seem to stitch the viewer in, does no more

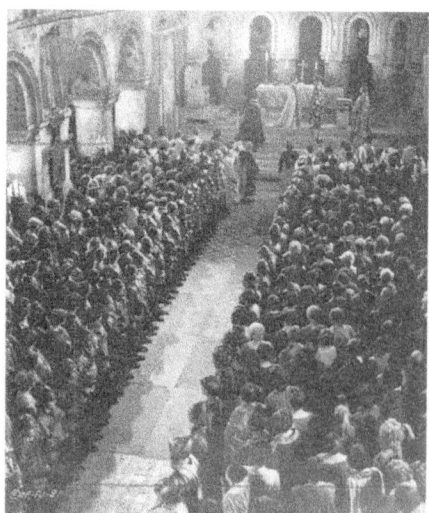

Figure 56. Source photograph for "Two Crowds with Shape of Reason Missing." Courtesy John Baldessari.

than formalize what is already there in the source pictures as a white space of meaning—a circular clearing, an aisle—where the crowd closes on or opens to the spacing of a performance. In one place, the crowd must accommodate to the divisions and limits of a preexistent architectural script. In the other, we seem to see the ancient shape of pure spontaneity, bound by no outer limit, with a vortex at its center across which, as in an arena, the crowd is exhibited to itself in an intensifying spiral of self-identification. And if we are troubled by images of a crowd that has lost its reason, we can, on the other hand, see that the crowd supplies its own logic and its own architecture, more than a backdrop to history to set off the significant players, more than a context lacking focus, more than disorder wanting sense. If the crowd is called forth by the event, it also constitutes a necessary stage and indispensable setting as, in more or less violent passivity, it asserts its role of spectator as the condition of a spectacular event that, in Baldessari's image, we can as yet only imagine: a performance of meaning in which some other may pronounce "I do," perhaps, or "I declare."

"I do" and "I declare": the pronouncements of marriage and war. We are in the classic space of the performative, here, in which, according to John Austin, utterance and context saturate each other as meaning is enacted to produce an effect that cannot be said to have existed before or outside language.[16] To speak is to act, but only here, in this well-understood social setting, before the appropriate witnesses.

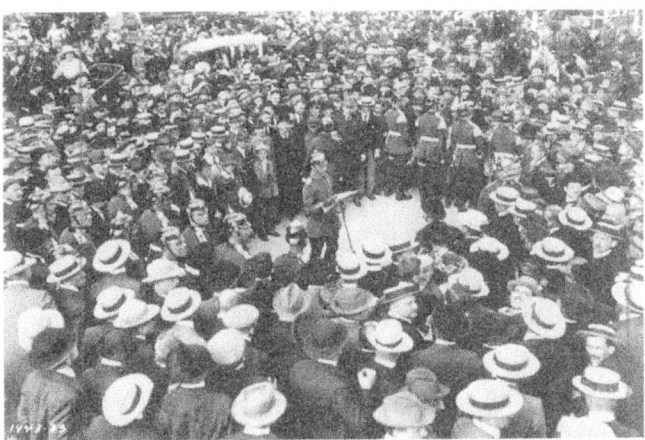

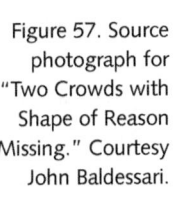
Figure 57. Source photograph for "Two Crowds with Shape of Reason Missing." Courtesy John Baldessari.

Writing on Austin's lectures on *How to Do Things with Words,* Jacques Derrida, however, rejects Austin's notion of the performative as a singular and original event of meaning in which the conscious intention of the speaker is unambiguously realized within the framework of a "total context."[17] For Derrida, the conventionality that determines meaning extends not just to the circumstance of the statement but also to what he calls "a certain intrinsic conventionality of that which constitutes the locution itself, that is, everything that might be quickly summarized under the problematic heading of the 'arbitrariness of the sign.'"[18] This "extends, aggravates, and radicalizes the difficulty," since it compels recognition that "Ritual is not an eventuality but, as iterability, is a structural characteristic of every mark."[19] The opposition between singular, univocal statement-events and statements that do not have the same specific context dependence is not, therefore, to the point. The "performative," too, is a coded or "iterable" inscription, of which intention, consciousness, presence, and meaning are not preconditions but can only be analyzed as effects.[20]

It follows that what must also be displaced is the concept of or quest for an "exhaustively determinable" context of meaning: a context for which a conscious intention must provide the determining focus.[21] Yet Derrida's point is not that the inscription Austin calls "performative" is valid outside its context but "on the contrary that there are only contexts without any centre of absolute anchoring."[22] It is not that there is no relative specificity of the effects of consciousness, of speech, of presence, and of the performative: "It is simply that these effects do not exclude what is generally opposed to them term by term, but on the contrary presuppose it in dissymmetrical fashion, as the general space of their possibility."[23] There is no primal scene or last instance of meaning, only spacing and temporizing—a play of *différance*—that erodes all closures and opens an abyss in the midst of the performative act, deconstructing the presence of event and context.

For Foucault, too, the discursive event—though event nonetheless—is neither discrete nor dissolved into the formless unity of contextualization, the intentionality of a subject, or some great external causal process. Instead, it is traced on what Foucault calls "those diverse converging, and sometimes divergent, but never autonomous series that enable us to circumscribe the 'locus' of an event, the limits to its fluid-ity and the conditions of its emergence."[24] The event is not what fits a hole in a context, but neither does it carry its reason in itself. The fun-damental notions to be brought to the analysis of the discursive event are no longer those of consciousness and continuity, but neither are they those of sign and structure. Foucault's conception of discourse is not, therefore, to be confused with the structuralist model of language as an available resource with the potential to generate all possible, and no im-possible, statements. All possible statements do not occur, while others continue to be reinscribed and to furnish criteria for policy and indi-vidual conduct, regardless of assessments of their value and use. It is this rarefaction of discursive events that interests Foucault: their "rules of appearance" and "conditions of appropriation and operation," which immediately raise the question of power and focus attention on the strategic role of discursive systems, on the domains of objects and forms of knowledge they make possible, and on the administrative effects they engender.[25]

There is, then, at least this much in common with Austin's perfor-mative: that discourse for Foucault is not a purely linguistic phenome-non, for the elements of a discursive system may not be in words at all. (Confessional rituals, for example—whether in the church or in the ana-lyst's office—involve not just certain kinds of speaking and hearing but also specially designed spaces, particular techniques and bodily postures, and special kinds of priestly or psychoanalytical training. And we can readily see how this could be extended to the rituals of connoisseurship or art historical judgment, as to other scenes where it is the attentive-ness of the eye, rather than that of the ear, that is in play.) It is not, then, a matter of the history of ideas. The field of discourse is a field of mate-rial acts. "Violent, discontinuous, querulous, disordered even and peril-ous,"[26] as Foucault describes it; it is a field that takes shape under a set of incitements and constraints that operate to control, select, organize, and redistribute the production of discourse and "to evade its ponderous, awesome materiality."[27]

In "The Discourse on Language," Foucault's inaugural lecture at the Collège de France, such incitements and constraints are divided into the categories of "exterior" and "internal" rules:[28] on the one hand, rules of exclusion, prohibition, division, and rejection, governing the hazards of the appearance of discourse; on the other hand, rules of identity, typology, origin, and disciplinary formation, and rules of employment and subjection, distributing speakers among discourses and discourses to subjects. Foucault's stress on "exteriority" and "external conditions of existence"[29] as fundamental principles of the genealogy of discursive formations may seem problematic here, reiterating a division of internal and external that he rejects in the traditional history of ideas. In effect, however, this stress functions as a rhetorical counter to notions of "signification"[30] as the determinant effect of a deep and exhaustive structure, and it takes Foucault into a territory that he now defies his critics to call "structuralism."[31]

What is crucial in this new territory is the emerging theme that the production of discourse is inseparable from the action and generation of power effects. And already, at the time of his lecture "The Discourse on Language," before the writing of *Discipline and Punish*, Foucault's conception of this relation of power and sense is not focused only on negation—on cutting out, rarefaction, and the prohibition of certain objects, practices, and performances of discourse. Equally, it seeks to follow the ways in which the operations of power on and in discourse are productive: productive of reason and truth; productive of textual hierarchies, unifying principles, and orders of discourse; productive of subjects and fellowships of discourse. Not only is the formation of a field of sense an effective formation of control, but control is also effective as a formation of sense. It is a violence that is done to us and that we do to things.[32] But it is a field of violence that takes effect as an incessant, scattered, and discontinuous production of discourse that would evade "its character as an event"[33] or series of "events" that always "have their place."[34]

Power and place: the terms of analysis of discourse have begun to pass from the rules of formation of statements, what governs them and the ways they govern each other, to a politics of sense, to an analysis of the "discursive régime,"[35] which can no longer be confused with a formal paradigm and for which the appropriate model is not the linguistic system but war and battle: "relations of power, not relations of meaning."[36] As in Derrida's analysis of the frame or *parergon*,[37] it no longer has any meaning, therefore, to ask whether the structures Foucault enumerates are "inside" or "outside": They *institute* discourse, and their location eludes both an internalizing formalism and a sociologism of the external.

The convergence of views between Derrida and Foucault is striking here, despite the two philosophers' well-documented disagreements.[38] Inside and outside, event and context, work and setting, the structural and the empirical: These coupled terms—familiar to us as those that fix the polarities of an interminable methodological debate in art history— are radically displaced by Foucault's conceptualization of the discursive event and the discursive field. Yet the effects of these dualisms persist, with all that depends from the separations they inscribe, between the pure interiority of form and the determinant exteriority of context and "social" history. To understand what supports this seemingly unsurmountable separation, we must look to the apparatus that keeps it so squarely in place:

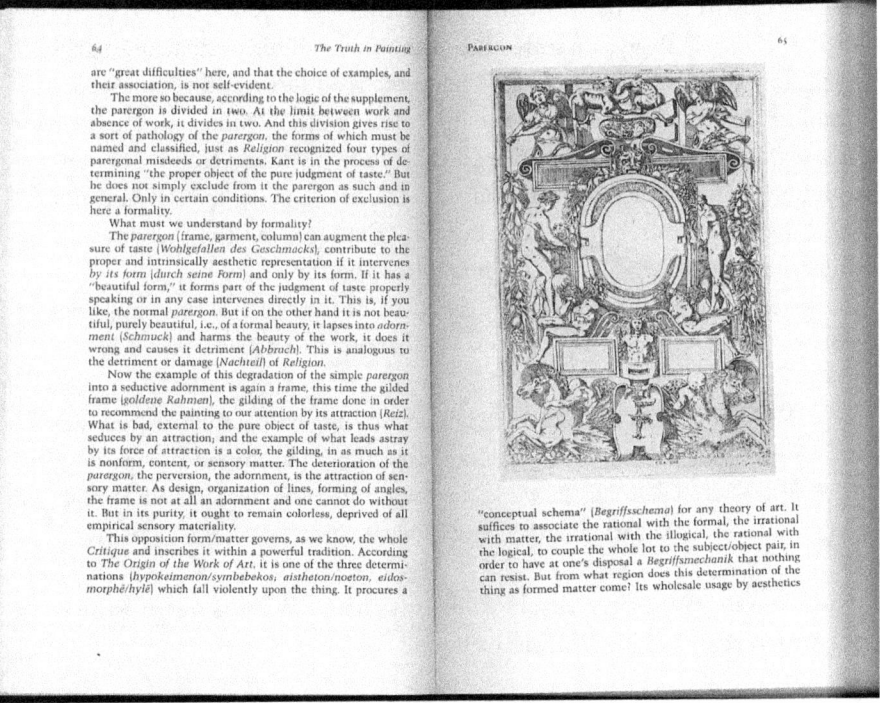

Figure 58. Antonio Fantuzzi, ornamental panel with empty oval, 1542–43. From Jacques Derrida, *The Truth in Painting* (Chicago and London: University of Chicago Press, 1987), 64–65.

to the action of what Derrida calls the frame, which, one can argue, is precisely an apparatus—a *dispositif*—in the fullest sense of Foucault's term.[39]

It is the frame, Derrida argues, that "*gives rise* to the work,"[40] in that it produces the distinction between the internal and proper sense and the circumstances, which organizes all Western philosophical discourse on art and meaning.[41] Yet the frame also troubles the very division it brings into existence. Like the supplement, the frame is an adjunct that is neither inherent nor dispensable. Marking a limit between the intrinsic and the extrinsic, it is neither inside nor outside, neither above nor below. Its thickness and depth separate it both from the integral inside of the so-called work itself and from the outside, from the wall or the space in which the work is sited, then, "step by step, from the whole field of historical, economic, political inscription in which the drive to signature is produced."[42] The frame thus stands out against the two grounds that it constitutes—the work and the setting—and yet, with respect to each of these, it always dissolves into the other.[43] This oscillation marks its presence and effaces its effect. The frame is all show, and yet it escapes visibility, like the labia that, to the infibulating eye Freud gives the little boy, already present the desolate spectacle of "nothing" to be seen, enframing the sight of pure difference.[44] The frame, too, is seen and not seen, disavowed, already at work in fixing the look and the givenness of difference, yet always denied or multiplied to infinity.

Across this denial, however, the work of the frame—this supposed adjunct to the work itself—returns. As Derrida insists:

> That which puts in place—the instances of the frame, the title, the signature, the legend, etc.—does not stop disturbing the *internal* order of discourse on painting, its works, its commerce, its evaluations, its surplus-values, its speculation, its law, and its hierarchies.[45]

The instability of difference always betrays itself. What is put at issue is the structure of the institution itself, and

> No "theory," no "practice," no "theoretical practice" can intervene effectively in this field if it does not weigh up and bear on the frame, which is the decisive structure of what is at stake, at the invisible limit to (between)

the interiority of meaning (put under shelter by the whole hermeneuticist, semioticist, phenomenologicalist, and formalist tradition) *and* (to) all the empiricisms of the extrinsic which, incapable of either seeing or reading, miss the question completely.[46]

Note the terms here: "formalist tradition" and "empiricisms of the extrinsic." Once more, the familiar polarities and unsettleable differences of art history are drawn out and reinscribed within the institution on which they hang. Once more, we find ourselves at a cutoff point, in a bounded space, up against the frame.

The Apparatus

Like the populous settings engraved by Antonio Fantuzzi that exemplify the frame in Derrida's text, the crowd in Baldessari's image is both present and absent. Describing a void, it belongs to a whole surrounding apparatus of presentation. Yet, in opening that space as a space of discourse, it is traced on the very constitution of what is presented as the event of meaning itself. This elusive limit between event and setting is scored out here by the cut of a knife that pointedly inverts the relation of image and mount. We see, however, that Baldessari has cut into his images more than once. The cut in each interior visibly frames a void that puts before us the question of the intrinsic and the extrinsic, event and setting, meaning and context. But Baldessari has also made a cut a second time, in a way that is obvious yet escapes us, cropping out unwanted meanings and spatial cues to give each print the edge of authority and the finality of a frame. So if we extend the logic of Baldessari's staging of the event of representation, what we have here are the shapes of two reasons for which the larger crowds are missing: the crowds that gather beyond the edges, beyond the crop marks, beyond the viewfinder of the camera at the scene, beyond the limits of the film set or the street, beyond whatever frame. What crowds must we now imagine into which these pictures may be fitted as the shapes of reason?

Each cut marks a threshold: "the decisive structure [as Derrida says] of what is at stake."[47] It is the historical trace of an institution of knowledge, where the object of knowledge takes its place in an architecture of presentation or places this architecture in question. It is the uncertain edge at which a proper attention—looking, listening, reading—is invoked and engaged or frustrated. It is the never-settled threshold at which a legitimized discourse is allowed to begin—like the discourse of art history, shall we say, mounting its precious or even delinquent objects in the white spaces of the modern museum, the university lecture hall, or the pages of the publishing industry and bringing to bear the full authority of its gaze.

Another crowd gathers around another void: a vacant white oblong waiting the projection of meaning, for which it has been prepared in advance. It is along its edges that a historical deconstruction might begin to operate with effect, on "the decisive structure" of the institution itself, on the order of externality and interiority it demarcates, and on the laws, evaluations, structures of knowledge, forms of spectacle, and types of commerce this order makes possible. What might be the outlines of such an operation? How might one begin to "bear on the frame" in art history, the frame of art history?

The function of the frame, like that of the prepared ground, is, as Meyer Schapiro has told us, "an advanced artifact" presupposing a long historical development.[48] Not until late in the second millennium BCE did the variable elements of frame and ground come together to constitute that closure and smoothness through which the image, in the West, acquired what Schapiro calls "a definite space of its own,"[49] marking a "fundamental change in art which is basic for our own imagery, even for the photograph, the film and the television screen."[50] Yet, Schapiro argues, just as the cropped rectangular picture without frame or margin became a commonplace of photographic illustration that seemed to appeal to immediacy and the momentary gaze, so "The frame was dispensable when painting ceased to represent deep space and became more concerned with the expressive and formal qualities of the non-mimetic marks than with their elaboration into signs."[51]

If Schapiro is right, then this would seem to be an end to it: The frame falls as artists strive to overthrow every convention in their restless search for that new idiom which is the mark of their freedom. (We might think of Jackson Pollock in Hans Namuth's photographs, if Baldessari had not been there before us and, taking his knife to Pollock's image, marked the space of the heroic artistic subject as another candid void.) But Schapiro is short of the mark, because his analysis is confined to the frame as a nonmimetic element of the image-sign. But, for Derrida, the frame is not a semantic element of a historically developed signifying system but, rather, the margin of certainty where the supposed interiority of such a system is set in place, at the price of disclosing that system's incompleteness to itself. Beyond this, what Schapiro also neglects is that, as part of the very process by which the authority of pictorial conventions and hierarchies of genre came to be weakened, the function of the frame had been absorbed into the wall and, more extensively, into the space of the gallery and then of the museum itself.[52]

Like the frame, the space of the museum encloses and displays. It cuts an inside from an outside, closing that inside on itself as pure interiority and surrounding it with value—of which the gilt of the frame is an embracing sign. What defines the museum as frame is thus the constitution of the space that constitutes art yet effaces itself in the visibility of its works. At the same time, as Jean-Claude Lebensztejn has shown, the museum can only make this cut by excluding what remains as other, its heterogeneity reduced to the status of nonart. "Everything the museum excludes from its space [Lebensztejn writes] becomes, by this exclusion, an undefined murmur, a level of noise against which art defines its difference."[53] "Such, in the last instance, is the function of the museum. It gives art its proper status by separating it from the remainder and, by its integrative function, conceals the cut that gives it the status of art."[54] Yet this remainder continues to taint the enclosure that guarantees the pure, hygienic space of art. Within the museum, the reserve collection, closed as it is to the public and consigned to secondary status, marks the trace of this undisplayable surplus. And in the silent galleries themselves, the very wall that stands for the infinite void in which art is apparently self-enclosed and self-defined also doubles as the *murmur*—the white noise of that unnameable production through whose exclusion, by the action of the frame, the wall, and the space of the museum, art is defined.

The canonicity of the museum collection is therefore haunted by a loss, and the pure interiority of its art is always tarnished by the trace of its other. It is this loss that the museum would make good in the imaginary of what Stephen Bann has called the museum's "poetics":[55] the

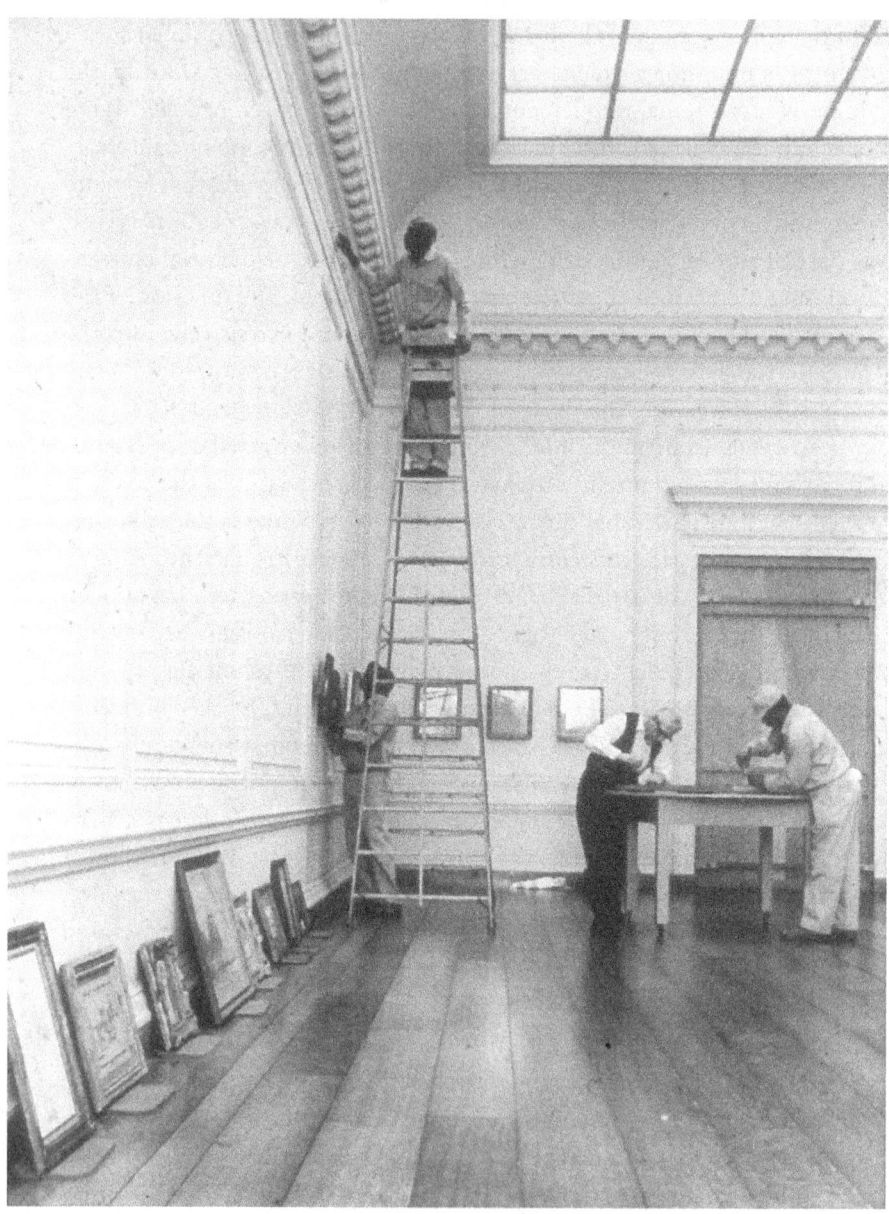

Figure 59. Installing the exhibit French Paintings from the Collections of Mr. and Mrs. Paul Mellon and Mrs. Mellon Bruce at the National Gallery of Art in Washington, D.C., 1966. Gallery Archives, National Gallery of Art, Washington, D.C.

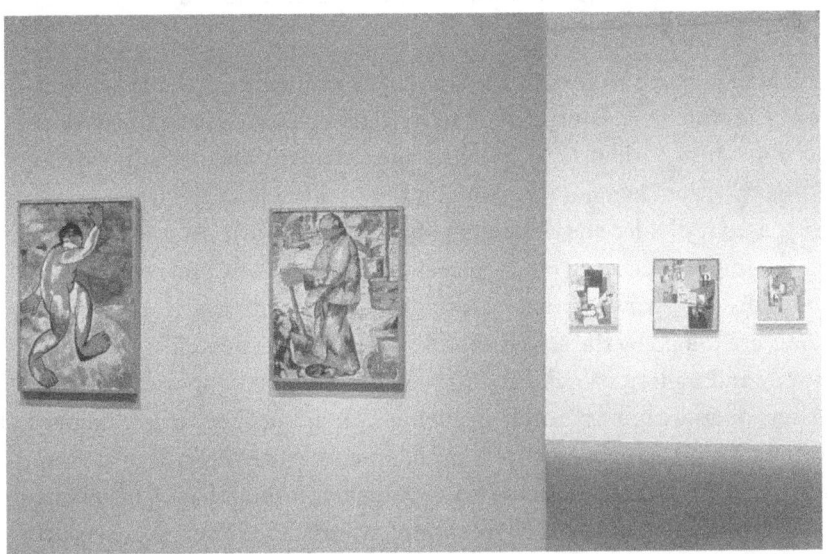

Figure 60. Installation view of the exhibit Kazimir Malevich, 1878–1935 at the National Gallery of Art in Washington, D.C., 1990. Kathleen Buckalew, Gallery Archives, National Gallery of Art, Washington, D.C.

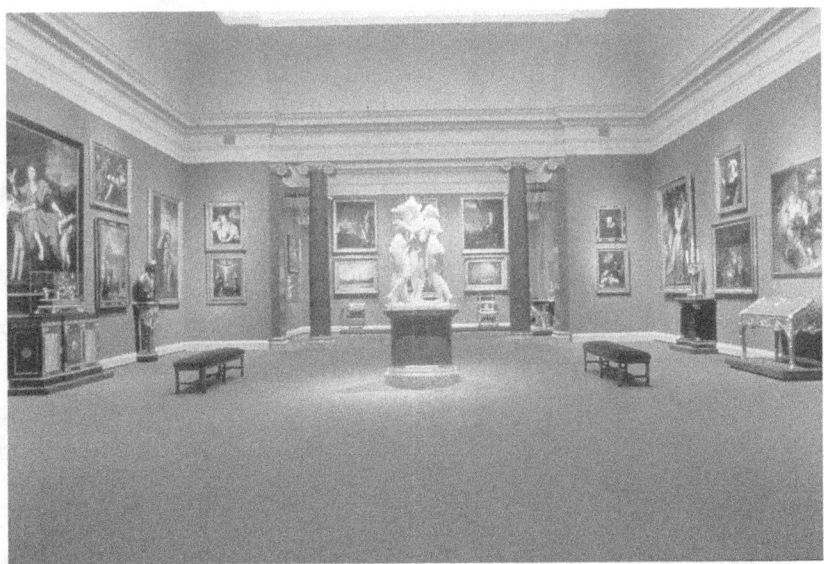

Figure 61. Installation view of the exhibit The Treasure Houses of Britain: Five Hundred Years of Private Patronage and Art Collecting, Waterloo Gallery at the National Gallery of Art, Washington, D.C., 1985. Gallery Archives, National Gallery of Art, Washington, D.C.

figures of a desire to restore the wholeness of history in the ideal totality of the historicist construction or in the reconstitution of an enveloping illusion of authenticity. We may note that the rhetorical polarities
of this "poetics" hang, once again, on the oscillation of the frame across
the spaces it divides and defines, from work to context. At one pole, the
metonymic sequences of masterpieces, schools, nations, and centuries, in
which disjunct paradigmatic objects, each systematically isolated in its
frame, are joined by the continuous wall in syntagmatic chains, from wall
to wall and gallery to gallery. At the other pole, metaphoric representations of an imaginary totality in which the frame, itself now a sign of
periodicity, links the picture to a larger ensemble or syntagma of authenticity—a contextuality offered to experience, rather than a rationalist
reconstruction of an ideal progression. And between these poles—which
are rarely present in their singular form—the narrative conflation of
artist and oeuvre serves as a kind of relay: presenting an ordered stylistic sequence, governed by evolutionary law, as a lived totality of which

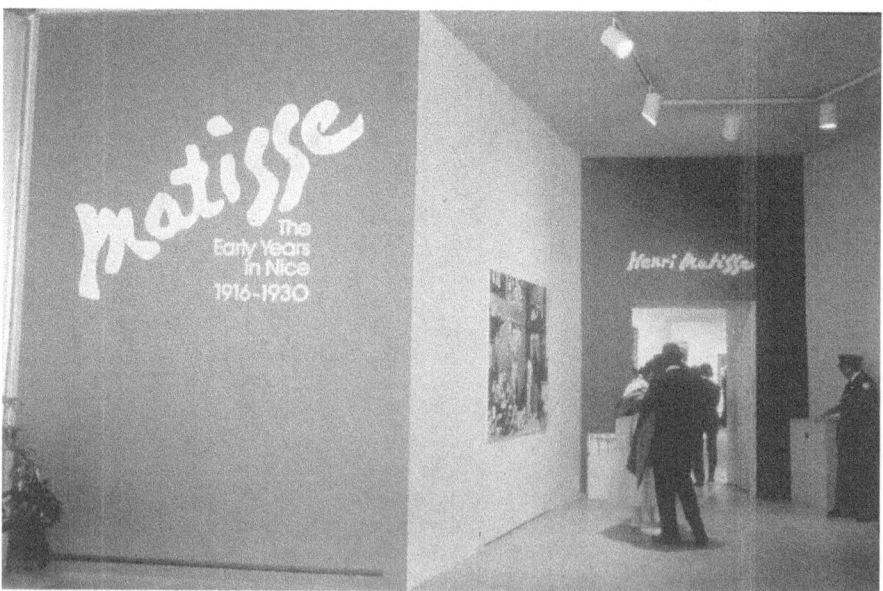

Figure 62. Entrance to the exhibit Matisse: The Early Years in Nice, 1916–1930 at the
National Gallery of Art in Washington, D.C., 1986–87. Gallery Archives, National
Gallery of Art, Washington, D.C.

KAZIMIR MALEVICH
1878–1935

Exit Only
Exhibition begins on the Mezzanine

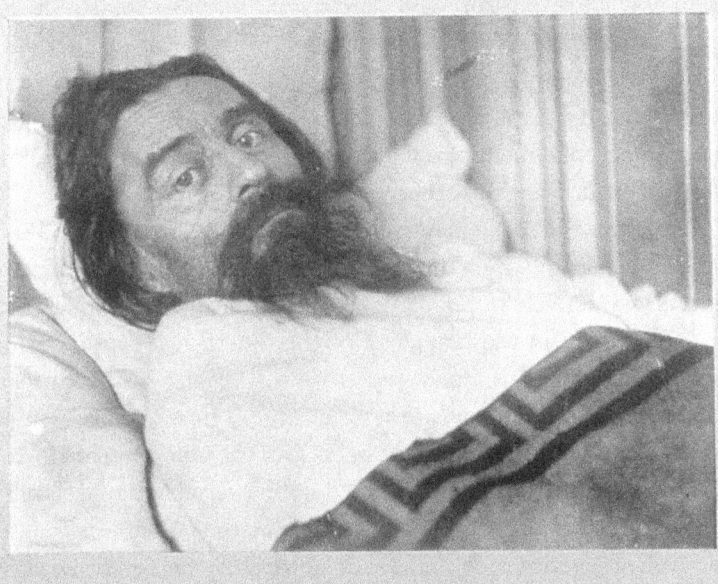

Figure 63. Exhibition panel from the exhibit Kazimir Malevich, 1878–1935 at the National Gallery of Art in Washington, D.C., 1990. Kathleen Buckalew, Gallery Archives, National Gallery of Art, Washington, D.C.

the index is the *signature*—that tear in the space of the enframed, which repeats itself countless times, in the label, in the catalog, in the spin-offs of the marketing machine, and in the lure of the name that draws us on through the sequential installation of the monographic show, from the street to the entrance and from room to room, to the exit that marks a death and the end of a series.

In the signature is written the promise of authenticity and order, the presence of the author and the integrity of the oeuvre, singularity and exchangeability, the unique and the taxonomic combined.[56] But what is also inscribed is the promise of identification with an exemplary subject—a mirror for our selves—for the frame of the museum orders meaning and knowledge, pleasure and perception, but also the structure of identification and subjection. The frame is a frame of differentiation that directs and delimits the field of visuality, setting in place a distance and separation that regulates desire and positions the viewing subject—a subject whose enjoyment of the look is exercised only through submission to the authority of the other: the gaze of the museum.[57]

Thus, if pleasure is in play in the museum, it is also at work. It is invoked to be organized. The museum orders subjectivities just as it does the objects it selectively displays. And this goes beyond the explicit moral mission, developed in the latter half of the nineteenth century, to join curatorship of culture to a pedagogy that will displace "idle curiosity" and cultivate the useful disposition of leisure—a mission in which each display case, frame, and label would be, as George Goode wrote in 1893, "a perpetual lecturer . . . constantly on duty in every large museum."[58] It was not only on this level of consciously articulated policy, however, that the museum effectively took shape as an apparatus of visual ordering and visual training: a space for the ordered production of knowledge and pleasure, where spectacle and discipline met.

Emerging across these two intersecting regimes of power, sense and vision, between the formations of spectacle and discipline, the museum, which took form as a sanctuary against the unceasing dispersal of space and time, was marked as the product of the double and conflictual drives of Western modernization. At one level, just as the museum in the West became, in a sense, a condition of everyday life through the "ordering up of the world itself as an endless exhibition,"[59] so too, within its walls, it

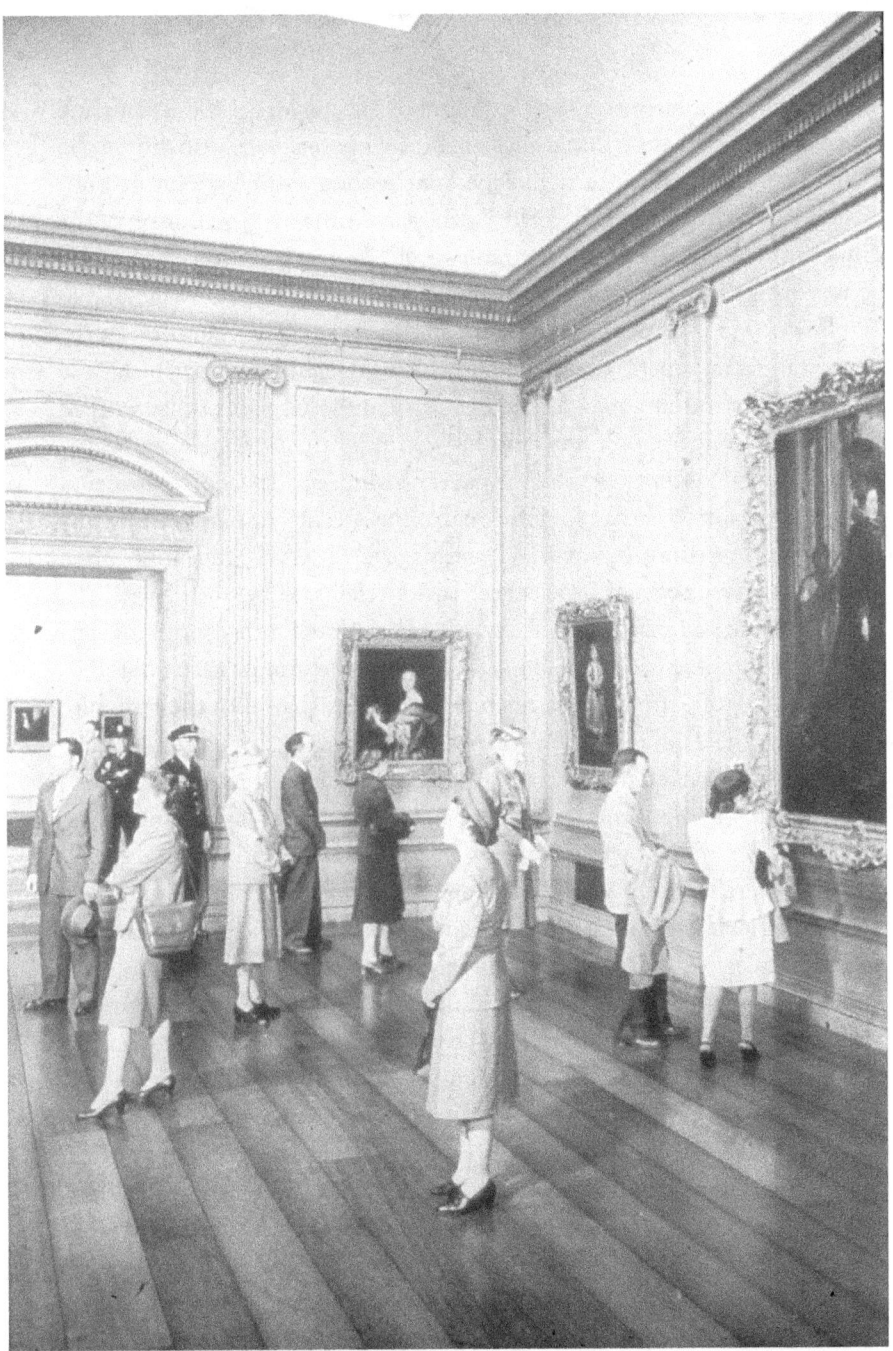

Figure 64. Visitors to the National Gallery of Art in Washington, D.C., 1947. Gallery Archives, National Gallery of Art, Washington, D.C.

was fully invested in the new economy of spectacle, reproduction, and accelerating exchange that transformed the operation of visuality in the capitalist states of western Europe and in the colonialist culture they extended to the rest of the world. At the same time, the institution of the museum was equally and inseparably implicated in what Jonathan Crary has seen as those "new forms by which vision itself became a kind of discipline or mode of work."[60] As in the disciplinary reconfiguration of the hospital, factory, prison, and school, which Foucault has described,[61] the museum instituted a new disposition of bodies and spaces that worked to procure a docile consumption in what might otherwise have been a dangerously contentious public space. Within this space, the museum set in place a new technology for managing attention, partitioning and cellularizing vision, fixing and isolating the observer, and imposing a homogeneity on visual experience. In its effects, it belonged with the development and marketing of a whole set of nineteenth-century optical and photographic products and devices, from the diorama to the stereoscope and, later, the cinema. Such technologies shattered the structure of existing fields of vision. But this was the condition for their reframing or, as Deleuze and Guattari would say, their "re-territorialization" into new institutions, new hierarchies, and new forms of exchange.[62]

The founding of art history as an academic discipline was also part of this reterritorialization. It, too, depended on the deployment of new technologies of vision, as much as it did on new modes of reproduction, circulation, indexing, and storage and on the creation of new public spaces for a culturally mobilized urban population. Yet the founders of modern art history, as Jonathan Crary has pointed out, excluded from their purview the very nineteenth-century art production whose making, consumption, and effectiveness depended on the apparatuses of vision, display, and reproduction that also made the academic practice of art history possible.[63] Only later were the categories and models developed in the analysis of the figurative art of antiquity and the Renaissance extended to the incorporation of more-recent phases of artistic production. A conflict is clearly sensed. Yet the paradox is not, as Walter Benjamin would have it, that nineteenth-century art history faced technical developments that promised to destroy forever the aura or cult value that had hitherto surrounded the work of art.[64] It is, rather, the reverse: that the technologies that marked so profound a discontinuity in the history of vision should themselves have furnished the apparatus to enframe "art" as integral, coherent, and structured internally by conventions whose authority and continuity could not be in doubt.

Once again, however, in tracing the "rules of appearance" and "conditions of appropriation" of academic art history, we are dealing with a multiple and overdetermined process. While art history emerged only through the discourses and technologies that shaped the museum, it was equally caught up in the emergence of an educational apparatus whose strategic aims and techniques of training were, in turn, to rechannel their effects into the workings of the museum. What I am thinking of here goes far beyond the usual treasured histories and anecdotes of émigré scholars and university traditions. It is the shaping of art history within the social dispersion of practices of cultural self-improvement, within the deployment of aesthetic disciplines in the school system, and within the tertiary-level training not only of a cohort of expert technicians and cultural bureaucrats but also of a cadre of "critical minds" capable of serving as trainers and exemplars in a new system of visual attentiveness as a technique of self-regulation.

A model for such a history can be found in Ian Hunter's remarkable "genealogy" of modern English criticism and literary education as "a specialised sector of the apparatus of popular education."[65] This apparatus itself was formed within the field of disciplinary techniques to which I have already referred. That is, it emerged in the dissemination of an unprecedented machinery of administration and regulation that began to surface in western Europe at the end of the eighteenth century and that, by the middle of the nineteenth century, had largely succeeded in reconstituting the everyday life of whole populations. The target of such administrative regulation was a new conception of the individual, whose health, moral conduct, criminal and sexual tendencies, and *culture* were constituted as the objects of new forms of governmental attention that aimed at reshaping the "moral and physical" order of the populace but that were made operative through forms of individual conscientiousness and disciplinary self-regulation.[66]

It is within this field of local disciplinary tactics that the deployment of "culture" in education has to be understood. For it was through this deployment that what Ian Hunter calls the "aesthetico-ethical practice" of a minority caste[67] acquired a new function by its insertion into the morally managed disciplinary environment of the public school. In the teaching of literature and criticism—and, by extension, in the teaching of art and art appreciation—an elite culture of the self was thus linked to the machinery of normalization and the corrective technologies of the public sphere, harnessing the ethical authority of the cultivated sensibility to an apparatus of governance through which the population internalized the disciplinary norms of "social" life as the seemingly spontaneous and individual project of self-realization. What such training worked to produce was not lovers of literature or art but a highly specific profile of cultural attributes necessary to the mobilization of a body of citizens or, as the British will have it, subjects. And, here, we might also remember that—as with the development of the museum—this educational strategy was and remained a national project, tying the teaching of language and literature, art and art history, into the differing forms of cultural articulation of the nationalist State.

In directing attention to the strategic effects of the museum apparatus, art history, and its pedagogical practice, I would want to stress, however, that there is no need here to conjure up a panoptic consciousness or a logic of ideology and the class State. We are dealing, for the most part, with piecemeal historical changes and technical transformations, local programmatic imperatives that take hold on the individual and the population in multiple and dispersed ways. There is no single rationality and no single outcome: no nineteenth-century observer, as Jonathan Crary would still have it, despite his doubts,[68] and no unified or stabilized discipline of art history; though that is not to say there are not always traceable limits to the possible, thinkable, or permissible mutations the field can undergo. However, we can very well think of art history, as Ian Hunter does of English literary studies and criticism, as a complex of administrative, pedagogical, ethical, and aesthetic techniques, invested in disciplinary technologies and articulated by supervisory goals that seek to exert specific effects on the constitution of a "social" field.[69] We might also want to note, in passing, the corollary that, if it is not fruitful to speculate on art history as if it assumed a singular form, then neither is it useful to expect it to respond to any single theoretical or political diagnosis or intervention. There is not only one hammer to take to this frame.

The End

These are no more than the tracings of outlines, no more than indications of possible directions. But they may be enough to show how far we would have to travel from a conception of art history as an array of methodologies, tractable to theoretical correction and ideology critique. Such indications describe a space of thinking made possible by the overlaying of the model of the apparatus and the model of the frame, that is, by the mutual pressures of Foucauldian genealogy and Derridean deconstruction. This may be surprising, especially since it implies an unfamiliar deconstruction, at least to those critics and proponents who have equated the insistence that everything is discourse or text with the unlikely belief that everything happens in books. (Some of the more fruitless standoffs in recent art historical debates begin here. But the aim, on all sides, has mostly been a coup in the boardroom and business as usual.) Yet Derrida has been clear enough that

> It is because deconstruction interferes with solid structures, "material" institutions, and not only with discourses or signifying representations, that it is always distinct from an analysis or a "critique." And in order to be pertinent, deconstruction works as strictly as possible in that place where the supposedly "internal" order of the philosophical is articulated by (internal *and* external) necessity with the institutional conditions and forms of teaching. To the point where the concept of institution itself would be subjected to the same deconstructive treatment.[70]

What follows for art history is not a form of conventional institutional history. But neither is it an endless metacommentary, generating a universe of tertiary texts that float in a self-sufficient space without coordinates, detached from the realm of the social and political. The very terms of this commonplace accusation merely repeat the action of the frame that deconstruction puts at issue. In their very implied promise of another space of genuinely political critique, necessarily "outside" textuality, these terms effectively remove the institution from the reach of political judgment. The deconstruction of the oppositions of internal to external, work to commentary, the rhetorical to the literal, texts to action, discourse to politics, and theory to practice transforms the concept of the institution and changes the conceptual space in which the political is thought.[71] It displaces those politics that seek to ground themselves on criteria that cannot themselves be grasped as political, because they are presented as the state of things, the literal or the real. It insists on the necessity of political judgments and strategic choices, not on the basis of the decoding of a hidden social content but on the basis of a positional calculation of the power effects of discursive practices on and in the field of sociality.

If deconstruction of the institution of art history withdraws from "social" critique, it does so, therefore, precisely in order to foreground the question of political and ethical practice, precisely in order to drive home the stakes of the discipline. But stakes are not interests. They are not the markers of what lies behind, so that this political practice cannot take the form of an unmasking. But neither can it stop at a mapping or traversal of the spaces, boundaries, closures, fractures, and linkages of the institutional formation. To question art history's finalities is to open the question of its ends. And when it is open, the question of ends compels contesting voices to speak to the stakes on which they are banking and to which they would have art history tied.

So art history is always tied to the stake. It seems we must prepare ourselves, therefore, for pain and suffering. The space in the crowd threatens to be that of a martyrdom. But what of the instability of structures? And what of dissidence, deviance, or resistance as pleasure and even joy?

Let us plunge into the crowd one final time. Back into the crowd of Canetti—the title of whose book, *Masse und Macht*, might more literally be translated as "Masses and Power." For Canetti, the crowd or mass does not conform to its image either in Marxism or in psychoanalysis, even in their structuralist variants. It is not the collective subject or the figure of the future whose allotted task in vulgar Marxist teleologies is to actualize a necessary moment of the historicist dialectic. Neither is it the regressive, infantile, primitive horde of psychoanalysis, bound by terror and guilt in submission to a masterful father-leader, on whom the horde projects a common ego ideal. No more is it the subject of structuralist interpolation, in which Freud's narrative of identification is transferred to the structure of the Law and the Ideological State Apparatus. By contrast, Canetti's account, as Michel Feher reads it, "does not consider mass in terms of revelation, regression, or submission, but in terms of the will for power."[72] The crowd is not contained by submission to the systematics of destiny or authority but is a contagious, turbulent pack—"a true incarnation of a multiplicity of disseminating effects"[73]— that breaks out whenever "events" call it forth and the systems that have worked to conjure its powers away find they have only the effect of focusing and exacerbating the crowd's disruptive drives.

This crowd does not, therefore, surge from "in itself" to "for itself," toward its own as yet undisclosed, historical reason. This crowd is not slave to a void into which it has projected the fantasized power of its own imaginary figure. This crowd is a pack, beyond all reason and restraint; a force field without shape that propagates the void only as the trace of its own internal limit, as unassignable drive turns into decline. This crowd is not, then, the model of a structuralist system; nor is it the docile subject of an omnipresent disciplinary power. It is dangerous and motile. It breaks all formal bounds. It erupts, like the crowd of White residents and servicemen in downtown Los Angeles who, over several nights in June 1943, savagely beat and stripped young Mexican American pachucos on the street in what, by a telling reversal, came to be dubbed the "zoot-suit riots."

This last image of the crowd framing the victims of racist policing in Los Angeles is one that we have encountered before. It may bring into the picture not only memories of more-recent events but also the terms of my earlier argument.[74] What this might signal here is that, if the crowd as a structure of closure is never predictable, stable, or fixed, then neither is the event of meaning ever stripped bare or contained en masse and utterly exhausted by its frame. The violence in Los Angeles was, as we saw, fired by a suit of clothes that insisted on drawing attention to itself, flaunting its excess and perversion of the proper form.[75] The language of the zoot suit, the language of *Caló*, the *mestizo* language of pachucos and pachucas, crossed over all borders. It evaded the spaces of separatism and segregation. It was mobile and inventive and disassembled the codes and protocols of Anglo and Mexican speech, dress, and culture to release a play of identity and difference that fitted no known frame.

In the face of the regimes that frame and enclose our lives, this is, then, more than resistance as negation, more than inversion, more than the recoil of suffering, constraint, and loss. It is the burden of lack lived as the exhilaration of incompletion; the pain of silence turned into exuberance beyond speech. I therefore offer the pachuca and pachuco again as shapes of another reason for a deconstructive art history on which their strategy will not be lost. As Lyotard said, the way beyond capital's hegemony and the "bloody impasses" of the great doctrinal systems lies not in the terror of legitimation through tradition or myth, which in the end amount to the same thing.[76] It comes

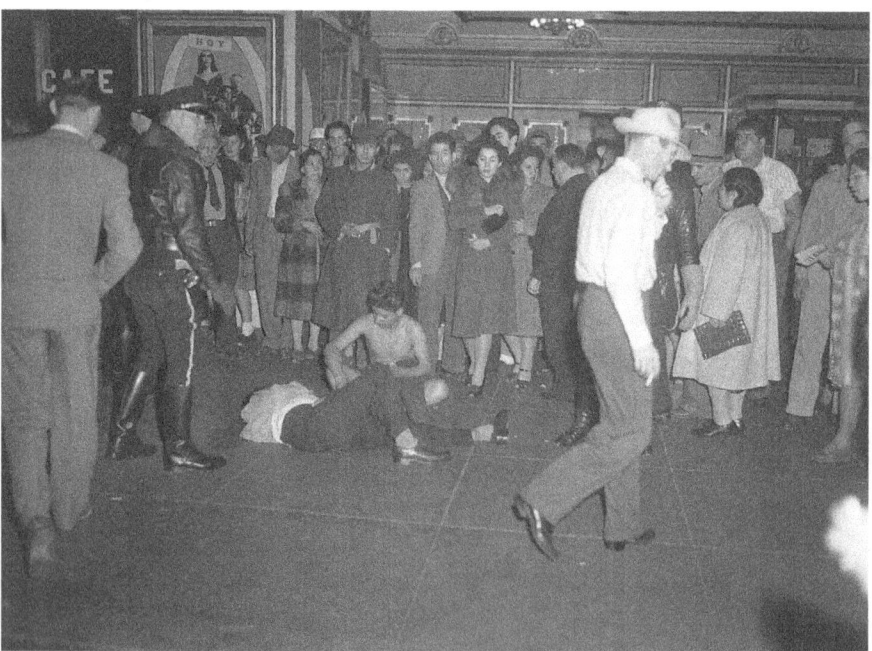

Figure 65. "These youths, one stripped of all his clothes, the others badly beaten, fell victim to raging bands of policemen who scoured the streets in Los Angeles on June 7, 1943, ferreting out and beating zoot-suited young hoodlums they blame for the numerous recent unprovoked assaults. Fifty or more zoot suiters had their clothing torn from them, police reported." Photography courtesy of AP Images/Harold P. Matosian.

when human beings who thought they could use language as an instrument of communication learn through the feeling of pain which accompanies silence (and of pleasure which accompanies the invention of a new idiom), that they are summoned by language, not to augment to their profit the quantity of information communicable through existing idioms, but to recognize that what remains to be phrased exceeds what they can presently phrase, and that they must be allowed to institute idioms which do not yet exist.[77]

Perhaps there is even an echo of Meyer Schapiro in this: If we are to live, we are all constrained to strike against the frame.

Notes

Introduction

1. W. G. Sebald, *The Emigrants*, trans. Michael Hulse (New York: New Directions Books, 1997).

2. Ibid., 39.

3. Ibid., 94–95.

4. Ibid., 186.

5. Ibid., 184.

6. Ibid., 235.

7. Ibid., 237.

8. Ibid., 239.

9. Brigitte Frase, *New York Newsday*, cited in ibid., i–ii.

10. Sebald, *Emigrants*, 25.

11. Champfleury [J.-F.-F. Husson], *Histoire de la caricature moderne* (Paris, 1865), 72, cited in T. J. Clark, *The Absolute Bourgeois: Artists and Politics in France, 1848–1851* (London: Thames and Hudson, 1973), 100. The lithograph in question is Honoré Daumier's "Vous avez la parole, expliquez-vous, vous êtes libre," which appeared in *La caricature*, no. 216, May 14, 1835.

12. Walter Benjamin, "Critique of Violence" (1921), in *One-Way Street and Other Writings*, trans. Edmund Jephcott and Kingsley Shorter (London: New Left Books, 1979), 132–54. I also draw here on Jacques Derrida's challenging reading of Benjamin's essay in "Force of Law: The 'Mystical Foundations of Authority,'" in *Deconstruction and the Possibility of Justice*, ed. Drucilla Cornell, Michel Rosenfeld, and David Gray Carlson (New York: Routledge, 1992), 3–67, and on Jean-François Lyotard's extraordinary meditation *The Differend: Phrases*

in Dispute, trans. Georges Van Den Abbeele (Minneapolis: University of Minnesota Press, 1988).

13. Thomas Byrnes, inspector of police and chief of detectives for New York City, oversaw the preparation of albums he called "probably the most complete criminal directory in the country." Ever eager to exploit public interest, Byrnes, like Philip Farley before him, published—"Pro Bono Publico"—a selection from this "Rogue's Gallery" in *Professional Criminals of America* (New York, 1885). It is this volume that contains, in the section "Why Thieves Are Photographed," between pages 52 and 53, the photographic illustration "The Inspector's Model," copyrighted by Byrnes himself in 1884 (Figure 3). Byrnes also coauthored, with Helen C. Campbell and Thomas W. Knox, *Darkness and Daylight, or Lights and Shadows of New York Life* (Hartford, Conn.: Hartford Publishing Co., 1899), which repeats the joke in the plate "An Unwilling Subject.—Photographing a Prisoner for the Rogue's Gallery at Police Headquarters" (Figure 5). Described as engraved after a photograph, the plate in fact shows what is necessarily elided in Byrnes's photographic version: the presence of the camera and camera operator. This is also the case with Sir Luke Fildes's earlier prototype "'The Bashful Model': Photographing a Prisoner in Gaol" (Figure 4), which was published in *Graphic* 8, no. 206 (Saturday, November 8, 1873), 440–41, and with C. Upham's sketch "Illinois—The Anarchist Trials at Chicago—A Scene at Police Headquarters—Photographing Criminals," for the cover of *Frank Leslie's Illustrated Newspaper*, week ending July 31, 1886.

The repeated play on "Rogue's Gallery"—not yet a dead metaphor—and on the comic foil of the studio portrait, the model, and the "bashful" beauty not only betrays a normative notion of gender, class, and the social relations of representation but also lets slip an anxiety about a difference that was being made but that was not yet to be taken for granted as a new economy of meaning was instituted. It is in the period of uncertainty that this little theater of justice, the camera, and the reluctant sitter, pictured by Fildes, Byrnes, and Upham, becomes a scene of fascination and contention to which the press and, especially, photographic journals—ever jealous of the status of the photograph and the interests of the photographic trade—would return again and again, beginning as early as the 1850s but with increasing insistence in the 1870s and '80s.

See also Philip Farley, Detective, *Criminals of America, or Tales of the Lives of Thieves: Enabling Every One to Be His Own Detective. With Portraits, Making a Complete Rogue's Gallery* (New York: Author's edition, 1876).

14. Jacques Lacan, *The Four Fundamental Concepts of Psycho-Analysis*, ed. Jacques-Alain Miller, trans. Alan Sheridan (Harmondsworth, U.K.: Penguin Books, 1979), 106.

15. Derrida, "Force of Law," 29.

16. For the concepts of the remainder, of linguistic mastery, and of language as a field of violent enunciative events, see Jean-Jacques Lecercle, "The Violence of Language," chap. 6 of *The Violence of Language* (London and New York: Routledge, 1990), 224–64.

17. For Foucault's opposition between the juridico-political edifice of sovereignty and rights and the material operations and techniques of discipline, domination, and subjugation, see Michel Foucault, "Two Lectures," chap. 5 of *Power/Knowledge: Selected Interviews and Other Writings, 1972–1977*, ed. Colin Gordon (Brighton, U.K.: Harvester Press, 1980), esp. "Lecture Two: 14 January 1976," 92–108. See also Michel Foucault, *Discipline and Punish: The Birth of the Prison*, trans. Alan Sheridan (New York: Vintage Books, 1979), 221–24.

18. See Foucault, *Discipline and Punish*, pt. 3, chap. 3, "Panopticism," 195–228, esp. 202–7. Foucault's use of "apparatus" as a term allied with "machine," "machinery," "technology of power," or "diagram" must be distinguished here from the use of "apparatus" as an abbreviation for "State Apparatus": see ibid., 213–17. See also Gilles Deleuze, "A New Cartographer (*Discipline and Punish*)," in *Foucault*, trans. Seán Hand (Minneapolis: University of Minnesota Press, 1988), 23–44.

19. John Tagg, introduction to *The Burden of Representation: Essays on Photographies and Histories* (London: Macmillan, 1988), 4–5. For Barthes's view of the photograph's "evidential force," see Roland Barthes, *Camera Lucida: Reflections on Photography*, trans. Richard Howard (London: Jonathan Cape, 1982), 88.

20. This phrase, which furnished the title of the book and took on an afterlife of its own in other fields, especially African American and postcolonial studies, was first used as the title of an essay in the independent journal *Ten: 8*; the essay was retitled for inclusion in the volume. See "The Burden of Representation: Photography and the Growth of the State," *Ten: 8*, no. 14 (1984): 10–12.

21. Geoffrey Batchen, *Burning with Desire: The Conception of Photography* (Cambridge, Mass., and London: MIT Press, 1997), 194; see also 7, 20–21, 176–77, 188–89.

22. John Tagg, "The Discontinuous City: Picturing and the Discursive Field," in *Grounds of Dispute: Art History, Cultural Politics, and the Discursive Field* (London: Macmillan; Minneapolis: University of Minnesota Press, 1992), 143.

23. "Introduction/Opening," in Tagg, *Grounds of Dispute*, 33.

24. Cf. Gilles Deleuze and Félix Guattari, chap. 13, "7000 B.C.: Apparatus of Capture," in *A Thousand Plateaus: Capitalism and Schizophrenia*, trans. Brian Massumi (Minneapolis: University of Minnesota Press, 1987), 424–73.

25. John Grierson, "Education and the New Order" (1941), in *Grierson on Documentary*, ed. Forsyth Hardy (New York: Harcourt, Brace, 1947), 235.

26. Grierson, "Education and Total Effort" (1941), in *Grierson on Documentary* (1947), 247.

27. Grierson, "The Challenge of Peace" (1945), in *Grierson on Documentary* (1947), 299.

28. Grierson, "The Nature of Propaganda" (1942), in *Grierson on Documentary* (1947), 211.

29. Lacan, *The Four Fundamental Concepts of Psycho-Analysis*, ix; Jean-François Lyotard, *The Inhuman: Reflections on Time*, trans. Geoffrey Bennington and Rachel Bowlby (Stanford, Calif.: Stanford University Press, 1991), 142–43; Julia Kristeva, *Black Sun: Depression and Melancholia*, trans. Leon S. Roudiez (New York: Columbia University Press, 1989), 13–15.

30. See James R. Hugunin, "Disputing Grounds," *Views* 13, no. 4, and 14, no. 1 (Winter 1993): 17.

31. Thus, the frame, which marks the institution of what is proper, what is interior, and what is exterior, cannot be dissolved, as Alan Trachtenberg would have it, into the externality of a defining "context" of "social use" that a diligent historian can, at least, aspire to reconstruct through the accumulation of appropriate "verbal documentation." See Alan Trachtenberg, "Introduction: Photographs as Symbolic History," in National Archives and Records Service, *The American Image: Photographs from the National Archives, 1860–1960* (New York: Pantheon Books, 1979), xxv, xxvi.

32. Ralph Ellison, *Invisible Man* (New York: Vintage Books, 1990), 441.

33. James Agee and Walker Evans, *Let Us Now Praise Famous Men: Three Tenant Families* (Boston: Houghton Mifflin, 1941).

34. Alain Robbe-Grillet, *Ghosts in the Mirror: A Romanesque*, trans. Jo Levy (New York: Grove Weidenfeld, 1988), 48.

35. Michel Foucault, "The Discourse on Language," trans. Rupert Swyer, appendix to *The Archaeology of Knowledge* (New York: Pantheon Books, 1972), 216, 229.

36. Cf. Karl Marx, "The Eighteenth Brumaire of Louis Bonaparte," in Karl Marx and Frederick Engels, *Collected Works* (London: Lawrence and Wishart, 1979), 11:176.

1. The One-Eyed Man and the One-Armed Man

1. Jacques Lacan, *The Four Fundamental Concepts of Psycho-Analysis*, ed. Jacques-Alain Miller, trans. Alan Sheridan (Harmondsworth, U.K.: Penguin Books, 1979), 112.

2. Cf. Gilles Deleuze and Félix Guattari, *A Thousand Plateaus: Capitalism and Schizophrenia*, trans. Brian Massumi (Minneapolis: University of Minnesota Press, 1987), 456–60.

3. Alan Trachtenberg, "Introduction: Photographs as Symbolic History," in National Archives and Records Service, *The American Image: Photographs from the National Archives, 1860–1960* (New York: Pantheon Books, 1979), xxv, xxviii, xx.

4. For a discussion of the emergence of this term, in a volume whose purpose was to propagate it, see A. L. Rees and Frances Borzello, introduction to A. L. Rees and F. Borzello, eds., *The New Art History: An Anthology* (London: Camden Press, 1985), 2–10.

5. T. J. Clark, "The Conditions of Artistic Creation," *Times Literary Supplement*, May 24, 1974, 562. See also T. J. Clark, chap. 1, "On the Social History of Art," in *Image of the People: Gustave Courbet and the 1848 Revolution* (London: Thames and Hudson, 1973), 9–20. The later expression of regret is found in the 1981 "Preface to the New Edition," in *Image of the People* (London: Thames and Hudson, 1982), 6. The phrase did not only appear in a chapter title, however. The "M.A. in the Social History of Art" was also the name Clark gave to the graduate program in art history that he founded in the Department of Fine Art at Leeds University in 1976.

6. The two symposia sessions were "What Use Is Deconstruction Anyway?" organized by Norman Bryson, and "Assessing the Marxist Tradition in U.S. Art History," convened by O. K. Werkmeister. See College Art Association of America, *Abstracts and Program Statements*, 76th Annual Meeting, Houston, February 11–13, 1988, 1–4, 10–22.

7. Centre for Contemporary Cultural Studies, *The Empire Strikes Back: Race and Racism in 70s Britain* (London: Hutchinson and the Centre for Contemporary Cultural Studies, University of Birmingham, 1984); first published in *Working Papers in Cultural Studies* in 1982.

8. See Clark, "The Conditions of Artistic Creation," 562: "For diversification, read disintegration."

9. I am thinking here of the description of the Commune's tactics in Kristin Ross, "The Transformation of Social Space," chap. 1 of *The Emergence of Social Space: Rimbaud and the Paris Commune* (Minneapolis: University of Minnesota Press, 1988), 32–46.

10. See Louis Althusser, "Ideology and Ideological State Apparatuses (Notes towards an Investigation)," in *Lenin and Philosophy and Other Essays*, trans. Ben Brewster (London: New Left Books, 1971), 121–73. This essay, completed in April 1970 and first published in *La pensée* the same year, dominated

discussions in Britain in the late 1970s and even the early 1980s and often represented the only text by Althusser that advocates could cite. The problem was that this attempt to escape the abstractions of *Reading Capital* and respond to events on the streets of Paris took Althusser back to the very theoretical terrain he had himself decisively undermined in his monumental essay "Contradiction et Surdetermination (Notes pour une recherche)," which appeared first in *La pensée* in December 1962 and was reprinted in his collection *Pour Marx* (Paris: Librairie François Maspero, 1965), 85–128; it appeared in English as "Contradiction and Overdetermination: Notes for an Investigation," in Louis Althusser, *For Marx*, trans. Ben Brewster (London: Allen Lane, 1969), 87–128.

11. See Paul Hill, Angela Kelly, and John Tagg, *Three Perspectives on Photography* (London: Arts Council of Great Britain, 1979); and Tagg, "Power and Photography—Part I: A Means of Surveillance. The Photograph as Evidence in Law," *Screen Education*, no. 36 (Autumn 1980): 17–55. The latter essay grew out of a lecture given in the series Over-Exposed: A Look at the Current Situation in Photography, organized by Sarah Kent at the Institute of Contemporary Arts, London, to coincide with the exhibition Photography as Art—Art as Photography, from January 10 to February 14, 1979.

12. John Tagg, "A Socialist Perspective on Photographic Practice," in Hill, Kelly, and Tagg, *Three Perspectives on Photography*, 71.

13. For a discussion of the critical inflation of the threat or promise of photographic technologies, see John Tagg, "Totalled Machines: Criticism, Photography, and Technological Change," *New Formations*, no. 7 (Spring 1989): 21–34; reprinted in Tagg, *Grounds of Dispute: Art History, Cultural Politics, and the Discursive Field* (London: Macmillan, 1992; Minneapolis: University of Minnesota Press, 1992), 115–33.

14. See Bernard Edelman, *Le droit saisi par la photographie* (Paris: Librairie François Maspero, 1973); translated by Elizabeth Kingdom as *Ownership of the Image: Elements for a Marxist Theory of Law* (London: Routledge and Kegan Paul, 1979).

15. Deleuze and Guattari, *A Thousand Plateaus*, esp. chap. 13, "7000 B.C.: Apparatus of Capture," 424–73.

16. Michel Foucault, *Discipline and Punish: The Birth of the Prison*, trans. Alan Sheridan (Harmondsworth, U.K.: Allen Lane, Penguin Press, 1977), 191.

17. See Michel Foucault, "The Eye of Power" (1977), in *Power/Knowledge: Selected Interviews and Other Writings, 1972–1977*, ed. Colin Gordon (Brighton, U.K.: Harvester Press, 1980), 159.

18. See John Tagg, "The Discontinuous City: Picturing and the Discursive Field," in Tagg, *Grounds of Dispute*, 134–56; reprinted in Norman Bryson,

Michael Ann Holly, and Keith Moxey, eds., *Visual Culture: Images and Interpretations* (Hanover, N.H., and London: Wesleyan University Press/University Press of New England, 1994), 83–103.

19. See Jeremy Bentham, *Panopticon, or The Inspection-House: Containing the Idea of a New Principle of Construction Applicable to Any Sort of Establishment, in Which Persons of Any Description Are to Be Kept under Inspection: And in Particular to Penitentiary-Houses, Prisons, Houses of Industry, Work-Houses, Poor-Houses, Manufactories, Mad-Houses, Lazarettos, Hospitals, and Schools: With a Plan of Management Adapted to the Principle: In a Series of Letters, Written in the Year 1787* (repr., London: T. Payne, 1791). For Foucault's discussion of Bentham's *Panopticon*, see Foucault, *Discipline and Punish*, "Panopticism," 195–228, and "The Eye of Power," 146–65. See also Jacques-Alain Miller, "Le despotisme de l'Utile: La machine panoptique de Jeremy Bentham," *Ornicar? Bulletin périodique du Champ freudien* 3 (May 1975).

20. Though this is not at all to say that the Panopticon is a metaphor or that Foucault deploys it as such. It is all the more regrettable, then, that this is how Allan Sekula seeks to dispose of the threat of Foucault's work, in a single footnote to his landmark essay "The Body and the Archive," *October*, no. 39 (Winter 1986): 9n13.

21. Michel Foucault, "The Discourse on Language," trans. Rupert Swyer, appendix to *The Archaeology of Knowledge* (New York: Pantheon Books, 1972), 220; originally *L'ordre du discours* (Paris: Gallimard, 1971).

22. *L'ordre du discours*, published by Gallimard in Paris in 1971, was the text of the inaugural lecture Foucault delivered at the Collège de France on December 2, 1970, following his election to the Chair in the History of Systems of Thought on April 12, 1970.

23. Foucault, "The Discourse on Language," 216.

24. Raymond Williams, *The Long Revolution* (London: Chatto and Windus, 1961), 64–65.

25. For the notion of "instigative violence," see the introduction above.

26. See, for example, Michel Foucault, "Powers and Strategies" (1977), in *Power/Knowledge*, 139–42.

27. Cf. Michel Foucault, "Truth and Power" (1977), in *Power/Knowledge*, 131.

28. On this mutation, see Michel Foucault, "Two Lectures" (January 7, 1976; January 14, 1976), in *Power/Knowledge*, 78–108. The full transcription of these lectures is found in Michel Foucault, *"Society Must Be Defended": Lectures at the Collège de France, 1975–1976*, ed. Mauro Bertani and Alessandro Fontana, trans. David Macey (New York: Picador, 2003), 1–41. For Foucault's phrase "general politics," see Foucault, "Truth and Power," 131.

29. Foucault, "Two Lectures," 99. See also Foucault, "The Eye of Power," 151, 155, 159; "Two Lectures," 103, 104; and "Truth and Power," 119, 125.

30. For Foucault's concepts of the "political economy of truth" and the "régime of truth," see "Truth and Power," 131–33. For the distinction between the open field of "sociality" and the unstable closure of "society," see Ernesto Laclau and Chantal Mouffe, "Beyond the Positivity of the Social: Antagonisms and Hegemony," chap. 3 of *Hegemony and Socialist Strategy: Towards a Radical Democratic Politics* (London and New York: Verso, 1985), 93–148.

31. Foucault, "The Eye of Power," 155.

32. Slavoj Žižek, "Enjoy Your Nation as Yourself!" in *Tarrying with the Negative: Kant, Hegel, and the Critique of Ideology* (Durham, N.C.: Duke University Press, 1993), 200.

33. Ibid., 202.

34. Ibid., 210, 203, 215.

35. Ibid., 203.

36. Ibid., 210.

37. Ibid., 206.

38. Ibid., 202.

39. Ibid., 220, 216.

40. See Foucault, *"Society Must Be Defended,"* chaps. 3 to 10, 43–238.

41. Stuart Hall, "The State in Question," in *The Idea of the Modern State*, ed. Gregor McLennan, David Held, and Stuart Hall (Milton Keynes, U.K., and Philadelphia: Open University Press, 1984), 1.

42. Philip Bobbitt, *The Shield of Achilles: War, Peace, and the Course of History* (New York: Alfred A. Knopf, 2002).

43. Ibid., 80, 83.

44. Ibid., 87.

45. Ibid., 97.

46. Ibid., 209.

47. Ibid., 67.

48. Ibid., 74.

49. Ibid., 107.

50. See ibid., 79, 83–85, 88, 100.

51. Pierre Clastres, *Society against the State*, trans. Robert Hurley (New York: Zone Books, 1989).

52. Ibid., 189.

53. Ibid., 212, 214, 215.

54. Ibid., 218.

55. Ibid., 205.

56. Deleuze and Guattari, *A Thousand Plateaus*, chap. 12, "1227: Treatise on Nomadology—The War Machine," Proposition 2, "The exteriority of the war machine is also attested to by ethnology (a tribute to the memory of Pierre Clastres)," 357–61, and chap. 13, "7000 B.C.: Apparatus of Capture," Proposition 11, "Which Comes First?" 427–37.

57. Deleuze and Guattari, *A Thousand Plateaus*, 359.

58. Ibid., 357–58.

59. Ibid., 429, 431.

60. Ibid., 360, 429.

61. Ibid., 430.

62. Ibid., 435.

63. Ibid., 435, 437.

64. Ibid., 352, 358, 424–25, 456–57.

65. Ibid., 434.

66. Ibid., 360.

67. Ibid., 360.

68. Ibid., 351, 424, 459.

69. Ibid., 424, 428, 456–58.

70. Ibid., 366.

71. Ibid., 362–63, 370, 380–82.

72. Ibid., 361, 364, 367, 369, 374.

73. Ibid., 364.

74. Ibid., 368.

75. Ibid., 354.

76. Michael Hardt and Antonio Negri, *Multitude: War and Democracy in the Age of Empire* (London and New York: Penguin Books, 2004).

77. The classic source for Marx's account is his three addresses on the Paris Commune in "The Civil War in France" (1871), in Karl Marx and V. I. Lenin, *Civil War in France: The Paris Commune* (New York: International Publishers, 1988), 23–85. This is, of course, the view of the State that Lenin takes up. See V. I. Lenin, *The State and Revolution* (Peking: Foreign Languages Press, 1965), also in *Selected Works of V. I. Lenin*, vol. 2, pt. 1 (Moscow: Foreign Languages Publishing House, 1952); and Lenin, "Writings on the Commune," in Marx and Lenin, *Civil War in France*, 89–129.

For Foucault's rejection of the notion of the State apparatus as the causative force in the development of new technologies of power, see earlier discussion in this chapter and Foucault, "Truth and Power," and, more expansively, *"Society Must Be Defended,"* especially Lecture One, January 7, 1976, and Lecture Two, January 14, 1976, 1–41.

78. See Foucault, *"Society Must Be Defended,"* esp. Lectures Six, February 11, 1976, and Seven, February 18, 1976, 115–66. We might contrast Foucault's notion of war as a schema for analyzing power and understanding the history of the State with Philip Bobbitt's sweeping view of the evolutionary interrelationship between revolutions in military tactics and strategy and the development of constitutional forms. See Bobbitt, *The Shield of Achilles,* esp. pt. 2, "A Brief History of the Modern State and Its Constitutional Orders," chaps. 5, 6, 7, 8, and 9, 67–209. As discussed above, Bobbitt's central thesis is that "it is the constitutional order of the State that tends to confer military advantage by achieving cohesion, continuity, and, above all, legitimacy for its strategic operations. And it is these strategic operations, through continuous innovation, that winnow out unsuccessful constitutional orders" (209). In relation to the period under discussion, Bobbitt argues that "Napoleon . . . forced every territorial state eventually to conform itself to the state-nation model if it was to compete militarily" (159). The state-nation model is "a state that mobilizes a nation—a national, ethnocultural group—to act on behalf of the State" (146). However, the arming of vast conscript armies and the political mobilization of the masses in defense of a national identity and the State that defined it involved definite dangers. The Prussian solution to this, as Bobbitt sees it, was the militarization of the entire society (203), a development that entailed a new State form and a new form of State power in which "the state undertook to guide and manage the entire society, because without the total effort of all sectors of society, modern warfare could not be successfully waged" (204).

79. Cf. Foucault, *"Society Must Be Defended,"* Lecture Two, January 14, 1976, where Foucault argues that "From the nineteenth century until the present day, we have then in modern societies, on the one hand, a legislation, a discourse, and an organization of public right articulated around the principle of the sovereignty of the social body and the delegation of individual sovereignty to the State; and we also have a tight grid of disciplinary coercions that actually guarantees the cohesion of that social body. Now that grid cannot in any way be transcribed in right, even though the two necessarily go together. A right of sovereignty and a mechanics of discipline. It is, I think, between these two limits that power is exercised" (37). What Foucault excludes here is a third mechanics, not of sovereignty or of discipline but of *Cultur.*

80. Cf. P. G. W. Glare, ed., *The Oxford Latin Dictionary* (Oxford: Clarendon Press, 1982), 466–67.

81. Cf. ibid., 329–30.

82. See, for example, Kant's usage in his *Critique of Pure Reason* of 1781 and his *Anthropologie* of 1798, as cited in A. L. Kroeber and Clyde Kluckhohn,

Culture: A Critical Review of Concepts and Definitions, Papers of the Peabody Museum of American Archaeology and Ethnology, Harvard University, vol. 42, no. 1 (Cambridge, Mass.: The Museum, 1952), 23–24.

83. Wilhelm von Humboldt, *Über die Kawi-Sprache* (Berlin, 1836).

84. Kroeber and Kluckhohn, *Culture.* See also Edward Burnett Tylor, *Primitive Culture: Researches into the Development of Mythology, Philosophy, Religion, Art, and Custom,* 2 vols. (London: J. Murray, 1871).

We might compare here the genealogy of "culture" offered in Raymond Williams's *Keywords: A Vocabulary of Culture and Society* (New York: Oxford University Press, 1985), 87–93. What Williams had tried to do in *Culture and Society, 1780–1950* (London: Chatto and Windus, 1958) and what he continued to attempt in *Keywords* was to historicize "culture" by plotting its changing patterns of usage across a crucial period of social transformation. What he envisaged was a "counter-appropriation" to oppose the appropriation and "short-circuiting" of the term "culture" in certain "reactionary" midcentury accounts, principally by T. S. Eliot and, behind him, F. R. Leavis. See Raymond Williams, "Culture and Society," in *Politics and Letters: Interviews with New Left Review* (London: Verso, 1981), 97–132. But he was also trying to avoid the hasty and reductive politicizations of literature in the Marxist criticism he encountered at Cambridge in the 1930s and 1940s. By contrast, Williams aimed to reconstruct the richness and "true complexity" of a historical process of debate and uncertainty that had produced a concentration of social thought around the term "culture." What he wanted to find in this process was an alternative "tradition" of social thought and literature—a tradition that might then reawaken debate about the cultural effects of industrialization while simultaneously combating the economism of the British labor movement and reanimating left politics.

Keywords traces the emergence of "culture" as an abstract category from a noun of process that had been applied metaphorically from husbandry to the cultivation of the mind and thence to its products. Williams adds, however, that the development of new meanings in English was crucially inflected in the late eighteenth century by a "new social and intellectual movement" (88) in Germany, beginning with Johann Gottfried von Herder in his *Ideen zur Philosophie der Geschichte der Menschheit* of 1784, or even earlier, perhaps, in his *Auch eine Philosophie der Geschichte zur Bildung der Menschheit* of 1774. What these texts by Herder introduced, Williams argues, was the notion of a historical approach to the plurality of human cultures, which meant seeing them as the product of a law of development driven by the contradiction between individuation and the whole of history. Across the next century, Williams's account suggests, Herder's organic conception of culture was to be amplified through a contrast with the mechanical character of the new civilization then emerging. A decisive step, Williams says, was taken in the works of the German anthropologist Gustav Friedrich Klemm, in his *Allgemeine Kulturgeschichte der Menschheit* [*sic*] of 1843–52 and his *Allgemeine Kulturwissenschaft* [*sic*] of 1854–55 (as Williams cites the titles), elaborating an anthropological conception of culture as the entire matrix of human activities peculiar to a people that was to pass into English in Tylor's *Primitive Culture* of 1870 (Williams's date is inaccurate; see above).

The glaring omission in Williams's genealogy is any discussion of Hegel, from whose philosophy of history Klemm's three stages of human history appear to have directly derived. What escapes Williams, therefore, is that between Hegel and Klemm, a crucial shift takes place in which the burden of Hegel's historical conception of the State as the embodiment of an ethical form of life of a people is displaced onto the term *Cultur*, which comes to underpin a notion of nationhood around which a new formation of the nation-state begins to be centered. (Tellingly, there is no entry in Williams's *Keywords* under "State.")

85. In 1843, Gustav Friedrich Klemm (1802–67) published the first volume of his *Allgemeine Cultur-Geschichte der Menschheit* (Leipzig: B. G. Teubner, 1843–52), whose ten volumes were completed in 1852. In 1854 and 1855, he published the two further volumes of his *Allgemeine Culturwissenschaft* (Leipzig: Romberg, 1854–55), his systematic science of culture.

86. Klemm, *Allgemeine Cultur-Geschichte*, 1:18; quoted in Kroeber and Kluckhohn, *Culture*, 10.

87. Kroeber and Kluckhohn, *Culture*, 19.

88. Ibid., 18.

89. Ibid., 18. See also 19.

90. Johann Christoph Adelung (1732–1806), *Versuch einer Geschichte der Cultur des menschlichen Geschlechts* (Leipzig: C. G. Hertel, 1782); Johann Gottfried Herder (1744–1803), *Ideen zur Philosophie der Geschichte der Menschheit*, 4 vols. (Riga and Leipzig: J. F. Hartknoch, 1784, 1785, 1787, 1791).

91. Kroeber and Kluckhohn, *Culture*, 26.

92. Cf. Heinrich Rickert, *Kulturwissenschaft und Naturwissenschaft* (1898). From the point of view of art history, the place of Jacob Burckhardt in this development is extremely interesting. In 1860, he published the great study that is translated into English as *The Civilization of the Renaissance in Italy* but that he titled *Der Cultur der Renaissance in Italien: Ein Versuch* (*Werke*, vol. 4, ed. Hiroyuki Numata and Peter Ganz [Munich: C. H. Beck; Basel: Schwabe, 2000]). A decade later, in notes for lectures delivered at the university in Basel between 1868 and 1871, he wrote, "Culture [*Die Cultur*] may be defined as the sum total of those mental developments [*Entwicklungen des Geistes*] which take place spontaneously

and lay no claim to universal or compulsive authority. . . . Culture is, further, that millionfold process by which the spontaneous, unthinking activity of a race [*das Naive und Racenmässige Thun*] is transformed into considered action, or indeed, at its last and highest stage, in science [*Wissenschaft*] and especially philosophy, into pure thought. Its total external form, however, as distinguished from the State and religion, is society in its broadest sense." Burckhardt, *Reflections on History*, trans. M. D. Hottinger (Indianapolis, Ind.: Liberty Classics, 1979), 93; *Über das Studium der Geschichte*, in *Werke*, ed. Peter Ganz (Munich: C. H. Beck; Basel: Schwabe, 2000), 10:180.

A little earlier in these lectures, he had offered another equally totalizing and equally post-Hegelian definition: "Culture [*Die Cultur*], which meets material and spiritual need in the narrower sense, is the sum of all that has spontaneously arisen for the advancement of material life and as an expression of spiritual and moral life—all social intercourse, technologies, arts, literatures, and sciences." *Reflections on History*, 59–60; *Werke*, 10:161.

93. Cf. Beat Wyss, *Hegel's Art History and the Critique of Modernity*, trans. Caroline Dobson Saltzwedel (Cambridge: Cambridge University Press, 1999).

94. In his essay "Faith and Knowledge," published in 1802 in the first issue of the second volume of *Kritische Journal der Philosophie*, the critical journal of philosophy he edited with Friedrich Schelling, Hegel uses both *Cultur* and *Bildung*, sometimes on the same page, but not at all interchangeably. See G. W. F. Hegel, *Glauben und Wissen, oder Die Reflexionsphilosophie der Subjectivität in der Vollständigkeit ihrer Formen, als Kantische, Jacobische, und Fichtesche Philosophie, Kritische Journal der Philosophie* 2, no. 1 (Tübingen, July 1802), in *Jenaer Kritische Schriften*, ed. Hartmut Buchner and Otto Pöggeler, *Gesammelte Werke* (Hamburg: Felix Meiner Verlag, 1968), 4:313–414.

In every case but one, the seven uses of *Cultur* carry the sense of a general ethos or outlook, more broadly spread than the particular sphere of philosophy (see 315, 322, 323, 388, and 412). The one exception involves a reference to the philosophical culture of John Locke and David Hume (388). By contrast, the seven usages of *Bildung* (if we include the one appearance of *Bilden*) all connote the narrower sense of an intellectual culture or system of teaching, which also has the implication of a formative process rather than a general state of affairs (see 319, 348, and 413, where five of the seven uses appear). The distinction is significant. It points to a sense in which, for Hegel at this time, "just as the perfection of the fine arts is conditioned by the trajectory of mechanical skills" (413), so the complete development of philosophy as a system of teaching and an intellectual culture (*Bildung*) is embedded in the broader historical climate of ideas or cultural ethos (*Cultur*) to which it gives a more systematic, philosophical articulation.

Hegel's text has appeared in English as *Faith and Knowledge*, trans. Walter Cerf and H. S. Harris (Albany: State University of New York Press, 1977). The translation provides a lucid articulation into plainer English of Hegel's inordinate German sentences, in which subjects are left hanging and the conjugate verbs never seem to arrive. For present purposes, however, the translation is less useful, since it often does not regularly distinguish in the text between *Kultur* (*sic*) and *Bildung*, rendering *Cultur* variously as "civilization" (55, 63), "culture" (64 twice, 65), "cultural" (189), and "tradition" (154), while *Bildung* is translated as "culture" (60, 98, 189 twice), "the formative process of culture" (189, 190), and "cultural process" (189). The "Analytical Index" to the translation is indicative of the problem. It reads, "civilization (*Kultur*): see culture"; "culture (*Bildung*)" (199).

Henry Harris has described *Glauben und Wissen* as "Hegel's first attempt to survey the culture of the time, and to place all the signs of the advent of 'absolute knowledge' in an ideal context which would cause them to reveal their meaning." H. S. Harris, "Introduction to *Faith and Knowledge*," in Hegel, *Faith and Knowledge*, 4. The essay thus rehearses the argument that will fold out in the summation of Hegel's work at Jena to fill the final major section of the *Phenomenology of Spirit*, precisely the section "C." in which, in subsection (BB) vi. B., Hegel comes on to discuss the fractured world of modern values and intellectual culture (now uniformly *Bildung*) as a reflection of "Self-estranged Spirit" (*Der sich entfremdete Geist*).

95. See here, Terry Pinkard's compelling commentary on the *Phenomenology of Spirit* and the intellectual context it sought to reshape, in *Hegel: A Biography* (Cambridge: Cambridge University Press, 2000), esp. chap. 4, "Texts and Drafts: Hegel's Path to the *Phenomenology* from Frankfurt to Jena," 118–202, and chap. 5, "Hegel Finds His Voice: The *Phenomenology of Spirit*," 203–20. See also Walter Jaeschke, *Reason in Religion: The Foundation of Hegel's Philosophy of Religion*, trans. J. Michael Stewart and Peter C. Hodgson (Berkeley, Los Angeles, and Oxford: University of California Press, 1990), where it is argued that Hegel's speculative conception of religion laid stress not on doctrine but on *cultus*: "not on the knowledge of God established in the relationship-of-consciousness but on the self-certainty of the community," into which the moment of consciousness is sublated (192).

96. Georg Wilhelm Friedrich Hegel, *Phänomenologie des Geistes*, ed. Wolfgang Bonsiepen and Reinhard Heede, vol. 9 of *Gesammelte Werke* (Hamburg: Felix Meiner Verlag, 1980). First published as *System der Wissenschaft*, part 1, *Die Phänomenologie des Geistes* (Bamberg and Würzburg: Joseph Anton Goebhardt, 1807). Translated into English as *Phenomenology of Spirit*, trans. A. V. Miller

(Oxford and New York: Oxford University Press, 1977). This translation supersedes that of J. B. Baillie: *The Phenomenology of Mind*, trans. J. B. Baillie (London: George Allen and Unwin; New York: Macmillan, 1931).

97. See here, Stephen Houlgate, *Freedom, Truth, and History: An Introduction to Hegel's Philosophy* (London and New York: Routledge, 1991).

98. See Frederick Beiser, *Hegel* (New York and London: Routledge, 2005), 234. In his *Philosophy of Right*, Hegel argues that customs are ethical in that they embody the rationality of those whose customs they are. Playing on the linguistic linkage of the German terms, he suggests that custom (*Sitte*) is to the ethical (*das Sittliche*) as the Greek *ethos* is to *ethics*. See the translator's note to para. 151, in G. W. F. Hegel, *Hegel's Philosophy of Right*, trans. T. M. Knox (Oxford: Clarendon Press, 1942), 350.

99. On the way that an inadequate theory of language contaminates Hegel's system, see Paul de Man, "Hegel on the Sublime," in *Aesthetic Ideology* (Minneapolis: University of Minnesota Press, 1997), 105–18.

100. Hegel, *The Phenomenology of Mind*, trans. Baillie, 731. Miller's translation has "the immediate trust of the individuals in their nation as a whole." *Phenomenology of Spirit*, trans. Miller, 440. The German reads "dem unmittelbaren Vertrauen der Einzelnen zu dem Ganzen inhres Volkes." *Gesammelte Werke*, 9:389.

101. The difficulty here is the now familiar one that, throughout their English renderings of Hegel's *Phänomenologie des Geistes*, both Baillie and Miller translate *Bildung* as "culture."

102. Hegel, *Phenomenology of Spirit*, trans. Miller, 319.

103. Cf. *Hegel's Philosophy of Right*, especially part 3, "Ethical Life" (*Das Sittliche*), in which Hegel argues, "ethical life is the concept of freedom developed into the existing world and the nature of self-consciousness" (105, para. 142); "The ethical substance, as containing independent self-consciousness united with its concept, is the actual mind of a family and a nation" (110, para. 156); "The state is the actuality of the ethical idea" (155, para. 257); and, "since the state is mind objectified, it is only as one of its members that the individual himself has objectivity, genuine individuality, and an ethical life" (156, para. 258, Remarks). Hegel also declares, "Education is the art of making men ethical" (260, addition to para. 151). But in this text, which was first published in Berlin in 1821, it is interesting to note that the term he uses is not *Bildung* but *die Pädagogik*. G. W. F. Hegel, *Grundlinien der Philosophie des Rechts oder Naturrecht und Staatswissenschaft im Grundrisse*, vol. 7 of *Werke* (Frankfurt am Main: Suhrkamp Verlag, 1970), 302.

104. On this, see Pinkard, *Hegel*, chap. 10, "Berlin: Reform and Repression at the Focal Point (1818–1821)," 418–68.

105. Ian Hunter, *Culture and Government: The Emergence of Literary Education* (London: Macmillan, 1988), 70. Hunter's astute and unjustly neglected analysis examines what happens when this "caste practice," through which a minority of individuals seek to constitute themselves as subjects of moral action, enters the new social technology of public schooling and is absorbed into the machinery of literary education. Hunter's brief "genealogy" of the earlier emergence of "culture" in German idealist philosophy and pedagogy is, however, wholly reliant on translations and does not, therefore, mark the distinction between *Bildung* and *Cultur.* Focusing solely on Johann Gottlieb Fichte and Friedrich Wilhelm Joseph von Schelling, it also misses Hegel's distinctive intervention in debates at Jena, in the positing of an ethical substance that resides not in the cultivated individual but in the communal mutuality whose embodiment is the State.

106. Hunter, *Culture and Government,* 88.

107. The original subtitle to the *Phenomenology of Spirit* was *Science of the Experience (Erfahrung) of Consciousness.*

108. Cf. Hermann Lübbe, "Deutscher Idealismus als Philosophie Preussischer Kulturpolitik," in *Kunsterfahrung und Kulturpolitik im Berlin Hegels,* ed. Otto Pöggeler and Annemarie Gethmann-Siefert, Hegel-Studien, vol. 22 (Bonn: Bouvier Verlag Herbert Grundman, 1983), 3–27, and Walter Jaeschke, "Politik, Kultur, und Philosophie in Preussen," in Pöggeler and Gethmann-Siefert, *Kunsterfahrung und Kulturpolitik im Berlin Hegels,* 29–48.

109. The antithesis between the reified rational structures of *Bildung* and the organic community of belief is found in Hegel's *Phenomenology of Spirit,* written in Jena in 1807. See Hegel, *Phenomenology of Spirit,* trans. Miller, section (BB), VI, B, "Self-alienated Spirit. Culture (*Bildung*)," 294–363.

110. Kroeber and Kluckhohn, *Culture,* 28.

2. The Plane of Decent Seeing

1. Edward Steichen, "The F.S.A. Photographers," in *U.S. Camera Annual 1939,* ed. T. J. Maloney (New York: William Morrow, 1938), 43.

2. Beaumont Newhall's essay "Documentary Approach to Photography," for example, appeared in *Parnassus* 10, no. 3 (March 1938), and is already confident of its canon: Matthew Brady, Timothy O'Sullivan, Alexander Gardner, Charles Marville, Eugène Atget, Lewis Hine, Berenice Abbott, Walker Evans, Ralph Steiner, Margaret Bourke-White, Ansel Adams, Willard Van Dyke, and the photographers of the Farm Security Administration.

3. Steichen, "The F.S.A. Photographers," 44. How American People Live—the Historical Section exhibit of eighty-one prints selected and arranged

by Arthur Rothstein and Russell Lee—was a contribution to the First International Photographic Exposition, held to mark photography's centennial at the Grand Central Palace in New York, from April 18 until April 24, 1938.

4. Steichen, "The F.S.A. Photographers," 44.

5. Cf. Colin MacCabe's analysis of the "classic realist text" in "Realism and the Cinema: Some Notes on Brechtian Theses," *Screen* 15, no. 2 (Summer 1974); reprinted in *Tracking the Signifier. Theoretical Essays: Film, Linguistics, Literature* (Minneapolis: University of Minnesota Press, 1985), 33–57. See also the discussion of realism and semiological critiques of realism in Rosalind Coward and John Ellis, *Language and Materialism: Developments in Semiology and the Theory of the Subject* (London: Routledge and Kegan Paul, 1977), 35–60.

6. It is worth noting that, in contrast to the uncritical support of a political Left that could not go beyond notions of social security, the most trenchant criticisms of the Roosevelt administration's top-down social reforms as mechanisms of political and economic dependency came from Black leaders outside the Democratic Party—such as Ralph Bunche, John P. Davis, A. Philip Randolph, and W. E. B. Du Bois—and from isolated and dissatisfied African Americans inside the administration, including Forrester Washington, race adviser to the Federal Emergency Relief Administration, and Robert Weaver, chief assistant to the Interior Department. See John B. Kirby, *Black Americans in the Roosevelt Era: Liberalism and Race* (Knoxville: University of Tennessee Press, 1980), 127, 140–45, 149, 162–63, 173, 195, 206.

7. John Grierson, "Films and the Community" (part 1, "The Use of Radio and Films in the Classroom" [1936]; part 2, "The Film in the Service of Religion," *World Film News* [October 1938]), in *Grierson on Documentary*, ed. Forsyth Hardy (New York: Harcourt, Brace, 1947), 153, and in *Grierson on Documentary*, ed. Forsyth Hardy (London: Faber and Faber, 1966), 193. The first part of Grierson's essay, from which this quotation comes, is made up of an address to the National Union of Teachers in Southport, England, in 1936, that was originally titled "The Use of Radio and Films in the Classroom." The essay does not appear in either of the two later companion volumes of Grierson's writings, *Grierson on Documentary* and *Grierson on the Movies*, published in 1979 and 1981, to which I have also made reference.

The different editions of Grierson's collected writings on documentary, *Grierson on Documentary*, ed. Forsyth Hardy (London: William Collins Sons, 1946; New York: Harcourt, Brace, 1947; London: Faber and Faber, 1966; London and Boston: Faber and Faber, 1979), vary in their contents. I have therefore provided the title of the essay with the original date of publication in parentheses, as some indication of the phases, development, and consistency of Grierson's argument.

8. Grierson, "Education and Total Effort" (address at Winnipeg, Canada, 1941), in *Grierson on Documentary*, 1979 ed., 139; 1966 ed., 278. The italicization is Grierson's.

9. Grierson, "Education and Total Effort" (1941), 1966 ed., 278; 1979 ed., 139.

10. Roy E. Stryker, "Still Photography," undated four-page memorandum prepared for the Resettlement Administration for budgetary purposes in 1935, 3, Roy Emerson Stryker Papers, 1932–1964, NDA 25, Archives of American Art, Smithsonian Institution, Washington, D.C.

11. Roy E. Stryker, "Documentary Photography," in *The Complete Photographer*, ed. Willard D. Morgan, 4, no. 21 (April 10, 1942) (Chicago: National Educational Alliance, 1942), 1364.

12. Newhall, "Documentary Approach to Photography," 5.

13. Jeremy Bentham, *The Rationale of Evidence*, 12:321, quoted in Jacques-Alain Miller, "Le despotisme de l'Utile: La machine panoptique de Jeremy Bentham," *Ornicar? Bulletin périodique du Champ freudien* 3 (May 1975): 18.

14. Pare Lorentz, "Dorothea Lange: Camera with a Purpose," in *U.S. Camera Annual 1941*, ed. T. J. Mahoney, vol. 1, *America* (New York: Duell, Sloan and Pearce, 1941), 97.

15. See William Stott, *Documentary Expression and Thirties America* (Oxford and New York: Oxford University Press, 1973).

16. John Grierson, preface (1951) to the third edition of Paul Rotha, *Documentary Film* (Glasgow: University Press, 1952), 16.

17. Ibid., 18.

18. Bill Nichols is, perhaps, the only other commentator to have put forward an analysis of documentary that runs, in many important respects, parallel to the argument made here. See Bill Nichols, "Documentary Film and the Modernist Avant-Garde," *Critical Inquiry* 27, no. 4 (Summer 2001). In this essay, Nichols also argues for the historical specificity of documentary, rejecting the assumed existence of a continuous "documentary tradition" and arguing that "documentary film only takes form as an actual practice in the 1920s and early 1930s" (580). Nichols similarly regards the "new emphasis on the rhetoric of social persuasion" (580) and documentary's "distinct form of viewer engagement" (582) as defining elements of documentary, linking it to "the direct service of various, already active efforts to build national identity during the 1920s and 1930s" (581). The difference comes, however, when Nichols argues that what he regards as the necessary components of documentary—photographic realism, narrative structure, modernist fragmentation, and documentary oratory—were evident from the early 1920s in Soviet productions and in the work of the European

avant-garde. Nichols goes on to link documentary production in Great Britain and the United States in the 1930s to the deployment of documentary techniques by Joseph Goebbels in Germany and by Anatoly Lunacharsky and Andrey Zhdánov in the Soviet Union. By contrast, I have argued for the decisive linkage of documentary to a distinctively social democratic version of State corporatism, uniquely embodied in the economic, social, and cultural policies of the New Deal. Nichols, too, I might note, acknowledges that the desire to endow documentary with "institutional solidity and civic respectability" led Grierson to separate his conception of documentary as a participatory ritual of citizenship both from the Soviet model and from the practices of defamiliarization characteristic of the European avant-garde.

19. Boleslas Matuszewski, *Une nouvelle source de l'histoire (Création d'un dépôt de cinématographie historique)* (Paris: Imprimerie Noizetie, 1898); reprinted in *Bolesław Matuszewski I Jego Pionierska Mysl Filowa: Dokumenty i wstepne kometarze* (Warsaw: Filmoteka Polska, 1980).

20. John Grierson, "Flaherty's Poetic *Moana*," *New York Sun*, February 8, 1926, reprinted in *Grierson on the Movies*, ed. Forsyth Hardy (London and Boston: Faber and Faber, 1981), 23–25.

21. Ibid., 24.

22. John Grierson, "First Principles of Documentary," part 1, *Cinema Quarterly* (Winter 1932), in *Grierson on Documentary*, 1946 ed., 102; 1966 ed., 148; 1979 ed., 38.

23. John Grierson, movie review, *Clarion*, August 1929, in *Grierson on the Movies*, 30; and "Drifters," in *Clarion*, October 1929, in *Grierson on Documentary*, 1966 ed., 136; 1979 ed., 20.

24. Grierson, movie review, *Clarion*, August 1929, 30.

25. Grierson, "First Principles of Documentary" (part 1, 1932), 1966 ed., 145; 1979 ed., 35.

26. For this and other details of Grierson's career and critical evolution, I am chiefly reliant on Ian Aitken's account in *Film and Reform: John Grierson and the Documentary Film Movement* (London and New York: Routledge, 1990).

27. Cf. John Grierson, "Propaganda and Education" (address to the Winnipeg Canadian Club, October 19, 1943), in *Grierson on Documentary*, 1966 ed., 289–90; 1979 ed., 150–51.

28. Ibid., 1966 ed., 290; 1979 ed., 151.

29. Cf. Grierson, "Films and the Community" (part 1, 1936), 1966 ed., 189–94.

30. See John Grierson, "What Makes a Special," *Motion Picture News*, November 20, 1926; "The Product of Hollywood," *Motion Picture News*, November

27, 1926; "Putting Punch in a Picture," *Motion Picture News*, November 27, 1926; "Putting Atmosphere in a Picture," *Motion Picture News*, December 4, 1926; and "The Seven Obstacles to Progress," *Motion Picture News*, December 4, 1926. See also the discussion of these articles in Aitken, *Film and Reform*, 68–74.

31. The description is that of Leo Amery, at this time secretary of state for the dominions and colonies. See Leo Amery, *My Political Life* (London: Hutchinson, 1953), 352, quoted in Aitken, *Film and Reform*, 94.

32. See Aitken, *Film and Reform*, 97–102.

33. John Grierson, "The Nature of Propaganda," *Documentary News Letter* (1942), in *Grierson on Documentary*, 1966 ed., 246; 1979 ed., 109.

34. Cf. John Grierson, "The Course of Realism," in *Footnotes to the Film* (London: Peter Davies, 1937), in *Grierson on Documentary*, 1966 ed., 207; 1979 ed., 78; "The Documentary Idea: 1942," *Documentary News Letter* (1942), in *Grierson on Documentary*, 1966 ed., 250; 1979 ed., 113; "Propaganda and Education" (1943), 1966 ed., 289–90; 1979 ed., 150–51. See also John Grierson, "Documentary Photography—Motion Pictures: Part I: The Documentary Idea," in *The Complete Photographer*, ed. Willard D. Morgan, 4, no. 21 (April 10, 1942), and 4, no. 22 (April 20, 1942) (Chicago: National Educational Alliance, 1942), 1377, where Grierson insists of the documentary movement that "the origins of its form and theory are *educational* and *sociological*."

35. Grierson, "Films and the Community" (part 1, 1936), 1947 ed., 151; 1966 ed., 191.

36. John Grierson, "Education and the New Order," Democracy and Citizenship Series, Canadian Association for Adult Education, pamphlet no. 7 (1941), in *Grierson on Documentary*, 1966 ed., 261; 1979 ed., 122.

37. Grierson, "Documentary Photography—Motion Pictures" (1942), 1379.

38. John Grierson, "Searchlight on Democracy," *Documentary News Letter* (1939), in *Grierson on Documentary*, 1966 ed., 228; 1979 ed., 91.

39. Ibid., 1966 ed., 229; 1979 ed., 92; and cf. "Education and the New Order" (1941), 1966 ed., 261; 1979 ed., 122.

40. Grierson, "Searchlight on Democracy" (1939), 1966 ed., 228; 1979 ed., 91.

41. Ibid., 1966 ed., 228; 1979 ed., 91.

42. Grierson, "Propaganda and Education" (1943), 1966 ed., 290; 1979 ed., 151.

43. Grierson, "Education and the New Order" (1941), 1966 ed., 268; 1979 ed., 129; see also "Propaganda and Education" (1943), 1966 ed., 289; 1979 ed., 150.

44. Grierson, "Propaganda and Education" (1943), 1966 ed., 289; 1979 ed., 150.

45. Grierson, "The Documentary Idea: 1942" (1942), 1966 ed., 250; 1979 ed., 113; see also "Propaganda and Education" (1943), 1966 ed., 286; 1979 ed., 147.

46. John Grierson, "The Challenge of Peace" (address to the Conference of the Arts, Sciences, and Professions in the Post-War World, New York, June 1945), in *Grierson on Documentary*, 1966 ed., 325; 1979 ed., 175.

47. Grierson, "Education and the New Order" (1941), 1966 ed., 262; 1979 ed., 123.

48. Grierson, "The Nature of Propaganda" (1942), 1966 ed., 246; 1979 ed., 109.

49. Grierson, "Propaganda and Education" (1943), 1966 ed., 287; 1979 ed., 148.

50. Grierson, "Education and Total Effort" (1941), 1966 ed., 279; 1979 ed., 140.

51. Grierson, "Propaganda and Education" (1943), 1966 ed., 281; 1979 ed., 142. Cf. also "Education and the New Order" (1941), 1966 ed., 268; 1979 ed., 129; and "The Challenge of Peace" (1945), 1966 ed., 328; 1979 ed., 178.

52. Grierson, "Films and the Community" (1936), 1947 ed., 154; 1966 ed., 193.

53. Grierson, "Education and the New Order" (1941), 1966 ed., 268; 1979 ed., 129.

54. Grierson, "The Nature of Propaganda" (1942), 1966 ed., 246; 1979 ed., 109; "Education and Total Effort" (1941), 1966 ed., 277; 1979 ed., 138; "Propaganda and Education" (1943), 1966 ed., 289; 1979 ed., 150; "The Challenge of Peace" (1945), 1966 ed., 325; 1979 ed., 175.

55. Grierson, "Propaganda and Education" (1943), 1966 ed., 290; 1979 ed., 151.

56. Grierson, "Education and Total Effort" (1941), 1966 ed., 279; 1979 ed., 140. Cf. also "The Nature of Propaganda" (1942), 1966 ed., 246; 1979 ed., 109.

57. Grierson, "The Nature of Propaganda" (1942), 1966 ed., 246; 1979 ed., 109.

58. Grierson, "Education and the New Order" (1941), 1966 ed., 269; 1979 ed., 130.

59. Ibid., 1966 ed., 262; 1979 ed., 123.

60. Grierson, "The Nature of Propaganda" (1942), 1966 ed., 247; 1979 ed., 110. Cf. also "Education and Total Effort" (1941), 1966 ed., 275; 1979 ed.,

136; and "Propaganda and Education" (1943), 1966 ed., 286–87; 1979 ed., 147–48.

61. Grierson, "Education and Total Effort" (1941), 1966 ed., 278; 1979 ed., 139.

62. Grierson, "Propaganda and Education" (1943), 1966 ed., 290; 1979 ed., 151.

63. Ibid., 1966 ed., 286; 1979 ed., 147.

64. Grierson, "Education and the New Order" (1941), 1966 ed., 268; 1979 ed., 129.

65. Grierson, "Propaganda and Education" (1943), 1966 ed., 289; 1979 ed., 150.

66. Grierson, "Films and the Community" (part 1, 1936), 1947 ed., 154; 1966 ed., 194.

67. Grierson, "Education and the New Order" (1941), 1966 ed., 268; 1979 ed., 129. Cf. also "The Library in an International World" (address to the American Library Association, Buffalo, June 1946), in *Grierson on Documentary*, 1966 ed., 304; 1979 ed., 165.

68. Grierson, "The Nature of Propaganda" (1942), 1966 ed., 246; 1979 ed., 109.

69. Grierson, "Propaganda and Education" (1943), 1966 ed., 290; 1979 ed., 151.

70. Ibid., 1966 ed., 290; 1979 ed., 151.

71. Ibid., 1966 ed., 289; 1979 ed., 150.

72. Grierson, "The Documentary Idea: 1942" (1942), 1966 ed., 248; 1979 ed., 111; "Education and Total Effort" (1941), 1966 ed., 278; 1979 ed., 139.

73. Grierson, "Propaganda and Education" (1943), 1966 ed., 287, 289; 1979 ed., 148, 150.

74. Ibid., 1966 ed., 292; 1979 ed., 153.

75. Grierson, "Education and the New Order" (1941), 1966 ed., 268; 1979 ed., 129.

76. Grierson, "Documentary Photography—Motion Pictures" (1942), 1380.

77. Grierson, "The Nature of Propaganda" (1942), 1966 ed., 246; 1979 ed., 109.

78. John Grierson, "What I Look For" (1932), in *Grierson on the Movies*, 39. Part of this essay, originally published in the *New Clarion* (June 11, 1932), was included in earlier editions of *Grierson on Documentary*, in "The Role of the Critic," Forsyth Hardy's introduction to the section "Background to Documentary." See *Grierson on Documentary*, 1946 ed., 26–27.

79. Grierson, "What I Look For" (1932), 38.

80. Grierson, "The Nature of Propaganda" (1942), 1966 ed., 246; 1979 ed., 109.

81. Grierson, "The Challenge of Peace" (1945), 1966 ed., 326; 1979 ed., 176.

82. Cf. Grierson, "Education and Total Effort" (1941), 1966 ed., 277; 1979 ed., 138; and "Propaganda and Education" (1943), 1966 ed., 289; 1979 ed., 150.

83. Grierson, "The Challenge of Peace" (1945), 1966 ed., 327; 1979 ed., 177.

84. Grierson, "Films and the Community" (part 1, 1936), 1947 ed., 150; 1966 ed., 190.

85. Grierson, "The Documentary Idea: 1942" (1942), 1966 ed., 250; 1979 ed., 113.

86. John Grierson, "Postscript to the New Edition" (1965), in *Grierson on Documentary*, 1966 ed., 397; 1979 ed., 223.

87. Grierson, "Education and Total Effort" (1941), 1966 ed., 276; 1979 ed., 137; "Propaganda and Education" (1943), 1966 ed., 283; 1979 ed., 144.

88. Grierson, "Education and the New Order" (1941), 1966 ed., 262; 1979 ed., 123.

89. Grierson, "Education and Total Effort" (1941), 1966 ed., 276; 1979 ed., 137.

90. Ibid., 1966 ed., 276; 1979 ed., 137.

91. Grierson, "Education and the New Order" (1941), 1966 ed., 267–68; 1979 ed., 128–29.

92. Ibid., 1966 ed., 267; 1979 ed., 128.

93. Ibid., 1966 ed., 269; 1979 ed., 130.

94. Ibid.

95. Grierson, "Propaganda and Education" (1943), 1966 ed., 283; 1979 ed., 144.

96. Grierson, "Education and Total Effort" (1941), 1966 ed., 278; 1979 ed., 139.

97. Grierson, "The Challenge of Peace" (1945), 1966 ed., 320; 1979 ed., 170. For an earlier, and unintentionally revealing, view of propaganda, see Grierson's review of "Hell Divers," in *Everyman*, April 7, 1932, where he writes, "Propaganda is an excellent mistress, but a blustering fool of a matron. In more incidental function, she gives spice, purpose and most necessary prejudice to life. With right to command, she outbawls one's every instinct of proportion"; in *Grierson on the Movies*, 87.

98. Grierson, "The Nature of Propaganda" (1942), 1966 ed., 246; 1979 ed., 109.

99. Grierson, "Education and Total Effort" (1941), 1966 ed., 279; 1979 ed., 140.

100. Ibid.

101. Grierson, "Propaganda and Education" (1943), 1966 ed., 281; 1979 ed., 142.

102. Ibid., 1966 ed., 285; 1979 ed., 146.

103. Ibid.

104. Ibid.

105. Grierson, "Education and Total Effort" (1941), 1966 ed., 278; 1979 ed., 139.

106. Grierson, "Propaganda and Education" (1943), 1966 ed., 285; 1979 ed., 146.

107. Ibid., 1966 ed., 286; 1979 ed., 147.

108. Ibid., 1966 ed., 286 and 290; 1979 ed., 151 and 147.

109. On this, see Maren Stange, "'Symbols of Ideal Life': Tugwell, Stryker, and the FSA Photography Project," chap. 3 of *Symbols of Ideal Life: Social Documentary Photography in America, 1890–1950* (Cambridge and New York: Cambridge University Press, 1989), 89–131, though one cannot accept the duality of ideological instrumentalism and authentic social realism that underlies Stange's critique of Stryker and the photography of the FSA.

110. Cf. here Stuart Hall's notion of the "'logics' of social perception," as developed in his unsurpassed essay "The Social Eye of *Picture Post*," *Working Papers in Cultural Studies* (Birmingham Centre for Contemporary Cultural Studies), no. 2 (Spring 1972): esp. 87–88.

111. Grierson, preface (1951) to Rotha, *Documentary Film*, 17.

112. Ibid., 18. On Grierson's view of the role of the documentary film movement in electing a Labour government in 1945, by "making the patterns of social justice patent to everyone," see also John Grierson, "Robert Flaherty," *Reporter*, October 16, 1951, in *Grierson on the Movies*, 178. For his insistence on the primacy of the British documentary school, see John Grierson, "Documentary: A World Perspective" (1963?), in *Grierson on Documentary*, 1966 ed., 365–71; 1979 ed., 203–9. I obviously take issue with this view and with Forsyth Hardy's representation of American documentary initiatives as "isolated efforts, not part of a movement as in Britain." Forsyth Hardy, introduction to *Grierson on Documentary*, 1947 ed., 16; 1966 ed., 24.

113. "American Memory" is the title of the U.S. Library of Congress's Internet-accessible collections of Americana, including "historic maps, photos,

documents, audio and video" (http://www.loc.gov/index.html). See Library of Congress, "American Memory: America from the Great Depression to World War II. Black-and-White Photographs from the FSA-OWI, 1935–1945," http://memory.loc.gov/ammem/fsahtml/fahome.html.

114. Steichen, "The F.S.A. Photographers," 44. The photographs concerned, unattributed on the page, are Dorothea Lange's "Hoe Culture in the South. Near Eutaw, Alabama," July 1936 (LC-USF34-009539-C; identifiers that begin "LC" refer to the RA/FSA/OWI file in the Library of Congress, Prints and Photographs Division), the negative itself being marked up for cropping as reproduced at the head of Steichen's essay; Russell Lee's "An Organ Deposited by the Flood on a Farm Near Mount Vernon, Indiana," February 1937 (LC-USF341-010435-B); together with thirty-nine other photographs, totaling forty-one images by Walker Evans (five), Theodor Jung (one), Dorothea Lange (eleven), Russell Lee (twelve), Ed Locke (one), Arthur Rothstein (six), Ben Shahn (four), and John Vachon (one).

115. Jacques Lacan, *The Four Fundamental Concepts of Psycho-Analysis*, ed. Jacques-Alain Miller, trans. Alan Sheridan (Harmondsworth, U.K.: Penguin Books, 1979), 89. First published as Jacques Lacan, *Le séminaire*, book 11, *Les quatre concepts fondamentaux de la psychanalyse, 1964*, text established by Jacques-Alain Miller (Paris: Editions du Seuil, 1973).

116. Lacan, *The Four Fundamental Concepts of Psycho-Analysis*, 109.

117. Ibid., 101.

118. Ibid., 100.

119. Ibid., 103 and 112.

120. Ibid., 94.

121. Ibid., 86, 92–94.

122. Ibid., 89.

123. Ibid., 96.

124. Ibid., 115. See also 86: "This construction allows that which concerns vision to escape totally."

125. Cf. ibid., 72, 75, 105–6.

126. See ibid., 96. The English translation by Alan Sheridan oddly turns this into a negative: "I am not simply that punctiform being located at the geometral point from which the perspective is grasped. No doubt, in the depths of my eye, the picture is painted. The picture, certainly, is in my eye. But I am not in the picture." The original reads: "Mais moi, je suis dans le tableau." Lacan, *Les quatre concepts fondamentaux de la psychanalyse*, 89. Cf. also ". . . that which turns *me* into a picture." Lacan, *The Four Fundamental Concepts of Psycho-Analysis*, 105.

127. Lacan, *The Four Fundamental Concepts of Psycho-Analysis*, 82.

290 – NOTES TO CHAPTER 2

128. Ibid., 92.

129. Ibid.

130. Cf. ibid., 85–89, 92. Hans Holbein the Younger's double portrait of Jean de Dinteville (1504–55), seigneur de Polisy, bailly of Troyes, knight of St. Michael, and French ambassador at the court of Henry VIII, and Georges de Selve (1509–41), bishop of Lavaur and French ambassador to Venice, *The Ambassadors*, was painted in 1533 for Dinteville's château at Polisy in Burgundy. Holbein pointedly added the name of Polisy to the terrestrial globe on the lower shelf of the whatnot between the figures, though the name does not appear on Johann Schöner's 1523 globe, which served as Holbein's model. Other objects filling the shelves include a lute with a broken string, a case of flutes, an open hymnbook with music, a book of arithmetic, a pair of compasses, a celestial globe, a portable sundial, two kinds of quadrant, an unidentified instrument, and a torquetum and semiss, used for determining the position of celestial bodies. Lacan closely follows Jurgis Baltrusaitis's reading of the painting, often to the word, both in linking anamorphosis and trompe l'oeil as practices of the same order of "false measurement and fake reality" and in interpreting the still life as a *vanitas* and the skull as a memento mori, condensing the meaning of the entire work as a meditation on the vanity of human knowledge. Against this reading, the immense detail of the scientific objects might equally argue for Holbein's interest in them as much for their own sake and for their personal associations for the sitters as for their metaphysical symbolism. The lute with a broken string, the open page of the third volume of Peter Apian's manual of merchants' arithmetic, and the hymnal open to Martin Luther's German rendering of "Veni Creator Spiritus" and his shortened version of the Ten Commandments may have been emblematic of an appeal to heal division, possibly with contemporary religious and political meaning. Even the distorted skull in the foreground echoes the silver skull ornament on Dinteville's cap brooch, not mentioned by Baltrusaitis, perhaps indicating that Dinteville, whose love of learned allusion is known from other portraits by Francesco Primaticcio and Felix Chrétien, had adopted the skull as his device. This iconographic and historical emphasis would tend to undermine Baltrusaitis's ingenious synthetic interpretation of the painting, but it would not erase the picture's calculated and meticulous undoing of perspectival vision, which seems to have been designed to produce its effect in a particular architectural setting. See Jurgis Baltrusaitis, "'Les Ambassadeurs' de Holbein," chap. 7 of *Anamorphoses ou magie artificielle des effets merveilleux* (Paris: Olivier Perrin Editeur, 1969), 91–116; Michael Levy, *National Gallery Catalogues: The German School* (London: National Gallery Publications Department, 1959), 47–54; and Mary F. S. Hervey's remarkable study, *Holbein's "Ambassadors": The*

Picture and the Men (London: George Bell and Sons, 1900), esp. pt. 4, "The Details of the Picture," 195–236.

131. Lacan, *The Four Fundamental Concepts of Psycho-Analysis*, 86.

132. Ibid., 71.

133. Ibid., 74.

134. Cf. ibid., 55, 60, 69, 79, 80.

135. Ibid., 83.

136. Ibid., 116.

137. Ibid., 87.

138. Cf. ibid., 74.

139. Ibid., 117.

140. Arthur Rothstein, "Direction in the Picture Story," in *The Complete Photographer*, ed. Willard D. Morgan, 4, no. 21 (April 10, 1942) (Chicago: National Educators Alliance, 1943), 1357.

141. Lacan, *The Four Fundamental Concepts of Psycho-Analysis*, 112.

142. Cf. ibid., 74 and 72.

143. Ibid., 84.

144. Ibid., 83.

145. Ibid., 107.

146. Ibid., 73. One should emphasize here, perhaps belatedly, that the split, for Lacan, is between the *eye* and the gaze—"L'oeil et le regard." Lacan, *Les quatre concepts fondamentaux de la psychanalyse*, 70. The separation between the *look* and the gaze, which distracts from Lacan's distinction, is one that has been introduced in commentaries in English but is not present in French in the original text. See, in particular, Kaja Silverman, "Fassbinder and Lacan: A Reconsideration of Gaze, Look, and Image," *Camera Obscura*, no. 19 (January 1989): 55–84, reprinted as chap. 3 of Silverman, *Male Subjectivity at the Margins* (London and New York: Routledge, 1992), 125–56. Silverman extends and defends her distinction in *The Threshold of the Visible World*, esp. chap. 4, "The Gaze"; chap. 5, "The Look"; and chap. 6, "The Screen" (New York and London: Routledge, 1996), 125–227.

147. Lacan, *The Four Fundamental Concepts of Psycho-Analysis*, 106.

148. The final prospectus for *Life*, June 1936, quoted in Loudon Wainwright, *The Great American Magazine: An Inside Story of "Life"* (New York: Alfred A. Knopf, 1986), 33.

149. Lacan, *The Four Fundamental Concepts of Psycho-Analysis*, 113.

150. Ibid., 113; and Lacan, *Les quatre concepts fondamentaux de la psychanalyse*, 104.

151. Lacan, *The Four Fundamental Concepts of Psycho-Analysis*, 115.

152. See, for example, "Children of the Forgotten Man! . . . LOOK Visits the Sharecropper," *Look*, March 1937, 18–19.

153. *Midweek Pictorial*, October 17, 1936, 23. The editorial commentary concludes: "An enlightened nation looks to its government." Ibid.

154. The word "shoot" (*pousse*) is Lacan's: *The Four Fundamental Concepts of Psycho-Analysis*, 72. The seer's "shoot" is "something prior to his eye" (72), like the machinery of photographic staging, though Lacan's "shoot" is organic, an outgrowth striving toward the light. In English, the notion of the photographic shoot opens an even richer vein of multiple meanings.

155. Paul A. Baran and Paul M. Sweezy, *Monopoly Capital: An Essay on the American Economic and Social Order* (New York: Monthly Review Press, 1966), 235.

156. The bibliography here is obviously vast, but for criticisms of the New Deal's social, economic, procorporate, and centralizing policies, see, for example, Baran and Sweezy, *Monopoly Capital*, esp. chap. 8, "On the History of Monopoly Capitalism," 215–43; Ronald Radosh, "The Myth of the New Deal," in *A New History of Leviathan: Essays on the Rise of the American Corporate State*, ed. Ronald Radosh and Murray Rothbard (New York: E. P. Dutton, 1972), 146–87; Kirby, *Black Americans in the Roosevelt Era*, esp. chap. 5, "Black Americans and the Coming of the New Deal," and chap. 6, "Blacks in the New Deal," 106–51; Lloyd C. Gardner, "The New Deal, New Frontiers, and the Cold War: A Reexamination of American Expansion, 1933–1945," in *Corporations and the Cold War*, ed. David Horowitz (New York and London: Monthly Review Press, 1969), 105–41; and James Weinstein, *Ambiguous Legacy: The Left in American Politics* (New York: New Viewpoints, 1975), chap. 3, "The Popular Front," 57–86. For general accounts, see, for example, Alonzo L. Hamby, ed., *The New Deal: Analysis and Interpretation* (New York and London: Longman, 1981); William E. Leuchtenburg, *Franklin D. Roosevelt and the New Deal, 1932–1940* (New York: Harper and Row, 1963); Donald R. McCoy, *Coming of Age: The United States during the 1920s and 1930s* (Harmondsworth, U.K.: Penguin Books, 1973); Robert S. McElvaine, *The Great Depression: America, 1929–1941* (New York: Times Books, 1993); and Arthur M. Schlesinger Jr., *The Age of Roosevelt*, 3 vols. (Boston: Houghton Mifflin, 1957–60).

157. On governance and the apparatuses of security, see especially Michel Foucault's course summaries from the Collège de France, "Security, Territory, and Population" (1977–78), "The Birth of Biopolitics" (1978–79), and "On the Government of the Living" (1979–80), in *The Essential Works of Foucault, 1954–1984*, vol. 1, *Ethics: Subjectivity and Truth*, ed. Paul Rabinow, trans. Robert Hurley et al. (New York: New Press, 1997), 67–85; and Foucault, "Governmentality"

(1978) and "The Risk of Security" (1983), in *The Essential Works of Foucault, 1954–1984*, vol. 3, *Power*, ed. James D. Faubion, trans. Robert Hurley et al. (New York: New Press, 2000), 201–22 and 365–81.

158. Hall, "The Social Eye of *Picture Post*," 87–88.

159. Holger Cahill, speech to the John Dewey Eightieth Birthday Celebration, in New York, October 28, 1939; subsequently presented as the foreword to an anthology of writings on the Federal Art Project, first conceived as a national progress report in 1936 and revised for publication in 1939: "American Resources in the Arts," in *Art for the Millions*, ed. Francis O'Connor (Boston: New York Graphic Society, 1975), 38.

160. Holger Cahill, "New Horizons in American Art," introduction to *New Horizons in American Art* (New York: Museum of Modern Art, 1936), 18, 40, and 41.

161. Ibid., 40.

162. Cahill, "American Resources in the Arts," 44. For Cahill's concept of "a usable past that is a powerful link in establishing the continuity of our culture," see "American Resources in the Arts," 43, as well as "New Horizons in American Art," 14 and 24.

163. Archibald MacLeish, "Unemployed Arts: WPA's Four Arts Projects. Their Origins, Their Operation," *Fortune*, May 1937, 108–17ff., quoted in Cahill, "American Resources in the Arts," 39.

164. Cahill, "New Horizons in American Art," 20.

165. Stuart Davis, "Abstract Art Today—Democracy—and Reaction" (August 11, 1939), the first draft of an essay that became "Abstract Painting Today," in O'Connor, *Art for the Millions*, 122.

166. On the deployment of documentary techniques and technologies across this formidable range of federal agencies, see P. Daniel, M. A. Foresta, M. Stange, and S. Stein, *Official Images: New Deal Photography* (Washington, D.C., and London: Smithsonian Institution Press, 1987). Of the agencies cited, it was the Resettlement Administration under Rexford Tugwell that was most vehemently attacked as "one of the most far-flung experiments in paternalistic government ever attempted in the U. S." See Felix Bruner, "Utopia Unlimited: Executive Order Gives Tugwell Power to Administer Projects Calling for $364,790,000," *Washington Post*, February 10, 1936, quoted in Nicholas Natanson, *The Black Image in the New Deal: The Politics of FSA Photography* (Knoxville: University of Tennessee Press, 1992), 51. For the history, structure, and function of the Resettlement Administration–FSA photographic file, see Carl Fleischhauer and Beverly W. Brannan, eds., *Documenting America, 1935–1943* (Berkeley, Los Angeles, and London: University of California Press, 1988), esp. the appendix,

"The FSA-OWI Collection," 330–42; and Alan Trachtenberg, "From Image to Story: Reading the File," in Fleischhauer and Brannan, *Documenting America, 1935–1943*, 43–73.

167. Rothstein, "Direction in the Picture Story," 1356.

168. Ibid., 1360.

169. Stryker, "Still Photography," 1.

170. Ibid., 2.

171. Ibid., 4.

172. Ibid., 1.

173. Ibid.

174. Ibid.

175. Ibid.

176. Judith Butler, *The Psychic Life of Power: Theories in Subjection* (Stanford, Calif.: Stanford University Press, 1997), 191.

177. Stryker, "Documentary Photography," 1365.

178. Ibid., 1369.

179. Grierson, "Documentary Photography—Motion Pictures," 1377. (Stryker's "Documentary Photography" also appeared in the same issue.)

180. Ibid., 1377. Though used repeatedly in his writings from the early 1940s (see also note 53 above), the phrase "the crystallizing of new loyalties" has a much longer history in the development of Grierson's thought, going back, at least, to 1932 and the essay "What I Look For," 38.

181. Jean-François Lyotard, "The Zone," in *Postmodern Fables*, trans. Georges Van Den Abbeele (Minneapolis and London: University of Minnesota Press, 1997), 31.

3. Melancholy Realism

For their considerable assistance, I wish to thank the staff of the Archives of American Art, Washington, D.C.; of the Library of Congress, Prints and Photographs Division; and of the E. S. Bird Library, Department of Special Collections, at Syracuse University. I owe a special debt to the generosity of colleagues in the Department of Photographs at the Metropolitan Museum of Art, New York, above all to Jeff Rosenheim, whose insight into the work of Evans and whose knowledge of the Walker Evans Archive have no rival. A shorter version of this chapter was delivered as a keynote address at Narrative: An International Conference, organized by the Society for the Study of Narrative Literature at the Kellogg Center, Michigan State University, in April 2002. It was subsequently published in *Narrative: The Journal of the Society for the Study of Narrative Literature* 11, no. 1 (January 2003): 3–77.

1. Walter Benjamin, *The Origin of German Tragic Drama*, trans. John Osborne (London: New Left Books, 1977), 27; translated from *Ursprung des deutschen Trauerspiels* (Frankfurt am Main: Suhrkamp Verlag, 1963), written between 1924 and 1925 and first published in 1928.

2. Paul de Man, *Allegories of Reading: Figural Language in Rousseau, Nietzsche, Rilke, and Proust* (New Haven, Conn., and London: Yale University Press, 1979), ix.

3. Ibid.

4. The comments on Evans come from Lincoln Kirstein's unpublished diary, in the entries for April 15 and June 13, 1931, "1930–1931 Diary," Lincoln Kirstein Papers, New York Public Library for the Performing Arts, Jerome Robbins Dance Division, (S)*MGZMD 123, box 3, folder 14, 280, 371, 372.

5. This is, of course, how—or where—Barthes begins his famous reading of a cover of *Paris-Match*. Casting the event in the barbershop allows Barthes to place his object—the magazine, the example—in a little theater of popular culture while simultaneously assuring us that he is not himself a subscriber. See Roland Barthes, *Mythologies* (Paris: Editions du Seuil, 1957), 201; selected and translated by Annette Lavers as *Mythologies* (London: Jonathan Cape, 1972), 116.

6. The projected figure comes from the first, mid-1936, prospectus for Henry Luce's proposed "Picture Magazine," then called *Dime*. See Loudon Wainwright, *The Great American Magazine: An Inside History of "Life"* (New York: Alfred A. Knopf, 1986), 32.

7. See Wainwright, *The Great American Magazine*, 63, 74. Wainwright's figures are, however, inconsistent and may be exaggerated. On page 81, he says, "All 250,000 newsstand copies of Vol. 1, No. 1 sold out the first day." He goes on to claim, "Within three months, the Donnelley presses were turning out 1 million copies a week." The numbers Wainwright cites also conflict with the circulation figures given in the January 4, 1937, issue of *Life* itself, where the paid circulation figure for the first issue, November 23, 1936, is put at 380,000 and the print order for the magazine is said to have climbed to 650,000 by the beginning of January 1937. See "With This Issue *Life* Prints 650,000 Copies," *Life*, January 4, 1937, 2–3.

8. See Wainwright, *The Great American Magazine*, 41, 42, and 81.

9. Ibid., 81–82.

10. Quoted in ibid., 83.

11. See "Pictures to the Editors," *Life*, February 8, 1937, 67. A reader, Charles J. Levine of Rochester, New York, had sent in a photograph of a window display of the January 11, 1937, issue at Lapidus's newsagent shop: "At the end

of the first day, Mr. Lapidus estimated that nearly 3,000 Rochesterians stopped to view *Life*—free of charge."

12. Wainwright, *The Great American Magazine*, 98. The study was commissioned by *Life* and reported in an advertisement in the magazine on December 12, 1938.

13. Quoted in Wainwright, *The Great American Magazine*, 94. Luce's speech was delivered in April 1937.

14. Bernard DeVoto, *Saturday Review of Literature*, January 29, 1938, quoted in W. A. Swanberg, *Luce and His Empire* (New York: Charles Scribner's Sons, 1972), 145.

15. Henry Luce's apology for the third trial dummy of the magazine that became *Life*, quoted in Wainwright, *The Great American Magazine*, 12. In 1923, Henry Luce had been a cofounder of *Time* as a national weekly digest of news. In 1931, he launched *The March of Time*, a weekly radio dramatization of the news that, in 1935, also lent its name to a monthly filmic version.

16. Henry Luce's notes for a prospectus for a "Picture Magazine," written mid-1936, quoted in Wainwright, *The Great American Magazine*, 29.

17. Daniel Longwell's memorandum accompanying a sixteen-page demonstration picture supplement that he produced in 1935, putatively to show what might be done with *Time* but implicitly to reenthuse Luce about the potentialities of a picture magazine. Quoted in Wainwright, *The Great American Magazine*, 21.

18. Opening text for *Four Hours a Year*, a seventy-two-page, large-format, hardcover, illustrated book published in 1936, under Luce's direct supervision, to celebrate and promote the *March of Time* newsreels. The volume was later to serve as what Longwell called *Life*'s "Bible" or "Magna Carta." See Wainwright, *The Great American Magazine*, 24, 25. The words may actually have been written by Luce, since they are repeated almost verbatim in a letter from Henry R. Luce to prospective charter subscribers to a magazine called *The Show-Book of the World*, September 8, 1936, Margaret Bourke-White Papers, box 49, Department of Special Collections, E. S. Bird Library, Syracuse University.

19. Quoted in Wainwright, *The Great American Magazine*, 7.

20. *Four Hours a Year*, caption to pictures taken from the publicity handouts of various beauty queens, quoted in Wainwright, *The Great American Magazine*, 25.

21. *Fortune*, December 1936. The advertisement goes on: "The Great Inquisitiveness makes you and your banker react to pictures much as your cook does, or your taxi-driver."

22. *Four Hours a Year*, quoted in Wainwright, *The Great American Magazine*, 26.

23. Margaret Bourke-White, *Portrait of Myself* (New York: Simon and Schuster, 1963), 137. Bourke-White was commenting on the absolute aptness of the title Erskine Caldwell had found for their 1937 collaborative photo-documentary book, *You Have Seen Their Faces* (New York: Modern Age Books, 1937).

24. First prospectus for a picture magazine then called *Dime*, mid-1936, quoted in Wainwright, *The Great American Magazine*, 30.

25. The opening of the final prospectus, June 1936, based on a text by Henry Luce, quoted in Wainwright, *The Great American Magazine*, 33. See also the variation on the same wording in the letter from Henry R. Luce to prospective charter subscribers to a magazine called *The Show-Book of the World*, September 8, 1936, Margaret Bourke-White Papers, box 49.

26. Modifying Debord, one might say the spectacle is the image to such a degree of accumulation that it becomes capital. It is the moment when the occupation of social life has become commodity. See Guy Debord, *Society of Spectacle* (Detroit, Mich.: Black and Red, 1970), chap. 2, nos. 34 and 42. For the concept of consummativity, *consommativité*, see Jean Baudrillard, "The Ideological Genesis of Needs," chap. 2 of *For a Critique of the Political Economy of the Sign*, trans. Charles Levin (St. Louis, Mo.: Telos Press, 1981), 82–84.

27. *Life*, February 1, 1937, 16–17.

28. *Life*, February 8, 1937, 9–23; followed by "Faces in the Flood," 46–47 (including, on page 47, a photograph by Margaret Bourke-White of a Black baby bundled up on a schoolroom chair next to a blanketed birdcage), and "Railroading in the Land of High Water," 48–49.

29. *Life*, February 8, 1937, 12.

30. *Life*, February 15, 1937, 9. By the following issue, it might be noted, the story had run down to one photograph of undermined tracks in Cincinnati's railroad yards, at the bottom of page 16. *Life* had moved on to Leon Trotsky in exile, Adolf Hitler in full pomp, President Roosevelt's struggle with the Supreme Court, and Tallulah Bankhead. See *Life*, February 22, 1937.

31. See, for example, the direct imitation of *Life*'s feature "Speaking of Pictures" in the movie advertisement "Speaking of Motion Pictures," *Life*, February 22, 1937, 6. Or, following the Louisville story, the timely advertisement for Goodrich Silvertown Tires, "How Trucks Rushed Food to Stricken Flood Area," *Life*, February 15, 1937, 63. *Life*'s picture editor and office manager, Daniel Longwell, readily admitted that *Life* "came right out of the advertising world of the United States." Quoted in Wainwright, *The Great American Magazine*, 14. On the other hand, completing the circle, Luce urged advertisers to "compete photographically with the editorial content"—a call to which many were eager

to respond. Luce, notes for a prospectus for a picture magazine, 1936, quoted in Wainwright, *The Great American Magazine*, 29. Wainwright reports one advertising executive boasting in 1936: "We're going to run you ragged—copy your technique so that you can't tell ads from editorial pages" (42). He also records that in *Life*'s first twenty years, advertisers spent more than $1 billion promoting products in its pages (94).

32. The phrase initially appears in the first prospectus for the magazine with the provisional title *Dime*, in 1936; see Wainwright, *The Great American Magazine*, 30–31. It is still retained as a name for the lead in the confidential memorandum titled "Redefinition" that Luce wrote in March 1937, looking back on the first twelve issues of *Life* and reconsidering the original prospectus. See Wainwright, *The Great American Magazine*, 89.

33. Quoted in Wainwright, *The Great American Magazine*, 89.

34. Newspaper Enterprise Association magazine article, 1929, quoted in Vicki Goldberg, *Margaret Bourke-White: A Biography* (New York: Harper and Row, 1986), 99. See also Marjorie Lawrence, "Dizzy Heights Have No Terrors for This Girl Photographer," *New York Sun*, April 25, 1929. Bourke-White was later to write to Daniel Longwell at *Life*: "I can't seem to get over being tired since the flood—I suppose because it was so continuous and strenuous." Letter dated "Wednesday evening" [1937], Margaret Bourke-White Papers, box 49.

35. Confusingly, Goldberg says in the anecdote that Bourke-White was photographing the Capitol, but this would suggest she was working on an assignment for an earlier February issue, to photograph Roosevelt's second, rain-soaked inaugural. See Goldberg, *Margaret Bourke-White*, 186. For Bourke-White's photograph of the Capitol beyond a sea of umbrellas, see *Life*, February 1, 1937, 12. This was also the issue in which the first pictures of the floods were printed: "Floods Drive 288,000 People from Their Homes," *Life*, February 1, 1937, 16–17. Bourke-White's photo-essay on the Supreme Court appears in the same issue as the photograph of Louisville flood victims and concentrates largely on the lavish fabric and domestic life of the new Supreme Court building, as light relief, one takes it, from the story of Roosevelt's attempt to force six of the nine justices to retire, following the invalidation of the National Recovery Act. See *Life*, February 15, 1937, 20–23.

36. In a confidential memorandum written in March 1937 reassessing the original 1936 prospectus for *Life*, Henry Luce opined, "You can pick practically any damn human or sub-human institution or phenomenon under the sun, turn a crack photographer on it (after a little lecture by a journalist) and publish with pleasure in eight pages the resultant *photographic essay*. Fifty or twenty years ago, people used to write "essays" for magazines. . . . The essay is no longer a vital

means of communication. But what is vital is *the photographic essay.*" Quoted in Wainwright, *The Great American Magazine,* 89.

37. See Goldberg, *Margaret Bourke-White,* 195 and 343.

38. This was the case within a year and a half of the start of Bourke-White's career in 1927, even before she definitively gave up commercial and industrial photography for photojournalism; see Goldberg, *Margaret Bourke-White,* 98–99, and note 34 above.

39. Goldberg, *Margaret Bourke-White,* 186.

40. Bourke-White, *Portrait of Myself,* 149.

41. *U.S. Camera,* May 1940, 43; quoted in Goldberg, *Margaret Bourke-White,* 194. See also Margaret Thomsen Raymond, "Girl with a Camera, Margaret Bourke-White," in *Topflight: Famous American Women,* ed. Anne Stoddard (New York: Thomas Nelson and Sons, 1946). Even at the end of her life, Bourke-White would be the subject of *The Margaret Bourke-White Story,* broadcast on national television in 1960, with Teresa Wright as Margaret Bourke-White.

42. The phrase is John Grierson's; see John Grierson, "What I Look For" (1932), in *Grierson on the Movies,* ed. Forsyth Hardy (London and Boston: Faber and Faber, 1981), 38. The essay was originally published in the *New Clarion,* June 11, 1932.

43. Erskine Caldwell, interview with Vicki Goldberg, December 1, 1982, quoted in Goldberg, *Margaret Bourke-White,* 168.

44. The technical specifications for this photograph were recorded at the time of the exhibition Photography, 1839–1937, at the Museum of Modern Art, New York, in a letter to Beaumont Newhall from Margaret Smith, secretary to Bourke-White, dated March 5, 1937: "When the Flood Receded—taken in February 1937, at Louisville, Kentucky, with 3¼ × 4¼ Linhof camera, Zeiss Tessar lens, 15 inches." Margaret Bourke-White Papers, box 31.

45. In a letter to Beaumont Newhall dated June 28, 1937, Bourke-White wrote, "I am deeply impressed with the possibilities of flash bulbs distributed through the room instead of using one attached to the camera in the usual way. I work mine with extension cords from a synchronizer attached directly to the shutter but always use two sources of light and sometimes three or four or even six distributed around the room." "I use a strong light to the side with a small light to the front. The flashlight gives a soft, very fine quality. The beauty of it of course is that you can watch your subject until they show just the expression or movements you wish and then release your flash." Margaret Bourke-White Papers, box 31.

46. Quoted in Goldberg, *Margaret Bourke-White,* 206. For Bourke-White's technique, see Goldberg, *Margaret Bourke-White,* 148, 168, 176, 206, and 231.

47. We may guess from its proportions that the image was printed in the magazine nearly full frame. When Bourke-White submitted her photographs, she insisted that her negatives be printed to the edge, initiating a practice that, in *Life*'s photo-lab, came to be called "printing black," in which the photographic image is bordered by a black margin as proof that it has not been cropped. This did not mean, however, that Bourke-White would raise objections to her pictures being cropped in the editorial process. See Goldberg, *Margaret Bourke-White*, 185.

48. Bourke-White, *Portrait of Myself*, 150.

49. Vicki Goldberg comments, "As she had known how to simplify industrial subjects and present the detail that summed up a process, so she knew how to simplify her human subjects and present a moment that would instantly telegraph a message on the page." Goldberg, *Margaret Bourke-White*, 188. Elsewhere, more critically, she adds, "Margaret could produce with surety and apparent ease the summaries that made good journalism in the thirties and still constitute a major part of it today. However much she longed to find greater insight with her camera, much of her work was clearly intended to be the most efficient and pointed reporting of surfaces." Goldberg, *Margaret Bourke-White*, 190.

Looking back, Roy Stryker, chief of the Resettlement Administration/Farm Security Administration/Office of War Information (RA/FSA/OWI) Historical Section, would characterize photojournalism at this time as "noun" and "verb" pictures, adding that "our kind of photography is the adjective and adverb." Roy Emerson Stryker, "The FSA Collection of Photographs," in Roy E. Stryker and Nancy Wood, *In This Proud Land: America, 1935–1943, as Seen by the FSA Photographers* (London: Secker and Warburg, 1973), 8.

50. Bourke-White, *Portrait of Myself*, 150.

51. Bourke-White's biographer calls this "the symbolic detail," "the symbolic expression," or "the symbolic moment": "opinions that have been compressed to the size of an aphorism to be instantly grasped by the viewer," often "a stereotype in a more visually compelling form than it usually commands." Goldberg, *Margaret Bourke-White*, 190. Elsewhere, Goldberg suggests, "The muscular compression of forms in a small space, the masterly distribution of design elements, give her photographs a poster-like clarity and power. The symbolic content is equally clear, the message unambiguous and instantly telegraphed, as it must be in a mass medium. . . . At times she reduced men and women to the status of message carriers; she saw them less as individuals than as symbols or universals" (317–18). Bourke-White herself was well aware of the established tropes of rhetoric and their function in advertising and journalism, remarking of one photograph made at the Oliver Chilled Plow Company in

1929, for the *Fortune* story "The Unseen Half of South Bend": "I made a picture of plow blades, plow handles which symbolized the whole plow factory." In Rosa Reilly, "Why Margaret Bourke-White Is at the Top," *Popular Photography*, July 1937, 68, quoted in Goldberg, *Margaret Bourke-White*, 190.

52. Cf. Colin MacCabe's analysis of the hierarchy of discourses composing what he calls the "classic realist text," in "Realism and the Cinema: Notes on Some Brechtian Theses," in *Tracking the Signifier. Theoretical Essays: Film, Linguistics, Literature* (Minneapolis: University of Minnesota Press, 1985), 33–57; first published in *Screen* 15, no. 2 (Summer 1974). MacCabe writes, "In the classic realist novel the narrative prose functions as a metalanguage that can state all the truths in the object language—those words held in inverted commas—and can also explain the relation of this object language to the real. . . . [A metalanguage] is exactly that language which, while placing other languages between inverted commas and regarding them as certain material expressions which express certain meanings, regards those same meanings as finding transparent expression within the metalanguage itself. Transparent in the sense that the metalanguage is not regarded as material; it is dematerialized to achieve perfect representation." "Realism and the Cinema," in *Tracking the Signifier*, 35.

53. *Life*, February 15, 1937, 9.

54. Letter to Miss Margaret Bourke-White from Beaumont Newhall, director, Exhibition Photography, 1839–1936, Museum of Modern Art, New York, February 16, 1937, Margaret Bourke-White Papers, box 31. Newhall refers to the photograph in what was the current issue of *Life* as "When the Flood Receded." Number 394 in the exhibition catalog, the Louisville photograph would be one of five pictures by Margaret Bourke-White in the show.

55. On the timing of the billboard campaign, see the letter reporting on the outdoor advertising program from F. D. Richards, president of Campbell-Ewald Company of New York, to Walter B. Weisenburger, executive vice president of the National Association of Manufacturers of the United States of America, October 16, 1936, Exhibit 5505 in U.S. Senate, *Hearings before a Subcommittee of the Committee on Education and Labor, United States Senate, Seventy-Fifth Congress, Pursuant to Senate Resolution 266 (74th Congress), A Resolution to Investigate Violations of the Right of Free Speech and Assembly and Interference with the Right of Labor to Organize and Bargain Collectively*, 75 parts (Washington, D.C.: Government Printing Office, 1936–1941), part 35, *Supplementary Exhibits, the National Association of Manufacturers and the National Industrial Council*, January 16, 1939 (Washington, D.C.: Government Printing Office, 1939), 14466–67. The billboard campaign was held over by the advertising agency until December 1, 1936—after the presidential election campaign—specifically to avoid

confusion with party political propaganda. Richards argued, "Industry's important job is to establish and confirm confidence in the American way of doing
things in the minds of the great mass of people all over the nation. This isn't a
political issue" (14467). Earlier in the same letter, however, Richards had already
conceded that "the posters had to be non-political in character in order that the
plant operators and the outdoor industry would not be subject to criticism in
return for their free co-operation, and they had to be of a character that would
do a good job with the great mass of people who make up the outdoor audience"
(14466).

56. Edwin Locke, "Billboard in Memphis during the Flood. Memphis,
Tennessee," February 1937 (LC-USF33-4211-M2) and the series of frames of
"Road Sign near Kingwood, West Virginia," February 1937 (LC-USF33-
004228-M2/M3/M4/M5); Arthur Rothstein's series of 35 mm shots of "A Billboard. Birmingham, Alabama," February 1937 (LC-USF33-2393-M2/M3, and
M1 and M4, which were punched with holes by Roy Stryker); Dorothea Lange's
larger-format photographs of three different posters, all titled "Billboard on
U.S. Highway 99 in California. National Advertising Campaign Sponsored
by National Association of Manufacturers," March 1937 (LC-USF34-16209-
C/16211-C/16213-C). Subsequent billboard campaigns were also recorded in
1939 in Georgia and Alabama by Marion Post Wolcott and in 1940 in Iowa by
John Vachon.

57. For details of the campaign, see the letter from F. D. Richards to Walter B. Weisenburger, October 16, 1936, Exhibit 5505 in U.S. Senate, *Hearings
before a Subcommittee of the Committee on Education and Labor*, pt. 35, 14466–67.
See also the announcement from Ernest T. Weir, chairman of the National
Industrial Information Committee of the National Association of Manufacturers of the USA, Exhibit 5485-E in ibid., pt. 35, 14411; and the letter from T. J.
Needham Jr. of Campbell-Ewald Company of New York to Walter B. Weisenburger of the National Association of Manufacturers, October 15, 1936, Exhibit
5504 in ibid., pt. 35, 14465.

58. See U.S. Senate, *Hearings before a Subcommittee of the Committee on
Education and Labor. Life*, too, paid early attention to the work of this committee,
chaired by Robert M. La Follette Jr. (D–Wisc.), running a full-page story on the
committee's inquiry into the strike-breaking role of the Pinkerton National
Detective Agency: "Life on the American Newsfront: Two Famous Names Clash
at a Senate Hearing," *Life*, February 22, 1937, 19. I am grateful to Patrick Kane
for first drawing my attention to the subcommittee records.

59. For the organization's public mission, see the *Constitution of the
National Association of Manufacturers of the United States of America*, Article II,

section 2, Exhibit 3788-A in U.S. Senate, *Hearings before a Subcommittee of the Committee on Education and Labor,* pt. 17, March 2 and 3, 1938 (Washington, D.C.: Government Printing Office, 1938), 7486.

Founded originally as a voluntary association, the National Association of Manufacturers was subsequently incorporated in 1905 as a nonprofit membership association under the Membership Corporation Law of the State of New York. The first suggestion for such a national association had come from the southern journalist Thomas H. Martin, editor of the *Dixie Manufacturer* in Atlanta, Georgia, whose editorials during the industrial depression of 1894 greatly impressed Thomas P. Egan of J. A. Fay and Egan Company, leading the latter to invite manufacturers and businessmen from all parts of the country to a gathering in Cincinnati, Ohio, on January 22, 1895. See the response by the National Association of Manufacturers of the USA to a questionnaire from the Special Committee of the U.S. Senate to Investigate Lobbying Activities, January 24, 1936, Exhibit 5253 in U.S. Senate, *Hearings before a Subcommittee of the Committee on Education and Labor,* pt. 35, 14023–25.

60. Clarence Bonnett, *A History of Employers' Associations in the United States* (New York: Vantage Press, 1956), 396.

61. *American Industries,* Boycott Supplement, National Association of Manufacturers, New York, August 15, 1904, 4, Exhibit 3803 in U.S. Senate, *Hearings before a Subcommittee of the Committee on Education and Labor,* pt. 17, 7547.

62. John Kirby Jr., president of the National Association of Manufacturers, *Proceedings of the Annual Convention of the National Association of Manufacturers,* 1911, 86, Exhibit 3804 in U.S. Senate, *Hearings before a Subcommittee of the Committee on Education and Labor,* pt. 17, 7547.

63. See, for example, *Life's* coverage of the sit-down strike in its January 18 and 25, 1937, issues: "U.S. Labor Uses a Potent New Tactic—The Sit-Down Strike," *Life,* January 18, 1937, 9–15, and "Governor Murphy and the National Guard Bring a Truce to the Automobile Strike," *Life,* January 25, 1937, 18–19. See also the coverage of the sit-down strike at the General Motors plant in Flint, Michigan, in the February 15 issue that contained Bourke-White's Louisville photograph: *Life,* February 15, 1937, 16–17.

64. See the testimony of Walter B. Weisenburger, executive vice president of the National Association of Manufacturers, U.S. Senate, *Hearings before a Subcommittee of the Committee on Education and Labor,* pt. 17, 7378–79.

65. In 1936, around four thousand members and contributors gave the National Association of Manufacturers an income of $1,171,390; of that, $572,761, or 48.9 percent, came from 207 companies, representing 5 percent of the total membership. See the testimony of Robert Wohlforth, secretary to the

Committee, U.S. Senate, *Hearings before a Subcommittee of the Committee on Education and Labor*, pt. 17, 7381–82, 7385–87, and Exhibit 3798, p. 7540.

66. U.S. Senate, *Hearings before a Subcommittee of the Committee on Education and Labor*, pt. 17, 7389.

67. The characterization of the National Association of Manufacturers' activities comes from the National Labor Relations Board Annual Report to the President, January 4, 1937. See the National Association of Manufacturers' letter to the National Labor Relations Board of March 31, 1937, Exhibit 3863 in U.S. Senate, *Hearings before a Subcommittee of the Committee on Education and Labor*, pt. 18, March 4, 7, and 8, 1938 (Washington, D.C.: Government Printing Office, 1938), 8015.

68. Speech by J. Phillip Bird, general manager of the National Association of Manufacturers, *American Industries*, December 1911, 41, Exhibit 3805 in U.S. Senate, *Hearings before a Subcommittee of the Committee on Education and Labor*, pt. 17, 7547.

69. See the *Constitution of the National Association of Manufacturers of the United States of America*, Article II, section 1, Exhibit 3788-A in U.S. Senate, *Hearings before a Subcommittee of the Committee on Education and Labor*, pt. 17, 7486.

70. See the circular letter from the chairman of the National Industrial Information Committee, February 27, 1937, Exhibit 3836 in U.S. Senate, *Hearings before a Subcommittee of the Committee on Education and Labor*, pt. 17, 7686.

71. National Association of Manufacturers of the USA, Memorandum on Community Public Information Programs to Combat Radical Tendencies and Present the Constructive Story of Industry, Exhibit 3866 in U.S. Senate, *Hearings before a Subcommittee of the Committee on Education and Labor*, pt. 18; also quoted in U.S. Senate, *Hearings before a Subcommittee of the Committee on Education and Labor*, pt. 34, *"Little Steel," Republican Steel Corporation, Labor Relations Policy and Practices, Espionage, and Violence, Refusal to Sign Union Contract*, August 11, 1938 (Washington, D.C.: Government Printing Office, 1938), 13865.

72. Robert L. Lund, *A Consideration of the Policies and Program of the National Association of Manufacturers*, National Association of Manufacturers, Law Department, Washington, D.C., September 7, 1933, Exhibit 3807 in U.S. Senate, *Hearings before a Subcommittee of the Committee on Education and Labor*, pt. 17, 7550.

73. Letter from H. O. Patton, for the Board of Directors of the National Association of Manufacturers, to Horace Hayden Jr., September 24, 1937, Exhibit 3838 in U.S. Senate, *Hearings before a Subcommittee of the Committee on Education and Labor*, pt. 17, 7693.

74. Ibid.

75. See the testimony of the committee chairman, Ernest T. Weir, chairman of the National Steel Corporation, U.S. Senate, *Hearings before a Subcommittee of the Committee on Education and Labor*, pt. 17, 7458; and the statement of Walter B. Weisenburger, executive vice president of the National Association of Manufacturers, U.S. Senate, *Hearings before a Subcommittee of the Committee on Education and Labor*, pt. 18, 7861–62.

76. Statement of Walter B. Weisenburger, executive vice president of the National Association of Manufacturers, U.S. Senate, *Hearings before a Subcommittee of the Committee on Education and Labor*, pt. 18, 7851.

77. The income figures for the Public Information Program were $36,500 in 1934; $112,659.58 in 1935; $467,759.98 in 1936; $793,043.06 in 1937. The total income for the National Association of Manufacturers in this period was $480,317.52 in 1934; $617,143.75 in 1935; $1,171,390.83 in 1936; $1,439,548.06 in 1937. U.S. Senate, *Hearings before a Subcommittee of the Committee on Education and Labor*, pt. 18, 7828, and U.S. Senate, *Hearings before a Subcommittee of the Committee on Education and Labor*, pt. 17: Exhibit 3794, p. 7538; Exhibit 3834-B, p. 7587; Exhibit 3824-C, p. 7587; Exhibit 3824-D, p. 7588; and Exhibit 3824-E, p. 7588.

78. *Industry Must Speak!* National Industrial Information Committee, n.d., Exhibit 3839 in U.S. Senate, *Hearings before a Subcommittee of the Committee on Education and Labor*, pt. 17, 7693–96.

79. Minutes of the Committee on Public Relations of the National Association of Manufacturers, April 19, 1937, Exhibit 5485 in U.S. Senate, *Hearings before a Subcommittee of the Committee on Education and Labor*, pt. 35, 14384.

80. Letter from Charles A. MacDonald, president of MacDonald-Cook Company, to C. M. Chester, March 25, 1937, Exhibit 3852 in U.S. Senate, *Hearings before a Subcommittee of the Committee on Education and Labor*, pt. 18, 7895. See also U.S. Senate, *Hearings before a Subcommittee of the Committee on Education and Labor*, pt. 36, *Supplementary Exhibits, the MacDonald-Cook Co. and the National Association of Manufacturers, the "Harmony Ads"* (Exhibits 5540–5624), January 16, 1939 (Washington, D.C.: Government Printing Office, 1939).

81. See the testimony of Walter Weisenburger, in U.S. Senate, *Hearings before a Subcommittee of the Committee on Education and Labor*, pt. 18, 7776; also Exhibit 3853, p. 7895.

82. *Industrial Strife and the Third Party*, unsigned pamphlet distributed by the National Industrial Council, July 1937, Exhibit 3873 in U.S. Senate, *Hearings before a Subcommittee of the Committee on Education and Labor*, pt. 18, 8031.

83. *Industry Must Speak!* National Industrial Information Committee, n.d., Exhibit 3839 in U.S. Senate, *Hearings before a Subcommittee of the Committee on Education and Labor,* pt. 17, 7695.

84. Statement of Walter B. Weisenburger, executive vice president of the National Association of Manufacturers, U.S. Senate, *Hearings before a Subcommittee of the Committee on Education and Labor,* pt. 18, 7862.

85. Ibid. See also "The American Way," Exhibit 5485-J in U.S. Senate, *Hearings before a Subcommittee of the Committee on Education and Labor,* pt. 35, 14433–39, and the promotional poster for schools and colleges, Exhibit 5514 in ibid., pt. 35, 14480.

86. Form letter from the president of the National Association of Manufacturers, November 29, 1937, Exhibit 3850 in U.S. Senate, *Hearings before a Subcommittee of the Committee on Education and Labor,* pt. 17, 7762. See also letter from L. J. Mulhearn, National Association of Manufacturers officer in charge of community programs, to Carl H. Bischoff, December 15, 1937, Exhibit 4047 in U.S. Senate, *Hearings before a Subcommittee of the Committee on Education and Labor,* pt. 19, March 10–12, 18, and 19, 1938 (Washington, D.C.: Government Printing Office, 1938), 8740–41. The budget figure for artwork, printing, and shipping for twenty thousand copies of three different poster designs comes from a letter from T. J. Needham Jr. of Campbell-Ewald Company of New York, to W. B. Weisenburger of the National Association of Manufacturers, October 15, 1936, Exhibit 5504 in U.S. Senate, *Hearings before a Subcommittee of the Committee on Education and Labor,* pt. 35, 14465. In the letter to W. B. Weisenburger from F. D. Richards of Campbell-Ewald, October 16, 1936, it is reported that "some idea of the extent of the co-operation offered [by outdoor advertising plant owners] may be found in the fact that the cost of these boards, if the space had to be paid for, would be about $335,000 per month, or over a million dollars worth of space during the three months' period. The labor cost alone in just posting the paper on the boards would amount to over $180,000 to plant operators." Exhibit 5505 in U.S. Senate, *Hearings before a Subcommittee of the Committee on Education and Labor,* pt. 35, 14466–67.

87. Testimony of Walter B. Weisenburger, U.S. Senate, *Hearings before a Subcommittee of the Committee on Education and Labor,* pt. 17, 7466.

88. Publicity circular, "Along the Highways of America," issued by Ernest T. Weir, chairman of the National Industrial Information Committee of the National Association of Manufacturers, Exhibit 5485-E in U.S. Senate, *Hearings before a Subcommittee of the Committee on Education and Labor,* pt. 35, 14411. The circular included a reproduction of all three billboard designs, under the heading "Industry Speaks to Millions—With Color, Pictures, Facts" (14412).

89. Bourke-White, *Portrait of Myself*, 107–13.

90. It was these "husky" advertising accounts that kept her penthouse studio in the Chrysler Building afloat for the six months each year in which she was not working for *Fortune*. See Bourke-White, *Portrait of Myself*, 80. Bourke-White's relinquishing of advertising photography coincided not only with her collaboration with Erskine Caldwell on *You Have Seen Their Faces*, from July to August 1936, but also with her being hired in September of the same year by *Life*, then two months away from its first issue. *Life*, to which Bourke-White said her first loyalty belonged, paid her a minimum of $12,000 a year, with two months free to do work that did not compete with Time Inc. publications. See Bourke-White, *Portrait of Myself*, 159; see also the Agreement between Margaret Bourke-White and Time, Incorporated, dated September 4, 1936, Margaret Bourke-White Papers, box 49.

91. On October 15, 1936, Bourke-White wrote from New York to her friend Dr. Francois Archibald Gilfillan: "The new job will give me more opportunity to work with creative things like this [*You Have Seen Their Faces*]—real life rather than attractive poses. I have had to do such a great amount of advertising photography in the last few years. . . . I am delighted to be able to turn my back on all advertising agencies and go on to life as it really is." Margaret Bourke-White Papers, box 20.

92. Bourke-White, *Portrait of Myself*, 80.

93. Margaret Bourke-White, letter to Mr. Caldwell, March 9, 1936, Erskine Caldwell Papers, Department of Special Collections, E. S. Bird Library, Syracuse University, box 1. The letter, attempting to persuade Caldwell to work with her on his documentary book project, also included the gift of a photograph, "Three Women Eating."

94. Bourke-White, *Portrait of Myself*, 127–28.

95. Ibid., 128.

96. Ibid., 112. See also Goldberg, *Margaret Bourke-White*, 159–60, where, subject to further (secondary or tertiary) revision, the dream acquires "metal beasts of prey" but gives rise to no uncertainty about its dating ("early in 1936"), about its authenticity, or about its reported immediate consequences.

97. See, for example, Mydans's 35 mm shot of the flooding in Louisville, "Louisville Ky. Mar 1936. The Ohio River flooding the Streets" (LC-USF-33-569-M4).

98. In his red-leather-bound "Diary 1937," Evans made the following entry on Wednesday, January 27: "Mercy, Stryker suggested quick trip to flood. I got Ed. Locke company." Walker Evans Archive, Diaries, 1994.250.98, Metropolitan Museum of Art, New York.

99. According to a letter from William D. Littlejohn, chief of the Appointment Section, on September 16, 1935, Evans was first appointed assistant specialist in information, CAF-7, at a salary of $7.22 per day, effective September 24, 1935, through June 30, 1937. A subsequent letter from Littlejohn, on October 1, 1935, changed this, however, to information specialist, P-2, promoted from a salary of $2,600 per annum to $3,000 a year, effective October 21, 1935. Information specialist is also the title that the chief of the Historical Section, Roy Stryker, used when writing to Miss McKinney of the Division of Information on October 9, 1935, confirming Evans's permanent appointment. It is only in the description of duties in this letter that Stryker refers to the position as "Senior Information Specialist," "with wide latitude for the exercise of independent judgment and decision." See correspondence in the Roy Emerson Stryker Papers, 1932–1964, NDA 25, Archives of American Art, Smithsonian Institution, Washington, D.C. Despite being urged by Stryker to get to Washington and out into the field as soon as possible, Evans did not actually begin work for Stryker's unit until October 29, 1935. He himself recorded having first asked for $3,600 while negotiating his appointment with Stryker. See Evans's entries for Friday, August 30, and Monday, October 28, 1935, in his "Diary 1935," Walker Evans Archive, Diaries, 1994.250.97. At the time of the flood assignment, Evans's entries in his "Diary 1937" for Thursday, January 28, and Monday, February 15, and the accounts pages at the back of the volume show that, in addition to $283.60 travel expenses, he received salary payments of $120.90, $128.96, and $104, covering the periods from January 1 to January 31 and from February 15 to February 28, 1937.

100. Locke was, in fact, Stryker's assistant chief, appointed to the position on April 16, 1936. Despite this, in later years, Stryker remembered him as "an extremely able, but unstable young man." See F. Jack Hurley, *Portrait of a Decade: Roy Stryker and the Development of Documentary Photography in the Thirties* (Baton Rouge: Louisiana State University Press, 1972), 182n47.

101. Evans, "Diary 1937," entry for Tuesday, February 2, 1937.

102. Edwin Locke to Roy Stryker, from "Locke-Evans Hdqs" at Hotel Chisca, Memphis, Tennessee, February 4, 1937, Roy Emerson Stryker Papers, 1932–1964, NDA 25. Locke adds, "My God, we are tired tonight! Got up at 6 this morning, worked until 5:30 PM, made the 6:20 PM train back to Memphis."

103. Evans recorded in his diary: "Much land flooded after leaving Memphis, water swift and deep and frightening. Auto road under water. Train tracks dry." "Diary 1937," entry for Wednesday, February 3, 1937.

104. Evans first drove through southern states in January 1934, on his way to the winter resort of Hobe Sound, Florida. He called it "a real revelation."

"Rural Carolina and Georgia" were "simply unbelievable for nostalgia and incidentally for poverty." Evans made a dozen photographs on his way back to New York, including a street scene in Fort Motte, South Carolina, but his first sustained photographic excursion came in February 1935, when he was commissioned to photograph Greek Revival architecture in the South, especially Savannah, Georgia, New Orleans, and Louisiana north to Natchez, Mississippi. He first photographed Black street life in the South and the segregated housing of "the Negro Quarter" in Savannah and New Orleans at this time, but he returned to the theme in a concerted way on his long, two-stage swing through the South for the Resettlement Administration, beginning in November 1935 and ending in April 1936. On the first stage of this trip, in December, Evans photographed in Alabama, especially in Selma, and in Louisiana, in and around New Orleans. Returning south in the second week of February 1936, on the second leg of his major assignment, Evans continued photographing Black living conditions in Louisiana, around New Orleans; in Vicksburg and Tupelo, Mississippi; in Birmingham, Alabama; and in Atlanta, Georgia, on his way to the Atlantic coast and the return route northward to Washington, D.C. See Jeff L. Rosenheim, "'The Cruel Radiance of What Is': Walker Evans and the South," in Maria Morris Hambourg, Jeff L. Rosenheim, Douglas Eklund, and Mia Fineman, *Walker Evans* (New York: Metropolitan Museum of Art, 2000, in association with Princeton University Press), 54–105.

105. Evans, "Diary 1937," entry for Thursday, February 4, 1937. In his letter to Roy Stryker of February 4, 1937, Locke wrote, "The Negro camp: Overcrowded. There are many more negroes than whites affected by flood in this area. Found 11 in one tent. They are not 'happy-go-lucky' about it, but dazed, apathetic, and hopeless. There is a good deal of illness: excruciating coughs, pneumonia and influenza cases laying in a dark cotton warehouse." Roy Emerson Stryker Papers, 1932–1964, NDA 25.

106. Stryker professed himself pleased with the results. Letter to Ed Locke, February 13, 1937, Roy Emerson Stryker Papers, 1932–1964, NDA 25. The negative judgment is that of later critics and biographers. James R. Mellow, for example, writes, "It had not been a successful assignment nor had it given Evans much satisfaction, partly because of his illness, partly perhaps because of a lack of interest in what he was doing." Mellow, *Walker Evans*, 348. Evans himself wrote to his friend, Jay Leyda, on March 17 that "I had the flu but the flood was damned interesting, highwater refugees and all that." Walker Evans, letter to Jay Leyda, Memphis, February 17, 1937, Jay and Si-ian Chen Leyda Papers, New York University, Tamiment Library, TAM 83, Series II (Correspondence), Sub-series A, box 3. In the midst of his shooting, in a "Diary 1937" entry for

Monday, February 8, Evans also noted, "Developed some of the Forrest City films; some good."

107. It was Evans's practice throughout his government employment to reserve certain negatives and duplicated images in this way for his own files. Moreover, correspondence between Evans, Stryker, and Tom Mabry, executive director of the Museum of Modern Art, indicates that, for the most part, only prints already in Evans's possession in New York were used in the production of *American Photographs*. See Evans's letters to Stryker, April 21, 1938, and June 17, 1938, Roy Emerson Stryker Papers, 1932–1964, NDA 25, and Tom Mabry's letter to Roy Stryker, June 20, 1938, Walker Evans Archive, American Photographs, 1994.250.57, folder 36. Another exposure of the same sleeping woman (LC-USF34-8202C) can be found in the RA/FSA file. It is this photograph, giving a fuller view of the face of the woman and the child lying watchfully next to her, that was hung in the exhibition, alongside a startling image of refusal (LC-USF34-8205C), showing only the feet and part of the upper face of an African American man whose eyes stare back through a gap in a tent of blankets hung for privacy, defying the camera's gaze. Both images, numbered 44 and 43 on the exhibition checklist, were severely cropped for the exhibition, to remove distracting figures. See the graphic reconstruction of the original hanging in Gilles Mora and John T. Hill, *Walker Evans: The Hungry Eye* (New York: Harry N. Abrams, 1993), 180.

108. See Walker Evans, *American Photographs* (New York: Museum of Modern Art, 1938).

109. This despite the best efforts of Evans's friend and collaborator, Lincoln Kirstein, whom Evans remembered "helping me very much compose the thing" and who, following Evans's own emphasis on the work being "arranged and divided and ordered by him," stressed in his catalog essay for *American Photographs* that "the photographs are arranged to be seen in their given sequence." Much influenced by Sergey Eisenstein's theory of montage, however, Kirstein also saw in the juxtapositions within Evans's photographs "living citations of the Hegelian theory of opposites." Lincoln Kirstein, "Photographs of America: Walker Evans," in Evans, *American Photographs*, 198, 195. For Evans's later recollections of Kirstein, see the edited transcript of a taped interview by Leslie Katz, 33–34, in the Walker Evans Archive, and the published excerpts, "Interview with Walker Evans," by Leslie Katz, *Art in America* 59, no. 2 (March–April 1971): 83. For Evans's stress on the arrangement of the photographs, in his notes for the inside front flap of *American Photographs*, see the one-page manuscript titled "PLAN OF ARRANGEMENT OF MUSEUM BOOK," Walker Evans Archive, American Photographs, 1994.250.57, folder 7.

110. The photograph is filed in the Resettlement Administration/Farm Security Administration collection at the Library of Congress as "Forrest City, Ark. Feb 1937. Negroes standing in line for food at the camp for flood refugees" (LC-USF33-009217-M3).

111. The faces actually appear in an adjacent image, LC-USF33-9217-M5, showing the young teenage woman, who holds the tin plate, between two older figures, who may be her mother and father, the latter a robust, smiling man in a hat whom it is hard to connect to the truncated arm in the better-known frame.

112. The Exposition and the Farm Security Administration contribution, "How American People Live," opened on April 18, 1938, and ran through April 24, after which the FSA section was transferred to Washington, D.C., and shown again, on the patio of the Department of Agriculture, from June 20 to July 2, 1938. The Museum of Modern Art in New York also offered to tour the FSA exhibit throughout the United States.

113. Walker Evans, letter to Roy Stryker, April 21, 1938, Roy Emerson Stryker Papers, 1932–1964, NDA 25.

114. Roy Stryker, letter to Edwin Locke, April 26, 1938, Roy Emerson Stryker Papers, 1932–1964, NDA 25.

115. Edward Steichen, "The F.S.A. Photographers," *U.S. Camera Annual 1939*, ed. T. J. Maloney (New York: William Morrow, 1938), 43–66. Of the forty-one photographs included, five were by Evans. One of these, "Graveyard, Houses, and Steel Mill, Bethlehem, Pennsylvania," November 1935 (LC-USF342-1167A), an eight-by-ten photograph of a cemetery, workers' housing, and a steel plant, was reproduced, cropped on all four sides, and bled to the edge of the page, across an entire double spread of the spiral-bound annual.

116. Roy Stryker, letter to Dorothea Lange, December 22, 1938, quoted in Hurley, *Portrait of a Decade*, 136.

117. Steichen, "The F.S.A. Photographers," 44. Steichen's comment refers to Evans's 35 mm picture of African Americans in Arkansas standing in a bread-line (LC-USF-33-009217-M3), which appears on page 46 of *U.S. Camera Annual 1939*, but also to Evans's "Graveyard, Houses, and Steel Mill, Bethlehem, Pennsylvania," which fills a double-page spread on pages 64 and 65. The second of Evans's flood refugee pictures, of Black children waiting in line in Forrest City, Arkansas (LC-USF33-9231-M1), appears on page 53, tellingly below Evans's Alabama "Minstrel Showbill" of 1936 (LC-USF342-1137A): precisely the juxtaposition Evans was to avoid in *American Photographs*.

118. Richard Wright, *12 Million Black Voices: A Folk History of the Negro in the United States*, photo-direction [*sic*] by Edwin Rosskam (New York: Viking,

1941). The second image, "A Sharecropper's Grave, Alabama," appears on page 55 in Part Two, "Inheritors of Slavery."

119. Evans, "Diary 1937," entry for Thursday, February 4, 1937.

120. The reference to Evans wanting to go on to Paducah and Louisville once he recovered from influenza comes in Ed Locke's letter to Roy Stryker from Memphis on February 11, 1937, Roy Emerson Stryker Papers, 1932–1964, NDA 25. Locke made four photographs of the National Association of Manufacturers' billboard, all filed under the title "Road sign near Kingwood, West Virginia" (LC-USF33-004228-M2/M3/M4/M5). As noted above, Locke also photographed the billboard campaign in Memphis, during the flood (LC-USF33-4211-M2).

121. Evans, "Diary 1937," entry for Saturday, March 20, 1937. The complete entry reads: "tacked poster show prints / lunch with R. Stryker / extraordinary conversation. / spent evening in Arlington / with P. Taylor."

122. The official communication simply read, "Reasons for action: Services no longer needed." National Personnel Records Center, St. Louis, quoted in Mellow, *Walker Evans*, 348. Oddly, Evans would file one further picture series with the RA/FSA collection in Washington, D.C.: a study of a single New York City block on East Sixty-first Street, between First and Second avenues, which he completed in August 1938 with a 35 mm camera. Fifty of Evans's negatives entered the file, but nothing in the written records explains how the assignment was selected or whether Evans was paid. See "New York City, 1938," in *Walker Evans: Photographs for the Farm Security Administration, 1935–1938*, introduced by Jerald C. Maddox (New York: Da Capo Press, 1975), nos. 451–88, and "New York City Block: Walker Evans," in *Documenting America, 1935–1943*, ed. Carl Fleischhauer and Beverly W. Brannan (Berkeley, Los Angeles, and London: University of California Press, in association with the Library of Congress, 1988), 128–31.

123. Archibald MacLeish, *Land of the Free* (New York: Harcourt, Brace, 1938). The caption for Evans's photograph is given on page 91.

124. Roy Stryker, letter to Russell Lee, April 1937, quoted in Nicholas Natanson, *The Black Image in the New Deal: The Politics of FSA Photography* (Knoxville: University of Tennessee Press, 1992), 203.

125. MacLeish, *Land of the Free*, "Notes," 89. The characterization of the "choral voice" came in a later interview, in Bernard A. Drabeck and Hellen E. Ellis, eds., *Archibald MacLeish: Reflections* (Amherst: University of Massachusetts Press, 1986), 95. It may be worth noting that Lorentz's *The Plow That Broke the Plains* derived from an essay of the same title that MacLeish had written for *Fortune* on winter wheat farming in Montana; see Drabeck and Ellis, *Archibald MacLeish*, 80.

126. MacLeish, in Drabeck and Ellis, *Archibald MacLeish*, 95. The term "Sound Track" is also MacLeish's and is inscribed on the recto of page 1, above the running black line that recurs on every page of text throughout the book, like the continuous optical sound track strip on a cinematic film. See also Archibald MacLeish, "The Soundtrack-and-Picture Form: A New Direction," in *New Directions in Prose and Poetry* (Norfolk, Conn.: New Directions, 1938), 3:167–70.

127. MacLeish, *Land of the Free*, 29, 87.

128. Ibid., 3.

129. Ibid.: "We're not telling," 33, 40, 41, 43, 46, 47; "we can't say," 30, 34, 39, 84; "we don't know," 1, 15, 31, 80, 88; "we aren't sure," 2, 35, 39, 84; "we get wondering," 9, 22, 23, 29, 49, 79, 88; "We're asking," 88.

130. See the "Index of Pictures," in ibid., 91.

131. Ibid., "Notes," 89.

132. MacLeish, in Drabeck and Ellis, *Archibald MacLeish*, 80.

133. Ruth Lechlitner, "Now the Land Is Gone: Magnificent Pictures of America Matched with a Rhythmic Text," *New York Herald-Tribune Books*, April 10, 1938, 6, section 9.

134. Peter Monro Jack, "Archibald MacLeish's Poem for Our Day," *New York Times Book Review*, May 8, 1938, 2, section 7.

135. Evans, letter to Roy Stryker, June 17, 1938, Roy Emerson Stryker Papers, 1932–1964, NDA 25. Evans added, "They even reproduced one of the great M. de Bourke-White pictures without mentioning that august name."

136. Two pages of grouped handwritten manuscript notes in ink, 1935, Walker Evans Archive, Miscellaneous Notes 1920s–1930s, 1994.250.4, folder 12. Under "Want": fourteen lines, including "all rights retained by me" and "guarantee of one-man performance." Under "Will give": two lines, "1 complete set prints and word records."

137. See Walker Evans Archive, Miscellaneous Notes 1920s–1930s, 1994.250.4, folder 18: "file on STRYKER / Among things you really think of me / (1) that you picked me up from a state of obscure poverty / 2 that I benefited by having a good job / 3 that you gave me my chance and defended my kind of work." And see also 1994.250.4, folder 26: two handwritten manuscript pages: "Stryker's background," and "Stryker & hole punching."

138. Typed letter with carbon, from Walker Evans to Roy Stryker, dated July 16, 1938, but unsigned, Walker Evans Archive, American Photographs, 1994.250.57, folder 57. See also Evans's letter to Stryker, June 15, 1938, Walker Evans Archive, American Photographs, 1994.250.57, folder 35, in which, five days after Mabry had written to Stryker about the proposed "general review" of Evans's work, Evans casually described the Museum of Modern Art show but was

careful not to ask for permission himself. Tom Mabry's letter to Roy Stryker, June 10, 1938, is in Walker Evans Archive, American Photographs, 1994.250.57, folder 34.

139. Letter from Roy Stryker to Mrs. L. A. Collins Jr. (Frances Strunsky Collins, head of publications at the Museum of Modern Art), October 19, 1938, Walker Evans Archive, American Photographs, 1994.250.57, folder 41.

140. Five pages of manuscript notes on small notepaper concerning the contract for *American Photographs*, Walker Evans Archive, American Photographs, 1994.250.57, folder 12.

141. One-page manuscript, "PLAN or ARRANGEMENT OF MUSEUM BOOK," Walker Evans Archive, American Photographs, 1994.250.57, folder 7. In the text, "more or less independently" is then crossed out.

142. One-page manuscript, "PEOPLE [FACES (deleted)] BY PHOTOGRAPHY," Walker Evans Archive, American Photographs, 1994.250.57, folder 8.

143. The Walker Evans Archive has three different versions of the 1938 draft "NOTE" for *American Photographs;* the note was never published. Miscellaneous Notes 1920s–1930s, 1994.250.4, folder 23, contains a one-page manuscript, in pencil, on the verso of a letter from Edith McCombe, secretary to Joseph Verner Reed, dated June 29, 1938, that includes draft notes for the unpublished "NOTE" and for unpublished acknowledgments. In addition, the American Photographs box, 1994.250.57, contains two typescript versions of the unpublished "NOTE": folder 17, a fifteen-page typewritten carbon of Lincoln Kirstein's "Photographs of America by Walker Evans," which includes on its final page a one-page text of a "NOTE" by Evans, amended by him in pencil, with further notes on its reverse; and folder 11, a two-page typewritten carbon that incorporates the editing of the earlier typewritten draft but is itself further revised in pencil by Evans, each page having further pencil notes on the verso.

144. Two-page typewritten carbon amended by Evans in pencil, 1, Walker Evans Archive, American Photographs, 1994.250.57, folder 11.

145. Ibid., 1.

146. Ibid., 2.

147. Jane Smith Ninas, who had met Evans in New Orleans in February 1935 and had accompanied him on his first photographic exploration of the Greek Revival architecture of Louisiana plantation houses. After a hiatus in their relationship, following a traumatic scene with Smith Ninas's husband in February 1936, Smith Ninas and Evans renewed their relationship in June 1939 and were married on October 27, 1941. On December 21, 1955, they were divorced, and Evans made a point of deleting the dedication from the republished version of *American Photographs* that came out in 1962. A three-by-five

notecard in the Walker Evans Archive has the curt penciled reminder "remove J. S. N. dedication." Walker Evans Archive, American Photographs exhibition and book reissue 1962, 1994.250.58, folder 27.

148. Evans, *American Photographs*, n.p.

149. Caldwell and Bourke-White, *You Have Seen Their Faces*. See also Elizabeth McCausland, "Photographic Books," in *The Complete Photographer*, ed. Willard D. Morgan, 8, no. 43 (November 20, 1942) (Chicago: National Educational Alliance, 1942), 2783–94, and Edwin Rosskam, "Not Intended for Framing: The FSA Archive," *Afterimage* 18, no. 8 (March 1981): 9–11.

150. See Peter Galassi, "A Note on the Fiftieth-Anniversary Edition," in Evans, *American Photographs*, 201. The designation "Bible cloth" was Evans's own.

151. Evans's first exhibition at the Museum of Modern Art took place between November 16, 1933, and January 1, 1934, displaying thirty-nine of the one hundred prints of American nineteenth-century architecture that had been donated to the museum's permanent collection by Lincoln Kirstein and that would be circulated as a traveling exhibit until 1940. In the same year, 1933, through the Downtown Gallery, Evans photographed Mayan and Aztec objects for Holger Cahill's exhibition American Sources of Modern Art, principally motivated by his effort to earn much-needed cash. More officially, in 1935, with the support of a grant from the General Education Board, Evans was commissioned by Alfred Barr and Tom Mabry to photograph all five hundred exhibits in the African Negro Art exhibition and to prepare seventeen portfolios of his complete prints. Over the next two years, the museum also included Evans's work in two major survey exhibitions: Barr's Fantastic Art, Dada, and Surrealism, in 1936, and Newhall's Photography, 1839–1937, in 1937. Then, in spring 1938, Tom Mabry engineered the purchase of work by Evans for the permanent collection, a purchase that was to precipitate the hastily scheduled solo exhibition, the museum's first for a photographer, from September 28 to November 18, 1938, accompanying the publication of *American Photographs*. It was Mabry and Kirstein, and later Frances Collins, who represented Evans's main supporters at the museum. Without much cause, Evans thought a great deal less of director Alfred H. Barr and museum librarian Beaumont Newhall. Even while negotiating the African Art commission, Evans made an entry in his "Diary 1935" on Saturday, April 13, 1935, that reads, "Barr so nice and so confused. Quite a *useless* man, I'd say; though a sweet one." Walker Evans Archive, Diaries, 1994.250.97. Three years later, worrying about misreadings of his forthcoming exhibition and book, Evans composed a defensive letter to Stryker, dated July 16, 1938, that ends with a crossed-out passage: "When I say Museum I do not mean their so called curator of photography who, a[s] I told you, has had and will have

nothing to do with my book or exhibition, and who as a matter of fact has not the right to use that title." Walker Evans Archive, American Photographs, 1994.250.57, folder 57.

152. Evans letter to Stryker, dated July 16, 1938. Walker Evans Archive, American Photographs, 1994.250.57, folder 57.

153. See Walker Evans, "The Reappearance of Photography," *Hound and Horn* 5, no. 1 (October–December 1931): 125–28. The definition of his work as "documentary, non-artistic photographs" comes from Evans's draft application to the Ford Foundation Fellowship Program for Studies in the Creative Arts, dated April 28, 1960, Walker Evans Archive, Grants and Foundations, 1994.250.85. The draft proposal begins, "My project is a book of documentary, non-artistic photographs, with text essay and extended captions, recording aspects of American society as it looks today. This work is in the field of non-scholarly, non-pedantic sociology. It is a visual study of American civilization of a sort never undertaken at all extensively by photographers, who are all either commercial, journalistic, or 'artistic.'" Some few years later, revising his publisher's proposed jacket text for the 1966 reprint of *Let Us Now Praise Famous Men*, Evans wrote, "If most professional photography is dominated by the commercial stance or the artistic posture, Evans is in recoil from these." Quoted in *Walker Evans at Work* (London: Thames and Hudson, 1983), 136.

154. Transcript of a tape-recorded interview of Walker Evans by Paul Cummings, October 13, 1971, Archives of American Art, quoted in Alan Trachtenberg, "A Book Nearly Anonymous," chap. 5 of *Reading American Photographs: Images as History, Mathew Brady to Walker Evans* (New York: Hill and Wang, 1989), 238.

155. Beaumont Newhall letter to Walker Evans, September 27, 1938, quoted in Mellow, *Walker Evans*, 388.

156. "Interview with Walker Evans," by Katz, 86.

157. It may be worth noting that Evans sold 171 photographs to the museum for the exhibition, at $25.00 each, for a total of $4,275.00—rather more than his annual salary at the Resettlement Administration. See the invoice sent to Evans by Dorothy H. Dudley, registrar of the Museum of Modern Art, September 19, 1938, Walker Evans Archive, American Photographs, 1994.250.57, folder 25. The book was less profitable. He received a $260.00 advance royalty on the 1,300 copies of the book distributed to members, half on signing the contract, half on delivering the final material. See the contract for "Photographs by Walker Evans," May 6, 1938, Walker Evans Archive, American Photographs, 1994.250.57, folder 30. Between January 1, 1939, and June 30, 1944, he received a further $249.25 in royalties on 1,071 sales and review copies. Statements of royalties due on *American Photographs* to Walker Evans, July 11, 1939, to July 28,

1944, Walker Evans Archive, American Photographs, 1994.250.57, folder 55. The book sold for $2.00 to members and $2.50 to the public.

158. Mabry letter to Lincoln Kirstein, April 29, 1938; quoted in Mellow, *Walker Evans*, 368.

159. Ibid.

160. Walker Evans Archive, American Photographs, 1994.250.57, folder 21.

161. Kirstein, "Photographs of America," 198.

162. Four-page typewritten carbon of a list of plates, annotated in pencil and ink, Walker Evans Archive, American Photographs, 1994.250.57, folder 1.

163. See Trachtenberg's intense reading of Evans's *American Photographs* in "A Book Nearly Anonymous," 265.

164. Kirstein, "Photographs of America," 195, 193.

165. Ibid., 196.

166. James Agee wrote to Evans, June 20, 1938: "I had heard from Via [Via Agee] that you felt thoroughly well over Lincoln's introduction [*sic*]." Agee Papers, Harry Ransom Humanities Research Center, University of Texas, Austin, quoted in Belinda Rathbone, *Walker Evans: A Biography* (Boston and New York: Houghton Mifflin, 1995), 159. See also "Interview with Walker Evans," by Katz, 83, and the longer transcript of his taped interview, quoted in Mellow, *Walker Evans*, 370, 377. These latter testimonies to Kirstein come later in Evans's life. Ten years earlier, however, Evans had drafted the one-page typescript annotated carbon of his unpublished "NOTE" for the reprint edition of *American Photographs* by the Museum of Modern Art and Doubleday, stamped November 29, 1961, and marked "revision." Walker Evans Archive, American Photographs exhibition and book reissue 1962, 1994.250.58, folder 5. Here, Evans concludes, "In addition, Lincoln Kirstein's accompanying essay stands out as one of the few intelligible, knowledgeable, illuminating statements made for the field of still photography, a field commonly muddled and corrupt as a cistern."

167. Letter to Walker Evans from "F" (Frances Collins), May 4, 1938, Walker Evans Archive, American Photographs, 1994.250.57, folder 29.

168. Eleanor Roosevelt drew attention to Evans's book in her My Day column, *New York Telegram*, September 30, 1938.

169. Edward Alden Jewell, *New York Times*, Sunday, October 2, 1938, section 9, 9.

170. H. B., "This, Our Native Land: America, the Beautiful," *Washington Daily News*, October 15, 1938.

171. Carl Van Vechten, *New York Herald Tribune*, Books Section, October 16, 1938, 4.

172. David Wolff, *New Masses*, October 4, 1938.

173. William Carlos Williams, "Sermon with a Camera," *New Republic*, October 12, 1938, 282.

174. *Washington Post*, October 7, 1938.

175. *San Francisco News*, December 17, 1938.

176. Kirstein, "Photographs of America," 198. S. T. Williamson, *New York Times Book Review*, November 27, 1938, 6.

177. Ansel Adams, letter to Edward Weston, September 23, 1938, quoted in Rathbone, *Walker Evans*, 166; Ansel Adams letter to Georgia O'Keeffe, quoted in Mellow, *Walker Evans*, 381.

178. Pare Lorentz, *Saturday Review of Literature*, December 19, 1938, 6.

179. Kirstein, "Photographs of America," 193.

180. Thomas Mabry, *Harper's Bazaar*, November 1, 1938, 84.

181. Jewell, *New York Times*, Sunday, October 2, 1938, 9.

182. S. T. Williamson, *New York Times Book Review*, 6.

183. Wolff, *New Masses*, October 4, 1938.

184. Ibid.

185. Williams, "Sermon with a Camera," 282.

186. Evans, unfinished draft of a two-page letter in ink on hotel stationery to Ernestine Evans, from Hobe Sound, Florida, dated February 1934, Walker Evans Collection, Getty Museum, JPGM 84.XG.963.42, published in *Walker Evans at Work*, 98.

187. See Stryker, "The FSA Collection of Photographs," 7, and "Selected Shooting Scripts," 187–88, in Stryker and Wood, *In This Proud Land*.

188. One-page manuscript in an envelope marked "Lists for *American Photographs*?" Walker Evans Archive, American Photographs, 1994.250.57, folder 4.

189. One-page manuscript, Walker Evans Archive, American Photographs, 1994.250.57, folder 5.

190. See the subject dividers for Evans's postcard collection, Walker Evans Archive, 1994.264; see also "Collections," in Jeff L. Rosenheim and Douglas Eklund, *Unclassified: A Walker Evans Anthology* (New York: Metropolitan Museum of Art; Zurich: Scalo, 2000), 199–245. See further the publications drawn by Walker Evans from his postcard collection: "When 'Downtown' Was a Beautiful Mess," *Fortune*, January 1962, 100–106, and "Come On Down," *Architecture Forum*, July 1962, 96–100.

191. See Evans's comments on Kirstein's "helping me very much compose the thing," in the transcript of his taped interview with Leslie Katz; quoted in Mellow, *Walker Evans*, 370. On Barthes's method of writing on index cards, see Louis-Jean Calvet, *Roland Barthes*, trans. Sarah Wykes (Bloomington and Indianapolis: Indiana University Press, 1994), 59, 189.

192. Kirstein, "Photographs of America," 196. Evans was an avid filmgoer, a particular fan of newsreels, and a would-be filmmaker on at least two occasions during the 1930s, in quite separate contexts. His first effort was made during a voyage as official photographer aboard the schooner *Cressida* that took him to the Marquesas Islands, to Tahiti, and to the neighboring Society Islands in the first four months of 1932. His second engagement with film came in the fall and winter of 1936, when he tried to develop a number of film projects, first with Ben Shahn and then with James Agee, the proposed scenarios ranging from Resettlement Administration greenbelt rehousing projects, to unemployment and slums, to a film version of the tenant farmer book. From spring 1943 to September 1945, Evans also worked as a cinema critic for *Time*. For Evans's involvements with film, see Mellow, *Walker Evans*, 153–56, 336–43, 469–75. Tellingly, after returning from the South Pacific and after viewing his footage, Evans wrote to his friend Hanns Skolle, "Movies are more difficult than I realized. I seem to be able to get striking individual pictures but have difficulty in composing any significant sequence." Evans, letter to Hanns Skolle, May 19, 1932, Walker Evans Archive, Correspondence: Evans to Hanns Skolle, 1928–1933, 1994.260.25, folder 35.

193. Kirstein, "Photographs of America," 196–97, 193, 195, 195, 196.

194. For the best of these in recent years, see Trachtenberg, "A Book Nearly Anonymous." While taking up Kirstein's notion of the dialectics of montage, Trachtenberg himself concedes that "The very openness of *American Photographs* implies skepticism toward closed forms and fixed meanings" (258).

195. For the interlinked functions of the Greek archive (αρκηειον) as magistrate's house, guardian of records, and place of adjudication, see Jacques Derrida, *Archive Fever: A Freudian Impression*, trans. Eric Prenowitz (Chicago and London: University of Chicago Press, 1996), esp. 1–5.

196. See Stryker, letter to Mrs. L. A. Collins Jr., October 19, 1938, Walker Evans Archive, American Photographs, 1994.250.57, folder 41, and Lorentz, *Saturday Review of Literature*, 6.

197. See Evans's letters to Stryker, April 21, June 15, and June 17, 1938, Roy Emerson Stryker Papers, 1932–1964, NDA 25.

198. Tom Mabry, letter to Roy Stryker, June 20, 1938, Walker Evans Archive, American Photographs, 1994.250.57, folder 36: "Since we are rather pressed for time and Mr. Evans is at work on another book we have decided to use only those extra prints which he happens to have in New York." Mabry was replying to a letter from Stryker, dated June 16, 1938, that gave permission for the inclusion of photographs made under Resettlement Administration auspices in the museum's exhibition and that offered to make arrangements for Evans to make his own prints from file negatives. See also note 107 above.

199. One-page manuscript on the verso of a note from Evans's house-cleaner, Jacqueline, concerning her hours of work and pay (forty-three cents per hour), Walker Evans Archive, Miscellaneous Notes, 1920s–1930s, 1994.250.4, folder 17.

200. For a precise description of the development and structure of the file, see "Appendix: The FSA–OWI Collection," in Fleischhauer and Brannan, *Documenting America, 1935–1943*, 330–42. For a reading of the file as "one of the prime cultural artefacts of the New Deal," see Alan Trachtenberg, "From Image to Story: Reading the File," in Fleischhauer and Brannan, *Documenting America, 1935–1943*, 43–73.

In Stryker's working picture file, mounted and captioned prints were stored in vertical storage cabinets, mostly placed by state and assignment, but some grouped by subject. The inefficiency and confusion of this arrangement led Stryker to hire the museum librarian and archivist, Paul Vanderbilt, in 1942 to restructure and systematize the filing system. Vanderbilt first organized the augmented picture collection into 22,000 lots, more or less corresponding to the original shooting assignments or image sets, and preserved these primary groupings on microfilm, setting some aside for storage. He then oversaw the redistribution of some 88,000 prints from Stryker's original pool into a "classified file," arranged in six broad geographical regions, in a sequence of nine subdivided subject categories descending from "The Land," through "Cities and Towns," "People as Such," "Houses and Living Conditions," to "Transportation," "Work," "Organized Society," "War," and a range of social and intellectual institutions and practices.

201. "Still Photography," a memorandum prepared by Roy Stryker for budgetary purposes, undated, 1, Roy Emerson Stryker Papers, 1932–1964, NDA 4.

202. Paul Vanderbilt, "Reorganization Reports," 12, Paul Vanderbilt Papers, Archives of American Art, Smithsonian Institution, Washington, D.C.

203. Roy Stryker, undated letter to Walker Evans, at the Corroll Hotel, Vicksburg, Mississippi, Roy Emerson Stryker Papers, 1932–1964, NDA 25. Evans's photograph does, however, in an indirect way, undo Stryker's later claim that in its focus on the local, the ordinary, and the everyday, there is in the entire photographic collection "no record of big people" and "absolutely no celebrities." Cf. Stryker, "The FSA Collection of Photographs," 8.

204. Walker Evans, "Outline Memorandum," no date, Roy Emerson Stryker Papers, 1932–1964, NDA 25.

205. John Vachon, interview by Richard K. Doud, New York, April 28, 1965, Archives of American Art, Smithsonian Institution, Washington, D.C., quoted in Hurley, *Portrait of a Decade*, 156.

206. John Vachon, letter to Roy Stryker from the Hotel Canfield, Dubuque, Iowa, April 19 (1940?), Roy Emerson Stryker Papers, 1932–1964, NDA 26.

207. Vachon, interview by Doud, quoted in Hurley, *Portrait of a Decade*, 156.

208. The full caption reads: "Atlanta, Ga. May 1938. Houses and advertisements. LC-USF-34-8447-D. John Vachon."

209. Compare, here, Craig Owens, "Photography *en abyme*," *October*, no. 5 (Summer 1978): 85–86 and 88.

210. Cf. Rosenheim, "'The Cruel Radiance of What Is,'" 83, and Mellow, *Walker Evans*, 300. The Kimball House, 33 Pryor Street, Atlanta, was a local landmark dating back to 1870 but rebuilt around 1883. One block from the Five Points business hub, it was also a popular rendezvous for political leaders from the nearby Capitol. See Works Progress Administration, Federal Writers Program, *Georgia: The WPA Guide to Its Towns and Countryside*, introduced by Phinizy Spalding (Columbia: University of South Carolina Press, 1990), 174; originally published in the American Guide Series (Athens: University of Georgia Press, 1940).

Peter Sekaer, a Danish-born photographer and poster designer and one-time pupil of Berenice Abbott, had started working for Evans on August 19, 1935, helping print and mount the sets of photographs of African sculpture that Evans was contracted to produce for the Museum of Modern Art in New York. In Washington, that same year, while negotiating for his own position, Evans tried to get Sekaer a government job, but in his diary for October 10, 1935, he recorded "trouble," the next day adding that he did not think it would prove as good an offer as his own; see Evans, "Diary 1935." In the event, without any government position, Sekaer made the trip south with Evans in February 1936, photographing alongside him, when he could get a decent vantage point, and also capturing Evans at work with his view camera, as he had before in Bethlehem, Pennsylvania, in November 1935. Sekaer's photograph of Evans, head beneath his black cloth, is in the collection of the Metropolitan Museum of Art, New York (1994.305.1). See also Peter Sekaer, *American Pictures* (Andover, Mass.: Addison Gallery of American Art, Phillips Academy; New York: Howard Greenberg Gallery, 1999).

211. See Evans's "Itemized Schedule of Travel and Other Expenses," May 6, 1936, Roy Emerson Stryker Papers, 1932–1964, NDA 25. See also Evans, "Diary 1935."

212. See Roy Stryker's undated letter to Evans at the Corroll Hotel in Vicksburg, Mississippi (end of February, 1936), Roy Emerson Stryker Papers, 1932–1964, NDA 25.

213. Ibid. See also Stryker's undated letter to Evans at St. Marys, Florida [*sic*] (at the end of March or the beginning of April 1936), Roy Emerson Stryker Papers, 1932–1964, NDA 25. Evans eventually arrived back in Washington, D.C., on Monday April 13, 1936, having clocked 4,064 miles in his car since leaving Gulfport. See Rosenheim, "'The Cruel Radiance of What Is,'" 85.

214. See Evans letter to Roy Stryker, from New York City, July 16, 1937, correcting the impression that Ernestine Evans had been with him in Mississippi and Alabama, Roy Emerson Stryker Papers, 1932–1964, NDA 25.

215. African Americans made up one-third of Atlanta's population in the late 1930s, living in segregated but not clearly defined city districts. For Evans's photographs, see, for example, the various views of "Negro Houses" in Atlanta, LC-USF-342-8032-E/8033-A/8034-A/8035-A/8036-A and 8037-A. LC-USF-342-8033-A, "Negro Section, Atlanta," would later be reproduced in Works Progress Administration, Federal Writers Program, *Georgia: The WPA Guide*, between 292 and 293, though it would be erroneously attributed to the U.S. Housing Administration. The photograph, "Negro Barber Shop Interior, Atlanta, 1936" (LC-USF342-8100-A), would be included in part 1 of *American Photographs* as plate 6. Cf. Peter Sekaer's "Negroes' Barber Shop, Atlanta, Georgia," March 1936, Addison Gallery of American Art, Phillips Academy, Andover, Massachusetts.

216. Not all of these negatives were sent to Washington, since only the Cherokee Parts Store appears in the Resettlement Administration file (LC-USF342-8102-A). The other prints are now in the Walker Evans Archive at the Metropolitan Museum of Art, New York: 1994.257.37, 1994.257.88, 1994.253.346.2/3/ and 4, 1994.253.346.5, 1994.253.346.1.

217. Francis Trevelyan Miller, ed. in chief, *The Photographic History of the Civil War*, 10 vols. (New York: Review of Reviews, 1911). See, in particular, vol. 3, *The Decisive Battles*, "To Atlanta," 104–38, and, for example, the plates "The Ruins of Hood's Retreat—Demolished Cars and Rolling-Mill" (10:135), "The Atlanta Bank before the March to the Sea" (10:215), and "Ruins in Atlanta" (10:221). The notion of "photographic evidence" is underlined in volume 1, in the "Editorial Introduction" by Francis Trevelyan Miller (1:18), in Henry Wysham Lanier's essay "Photographing the Civil War" (1:30–54), and in George Haven Putnam's "The Photographic Record as History" (1:60–84), where Putnam writes, "These vivid pictures bring past history into the present tense" (1:60). In Pittsburgh, in December 1935, Evans also picked up Charles Frey's souvenir album of Richmond, published by Chisholm Brothers in Portland, Maine, which he was eager to compare with the New York volumes; see Evans's entry for Tuesday, December 3, in "Diary 1935."

218. Works Progress Administration, Federal Writers Program, *Georgia: The WPA Guide*, 160.

219. "A Negro House in the Greek Revival Style, New Orleans, Louisiana," January 1936 (LC-USF-342-1284-A), and "The Outskirts of the Factory District, New Orleans, Louisiana," February 1936 (LC-USF-342-1297-A). Traveling for the Resettlement Administration the previous year, in Carrollton, Kentucky, Evans had also noted, "Courthouse square / Main street 1870 architecture / Movie on main st. posters / wild west." Evans, entry for Saturday, December 7, in "Diary 1935."

220. See, for example, "Liberty Theater Front, New Orleans, Louisiana," December 1935 (LC-USF342-1285-A); "Billboard, Birmingham, Alabama," March 1936 (LC-USF342-8091-A); and the later "Movie Poster, Vicinity Moundville, Alabama," summer 1936 (LC-USF33-31340-M2).

221. "RA" Exposure Records, Walker Evans Archive, 1994.250.148. Evans carried the printed forms with him and filled them in somewhat sporadically. Forty-one such record sheets, covering the years 1935 and 1936, are in the Walker Evans Archive. When completely filled out, they registered the camera used, the negative number, the date, the place, a memorandum of the subject, the lens used, the shutter speed, the filter, aperture, light conditions, and time of day. No other RA/FSA photographer seems to have used these forms, perhaps because they were more reliable at keeping their own records for the Washington photo-lab.

222. Works Progress Administration, Federal Writers Program, *Georgia: The WPA Guide*, 162.

223. Though Vachon's image is not quite in focus, what we also see is that damage to the house on the right, to the balcony and to the house's siding, seems to have been repaired. On the other hand, the upper balcony of the house on the left has been cleared, the curtains have been stripped from the window, and there is an air of abandonment about the place.

224. For Evans's camera technique, see Jerry L. Thompson, "Walker Evans: Some Notes on His Way of Working," in *Walker Evans at Work*, 9–17. The two components of the triple convertible lens gave three possibilities: from "normal" (29 cm) in combination, to long focus (40 cm), to still longer (69 cm).

225. Ibid., 12.

226. De Man, *Allegories of Reading*, 299–300. The reference to de Man places Evans's image on the side of allegory. This is also where it would fall in Walter Benjamin's terms, set against Bourke-White's commitment to the symbol. See Benjamin, *The Origin of German Tragic Drama*.

227. Trachtenberg, "A Book Nearly Anonymous," 265; Rosenheim, "'The Cruel Radiance of What Is,'" 83. For Rathbone, it is the black eye that provides

the central metaphor not only for what has happened to the houses but for "a condition of love" that Evans, in flight from Jane Smith Ninas's husband, "now understood better than before." Rathbone, *Walker Evans*, 116.

228. *Dialogue Continuity on "Chatterbox,"* production 870, December 19, 1935, New York State Archives, Albany, New York.

229. "Broadway," 1930, in *Advertising and Selling*, June 24, 1931, cover.

230. "Carole Lombard in *Love before Breakfast*," picture 757, stamped February 26, 1936, New York State Archives, Albany, New York.

231. Cf. Rathbone, *Walker Evans*, 116. Rathbone also titles her chapter 7, on Evans's later marriage to Jane Smith Ninas and their life in New York City in the late 1930s and early 1940s, "Love before Breakfast."

Asked later in life by a University of Michigan student whether he photographed billboards with a sense of disdain or derision or whether he considered them beautiful, Evans replied, "Well, I love them, and I'm entertained by them. I feel they're stimulating and exciting and endearing." "Walker Evans, Visiting Artist: A Transcript of His Discussion with the Students of the University of Michigan" (October 29, 1971), in *Photography: Essays and Images. Illustrated Readings in the History of Photography*, ed. Beaumont Newhall (New York: Museum of Modern Art, 1980), 317.

232. Jacques Derrida, *Of Grammatology*, trans. G. C. Spivak (Baltimore, Md.: The Johns Hopkins University Press, 1976), 163.

233. Evans writes of himself: "Evans was and is interested in what the present would look like as the past." This self-description comes from the fifth of eight versions of a "NOTE," drafted for but never published in the 1962 reissue of *American Photographs* (repr., New York: Museum of Modern Art, n.d. [1962]; distributed by Doubleday).

When the Museum of Modern Art proposed this new edition, Evans was called on for a retrospective statement, and the whole tortured process of his attempts to write about *American Photographs* began again, even though it seems he was only providing material for a prefatory note that the distributors, Doubleday, wished to see written by an official of the museum. See the letter from T. O'Connor Sloane III, editor at Doubleday, to Monroe Wheeler, director of exhibitions and publications at the Museum of Modern Art, New York, dated July 11, 1961, but postmarked August 14, 1961, Walker Evans Archive, American Photographs exhibition and book reissue 1962, 1994.250.58, folder 20. This time, there are eight various texts worked on by Evans—penciled manuscripts, typescripts, carbons, scribbled notes on the back of a letter—all written in the third person and almost all subject to annotation and revision. Again, however, Evans's efforts would come to nothing, and very little of the precise tone and awkward tensions of what he wrote would survive untransformed in the bland introductory foreword published under the signature of Monroe Wheeler, director of exhibitions and publications at the Museum of Modern Art.

The manuscripts—all in Walker Evans Archive, American Photographs exhibition and book reissue 1962, 1994.250.58—are, in apparent order: (1) a one-page manuscript in pencil, written on the verso of a manuscript note to Evans from Lee Friedlander (folder 10); (2) a one-page manuscript in pencil (folder 9); (3) a one-page manuscript in pencil derived from the preceding draft, stamped "November 28, 1961," and marked "latest" (folder 8); (4) an unrevised typescript top copy titled "NOTE" (folder 7); (5) a one-page typewriter carbon of "NOTE," annotated in ink, pencil, and red crayon and stamped "November 28, 1961" (folder 6); (6) a one-page typescript titled "NOTE," annotated in pencil and ink, marked "revision," and stamped "November 29, 1961" (folder 5); (7) a one-page typewriter carbon of the revised "NOTE," annotated in pencil, marked "revision," and stamped "November 29, 1961" (folder 11); (8) a one-page undated typewriter carbon of Monroe Wheeler's "FOREWORD," amended in pencil by Evans (folder 31).

In the first hasty notes, Evans wrote, "Evans says he was historically minded in any event, and still is concerned with what the future will look like as the past" (folder 10). By the fifth draft, this had been changed in the typescript to "Evans was and is interested in what the present would look like as the past" (folder 6). But, the next day, even though Evans had already mailed the typescript of his statement to Monroe Wheeler, this was changed again in the "revision" to read "Evans was, and is, interested in what [a given (deleted)] [any (inserted)] present time will look like as the past" (folder 5; see also Evans's letter to Monroe Wheeler, dated November 28, 1961, of which there is a carbon copy in folder 28). In Wheeler's published foreword, this would become "Evans, then and now, contemplates the present as it might be seen at some future date." Walker Evans, *American Photographs* (repr., n.d. [1962]), 7.

What Wheeler misses is crucial. It lies at the heart of Evans's dislocation, for his purpose was not to preserve the present as a historical record for the future, and least of all was his purpose nostalgic. (For Evans's hatred of the term "nostalgia," see "Interview with Walker Evans," by Katz, 87.) His interest was not in rescuing the present but in seeing it gone, set at a distance as the past. His camera, therefore, is not a means of fixing the ephemeral in the present tense but a machine out of time that robs us of the present. It does not offer recognition. It does not appeal for identification. It is "disinterested" (see insertion to the fifth draft, folder 6) in the sense that it stands radically outside any present desire and any desire of presence. Dividing photographic time from itself, it sees the present as already an abandoned ruin. This is what makes its unflinching inventory so intense.

234. May Cameron, "A Note on the Photographs: Margaret Bourke-White Finds Plenty of Time to Enjoy Life along with Her Camera Work," from the *New York Post*, in "Notes and Appendices," in James Agee and Walker Evans, *Let Us Now Praise Famous Men: Three Tenant Families* (Boston: Houghton Mifflin Company, 1941), 450–54.

235. See William Stott, *Documentary Expression and Thirties America* (Oxford and New York: Oxford University Press, 1973), 218–23, 267–71. More surprising, perhaps, is that Paula Rabinowitz's "feminist" reading should find that Agee's and, later, Evans's "'vicious' critiques of Bourke-White *were* fully justified," that Bourke-White's red coat, "presumably paid for by the profits from her book," "makes Agee's and Evans's project all the more morally superior," and that "we are left feeling embarrassed by Bourke-White's efforts." See Paula Rabinowitz, "Margaret Bourke-White's Red Coat, or Slumming in the Thirties," chap. 3 of *They Must Be Represented: The Politics of Documentary* (London and New York: Verso, 1994), 70–71.

236. Bourke-White, *Portrait of Myself*, 87.

237. Draft of chapter 12 of *Portrait of Myself*, 13, Margaret Bourke-White Papers, box 62. A little earlier, in another passage deleted from the final text, Bourke-White recalls, "The Louisville flood [burst into the news almost overnight (handwritten insert)] [surged up so fast that there was no time to think about what the well-dressed photographer should wear to a flood. I was lucky to find I had a pair of old slacks at the office and an equally old sweater which I stuffed into a corner of my camera case (deleted)]" (12–13).

238. For details of Evans's consumer preferences in the 1950s and 1960s, see Rathbone, *Walker Evans*, 212, 216, 269, and Mellow, *Walker Evans*, 559. For correspondence on the car radio, see Evans's letter to Pyke Johnson, editor in chief, Anchor Books, Doubleday and Company, July 20, 1961, Walker Evans Archive, American Photographs exhibition and book reissue, 1962, 1994.250.58, folder 15.

239. See Rosenheim, "'The Cruel Radiance of What Is,'" 91, 93, 94, 104n202.

240. See, for example, Dale Maharidge and Michael Williamson, *And Their Children after Them: The Legacy of "Let Us Now Praise Famous Men": James Agee, Walker Evans, and the Rise and Fall of Cotton in the South* (New York: Pantheon Books, 1989).

241. Margaret Bourke-White, "Notes on Photographs," in Caldwell and Bourke-White, *You Have Seen Their Faces*, 51–54, and *Portrait of Myself*, 126–27.

For Evans's remarks as quoted by Stott, see Stott, *Documentary Expression and Thirties America*, 223.

242. The 1931 exhibition was Photographs by Three Americans, the third photographer being their mutual friend Ralph Steiner. In 1937, both Bourke-White and Evans were selected by Beaumont Newhall to contribute representative sets of prints to the exhibition Photography, 1839–1937, at the Museum of Modern Art.

243. On this, see the brief but instructive foreword by Alan Trachtenberg to the reprint by Brown Thrasher Books of Erskine Caldwell's and Margaret Bourke-White's *You Have Seen Their Faces* (Athens: University of Georgia Press, 1995), v–viii.

244. Walker Evans, lecture at Harvard University, April 8, 1975, an edited transcript of which is republished in Peter C. Bunnell, ed., *Degrees of Guidance: Essays on Twentieth-Century American Photography* (Cambridge: Cambridge University Press, 1993), 64. This transcription was first published as "Walker Evans on Himself," ed. Lincoln Caplan, *New Republic*, November 13, 1976, 23–27. Evans's comment is also cited on the back cover of Walker Evans, *First and Last* (London: Secker and Warburg, 1978).

245. "Interview with Walker Evans," by Katz, 84, 87.

246. Ibid., 84. See also Evans's comment in his 1975 Harvard lecture: "I believe in staying out, the way Flaubert does in his writing." Bunnell, *Degrees of Guidance*, 68.

247. Evans, "Unposed Photographic Records of People," unpublished draft text to accompany a volume of subway portraits, 1958–61, in *Walker Evans at Work*, 160.

248. Evans, "The Reappearance of Photography," 81.

249. See interview of Evans by Paul Cummings, 33, quoted in Trachtenberg, "A Book Nearly Anonymous," 238.

250. Kirstein, unpublished diary, entry for January 19, 1931, "1930–1931 Diary," Lincoln Kirstein Papers, 116.

251. Ibid., entry for April 15, 1931, 280.

252. Ibid., entry for June 13, 1931, 371.

253. Ibid., entry for June 13, 1931, 372.

254. Lincoln Kirstein, unpublished diary, entry for December 30, 1931, "1931–1932 Diary," Lincoln Kirstein Papers, (S)*MGZMD 123, box 3, folder 17, 133.

255. John Cheever, letter to his former Iowa graduate student, Allan Gurganus, March 28 [1974], in *The Letters of John Cheever*, ed. Benjamin Cheever (New York: Simon and Schuster, 1988), 304.

256. Kirstein, unpublished diary, entry for June 13, 1931, "1930–1931 Diary," Lincoln Kirstein Papers, 372.

257. Julia Kristeva, *Black Sun: Depression and Melancholia*, trans. Leon S. Roudiez (New York: Columbia University Press, 1989), 13. More generally, see chap. 1, "Psychoanalysis—A Counterdepressant," and chap. 2, "Life and Death of Speech," 1–68. See also Julia Kristeva, "Black Sun: Melancholia and Creativity," interview by Dominique Grisoni, *Magazine littéraire* (Summer 1987), reprinted in *Julia Kristeva: Interviews*, ed. Ross Mitchell Guberman (New York: Columbia University Press, 1996), 78–84.

258. Giorgio Agamben, *Stanzas: Word and Phantasm in Western Culture*, trans. Ronald L. Martinez (Minneapolis and London: University of Minnesota Press, 1993), 20.

One might compare, here, Slavoj Žižek's unconvincing assault on what he terms the "objective cynicism" of the "politically correct" reversal of Freud that asserts the conceptual and ethical primacy of melancholy as fidelity to what cannot be integrated through the work of mourning. Slavoj Žižek, "Melancholy and the Act," chap. 4 of *Did Somebody Say Totalitarianism? Five Interventions in the (Mis)Use of a Notion* (London and New York: Verso, 2001), 142 and 141. For Žižek, so far from displaying fidelity, the "melancholic passive stupor" (152) "obfuscates" (143) and engages in the "deceitful translation of lack into loss" (143), taking "an ordinary sensual and material object" and elevating it "into the Absolute" (144), treating "*an object that we still fully possess as if this object is already lost*" (146).

Žižek's account invokes Agamben but works its own transformative practices of translation upon Agamben's commentary on Freud's "attempt to gloss over the contradiction posed by a loss without an object." Agamben, *Stanzas*, 20. For Agamben, the melancholic has not "lost the way of his *desire*," as Lacan writes of Hamlet, but is prompted by "a frantic exacerbation of desire that renders its object inaccessible to itself in the desperate attempt to protect itself from the loss of that object and to adhere to it at least in its absence, so it might be said that the withdrawal of melancholic libido has no other purpose than to make viable an appropriation in a situation in which none is really possible" (20). "From this point of view," Agamben continues, "melancholy would be not so much the regressive reaction to the loss of the love object as the imaginative capacity to make an unobtainable object appear as if lost." By this strategy of simulation, "melancholy opens a space for the existence of the unreal and marks out a scene in which the ego may enter into relation with it and attempt an appropriation such as no other possession could rival and no loss possibly threaten" (20). It is thus precisely the melancholic who refuses to confuse lack with loss—with a loss that can be made good in the chain of substitutions and cycles of exchange that return the subject to a domesticated desire. Against this, melancholy holds to an impossible, induced, and hallucinatory realism, beyond all symbolic mediation—though this has nothing to do with the "reality" that, Žižek insists, the authentic ethical act "redefines." Žižek, "Melancholy and the Act," 172. See also Jacques Lacan, "Desire and the Interpretation of Desire in *Hamlet*," *Yale French Studies*, nos. 55–56 (1977): 11–52.

At the same time, Jacques Derrida's meditation on melancholy has compelled us to think of the contradictions of a melancholic stratagem of the self that, in order to preserve an impossible relation with what discourse more or less violently excludes, seeks to incorporate the other as other whole and untouched, by an act of encryption, burying it deep in a crypt, holding on to it at the price of rendering it untouchable, sealed up as an outcast outside inside the inside, "a foreign body preserved as foreign" and barred forever from "the loving, appropriating assimilation of the other" toward which the work of mourning strives. See Jacques Derrida, "FORS," trans. Barbara Johnson, *Georgia Review* 31, no. 1 (Spring 1977): 64–116.

259. Sigmund Freud, "Mourning and Melancholia" (1917), in *The Standard Edition*, ed. James Strachey (London: Hogarth Press and Institute of Psycho-Analysis, 1957), 14:243–58; Judith Butler, "Psychic Inceptions: Melancholy, Ambivalence, Rage," chap. 6 of *The Psychic Life of Power: Theories in Subjection* (Stanford, Calif.: Stanford University Press, 1997), 167–98.

For what it is worth, early in 1938, Evans was himself reading—or rereading—Freud. Making a mild dig in a letter to Roy Stryker, Evans tells him, "I came across an opinion on education in Freud's New Introductory Lectures on Psychoanalysis which made me think of you and your own child and your interest in education. If you want to look it up it is p 203 (in lecture XXXIV)." Walker Evans, letter to Roy Emerson Stryker, dated April 21, 1938, Roy Emerson Stryker Papers, 1932–1964, NDA 25. In Lecture 34, "Explanations, Applications, and Orientations" (1933), Freud remarks that "education must inhibit, forbid and suppress, and this it has abundantly seen to in all periods of history. But we have learnt from analysis that precisely this suppression of instincts involves the risk of neurotic illness." Freud goes on to suggest that in consequence, "the only appropriate preparation for the profession of educator is a thorough psycho-analytic training." See Sigmund Freud, *The Complete Introductory Lectures on Psychoanalysis*, trans. and ed. James Strachey (New York: W. W. Norton, 1966), 613–14.

260. Judith Butler, introduction to *The Psychic Life of Power*, 1–2.

4. Running and Dodging, 1943

1. The image I have here is of William Ellerton Fry in 1890, armed with his camera, searchlights, and surveying equipment, venturing north with the self-styled Pioneer Column into the land of the Shona and the Matabele as part of the British occupation force. For this, see Gordon Bleach, "On 'The Occupation of Mashonaland': Rendering the Itinerary by F. C. Selous and W. E. Fry," chap. 7 of "Visions of Access: Africa Bound and Staged, 1880–1940" (Ph.D. diss., Binghamton University, 2000).

Sir John Herschel's coinage of "photography," along with "photographic" and "photograph," occurred in a paper read before the Royal Society on March 14, 1839. His terms may have suggested themselves as a diplomatic, cross-Channel compromise between William Henry Fox Talbot's "photogenic" and Nicephore Nièpce's "héliographie." See Sir John Herschel, "Note on the Art of Photography, or The Application of the Chemical Rays of Light to the Purpose of Pictorial Representation," *Proceedings of the Royal Society* 4 (March 14, 1839): 131.

2. This project is, therefore, misread by Naomi Schor, for whom it seems to serve only as a cockshy and as a foil for her own enthusiasm. See Naomi Schor, "*Cartes Postales:* Representing Paris, 1900," *Critical Inquiry* 18, no. 2 (Winter 1992): 188–244. The point is made at somewhat greater length in chapters 1 and 2, above.

3. See John Tagg, "Evidence, Truth, and Order: Photographic Records and the Growth of the State," "A Means of Surveillance: The Photograph as Evidence in Law," and "God's Sanitary Law: Slum Clearance and Photography in Late Nineteenth-Century Leeds," in *The Burden of Representation: Essays on Photographies and Histories* (London: Macmillan, 1988), 60–65, 66–102, and 117–52, and Tagg, "The Proof of the Picture" and "The Discontinuous City: Picturing and the Discursive Field," in *Grounds of Dispute: Art History, Cultural Politics and the Discursive Field* (London: Macmillan, 1992), 97–114 and 134–56.

4. Cf. "The Plane of Decent Seeing," chapter 2, above. See also John Tagg, "The Currency of the Photograph: New Deal Reformism and Documentary Rhetoric," in Tagg, *The Burden of Representation*, 153–83.

5. Michel Foucault, "Powers and Strategies," in *Power/Knowledge: Selected Interviews and Other Writings, 1972–1977*, ed. Colin Gordon (New York: Pantheon Books, 1980), 142. The interview was originally published as "Pouvoirs et Stratégies," in *Les Révoltes Logiques*, no. 4 (1977). For other discussions by Foucault of the concept of resistance, see, for example, "Two Lectures" (1976), "Truth and Power" (1977), and "The Eye of Power" (1977), in *Power/Knowledge*, 78–108, 109–33, and 146–65; and "Clarifications on the Question of Power"

(1978), in *Foucault Live (Interviews, 1966–84)*, ed. Sylvère Lotringer (New York: Semiotext(e), 1989), 179–92.

6. References to what has come to be known as Farm Security Administration photography in fact conflate the work of a number of departments or divisions headed by Roy E. Stryker between 1935 and 1943, under a number of government agencies. Stryker was first tapped by Rexford Tugwell in July 1935 to set up a photographic record unit within the Resettlement Administration, which had been created by Executive Order 7027 on April 30, 1935, to consolidate an array of experimental New Deal programs formerly run by the Federal Emergency Relief Administration, the Agricultural Adjustment Administration, and the Department of the Interior. On January 1, 1937, however, the Resettlement Administration was incorporated into the Department of Agriculture through Executive Order 7530, and on September 1 of the same year, the RA's activities were further cut back and reorganized under the Bankhead-Jones Farm Tenancy Act. By order of the secretary of agriculture, Stryker's Historical Section of the Division of Information passed on to the new agency, the Farm Security Administration. The FSA itself was terminated in October 1942, at which point the photographic unit was transferred to the Office of War Information, first as the Division of Photography of the Bureau of Publications and Graphics, Domestic Operations Branch, and then, finally, as the Washington Section, Overseas Picture Division, following Stryker's resignation on September 14, 1943. On January 18, 1944, with Stryker gone and the integrity of the archive threatened, the librarian of Congress, Archibald MacLeish, accepted transfer of the custody of all files and equipment from Elmer Davis, director of the Office of War Information.

The Resettlement Administration/Farm Security Administration/Office of War Information archive, as it presently exists in the Library of Congress, comprises some 110,000 black-and-white prints, 182,000 negatives, and 1,600 color transparencies. Nicholas Natanson has estimated that approximately 75,000 of the prints can be connected to Stryker's period as director. See Nicholas Natanson, *The Black Image in the New Deal: The Politics of FSA Photography* (Knoxville: University of Tennessee Press, 1992), 269–70. The present arrangement of the archive is based on the systematic subject classification developed by Paul Vanderbilt only after January 1943. Earlier, the prints and negatives were filed by assignment, in series, as developed by the photographers on location, following the dozens of shooting scripts and hundreds of memos sent to them by Stryker, outlining thematic directions for their work in the field.

7. This is hardly the place to attempt to provide a bibliography of the social, political, and cultural history of the United States in the 1930s, impossible as

that would be, given the enormous literature on the period. My argument here is that the cultural and political formations and the economic and social policies that came, in the United States, to characterize the 1930s had already reached the limits of their development and effectivity even before the end of the decade and the mobilization for war, in 1941. On the limits of New Deal government spending and economic reform, see, for example, Paul A. Baran's and Paul M. Sweezy's classic analysis in *Monopoly Capital: An Essay on the American Economic and Social Order* (New York: Monthly Review Press, 1966); Barton J. Bernstein, "The New Deal: The Conservative Achievements of Liberal Reform," in *Towards a New Past*, ed. Barton J. Bernstein (New York: Pantheon, 1968), 263–88; and Ronald Radosh, "The Myth of the New Deal," in *A New History of Leviathan: Essays on the Rise of the American Corporate State*, ed. Ronald Radosh and Murray Rothbard (New York: E. P. Dutton, 1972), 146–87. On the political limits and the breakup of the New Deal coalition, see John M. Allswang, *The New Deal and American Politics: A Study in Political Change* (New York: Wiley, 1978); James T. Patterson, *Congressional Conservatism and the New Deal* (Lexington: University Press of Kentucky, 1967); and David L. Porter, *Congress and the Waning of the New Deal* (Port Washington, N.Y.: Kennikat, 1979). On the limits of 1930s leftism and the politics of the Popular Front, see James Weinstein, *Ambiguous Legacy: The Left in American Politics* (New York: New Viewpoints, 1975), and Christopher Lasch, *The Agony of the American Left: One Hundred Years of Radicalism* (Harmondsworth, U.K.: Penguin Books, 1973), esp. "The Collapse of Socialism and the Isolation of the Intellectuals," 42–63. On the demise of the left cultural movement, see James B. Gilbert, *Writers and Partisans: A History of Literary Radicalism in America* (New York: Wiley, 1968), and Daniel Aaron, *Writers on the Left* (Oxford and New York: Oxford University Press, 1977). And on the conditions of existence of the "documentary" movement, see William Stott, *Documentary Expression and Thirties America* (Oxford and New York: Oxford University Press, 1973).

8. The figures come from Baran and Sweezy, *Monopoly Capital*, 162; see also 175–76 and 237.

9. For a broad survey of these changes in the character and position of labor and the working class, see James Green, "Fighting on Two Fronts: Working-Class Militancy in the 1940's," *Radical America* 9, nos. 4–5 (July–August 1975): 7–47; and Mike Davis, *Prisoners of the American Dream: Politics and Economy in the History of the U.S. Working Class* (London: Verso, 1986).

10. Contrast Benjamin's view that "mechanical reproduction of art changes the reaction of the masses toward art. The reactionary attitude toward a Picasso painting changes into the progressive reaction toward a Chaplin movie. The progressive reaction is characterized by the direct, intimate fusion of visual and

emotional enjoyment with the orientation of the expert. . . . With regard to the screen, the critical and the receptive attitudes of the public coincide. The decisive reason for this is that individual reactions are predetermined by the mass audience response they are about to produce, and this is nowhere more pronounced than in the film. The moment these responses become manifest they control each other. . . . Although paintings began to be publicly exhibited in galleries and salons, there was no way for the masses to organize and control themselves in their reception." Walter Benjamin, "The Work of Art in the Age of Mechanical Reproduction," in *Illuminations*, ed. Hannah Arendt, trans. Harry Zohn (London: Fontana/Collins, 1973), 236–37.

11. See, for example, Karen Anderson, *Wartime Women: Sex Roles, Family Relations, and the Status of Women during World War II* (Westport, Conn.: Greenwood Press, 1981); D'ann Campbell, *Women at War with America: Private Lives in a Patriotic Era* (Cambridge, Mass.: Harvard University Press, 1984); Miriam Frank, *The Life and Times of Rosie the Riveter* (Emeryville, Calif.: Clarity Educational Productions, 1982); Sherna Berger Gluck, *Rosie the Riveter Revisited: Women, the War, and Social Change* (Boston: Twayne, 1987); Claudia Goldin, *The Role of World War II in the Rise of Women's Work* (Cambridge, Mass.: National Bureau of Economic Research, 1989); Susan Hartmann, *The Home Front and Beyond: American Women in the 1940s* (Boston: Twayne, 1982); Maureen Honey, *Creating Rosie the Riveter: Class, Gender, and Propaganda during World War II* (Amherst: University of Massachusetts Press, 1984); Ruth Milkman, "Redefining 'Women's Work': The Sexual Division of Labor in the Auto Industry during World War II," *Feminist Studies* 8 (Summer 1982): 337–72; Paddy Quick, "Rosie the Riveter: Myths and Realities," *Radical America* 9, nos. 4–5 (July–August, 1975): 115–31; Leila Rupp, *Mobilizing Women for War: German and American Propaganda, 1939–1945* (Princeton, N.J.: Princeton University Press, 1978); and Doris Weatherford, *American Women and World War II* (New York: Facts on File, 1990).

12. Louise Rosskam came to Washington, D.C., in 1938, following the hiring of her husband, Edwin Rosskam, as Roy Stryker's photo-editor and visual information specialist at the FSA. The Rosskams had previously worked for the *Philadelphia Record* as a photographic team. Martha McMillan Roberts arrived at Stryker's unit in 1940, from Black Mountain College, as an apprentice darkroom technician. Art school–trained photojournalist Esther Bubley was hired by Stryker in 1941 as a lab technician but was allowed to take up photographic assignments around 1942.

With the exception of the work of Lange and Post Wolcott, acknowledgment of the photographic activity of women employees of the Farm Security

Administration/Office of War Information was all but entirely absent from standard histories of the FSA's photography unit—such as F. Jack Hurley, *Portrait of a Decade: Roy Stryker and the Development of Documentary Photography in the Thirties* (Baton Rouge: Louisiana State University Press, 1972). This remained the case until the publication of Andrea Fisher, *Let Us Now Praise Famous Women: Women Photographers for the U.S. Government, 1935 to 1944: Esther Bubley, Marjory Collins, Pauline Ehrlich, Dorothea Lange, Martha McMillan Roberts, Marion Post Wolcott, Ann Rosener, Louise Rosskam* (London and New York: Pandora Press, 1987). Some discussion of the later work of Bubley, McMillan Roberts, and Louise Rosskam may be found in Steven W. Plattner, *Roy Stryker, U.S.A., 1943–1950: The Standard Oil (New Jersey) Photography Project* (Austin: University of Texas Press, 1983), and in Ulrich Keller, *The Highway as Habitat: A Roy Stryker Documentation, 1943–1955* (Santa Barbara, Calif.: University Art Museum, 1986). For Dorothea Lange, see George P. Elliott, *Dorothea Lange* (New York: Museum of Modern Art, 1966); Milton Meltzer, *Dorothea Lange: A Photographer's Life* (New York: Farrar Straus Giroux, 1978); Karin Becker Ohrn, *Dorothea Lange and the Documentary Tradition* (Baton Rouge: Louisiana State University Press, 1980); and Elizabeth Partridge, ed., *Dorothea Lange: A Visual Life* (Washington, D.C., and London: Smithsonian Institution Press, 1994). For Marion Post Wolcott, see Paul Hendrickson, *Looking for the Light: The Hidden Life and Art of Marion Post Wolcott* (New York: Alfred A. Knopf, 1992); F. Jack Hurley, *Marion Post Wolcott: A Photographic Journey* (Albuquerque: University of New Mexico Press, 1989); and Sally Stein, "Marion Post Wolcott: Thoughts on Some Lesser Known FSA Photographs," in *Marion Post Wolcott, FSA Photographs* (Carmel, Calif.: Friends of Photography, 1983), 3–10. See also the discussion of the work of Barbara H. Wright for the National Youth Administration in Sally Stein, "Figures of the Future: Photography of the National Youth Administration," in Pete Daniel, Merry A. Foresta, Maren Stange, and Sally Stein, *Official Images: New Deal Photography* (Washington, D.C.: Smithsonian Institution Press, 1987), 92–107.

13. Roy Stryker, letter to Marion Post (later Marion Post Wolcott), July 14, 1938, Stryker Correspondence, University of Louisville Photographic Archive, Louisville, Kentucky, quoted in Stein, "Marion Post Wolcott," 7. The complete quotation also demonstrates the way the constrictive framing of movement, space, and interpersonal contact by constructions of gender is also, inextricably and in the same moment, reinflected by questions of race and power: "There is another thing I raised with you the other day, that is the idea of your traveling in certain areas alone. I know that you have a great deal of experience in the field, and that you are quite competent to take care of yourself, but I do have grave doubts of the advisability of sending you, for instance, into certain

sections of the South. It would not involve you personally in the least, but, for example, negro people are put into a very difficult spot when white women attempt to interview or photograph them." And Stryker goes on, "I'm glad that you have learned you can't depend on the wiles of femininity when you are in the wilds of the South. Colorful bandannas and brightly colored dresses, etc. aren't part of our photographers' equipment. The closer you get to what the great back-country recognizes as the normal dress for women, the better you are going to succeed as a photographer. I know this will probably make you mad, but I can tell you another thing—that slacks aren't part of your attire when you are in the back-country. You are a woman, and 'a woman can't never be a man.'" Quoted in Claire Peeps, "Chronology and Correspondence," in *Marion Post Wolcott, FSA Photographs*, 45. Stryker had clearly not looked at the photographs Dorothea Lange was sending him.

14. Marion Post, letter to Roy Stryker, July 1939, Stryker Correspondence, quoted in Peeps, "Chronology and Correspondence," 45.

15. File-mount caption to Esther Bubley, LC-USW3-021005-E, Washington, D.C., April 1943 (punctuation as in the original). The other photographs discussed here are Marjory Collins, LC-USW3-026086-D, Buffalo, New York, May 1943; LC-USW3-23902-D, Buffalo, New York, May 1943; LC-USW3-22130-D, Baltimore, Maryland, April 1943; LC-USW3-7739-E, New York, New York, September 1942; and Esther Bubley, LC-USW3-40651-D, Washington, D.C., December 1943. All pictures were produced for the Office of War Information.

16. The file-mount caption for the earlier FSA photograph (LC-USF34-016119-C) reads, "Calipatria (vicinity), Calif. Feb 1937. Native of Indiana in a migratory labor contractor's camp. 'It's root, hog, or die for us folks.'" The image appeared in Archibald MacLeish's 1938 publication *Land of the Free* (New York: Harcourt, Brace, 1938), opposite 79, with the lines: "We're not talking now: / we only wonder." But it was not included in Lange's own work (with Paul Taylor) *An American Exodus: A Record of Human Erosion* (New York: Reynal and Hitchcock, 1939). The second photograph, "Richmond, California/1942," taken after Lange had left government employment, was added to the expanded 1969 republication of Lange's and Taylor's *An American Exodus: A Record of Human Erosion in the Thirties* (New Haven, Conn., and London: Yale University Press, 1969). It appears on page 120, in the section "End of the Road: The City," and Paul Schuster Taylor has added the caption "Work for all—now—regardless of sex or race."

17. Cf. Martha Rosler, "The Bowery in Two Inadequate Descriptive Systems" (1975), reproduced in *Three Works* (Halifax: Press of the Nova Scotia College of Art and Design, 1981), and Connie Hatch, "The De-Sublimation of

Romance" (1975–85), reproduced in shortened form as "The Desublimation of Romance," in "Sexuality: Re/Positions," ed. Sylvia Kolbowski, special issue, *Wedge*, no. 6 (Winter 1984): 20–23. For discussion of these works, see Allan Sekula, "Dismantling Modernism, Reinventing Documentary (Notes on the Politics of Representation)," in *Photography against the Grain: Essays and Photo Works, 1973–1983* (Halifax: Press of the Nova Scotia College of Art and Design, 1984), 53–75, and Abigail Solomon-Godeau, "Reconstructing Documentary: Connie Hatch's Representational Resistance," in *Photography at the Dock: Essays on Photographic History, Institutions, and Practices* (Minneapolis: University of Minnesota Press, 1991), 184–217.

18. See Plattner, *Roy Stryker, U.S.A., 1943–1950*, and Keller, *The Highway as Habitat*.

19. For Margaret Bourke-White, see Margaret Bourke-White, *Portrait of Myself* (New York: Simon and Schuster, 1963); Sean Callahan, ed., *The Photographs of Margaret Bourke-White* (Greenwich, Conn.: New York Graphic Society, 1972); and Vicki Goldberg, *Margaret Bourke-White: A Biography* (New York: Harper and Row, 1986). For Lee Miller, see Antony Penrose, *The Lives of Lee Miller* (New York: Holt, Rinehart, and Winston, 1985), and Penrose, ed., *Lee Miller's War: Photographer and Correspondent with the Allies in Europe, 1944–45* (Boston: Bulfinch Press, 1992).

20. Quoted in Plattner, *Roy Stryker, U.S.A., 1943–1950*, 45.

21. Richard Wright, *12 Million Black Voices: A Folk History of the Negro in the United States*, photo-direction [*sic*] by Edwin Rosskam (New York: Viking, 1941). In a radio interview with Edwin Seaver, broadcast on December 23, 1941, Wright affirmed that the text was written at the suggestion of Edwin Rosskam, though it echoed ideas he had had for "a series of historical novels telescoping Negro history in terms of the urbanization of a feudal folk." He also reported that "Ed Rosskam and I looked at thousands of pictures to get the 90 odd [*sic*] we used in the book. It [the FSA archive] is one of the most remarkable collections of photographs in existence, I think. If you want to get a comprehensive picture of our country, you should go through these files sometime. It's quite an education." "Readers and Writers," in *Conversations with Richard Wright*, ed. Keneth Kinnamon and Michel Fabre (Jackson: University Press of Mississippi, 1993), 44, 43.

It was following the 1940 publishing success of Wright's *Native Son* and the attention focused on rural–urban population shifts by the 1940–41 Tolan House Committee on Interstate Migration that the FSA photography unit began to investigate urban problems. Moved by Wright's novel, Edwin Rosskam—FSA photo-editing and visual information specialist—urged a collaboration with

Wright, focusing on a Chicago locale. Having secured the backing of Viking Press for a publication, Rosskam raised Wright's interest by sending him a selection of FSA images. In April 1941, Rosskam spent two weeks in Chicago with photographer Russell Lee, while Wright was still (secretly) preparing his manuscript. Rosskam then provided detailed "general captions" for the photographic prints, which he shared with Wright, together with a broad selection of images from the FSA file and a stream of other research materials. Finally, the two met in Washington over the summer of 1941 to coordinate the narrative text, the brief captions, and the evolving layout that had been modeled on an earlier draft, though Rosskam insisted that any rewrites stay within the exact lineage and wordage of his dummy. See Edwin Rosskam, "Not Intended for Framing: The FSA Archive," *Afterimage* 18, no. 8 (March 1981): 9–11, and Natanson, *The Black Image in the New Deal*, esp. chap. 5, "The Photo Series: Russell Lee, Chicago, and the 1940s," 142–202, and chap. 6, "The FSA Black Image in the Marketplace," 203–67, particularly 244–55. On the photo-documentary book as itself a hybrid form, see Elizabeth McCausland, "Photographic Books," in *The Complete Photographer*, ed. Willard D. Morgan, 8, no. 43 (November 20, 1942) (Chicago: National Educational Alliance, 1942), 2783–94.

Wright's *12 Million Black Voices* was first published in October 1941. In the foreword, Wright acknowledged his debt "to Mr. Horace R. Cayton, director of the Good Shepherd Community Center of Chicago, for his making available his immense files of materials on urban life among Negroes and, above all, for the advice and guidance which made sections of this book possible" (6). In his note on the photographs, Ed Rosskam thanked Roy E. Stryker and Horace R. Cayton, the latter (see note 27, below) "for his invaluable advice on the pictorial interpretation of the urban Negro" (149).

The photograph by Louise Rosskam, "At the Savoy in Harlem, New York, N.Y.," is reproduced on page 129, in Part Three, "Death on the City Pavements." Opposite and above the image, Wright writes, "We lose ourselves in violent forms of dances in our ballrooms. The faces of the white world, looking on in wonder and curiosity, declare: '*Only* the Negro can play!' But they are wrong. They misread us. We are able to play in this fashion because we have been excluded, left behind; we play in this manner because all excluded folk play. . . . our hunger for expression finds its form in our wild, raw music, in our invention of slang that winds its way all over America. Our adoration of color goes not into murals, but into dress, into green, red, yellow, and blue clothes. When we have some money in our pockets on payday, our laughter and songs make the principal streets of our Black Belts—Lenox Avenue, Beale Street, State Street, South Street, Auburn Avenue—famous the earth over" (128–29).

This less-than-positive assessment of contemporary Black popular culture seems to have been characteristic of Wright, who had joined the John Reed Club of Chicago and the Communist Party in 1933 and who, from 1935, had worked for the Works Progress Administration's Federal Writers' Project in Chicago and later New York. In a 1940 essay in the *Saturday Review of Literature*, analyzing the gestation of his novel *Native Son*, Wright had contrasted the visible and violent acts of rebellion against racism and segregation of those who inspired the character of Bigger Thomas with the "variations in the Bigger Thomas pattern," through which some "got religion" while others, "clinging still to that brief glimpse of post–Civil War freedom, employed a thousand ruses and stratagems of struggle to win their rights." "Still others," he went on, "projected their hurts and longings into more naive and mundane forms—blues, jazz, swing—and, without intellectual guidance, tried to build up a compensatory nourishment for themselves." "How 'Bigger' Was Born," *Saturday Review of Literature*, June 1, 1940; reprinted as the introduction to *Native Son* (New York: Harper and Row, 1940), xii–xiii.

Such ambivalence toward urban Black music, dance, and dress is already there in Wright's earlier work *Lawd Today*, even as its protagonist, Jake Jackson, stands before his wardrobe, fingering his ten suits and mulling over his collection of panchromatic shirts, ties, and shoes. As Jake carefully chooses the green suit with red suspenders, the low-cut brown suede shoes, the white spats, the lavender shirt, the wide yellow tie with blue half moons, the ruby pin, and the purple-embroidered orange handkerchief, Wright offers us an early symptom of the naive, commercially debased fantasy and violent sensuality that fatally sweep along Jake's barely half-conscious emotional life: the life of the "Flying Fool." Richard Wright, *Lawd Today* (1937) (repr., New York: Walker, 1963), 27–28.

22. Wright, *12 Million Black Voices*, 127.

23. Ralph Ellison, *Invisible Man* (New York: Vintage Books, 1990), 440.

24. Ibid.

25. Ibid., 441. The passages cited are well worth quoting at length: "What about those three boys, coming now along the platform, tall and slender, walking stiffly with swinging shoulders in their well-pressed, too-hot-for-summer suits, their collars high and tight about their necks, their identical hats of black cheap felt set upon the crowns of their heads with a severe formality above their hard conked hair? It was as though I'd never seen their like before: Walking slowly, their shoulders swaying, their legs swinging from their hips in trousers that ballooned upward from cuffs fitting snug about their ankles; their coats long and hip-tight with shoulders far too broad to be those of natural western men. These fellows whose bodies seemed—what had one of my teachers said of me?—

'You're like one of these African sculptures, distorted in the interests of a design.' Well, what design and whose? I stared as they seemed to move like dancers in some kind of funeral ceremony, swaying, going forward, their black faces secret, moving slowly down the subway platform, the heavy heel-plated shoes making a rhythmical tapping as they moved. Everyone must have seen them, or heard their muted laughter, or smelled the heavy pomade on their hair—or perhaps failed to see them at all. For they were men outside of historical time, they were untouched, they didn't believe in Brotherhood, no doubt had never heard of it; or perhaps like Clifton would mysteriously have rejected its mysteries; men of transition whose faces were immobile" (440). And: ". . . the boys speak a jived-up transitional language full of country glamour, think transitional thought, though perhaps they dream the same old ancient dreams. They were men out of time—unless they found Brotherhood. Men out of time, who would soon be gone and forgotten. . . . But who knew (and now I began to tremble so violently I had to lean against a refuse can)—who knew but that they were the saviours, the true leaders, the bearers of something precious? The stewards of something uncomfortable, burdensome, which they hated because, living outside the realm of history, there was no one to applaud their value and they themselves failed to understand it" (441). And: "For they were outside . . . running and dodging the forces of history instead of making a dominating stand" (441).

26. The oratorical roots of Wright's text in popular blues, spirituals, and sermons has been analyzed by John M. Reilly in "Reconstruction of Genre as Entry into Conscious History," *Black American Literature Forum* 13 (Spring 1979), and "Richard Wright Preaches the Nation," *Black American Literature Forum* 16 (Fall 1982). The relation of Wright's narration to documentary film is discussed in Jack B. Moore, "The Voice in *12 Million Black Voices*," *Mississippi Quarterly* 42, no. 4 (Fall 1989): 415–24. Neither author relates Wright's narrative of history to the didactic and reductive forms of "historical materialism" propounded by the Communist Party at this time as a Marxist theory of history. Wright remained a member of the Communist Party until his unpublicized withdrawal in 1942. His earlier adherence to its Stalinist policies may be summed up by his reported welcoming of the Nazi–Soviet Pact of 1939 as "a great step toward peace" that "struck a blow against the imperialist war intrigues of Chamberlain on the continent." "Negroes Have No Stake in This War, Wright Says," *Sunday Worker*, February 11, 1940, 7, reprinted in Kinnamon and Fabre, *Conversations with Richard Wright*, 25.

27. For the socioeconomic causes and effects of the Great Migration, see E. Marvin Goodwin, *Black Migration in America from 1915 to 1960: An Uneasy Exodus* (Lewiston, N.Y.: E. Mellen Press, 1990); George W. Groh, *The Black*

Migration: The Journey to Urban America (New York: Weybright and Talley, 1972); Alferdteen Harrison, ed., *Black Exodus: The Great Migration from the American South* (Jackson: University Press of Mississippi, 1991); and Nicholas Lemann, *The Promised Land: The Great Black Migration and How It Changed America* (New York: Alfred A. Knopf, 1991). For the social, political, and cultural impact on the cities of the Northeast and Midwest, see James Weldon Johnson, *Black Manhattan* (New York: Alfred A. Knopf, 1930); St. Clair Drake and Horace R. Cayton, *Black Metropolis: A Study of Negro Life in a Northern City*, with an introduction by Richard Wright (New York: Harcourt, Brace, 1945); Allan H. Spear, *Black Chicago: The Making of a Negro Ghetto, 1890–1920* (Chicago: University of Chicago Press, 1967); Mike Rowe, *Chicago Breakdown* (London: Eddison Press, 1973); and Robert Palmer, *Deep Blues* (New York: Viking, 1981). See also Claude McKay, *Harlem: Negro Metropolis* (New York: E. P. Dutton, 1940), almost contemporary with the Wright–Rosskam volume and illustrated by twenty-four largely agency and Black studio photographs.

28. Lemann, *The Promised Land*, 6.

29. Rowe, *Chicago Breakdown*, 27.

30. On the record of the New Deal in relation to the lives of African Americans and on issues of racism, see, for example, Leslie H. Fischel Jr., "The Negro in the New Deal Era," *Wisconsin Magazine of History* 48 (Winter 1964–65): 111–23, reprinted in Alonzo L. Hamby, ed., *The New Deal: Analysis and Interpretation* (New York and London: Longman, 1981), 177–87; John B. Kirby, *Black Americans in the Roosevelt Era: Liberalism and Race* (Knoxville: University of Tennessee Press, 1980); and Harvard Sitkoff, *A New Deal for Blacks: The Emergence of Civil Rights as a National Issue* (New York: Oxford University Press, 1978).

31. Lemann, *The Promised Land*, 6, 10–11.

32. On the economy of cotton production and the system of farm tenantry, see Charles S. Johnson, *Shadow of the Plantation* (Chicago: University of Chicago Press, 1934); Charles S. Johnson, Edwin R. Embree, and W. W. Alexander, *The Collapse of Cotton Tenancy: Summary of Field Studies and Statistical Surveys, 1933–35* (Chapel Hill: University of North Carolina Press, 1935); Charles S. Johnson, *Growing Up in the Black Belt: Negro Youth in the Rural South* (Washington, D.C.: American Council on Education, 1941); Lemann, *The Promised Land*; Dale Maharidge and Michael Williamson, *And Their Children after Them: The Legacy of "Let Us Now Praise Famous Men": James Agee, Walker Evans, and the Rise and Fall of Cotton in the South* (New York: Pantheon Books, 1989); and T. J. Woofter Jr., *Landlord and Tenant on the Cotton Plantation* (New York: New American Studies, 1969), originally published in 1936 by the Works Progress Administration, Division of Social Research.

33. Cf. Harrison, *Black Exodus.*

34. John Morton Blum, *V Was for Victory: Politics and American Culture during World War II* (New York and London: Harcourt Brace Jovanovich, 1976), chap. 6, "Black America: The Rising Wind," 182–220, esp. 183, 198. See also Neil A. Wynn, *The Afro-American and the Second World War* (New York: Holmes and Meier, 1976).

35. Blum, *V Was for Victory,* 197.

36. Ibid., 190.

37. Wright, *12 Million Black Voices,* 123.

38. For a memoir of the June 1943 riots in Detroit, see Charles Denby [Matthew Ward, pseud.], "Detroit Riots, 1943," chap. 8 of *Indignant Heart: The Testimony of a Black American Worker* (1952; repr. London: Pluto Press, 1979), 110–19. For the Harlem riots of August 1943, cf. Ellison, *Invisible Man,* esp. chap. 25, 535–71. Wright's view of the Harlem "disturbances" as "stemming mainly from the economic pinch" was reported in "Richard Wright Feels Grip of Harlem Tension," *PM Daily,* August 3, 1943, 8, reprinted in Kinnamon and Fabre, *Conversations with Richard Wright,* 49. See also Blum, *V Was for Victory,* 199–207.

39. See Alvin F. Harlow, *Old Bowery Days: The Chronicles of a Famous Street* (New York: D. Appleton, 1931); Lloyd Morris, *Incredible New York: High Life and Low Life of the Last Hundred Years* (New York: Random House, 1951); and Christine Stansell, *City of Women: Sex and Class in New York, 1789–1860* (Urbana and Chicago: University of Illinois Press, 1987), esp. 89–101.

40. Wright, *12 Million Black Voices,* 130.

41. Cf. Kobena Mercer, "Black Hair/Style Politics," *New Formations,* no. 3 (Winter 1987): 33–54; and Stuart Hall, "What Is This 'Black' in Black Popular Culture?" in *Black Popular Culture,* ed. Gina Dent (Seattle: Bay Press, 1992), 21–33.

42. Cf. Mauricio Mazón, *The Zoot-Suit Riots: The Psychology of Symbolic Annihilation* (Austin: University of Texas Press, 1984).

43. On the history of the zoot suit and of pachucos and pachucas in Los Angeles, see Beatrice Griffith, *American Me* (Boston: Houghton Mifflin, 1948); Ralph H. Turner and Samuel J. Surace, "Zoot-Suiters and Mexicans," in *Racism in California: A Reader in the History of Oppression,* ed. Roger Daniels and Spencer C. Olm (New York: Macmillan, 1972), 210–19; Arturo Madrid-Barela, "In Search of the Authentic Pachuco: An Interpretive Essay," *Aztlán* 4, no. 1 (Spring 1973): 31–60; José Montoya, *Pachuco Art: A Historical Update* (Sacramento, Calif.: Royal Chicano Air Force, 1977); Stuart Cosgrove, "The Zoot Suit and Style Warfare," in *Zoot Suits and Second-Hand Dresses: An Anthology of Fashion and Music,* ed.

Angela McRobbie (Boston: Unwin Hyman, 1988), 3–22, originally published in *History Workshop Journal*, no. 18 (Autumn 1984): 77–91; Steve Chibnall, "Whistle and Zoot: The Changing Meaning of a Suit of Clothes," *History Workshop Journal*, no. 20 (1985): 56–81; and Marcos Sanchez-Tranquilino and John Tagg, "The Pachuco's Flayed Hide: The Museum, Identity, and *Buenas Garras*," in *Chicano Art: Resistance and Affirmation, 1965–1985*, ed. Richard Griswold del Castillo, Teresa McKenna, and Yvonne Yarbro-Bejarano (Los Angeles: Wight Art Gallery, University of California, Los Angeles, 1991), 97–108.

44. Octavio Paz, "The *Pachuco* and Other Extremes," in *The Labyrinth of Solitude: Life and Thought in Mexico*, trans. Lysander Kemp (New York: Grove Press, 1961), 9–28. For a more extended analysis of this essay, see Marcos Sanchez-Tranquilino, "*Mano a mano*: An Essay on the Representation of the Zoot Suit and Its Misrepresentation by Octavio Paz," *Journal* (Los Angeles Institute of Contemporary Art) (Winter 1987): 34–42.

45. Gloria Anzaldúa, *Borderlands/La Frontera: The New Mestiza* (San Francisco: Spinsters/Aunt Luce, 1987), 5.

46. *Pochismos* or *Anglicismos* are translated and Hispanized English words taken over into southwestern interlingual slang. *Caló* draws on southwestern Spanish, regional dialect, Mexican slang, and words that have changed little in form and meaning from Spanish Gypsy slang of the fifteenth century, but it is also a language of constant innovation, kept in restrictive usage by frequent and rapid changes of content through the invention of new terms. See George Carpenter Barker, *Pachuco: An American-Spanish Argot and Its Social Functions in Tucson, Arizona, Social Science Bulletin*, no. 18, *University of Arizona Bulletin*, 21, no. 1 (January 1950). See also Haldeen Braddy, "The Pachucos and Their Argot," *Southern Folklore Quarterly* 24, no. 4 (December 1960); and Raphael Jesús Gonzáles, "Pachuco: The Birth of a Creole Language," *Arizona Quarterly* 23, no. 4 (Winter 1967): 343–56.

47. Anzaldúa, *Borderlands/La Frontera*, 3.

48. Again, the conjunctural specificity of this strategy must be emphasized. By contrast, see Robert D. Kaplan, "The Coming Anarchy," *Atlantic Monthly*, February 1994, 44–76, for a sobering view of the effect on sub-Saharan Africa of border breakdowns brought about by mass migration, urbanization, and refugee movements, simultaneously producing highly segmented and transnational cultural forms, framed by conditions of ecological depletion, environmental scarcity, demographic density, disease, ethnic and religious conflict, and the transformation brought about by the State's loss of its monopoly over the means of waging war. Against the *sapeurs* and *sapeuses* of Kinshasa has to be set the Somalian war-machine culture of technicals and khat, though, for Western

media, the latter has functioned rhetorically much as pachuco culture did in 1943.

49. The emergence of "youth" as a psychosocial category linked to the notion that the city was divided and organized into distinct "ecological" areas, each with its own "world," was developed by the Chicago school of social ecology from the late 1920s on. See R. E. Park and R. D. McKenzie, eds., *The City* (Chicago: University of Chicago Press, 1967), and R. E. Faris, *Chicago Sociology: 1920–1932* (Chicago: University of Chicago Press, 1967). For an application of this model to research on Chicano youth-gang members and *pintos* (prison inmates), see Joan W. Moore, *Homeboys: Gangs, Drugs, and Prison in the Barrios of Los Angeles* (Philadelphia: Temple University Press, 1978).

50. On the Bold Look of 1948 mainstream menswear, see Mercer, "Black Hair/Style Politics," 49. For the subsequent history of the zoot suit, see Chibnall, "Whistle and Zoot." And for the "updating" of the *Pachuco*, see Montoya, *Pachuco Art*, and Sanchez-Tranquilino and Tagg, "The Pachuco's Flayed Hide."

51. Much unique contemporary material is held in the Department of Special Collections at the University Research Library, UCLA. See Dan Luckenbill, *The Pachuco Era*, catalog of an exhibit at the University Research Library, Department of Special Collections, September–October 1990 (Los Angeles: University of California, Los Angeles, 1990).

52. Cf. Fredric Jameson, *Postmodernism, or The Cultural Logic of Late Capitalism* (Durham, N.C.: Duke University Press, 1991), esp. "The Cultural Logic of Late Capitalism," 1–54.

53. Cf. Jean Baudrillard, *Simulations*, trans. Paul Foss, Paul Patton, and Philip Beitchman (New York: Semiotext(e), 1983), and *Fatal Strategies: Crystal Revenge*, ed. Jim Fleming, trans. Philip Beitchman and W. G. J. Niesluchowski (New York and London: Semiotext(e)/Pluto, 1990).

54. Mercer, "Black Hair/Style Politics," 49.

55. See Karl Marx, *Capital: A Critique of Political Economy*, vol. 1, trans. Ben Fowkes (New York: Vintage Books, 1977): "The coat is a use-value that satisfies a particular need" (132). And: "If the use-values were not qualitatively different, hence not the products of qualitatively different forms of useful labour, they would be absolutely incapable of confronting each other as commodities. Coats cannot be exchanged for coats, one use-value cannot be exchanged for another of the same kind" (132). And: "Use-values like coats, linen, etc., in short, the physical bodies of commodities, are combinations of two elements, the material provided by nature, and labour. If we subtract the total amount of useful labour of different kinds which is contained in the coat, the linen, etc., a

material substratum is always left. This substratum is furnished by nature without human intervention" (133).

As Baudrillard has remarked, "By not submitting use value to [the] logic of equivalence in radical fashion, by maintaining use value as the category of 'incomparability,' Marxist analysis has contributed to the mythology (a veritable rationalist mystique) that allows the relation of the individual to objects conceived as use values to pass for a concrete and objective—in sum, 'natural'—relation between man's needs and the function proper to the object." Baudrillard, "Beyond Use Value," chap. 7 of *For a Critique of the Political Economy of the Sign,* trans. Charles Levin (St. Louis, Mo.: Telos Press, 1981), 134.

56. Stuart Hall, "The Social Eye of *Picture Post,*" *Working Papers in Cultural Studies* (Birmingham Centre for Contemporary Cultural Studies), no. 2 (Spring 1972): 71–120.

57. In May 1943, McKinley Morganfield, known as Muddy Waters since he was a child, left Clarksdale, in the heart of the Mississippi cotton belt, by train for Memphis and, from there, rode the Illinois Central north to Chicago. Here, in the segregated ghetto of the South Side, Muddy's harsh and emotional Delta country-blues was to be reamplified for a new Black urban–migrant market, through the entrepreneurial networks of nightclubs, independent recording companies, and trade journals that, between 1948 and the early 1950s, took his local success to a national level. A landmark in this passage was the January 1950 extracontractual recording session for Parkway, with Little Walter and "Baby Face" Leroy Foster, which produced the two unsurpassable versions of "Rollin' and Tumblin'."

5. The Pencil of History

1. O. K. Werkmeister's comments were made in an unpublished lecture for a conference entitled Culture and the State, in the series Current Debates in Art History, at Binghamton University in 1990. For Thomas Crow's review of Donald Preziosi's *Rethinking Art History: Meditations on a Coy Science,* see "Art History as Tertiary Text," *Art in America* 78, no. 4 (April 1990): 43–45.

2. William Henry Fox Talbot, *The Pencil of Nature* (1844) (New York: Da Capo Press, 1968), n.p.

3. Roland Barthes, *Camera Lucida: Reflections on Photography,* trans. Richard Howard (London: Jonathan Cape, 1982), 93.

4. Stephen Bann, *The Clothing of Clio: A Study of the Representation of History in Nineteenth-Century Britain and France* (Cambridge: Cambridge University Press, 1984), 3.

5. Ibid., 3–4.

6. H. D. Gower, L. Stanley Jast, and W. W. Topley, *The Camera as Historian* (London: Sampson Low, Marston and Co., 1916), iii.

7. Cf. Harry Milligan, "The Manchester Photographic Survey Record," *Manchester Review* 7 (Autumn 1958): 193–204, and John Tagg, *The Burden of Representation: Essays on Photographies and Histories* (London: Macmillan, 1988), 139.

8. Gower, Jast, and Topley, *The Camera as Historian,* v.

9. Ibid., vii.

10. Ibid., vii–viii.

11. Lynn Hunt, "History beyond Social Theory," in *The States of "Theory": History, Art, and Critical Discourses,* ed. David Carroll (New York: Columbia University Press, 1990), 95.

12. Mark Cousins, "The Practice of Historical Investigation," in *Poststructuralism and the Question of History,* ed. Derek Attridge, Geoff Bennington, and Robert Young (Cambridge and New York: Cambridge University Press, 1987), 126–36.

13. Cf. Michel Foucault, "The Discourse on Language," trans. Rupert Swyer, appendix to *The Archaeology of Knowledge,* trans. A. M. Sheridan Smith (New York: Pantheon Books, 1972): "History, as it is practiced today, does not turn its back on events; on the contrary, it is continually enlarging the field of events" (230).

14. Gower, Jast, and Topley, *The Camera as Historian,* 2–3.

15. A. Pugin and A. W. Pugin, *Examples of Gothic Architecture: Selected from Various Ancient Edifices in England,* 3 vols. (London: H. G. Bohn, 1850), quoted in ibid., 2.

16. Gower, Jast, and Topley, *The Camera as Historian,* 1.

17. Ibid.

18. Charles Alfred Stothard, *The Monumental Effigies of Great Britain, Selected from Our Cathedrals and Churches, for the Purpose of Bringing Together, and Preserving Correct Representations of the Best Historical Illustrations Extant, from the Norman Conquest to the Reign of Henry the Eighth* (London, 1817–33), quoted in Bann, *The Clothing of Clio,* 64.

19. Stothard, quoted in A. J. Kempe's introduction to *The Monumental Effigies of Great Britain,* 2, quoted in Bann, *The Clothing of Clio,* 65.

20. Bann, *The Clothing of Clio,* 67.

21. Gower, Jast, and Topley, *The Camera as Historian,* 80.

22. Ibid., 3.

23. Bann, *The Clothing of Clio,* 138. The problem is that, whereas Bann is concerned to reveal the morphology of nineteenth-century rhetorics of historical representation, he wants to insist on "the fundamental difference between historical discourse, on the one hand, and the photograph" (135). The difference,

for Bann, following Roland Barthes and John Berger and others, is rooted in the indexicality of the photograph as a guarantee of meaning outside the morphology of narrative and rhetorical structures that he analyzes. Photography, therefore, comes to take on the "unique function of representing the past, of making manifest to the spectator what Roland Barthes has called the 'having-been-there . . . the always stupefying evidence of *this is how it was*'" (134). This leads Bann even to propose the possibility of identifying Ranke's *wie es eigentlich gewesen* with the "having-been-there" that, for Barthes, inhabits the photograph.

Elsewhere, Bann writes of the photograph as "not simply an automatic, and to that extent a more efficient, means of reproduction" but as "a reproduction with a signature in time" (134). And in the context of discussing "the succession of technical developments, beyond the sphere of language, which offered a temporary or more long-lasting effect of illusory recreation"—an illusory re-creation central to "the new historical sensibility, striving to annihilate the gap between the model and the copy, and offering the Utopian possibility of a restoration of the past in the context of the present"—he suggests that "only the photograph, with its capacity to record and perpetuate light rays on a chemically-prepared surface, was able to achieve this effect with complete success" (138).

24. Ibid., 139.

25. Gower, Jast, and Topley, *The Camera as Historian*, 35.

26. Ibid., 213.

27. Ibid., 99–100.

28. Ibid., 6.

29. Ibid., 5.

30. Ibid., 6.

31. Ibid., 177.

32. Ibid., 160–61.

33. Ibid., 48.

34. Ibid., 80.

35. Ibid., 94.

36. Ibid.

37. Ibid., 96–97. It is worth noting that, of the authors, L. Stanley Jast was deputy chief librarian of Manchester Public Libraries and honorable secretary of the Library Association, while W. W. Topley was a member of Croydon Libraries Committee.

For the influence of bibliographic science on the organization of photographic archives, see Allan Sekula, "The Body and the Archive," *October*, no. 39 (Winter 1986): 56–57.

38. Gower, Jast, and Topley, *The Camera as Historian*, 71.

39. Ibid., 70.

40. Ibid.

41. See, for example, George Brown Goode (assistant secretary of the Smithsonian Institution in charge of the National Museum), "Report of the Assistant Secretary," *Report of the National Museum* (Washington: National Museum, 1893).

42. Frederick William True, "The United States National Museum," in *The Smithsonian Institution, 1846–1896: The History of Its First Half Century*, ed. George Brown Goode (Washington, D.C.: De Vinne Press, 1897), 335.

43. Sekula, "The Body and the Archive," 16.

44. Gower, Jast, and Topley, *The Camera as Historian*, 85.

45. Gower, Jast, and Topley's *Camera as Historian* is quite clear about the addressee of the Survey archive: "To the historian and the scientist the value of exact records, indisputably authentic, can hardly be overrated. Such are the primary requirements of their work, the raw materials necessary for their labours" (3). "The architect, and especially the student of architecture, will find there is no index to what has been accomplished so instructive as a series of photographs, comprehensively recording both broad outlines and details, compactly arranged and classified in such manner as to facilitate reference and comparison" (3). "The politician, in his efforts for the betterment of our social structure, must, if his constructive work is to stand the test of actual trial, take for his starting point the existing conditions of his time, and must duly weigh the evolutionary forces which have brought those conditions into being. For both purposes exact records of material conditions, chronologically arranged for purposes of comparison, furnish a valuable, indeed a necessary, basis for generalization" (3–4). "Nor is the work without value in a commercial and legal sense. Questions relative to property, and mutual rights therein, often arise, the solution of which requires evidence based on a state of things which has passed away" (4). "The value of adequate photographic records, kept as the common heritage of all, in fostering the civic spirit, is not to be overlooked. A healthy corporate consciousness constitutes a quality in our civic and national life which cannot be too highly valued or too sedulously fostered. . . . And in the fostering of such a consciousness exact records of fact, by reference to which misunderstandings and misapprehensions can be dispelled, have their fitting place" (4).

46. Jean-François Lyotard, *The Differend: Phrases in Dispute*, trans. Georges Van Den Abbeele (Minneapolis: University of Minnesota Press, 1988), 177, sec. 251.

47. Michel Foucault, *Discipline and Punish: The Birth of the Prison*, trans. Alan Sheridan (New York: Vintage Books, 1979), 190–91.

48. Sekula, "The Body and the Archive," 16. For the development in the nineteenth century of nonmimetic strategies of historical representation, see Bann, *The Clothing of Clio*, 138ff.

49. See, esp., John Tagg, "The Discontinuous City: Picturing and the Discursive Field," in *Grounds of Dispute: Art History, Cultural Politics, and the Discursive Field* (London: Macmillan, 1992), 134–56, and *The Burden of Representation*.

50. Jonathan Crary, "Modernizing Vision," in *Vision and Visuality*, ed. Hal Foster, Discussions in Contemporary Culture no. 2 (Seattle, Wash.: Bay Press, 1988), 43. See also Crary, *Techniques of the Observer: On Vision and Modernity in the Nineteenth Century* (Cambridge, Mass., and London: MIT Press/October Books, 1990), where he argues, somewhat differently, though still in terms of an epochal visuality, that "the camera obscura and the photographic camera, as assemblages, practices, and social objects, belong to two fundamentally different organizations of representation and the observer, as well as of the observer's relation to the visible. By the beginning of the nineteenth century the camera obscura is no longer synonymous with the production of truth and with an observer positioned to see truthfully. The regularity of such statements ends abruptly; the assemblage constituted by the camera breaks down and the photographic camera becomes an essentially dissimilar object, lodged amidst a radically different network of statements and practices" (32).

51. Lyotard, *The Differend*, 47, sec. 75.

52. Ibid., 44, sec. 68.

53. Ibid., 47, sec. 75.

54. Ibid., 50, sec. 81.

55. Ibid., 55, sec. 92.

56. Ibid., 53, sec. 88.

57. Ibid., 56, sec. 92.

58. Ibid., 55, sec. 92.

59. See ibid., 32–58. See also Bill Readings, *Introducing Lyotard: Art and Politics* (London and New York: Routledge, 1991), esp. chap. 3, "Politics and Ethics," 86–139.

60. Lyotard, *The Differend*, 181, sec. 263.

61. Ibid., 57, sec. 93.

62. Ibid., 53, sec. 88. One might compare Derrida's remark, in *Archive Fever*, that "each time a historian as such decides to 'step aside and let . . . speak,' for example to let a photographic specter . . . speak, it is the sign of a respect before the future to come of the future to come. Thus he is no longer a historian." Jacques Derrida, *Archive Fever: A Freudian Impression*, trans. Eric Prenowitz (Chicago and London: University of Chicago Press, 1996), 70.

63. Barthes, *Camera Lucida*, 93.

64. Ibid.

65. Ibid.

66. Ibid., 76.

67. Ibid., 87.

68. Ibid., 107.

69. Ibid., 87.

70. Karl Marx, "The Eighteenth Brumaire of Louis Bonaparte," in Karl Marx and Frederick Engels, *Collected Works*, vol. 11 (London: Lawrence and Wishart, 1979), 11:103. For Barthes's own comments on Marx's formulation, see "Le retour comme farce—Recurrence as Farce," in *Roland Barthes by Roland Barthes*, trans. Richard Howard (New York: Hill and Wang, 1977), 88–89.

71. Barthes, *Camera Lucida*, 87–88.

72. Ibid., 85.

73. Ibid., 87.

74. Ibid., 88–89.

75. Ibid., 80.

76. Ibid., 88.

77. Ibid., 96.

78. Cf. ibid., 73, 79, 85, and esp. 113.

79. Roland Barthes, "The Discourse of History," trans. Stephen Bann, in *Comparative Criticism: A Yearbook*, ed. E. S. Shaffer, no. 3 (Cambridge: Cambridge University Press, 1981), 18.

80. Ibid., 16.

81. Ibid., 11.

82. Ibid., 14.

83. Ibid., 17.

84. Ibid.

85. Ibid.

86. Ibid., 17–18.

87. Ibid., 18.

88. Ibid., 20n13. Cf. Roland Barthes, "Rhetoric of the Image," trans. Stephen Heath, in *Image-Music-Text* (Glasgow: Fontana/Collins, 1977), 32–51.

89. Barthes, "The Discourse of History," 18. See also 20n14.

90. Ibid., 18.

91. Barthes, *Camera Lucida*, 106.

92. Ibid., 89.

93. Ibid., 91.

94. Ibid.

95. Ibid., 90.

96. Ibid.

97. Ibid., 93.

98. Ibid.

99. Ibid., 94.

100. Ibid., 115; see also 116.

101. Roland Barthes, "Phases," in *Roland Barthes by Roland Barthes*, 145.

102. Barthes, *Camera Lucida*, 119.

103. Cf. ibid., 113.

104. Ibid., 119; see also 117.

105. Cf. Claude Lévi-Strauss, *The Savage Mind* (Chicago: University of Chicago Press, 1966), chap. 9, "History and Dialectic," esp. 258.

106. Geoff Bennington and Robert Young, "Introduction: Posing the Question," in Attridge, Bennington, and Young, *Poststructuralism and the Question of History*, 4.

107. Barthes, *Camera Lucida*, 119.

108. Ibid., 93.

109. Ibid., 119.

110. Ibid., 94. Cf. 65: "impossible for me to believe in 'witnesses'; impossible at least, to be one."

111. Jacques Derrida, "Cogito and the History of Madness," in *Writing and Difference*, trans. Alan Bass (Chicago: University of Chicago Press, 1978), 61. For Derrida's reading of Barthes's *Camera Lucida*, see Derrida, "The Deaths of Roland Barthes," trans. Pascale-Anne Brault and Michael Naas, in *Philosophy and Non-Philosophy since Merleau-Ponty*, ed. Hugh J. Silverman (New York and London: Routledge, 1988), 259–96, and Jacques Derrida and Marie-Françoise Plissart, "Right of Inspection," trans. David Wills, *Art and Text*, no. 32 (Autumn 1989): 20–97, esp. 90–92.

112. Jacques Derrida, "Parergon," in *The Truth in Painting*, trans. Geoff Bennington and Ian McLeod (Chicago and London: University of Chicago Press, 1987), 61.

113. Jacques Derrida, "Some Statements and Truisms about Neologisms, Newisms, Postisms, Parasitisms, and Other Small Seisisms," trans. Anne Tomiche, in Carroll, *The States of "Theory,"* 93.

114. Ibid., 92.

6. A Discourse with Shape of Reason Missing

The earliest version of this chapter was researched and written during my tenure as Ailsa Mellon Bruce Senior Fellow at the Center for Advanced Study in the

Visual Arts at the National Gallery of Art, Washington, D.C. It was first presented at a colloquium in the Center for Advanced Study in the Visual Arts in April 1991 and subsequently published in *Art History* 15, no. 3 (September 1992): 72–94.

1. Jean-François Lyotard, *The Differend: Phrases in Dispute*, trans. Georges Van Den Abbeele (Minneapolis: University of Minnesota Press, 1988), 41, sec. 62.

2. Jeremy Gilbert-Rolfe and John Johnston, eds., *Multiplicity, Proliferation, Reconvention*, special feature for *Journal: A Contemporary Art Magazine* 5, no. 42 (Fall 1985): 21–65.

3. Jeremy Gilbert-Rolfe and John Johnston, "Multiplicity, Proliferation, Reconvention," in Gilbert-Rolfe and Johnston, *Multiplicity, Proliferation, Reconvention*, 28.

4. Ibid.

5. Michel Feher, "Mass, Crowd, and Pack," in Gilbert-Rolfe and Johnston, *Multiplicity, Proliferation, Reconvention*, 45–49.

6. Ibid., 48. The reference to Baldessari's reading of Canetti is made in Coosje van Bruggen, *John Baldessari* (Los Angeles: Museum of Contemporary Art; New York: Rizzoli, 1990), 163.

7. Elias Canetti, *Crowds and Power*, trans. Carol Stewart (New York: Seabury Press, 1978), 180–81.

8. See ibid., 16–23, 73–74.

9. Ibid., 17.

10. Ibid., 20.

11. Ibid., 29.

12. Ibid., 73.

13. Ibid., 74.

14. John Baldessari, "Crowds with Shape of Reason Missing," in *Zone*, ed. Michel Feher and Sanford Kwinter, nos. 1–2 (New York: Urzone, n.d.), 32–39.

15. See Louis Althusser, "On the Young Marx," in *For Marx*, trans. Ben Brewster (London: Allen Lane, 1969), 63.

16. See J. L. Austin, *How to Do Things with Words* (New York: Oxford University Press, 1962).

17. Jacques Derrida, "Signature Event Context," in *Margins of Philosophy*, trans. Alan Bass (Chicago: University of Chicago Press, 1982), 322.

18. Ibid., 323.

19. Ibid., 324.

20. On "iterable," see ibid., 315 and 326. What follows from this concept for Derrida is that "above all, one then would be concerned with different types

of marks or chains of marks, and not with an opposition between citational state-ments on the one hand, and singular and original statement-events on the other" (326).

21. Ibid., 327.

22. Ibid., 320.

23. Ibid., 327; the text says "dyssemtrical fashion."

24. Michel Foucault, "The Discourse on Language," trans. Rupert Swyer, appendix to *The Archaeology of Knowledge*, trans. A. M. Sheridan Smith (New York: Pantheon Books, 1972), 230. Originally published as *L'ordre du discours* (Paris: Editions Gallimard, 1971).

25. Foucault, *The Archaeology of Knowledge*, 120.

26. Foucault, "The Discourse on Language," 229.

27. Ibid., 216.

28. Ibid., 220.

29. Ibid., 229.

30. Ibid., 230.

31. Ibid., 234.

32. Ibid., 229.

33. Ibid.

34. Ibid., 231.

35. Michel Foucault, "Truth and Power," in *Power/Knowledge: Selected Interviews and Other Writings, 1972–1977*, ed. Colin Gordon (New York: Pantheon, 1980), 113.

36. Ibid., 114.

37. See Jacques Derrida, "Passe-Partout" and "Parergon," in *The Truth in Painting*, trans. Geoff Bennington and Ian McLeod (Chicago and London: University of Chicago Press, 1987), 1–13 and 15–147.

38. Derrida's criticisms of Foucault's *Folie et déraison* and, specifically, of Foucault's reading of a passage from Descartes' *First Meditation* were first pre-sented in a lecture at the Collège de Philosophie on March 4, 1963, and were first published in the *Revue de métaphysique et de morale* (October–December 1963). Four years later, Derrida reprinted "Cogito et histoire de la folie" in *Ecriture et la différence* (Paris: Points-Seuil, 1967); see "Cogito and the History of Mad-ness," in *Writing and Difference*, trans. Alan Bass (Chicago: University of Chicago Press, 1978), 31–63. Foucault's response came only in 1971, in "Mon corps, ce papier, ce feu," first published in *Paideia* (September 1971) and reprinted at the end of the 1972 edition of *Histoire de la folie à l'âge classique* (Paris: Gallimard, 1972): see "My Body, This Paper, This Fire," trans. Geoff Bennington, *Oxford Literary Review* 4, no. 1 (1979): 9–28.

39. Cf. Michel Foucault, *Discipline and Punish: The Birth of the Prison*, trans. Alan Sheridan (London: Allen Lane, 1977), for example, pt. 3, chap. 3, "Panopticism," 195–228, and pt. 4, chap. 1, "Complete and Austere Institutions," 231–56.

40. Derrida, "Passe-Partout," 9.

41. Derrida, "Parergon," 45.

42. Ibid., 61.

43. Ibid.

44. Sigmund Freud, "Some Psychological Consequences of the Anatomical Distinction between the Sexes (1925)," in *Sexuality and the Psychology of Love*, ed. Philip Rieff (New York: Macmillan, 1963), 187.

45. Derrida, "Passe-Partout," 9.

46. Derrida, "Parergon," 61.

47. Ibid.

48. Meyer Schapiro, "On Some Problems in the Semiotics of Visual Art: Field and Vehicle in Image-Signs," *Semiotica* 1, no. 3 (1969): 223. See also 226–27: "Apparently it was late in the second millennium B.C. (if even then) before one thought of a continuous isolating frame around an image, a homogeneous enclosure like a city wall."

49. Ibid., 224.

50. Ibid.

51. Ibid., 227.

52. See Jean-Claude Lebensztejn, "L'espace de l'art," in *Zigzag* (Paris: Flammarion, 1981), 19–47, esp. 40–41. For a formalist analysis of the function of the gallery wall, see Brian O'Doherty, "Inside the White Cube: Notes on Gallery Space. Part I," *Artforum* 14, no. 7 (March 1976): 24–30; "Inside the White Cube: Part II. The Eye and the Spectator," *Artforum* 14, no. 8 (April 1976): 26–34; "Inside the White Cube: Part III. Context as Content," *Artforum* 15, no. 3 (November 1976): 38–44.

53. Lebensztejn, "L'espace de l'art," 42.

54. Ibid., 45.

55. Stephen Bann, "Poetics of the Museum: Lenoir and Du Sommerard," chap. 4 of *The Clothing of Clio: A Study of the Representation of History in Nineteenth-Century Britain and France* (Cambridge: Cambridge University Press, 1984), 77–92.

56. See Derrida, "Signature Event Context," 327–29; "Passe-Partout," 8; "Parergon," 78; and "Restitutions of the Truth in Pointing [*pointure*]," in *Truth in Painting*, 279, 301, 365. See also Jean Baudrillard, "Gesture and Signature: Semiurgy in Contemporary Art," chap. 4 of *For a Critique of the Political Economy of the Sign*, trans. Charles Levin (St. Louis, Mo.: Telos Press, 1981), 102–11.

57. Cf. Kaja Silverman, "Fassbinder and Lacan: A Reconsideration of Gaze, Look, and Image," *Camera Obscura*, no. 19 (January 1989): 55–84.

58. George Brown Goode (assistant secretary of the Smithsonian Institution in charge of the National Museum), "Report of the Assistant Secretary," *Report of the National Museum* (Washington, D.C.: National Museum, 1893), 23.

59. Timothy Mitchell, "The World as Exhibition," *Comparative Studies in Society and History* 31, no. 2 (1989): 218.

60. Jonathan Crary, *Techniques of the Observer: On Vision and Modernity in the Nineteenth Century* (Cambridge, Mass., and London: MIT Press/October Books, 1990), 18.

61. See especially Foucault, *Discipline and Punish*, and *Birth of the Clinic: An Archaeology of Medical Perception*, trans. A. M. Sheridan Smith (London: Tavistock, 1973).

62. Gilles Deleuze and Félix Guattari, *Anti-Oedipus: Capitalism and Schizophrenia*, trans. Mark Seem, Robert Hurley, and Helen Lane (New York: Viking, 1978), and *A Thousand Plateaus: Capitalism and Schizophrenia*, trans. Brian Massumi (Minneapolis: University of Minnesota Press, 1987).

63. Crary, *Techniques of the Observer*, 21–23.

64. Walter Benjamin, "The Work of Art in the Age of Mechanical Reproduction," in *Illuminations*, ed. Hannah Arendt, trans. Harry Zohn (New York: Schoken Books, 1969), 217–51.

65. Ian Hunter, *Culture and Government: The Emergence of Literary Education* (London: Macmillan, 1988), viii.

66. Cf. Foucault, *Discipline and Punish* and *Power/Knowledge*.

67. Hunter, *Culture and Government*, 3, 70, 153.

68. Crary, *Techniques of the Observer*, 6–7.

69. Hunter, *Culture and Government*, 153, 263.

70. Derrida, "Parergon," 19–20.

71. Cf. Bill Readings, "The Deconstruction of Politics," in *Reading De Man Reading*, ed. Lindsay Waters and Wlad Godzich (Minneapolis: University of Minnesota Press, 1989), 223–43.

72. Feher, "Mass, Crowd, and Pack," 49.

73. Ibid., 48.

74. See Marcos Sanchez-Tranquilino and John Tagg, "The Pachuco's Flayed Hide: The Museum, Identity, and *Buenas Garras*," in *Chicano Art: Resistance and Affirmation, 1965–1985*, ed. Richard Griswold del Castillo, Teresa McKenna, and Yvonne Yarbro-Bejarano (Los Angeles: Wight Art Gallery, University of California, Los Angeles, 1991), 97–108.

75. The relationship of *drapes* to *frame* might be pursued. Derrida's analysis of the frame departs from his reading of a passage in the first part of Kant's *Critique of Judgement*, on the analytic of the beautiful and judgments of taste, in which Derrida focuses on the anomalous position of *parerga*, or ornamentations: those adjuncts that, in Kant's words, run the risk of being mere "finery" and "enter into the composition of the beautiful form" of the work itself only insofar as they also augment the delight of taste by means of their form. Kant's examples of such *parerga* are the framings of pictures, the colonnades of palaces, and the *drapery* on statues. Cf. Immanuel Kant, *The Critique of Judgement*, trans. James Creed Meredith (Oxford: Clarendon Press, 1952), 68, and Derrida, "Parergon," esp. 52–82.

76. Lyotard, *The Differend*, 181, sec. 262.

77. Ibid., 13, sec. 23.

Bibliography

Aaron, Daniel. *Writers on the Left*. Oxford and New York: Oxford University Press, 1977.

Agamben, Giorgio. *Stanzas: Word and Phantasm in Western Culture*. Translated by Ronald L. Martinez. Minneapolis and London: University of Minnesota Press, 1993.

Agee, James, and Walker Evans. *Let Us Now Praise Famous Men: Three Tenant Families*. Boston: Houghton Mifflin, 1941.

Aitken, Ian. *Film and Reform: John Grierson and the Documentary Film Movement*. London and New York: Routledge, 1990.

Allswang, John M. *The New Deal and American Politics: A Study in Political Change*. New York: Wiley, 1978.

Althusser, Louis. *For Marx*. Translated by Ben Brewster. London: Allen Lane, 1969.

———. *Lenin and Philosophy and Other Essays*. Translated by Ben Brewster. London: New Left Books, 1971.

———. *Pour Marx*. Paris: Librairie François Maspero, 1965.

Anderson, Karen. *Wartime Women: Sex Roles, Family Relations, and the Status of Women during World War II*. Westport, Conn.: Greenwood Press, 1981.

Anzaldúa, Gloria. *Borderlands/La Frontera: The New Mestiza*. San Francisco: Spinsters/Aunt Luce, 1987.

Attridge, Derek, Geoff Bennington, and Robert Young, eds. *Poststructuralism and the Question of History*. Cambridge and New York: Cambridge University Press, 1987.

Austin, J. L. *How to Do Things with Words*. New York: Oxford University Press, 1962.

Baldessari, John. "Crowds with Shape of Reason Missing." *Zone,* ed. Michel Feher and Sanford Kwinter, nos. 1–2 (New York: Urzone, n.d.): 32–39.

Baltrusaitis, Jurgis. *Anamorphoses ou magie artificielle des effets merveilleux.* Paris: Olivier Perrin Editeur, 1969.

Bann, Stephen. *The Clothing of Clio: A Study of the Representation of History in Nineteenth-Century Britain and France.* Cambridge: Cambridge University Press, 1984.

Baran, Paul A., and Paul M. Sweezy. *Monopoly Capital: An Essay on the American Economic and Social Order.* New York: Monthly Review Press, 1966.

Barker, George Carpenter. *Pachuco: An American-Spanish Argot and Its Social Functions in Tucson, Arizona. Social Science Bulletin,* no. 18. *University of Arizona Bulletin* 21, no. 1 (January 1950).

Barthes, Roland. *Camera Lucida: Reflections on Photography.* Translated by Richard Howard. London: Jonathan Cape, 1982.

———. "The Discourse of History." Translated by Stephen Bann. In *Comparative Criticism: A Yearbook,* ed. E. S. Shaffer, no. 3. Cambridge: Cambridge University Press, 1981.

———. *Mythologies.* Paris: Editions du Seuil, 1957.

———. *Mythologies.* Translated by Annette Lavers. London: Jonathan Cape, 1972.

———. "Rhetoric of the Image." Translated by Stephen Heath. In *Image-Music-Text,* 32–51. Glasgow: Fontana/Collins, 1977.

———. *Roland Barthes by Roland Barthes.* Translated by Richard Howard. New York: Hill and Wang, 1977.

Batchen, Geoffrey. *Burning with Desire: The Conception of Photography.* Cambridge, Mass., and London: MIT Press, 1997.

Baudrillard, Jean. *Fatal Strategies: Crystal Revenge.* Edited by Jim Fleming. Translated by Philip Beitchman and W. G. J. Niesluchowski. New York and London: Semiotext(e)/Pluto, 1990.

———. *For a Critique of the Political Economy of the Sign.* Translated by Charles Levin. St. Louis, Mo.: Telos Press, 1981.

———. *Simulations.* Translated by Paul Foss, Paul Patton, and Philip Beitchman. New York: Semiotext(e), 1983.

Becker Ohrn, Karin. *Dorothea Lange and the Documentary Tradition.* Baton Rouge: Louisiana State University Press, 1980.

Beiser, Frederick. *Hegel.* New York and London: Routledge, 2005.

Benjamin, Walter. "Critique of Violence." In *One-Way Street and Other Writings,* trans. Edmund Jephcott and Kingsley Shorter, 132–54. London: New Left Books, 1979.

————. *The Origin of German Tragic Drama.* Translated by John Osborne. London: New Left Books, 1977.

————. *Ursprung des deutschen Trauerspiels.* Frankfurt am Main: Suhrkamp Verlag, 1963.

————. "The Work of Art in the Age of Mechanical Reproduction." In *Illuminations*, ed. Hannah Arendt, trans. Harry Zohn, 217–51. New York: Schoken Books, 1969.

Bennington, Geoff, and Robert Young. "Introduction: Posing the Question." In *Poststructuralism and the Question of History*, ed. Derek Attridge, Geoff Bennington, and Robert Young. Cambridge and New York: Cambridge University Press, 1987.

Bentham, Jeremy. *Panopticon, or The Inspection-House: Containing the Idea of a New Principle of Construction Applicable to Any Sort of Establishment, in Which Persons of Any Description Are to Be Kept under Inspection: And in Particular to Penitentiary-Houses, Prisons, Houses of Industry, Work-Houses, Poor-Houses, Manufactories, Mad-Houses, Lazarettos, Hospitals, and Schools: With a Plan of Management Adapted to the Principle: In a Series of Letters, Written in the Year 1787.* Reprint, London: T. Payne, 1791.

Berger Gluck, Sherna. *Rosie the Riveter Revisited: Women, the War, and Social Change.* Boston: Twayne, 1987.

Bernstein, Barton J. "The New Deal: The Conservative Achievements of Liberal Reform." In *Towards a New Past*, ed. Barton J. Bernstein. New York: Pantheon Books, 1968.

Bleach, Gordon. "Visions of Access: Africa Bound and Staged, 1880–1940." Ph.D. diss., Binghamton University, 2000.

Blum, John Morton. *V Was for Victory: Politics and American Culture during World War II.* New York and London: Harcourt Brace Jovanovich, 1976.

Bobbitt, Philip. *The Shield of Achilles: War, Peace, and the Course of History.* New York: Alfred A. Knopf, 2002.

Bonnett, Clarence. *A History of Employers' Associations in the United States.* New York: Vantage Press, 1956.

Bourke-White, Margaret. "Notes on Photographs." In Erskine Caldwell and Margaret Bourke-White, *You Have Seen Their Faces.* New York: Modern Age Books, 1937.

————. Papers. Department of Special Collections, E. S. Bird Library, Syracuse University.

————. *Portrait of Myself.* New York: Simon and Schuster, 1963.

Braddy, Haldeen. "The Pachucos and Their Argot." *Southern Folklore Quarterly* 24, no. 4 (December 1960).

Bruggen, Coosje van. *John Baldessari*. Los Angeles: Museum of Contemporary Art; New York: Rizzoli, 1990.

Bryson, Norman, Michael Ann Holly, and Keith Moxey, eds. *Visual Culture: Images and Interpretations*. Hanover, N.H., and London: Wesleyan University Press/University Press of New England, 1994.

Burckhardt, Jacob. *Der Cultur der Renaissance in Italien: Ein Versuch*. Edited by Hiroyuki Numata and Peter Ganz. Vol. 4 of *Werke*. Munich: C. H. Beck; Basel: Schwabe, 2000.

———. *Reflections on History*. Translated by M. D. Hottinger. Indianapolis, Ind.: Liberty Classics, 1979.

———. *Über das Studium der Geschichte*. Edited by Peter Ganz. Vol. 10 of *Werke*. Munich: C. H. Beck; Basel: Schwabe, 2000.

Butler, Judith. *The Psychic Life of Power: Theories in Subjection*. Stanford, Calif.: Stanford University Press, 1997.

Byrnes, Thomas. *Professional Criminals of America*. New York, 1885.

Byrnes, Thomas, Helen C. Campbell, and Thomas W. Knox. *Darkness and Daylight, or Lights and Shadows of New York Life*. Hartford, Conn.: Hartford Publishing Co., 1899.

Cahill, Holger. "American Resources in the Arts." In *Art for the Millions*, ed. Francis O'Connor. Boston: New York Graphic Society, 1975.

———. "New Horizons in American Art." Introduction to *New Horizons in American Art*. New York: Museum of Modern Art, 1936.

Caldwell, Erskine, and Margaret Bourke-White. *You Have Seen Their Faces*. New York: Modern Age Books, 1937.

Callahan, Sean, ed. *The Photographs of Margaret Bourke-White*. Greenwich, Conn.: New York Graphic Society, 1972.

Calvet, Louis-Jean. *Roland Barthes*. Translated by Sarah Wykes. Bloomington and Indianapolis: Indiana University Press, 1994.

Campbell, D'ann. *Women at War with America: Private Lives in a Patriotic Era*. Cambridge, Mass.: Harvard University Press, 1984.

Canetti, Elias. *Crowds and Power*. Translated by Carol Stewart. New York: Seabury Press, 1978.

Carole Lombard in "Love before Breakfast." Picture no. 757. February 26, 1936. New York State Archives, Albany, New York.

Carroll, David, ed. *The States of "Theory": History, Art, and Critical Discourses*. New York: Columbia University Press, 1990.

Centre for Contemporary Cultural Studies. *The Empire Strikes Back: Race and Racism in 70s Britain*. London: Hutchinson and the Centre for Contemporary Cultural Studies, University of Birmingham, 1984.

Cheever, Benjamin, ed. *The Letters of John Cheever.* New York: Simon and Schuster, 1988.

Chibnall, Steve. "Whistle and Zoot: The Changing Meaning of a Suit of Clothes." *History Workshop Journal,* no. 20 (1985): 56–81.

Clark, T. J. *The Absolute Bourgeois: Artists and Politics in France, 1848–1851.* London: Thames and Hudson, 1973.

———. "The Conditions of Artistic Creation." *Times Literary Supplement,* May 24, 1974, 562.

———. *Image of the People: Gustave Courbet and the 1848 Revolution.* London: Thames and Hudson, 1973.

Clastres, Pierre. *Society against the State.* Translated by Robert Hurley. New York: Zone Books, 1989.

Cosgrove, Stuart. "The Zoot Suit and Style Warfare." In *Zoot Suits and Second-Hand Dresses: An Anthology of Fashion and Music,* ed. Angela McRobbie, 3–22. Boston: Unwin Hyman, 1988. Originally published in *History Workshop Journal,* no. 18 (Autumn 1984): 77–91.

Cousins, Mark. "The Practice of Historical Investigation." In *Poststructuralism and the Question of History,* ed. Derek Attridge, Geoff Bennington, and Robert Young, 126–36. Cambridge and New York: Cambridge University Press, 1987.

Coward, Rosalind, and John Ellis. *Language and Materialism: Developments in Semiology and the Theory of the Subject.* London: Routledge and Kegan Paul, 1977.

Crary, Jonathan. "Modernizing Vision." In *Vision and Visuality,* ed. Hal Foster. Discussions in Contemporary Culture no. 2. Seattle, Wash.: Bay Press, 1988.

———. *Techniques of the Observer: On Vision and Modernity in the Nineteenth Century.* Cambridge, Mass., and London: MIT Press/October Books, 1990.

Crow, Thomas. "Art History as Tertiary Text." *Art in America* 78, no. 4 (April 1990): 43–45.

Daniel, P., M. A. Foresta, M. Stange, and S. Stein. *Official Images: New Deal Photography.* Washington, D.C., and London: Smithsonian Institution Press, 1987.

Davis, Mike. *Prisoners of the American Dream: Politics and Economy in the History of the U.S. Working Class.* London: Verso, 1986.

Davis, Stuart. "Abstract Painting Today." In *Art for the Millions,* ed. Francis O'Connor. Boston: New York Graphic Society, 1975.

de Man, Paul. *Aesthetic Ideology.* Minneapolis: University of Minnesota Press, 1997.

————. *Allegories of Reading: Figural Language in Rousseau, Nietzsche, Rilke, and Proust.* New Haven, Conn., and London: Yale University Press, 1979.

Debord, Guy. *Society of Spectacle.* Detroit, Mich.: Black and Red, 1970.

Deleuze, Gilles. *Foucault.* Translated by Seán Hand. Minneapolis: University of Minnesota Press, 1988.

Deleuze, Gilles, and Félix Guattari. *Anti-Oedipus: Capitalism and Schizophrenia.* Translated by Mark Seem, Robert Hurley, and Helen Lane. New York: Viking, 1978.

————. *A Thousand Plateaus: Capitalism and Schizophrenia.* Translated by Brian Massumi. Minneapolis: University of Minnesota Press, 1987.

Denby, Charles [Matthew Ward, pseud.]. *Indignant Heart: The Testimony of a Black American Worker.* London: Pluto Press, 1979.

Derrida, Jacques. *Archive Fever: A Freudian Impression.* Translated by Eric Prenowitz. Chicago and London: University of Chicago Press, 1996.

————. "Cogito et histoire de la folie." In *Ecriture et la différence.* Paris: Points-Seuil, 1967.

————. "The Deaths of Roland Barthes." Translated by Pascale-Anne Brault and Michael Naas. In *Philosophy and Non-Philosophy since Merleau-Ponty,* ed. Hugh J. Silverman, 259–96. New York and London: Routledge, 1988.

————. "Force of Law: The 'Mystical Foundations of Authority.'" In *Deconstruction and the Possibility of Justice,* ed. Drucilla Cornell, Michel Rosenfeld, and David Gray Carlson, 3–67. New York: Routledge, 1992.

————. "FORS." Translated by Barbara Johnson. *Georgia Review* 31, no. 1 (Spring 1977): 64–116.

————. *Of Grammatology.* Translated by G. C. Spivak. Baltimore, Md.: The Johns Hopkins University Press, 1976.

————. "Signature Event Context." In *Margins of Philosophy,* trans. Alan Bass. Chicago: University of Chicago Press, 1982.

————. "Some Statements and Truisms about Neologisms, Newisms, Postisms, Parasitisms, and Other Small Seisisms." Translated by Anne Tomiche. In *The States of "Theory": History, Art, and Critical Discourses,* ed. David Carroll. New York: Columbia University Press, 1990.

————. *The Truth in Painting.* Translated by Geoff Bennington and Ian McLeod. Chicago and London: University of Chicago Press, 1987.

————. *Writing and Difference.* Translated by Alan Bass. Chicago: University of Chicago Press, 1978.

Derrida, Jacques, and Marie-Françoise Plissart. "Right of Inspection." Translated by David Wills. *Art and Text,* no. 32 (Autumn 1989): 20–97.

Dialogue Continuity on "Chatterbox." Production no. 870. December 19, 1935. New York State Archives, Albany, New York.

Drabeck, Bernard A., and Hellen E. Ellis, eds. *Archibald MacLeish: Reflections.* Amherst: University of Massachusetts Press, 1986.

Drake, St. Clair, and Horace R. Cayton. *Black Metropolis: A Study of Negro Life in a Northern City.* New York: Harcourt, Brace, 1945.

Edelman, Bernard. *Le droit saisi par la photographie.* Paris: Librairie François Maspero, 1973.

———. *Ownership of the Image: Elements for a Marxist Theory of Law.* Translated by Elizabeth Kingdom. London: Routledge and Kegan Paul, 1979.

Elliott, George P. *Dorothea Lange.* New York: Museum of Modern Art, 1966.

Ellison, Ralph. *Invisible Man.* New York: Vintage Books, 1990.

Evans, Walker. *American Photographs.* New York: Museum of Modern Art, 1938.

———. *American Photographs.* Reprint, New York: Museum of Modern Art, n.d. [1962]. Distributed by Doubleday.

———. "Come On Down." *Architecture Forum,* July 1962, 96–100.

———. *First and Last.* London: Secker and Warburg, 1978.

———. "Interview with Walter Evans." By Leslie Katz. *Art in America* 59, no. 2 (March–April 1971).

———. Lecture at Harvard University, April 8, 1975. In *Degrees of Guidance: Essays on Twentieth-Century American Photography,* ed. Peter C. Bunnell. Cambridge: Cambridge University Press, 1993. Originally published as "Walker Evans on Himself," ed. Lincoln Caplan, *New Republic,* November 13, 1976, 23–27.

———. "The Reappearance of Photography." *Hound and Horn* 5, no. 1 (October–December 1931): 125–28.

———. Walker Evans Archive. Metropolitan Museum of Art, New York.

———. *Walker Evans: Photographs for the Farm Security Administration, 1935–1938.* New York: Da Capo Press, 1975.

———. "Walker Evans, Visiting Artist: A Transcript of His Discussion with the Students of the University of Michigan." In *Photography: Essays and Images. Illustrated Readings in the History of Photography,* ed. Beaumont Newhall. New York: Museum of Modern Art, 1980.

———. "When 'Downtown' Was a Beautiful Mess." *Fortune,* January 1962, 100–106.

Faris, R. E. *Chicago Sociology: 1920–1932.* Chicago: University of Chicago Press, 1967.

Farley, Philip. *Criminals of America, or Tales of the Lives of Thieves: Enabling Every One to Be His Own Detective. With Portraits, Making a Complete Rogue's Gallery.* New York: Author's edition, 1876.

Feher, Michel. "Mass, Crowd, and Pack." In *Multiplicity, Proliferation, Reconvention*, ed. Jeremy Gilbert-Rolfe and John Johnston. Special feature for *Journal: A Contemporary Art Magazine* 5, no. 42 (Fall 1985).

Fischel, Leslie H., Jr. "The Negro in the New Deal Era." *Wisconsin Magazine of History* 48 (Winter 1964–65): 111–23.

Fisher, Andrea. *Let Us Now Praise Famous Women: Women Photographers for the U.S. Government, 1935 to 1944. Esther Bubley, Marjory Collins, Pauline Ehrlich, Dorothea Lange, Martha McMillan Roberts, Marion Post Wolcott, Ann Rosener, Louise Rosskam*. London and New York: Pandora Press, 1987.

Fleischhauer, Carl, and Beverly W. Brannan, eds. *Documenting America, 1935–1943*. Berkeley, Los Angeles, and London: University of California Press, in association with the Library of Congress, 1988.

Foucault, Michel. *Birth of the Clinic: An Archaeology of Medical Perception*. Translated by A. M. Sheridan Smith. London: Tavistock, 1973.

———. *Discipline and Punish: The Birth of the Prison*. Translated by Alan Sheridan. New York: Vintage Books, 1979.

———. "The Discourse on Language." Translated by Rupert Swyer. Appendix to *The Archaeology of Knowledge*, trans. A. M. Sheridan Smith. New York: Pantheon Books, 1972. Originally published as *L'ordre du discours*. Paris: Editions Gallimard, 1971.

———. *The Essential Works of Foucault, 1954–1984*. Vol. 1, *Ethics: Subjectivity and Truth*. Edited by Paul Rabinow. Translated by Robert Hurley et al. New York: New Press, 1997.

———. *The Essential Works of Foucault, 1954–1984*. Vol. 3, *Power*. Edited by James D. Faubion. Translated by Robert Hurley et al. New York: New Press, 2000.

———. *Foucault Live (Interviews, 1966–84)*. Edited by Sylvère Lotringer. New York: Semiotext(e), 1989.

———. "My Body, This Paper, This Fire." Translated by Geoff Bennington. *Oxford Literary Review* 4, no. 1 (1979): 9–28. Originally published as "Mon corps, ce papier, ce feu." *Paideia*, September 1971.

———. *Power/Knowledge: Selected Interviews and Other Writings, 1972–1977*. Edited by Colin Gordon. Brighton, U.K.: Harvester Press, 1980.

———. "*Society Must Be Defended*": Lectures at the Collège de France, 1975–1976. Edited by Mauro Bertani and Alessandro Fontana. Translated by David Macey. New York: Picador, 2003.

Frank, Miriam. *The Life and Times of Rosie the Riveter*. Emeryville, Calif.: Clarity Educational Productions, 1982.

Freud, Sigmund. *The Complete Introductory Lectures on Psychoanalysis*. Translated and edited by James Strachey. New York: W. W. Norton, 1966.

———. "Mourning and Melancholia." In *The Standard Edition*, ed. James Strachey, 14:243–58. London: Hogarth Press and Institute of Psycho-Analysis, 1957.

———. "Some Psychological Consequences of the Anatomical Distinction between the Sexes (1925)." In *Sexuality and the Psychology of Love*, ed. Philip Rieff. New York: Macmillan, 1963.

Galassi, Peter. "A Note on the Fiftieth-Anniversary Edition." In Walker Evans, *American Photographs*. New York: Museum of Modern Art, 1988.

Gardner, Lloyd C. "The New Deal, New Frontiers, and the Cold War: A Re-examination of American Expansion, 1933–1945." In *Corporations and the Cold War*, ed. David Horowitz, 105–41. New York and London: Monthly Review Press, 1969.

Gilbert, James B. *Writers and Partisans: A History of Literary Radicalism in America*. New York: Wiley, 1968.

Gilbert-Rolfe, Jeremy, and John Johnston. "Multiplicity, Proliferation, Reconvention." In *Multiplicity, Proliferation, Reconvention*, ed. Jeremy Gilbert-Rolfe and John Johnston. Special feature for *Journal: A Contemporary Art Magazine* 5, no. 42 (Fall 1985).

Goldberg, Vicki. *Margaret Bourke-White: A Biography*. New York: Harper and Row, 1986.

Goldin, Claudia. *The Role of World War II in the Rise of Women's Work*. Cambridge, Mass.: National Bureau of Economic Research, 1989.

Gonzáles, Raphael Jesús. "Pachuco: The Birth of a Creole Language." *Arizona Quarterly* 23, no. 4 (Winter 1967): 343–56.

Goode, George Brown (assistant secretary of the Smithsonian Institution in charge of the National Museum). "Report of the Assistant Secretary." *Report of the National Museum*. Washington, D.C.: National Museum, 1893.

———, ed. *The Smithsonian Institution, 1846–1896: The History of Its First Half Century*. Washington, D.C.: De Vinne Press, 1897.

Goodwin, E. Marvin. *Black Migration in America from 1915 to 1960: An Uneasy Exodus*. Lewiston, N.Y.: E. Mellen Press, 1990.

Gower, H. D., L. Stanley Jast, and W. W. Topley. *The Camera as Historian*. London: Sampson Low, Marston, 1916.

Green, James. "Fighting on Two Fronts: Working-Class Militancy in the 1940's." *Radical America* 9, nos. 4–5 (July–August 1975): 7–47.

Grierson, John. "Documentary Photography—Motion Pictures: Part 1: The Documentary Idea." In *The Complete Photographer*, ed. Willard D. Morgan, 4, no. 21 (April 10, 1942), and 4, no. 22 (April 20, 1942). Chicago: National Educational Alliance, 1942.

———. *Grierson on Documentary*. Edited by Forsyth Hardy. London: William Collins Sons, 1946.

———. *Grierson on Documentary*. Edited by Forsyth Hardy. New York: Harcourt, Brace, 1947.

———. *Grierson on Documentary*. Edited by Forsyth Hardy. London: Faber and Faber, 1966.

———. *Grierson on Documentary*. Edited by Forsyth Hardy. London and Boston: Faber and Faber, 1979.

———. *Grierson on the Movies*. Edited by Forsyth Hardy. London and Boston: Faber and Faber, 1981.

Griffith, Beatrice. *American Me*. Boston: Houghton Mifflin, 1948.

Groh, George W. *The Black Migration: The Journey to Urban America*. New York: Weybright and Talley, 1972.

Hall, Stuart. "The Social Eye of *Picture Post*." *Working Papers in Cultural Studies* (Birmingham Centre for Contemporary Cultural Studies), no. 2 (Spring 1972): 71–120.

———. "What Is This 'Black' in Black Popular Culture?" In *Black Popular Culture*, ed. Gina Dent, 21–33. Seattle: Bay Press, 1992.

Hambourg, Maria Morris, Jeff L. Rosenheim, Douglas Eklund, and Mia Fineman. *Walker Evans*. New York: Metropolitan Museum of Art, 2000. Published in association with Princeton University Press.

Hamby, Alonzo L., ed. *The New Deal: Analysis and Interpretation*. New York and London: Longman, 1981.

Hardt, Michael, and Antonio Negri. *Multitude: War and Democracy in the Age of Empire*. London and New York: Penguin Books, 2004.

Harlow, Alvin F. *Old Bowery Days: The Chronicles of a Famous Street*. New York: D. Appleton, 1931.

Harrison, Alferdteen, ed. *Black Exodus: The Great Migration from the American South*. Jackson: University Press of Mississippi, 1991.

Hartmann, Susan. *The Home Front and Beyond: American Women in the 1940s*. Boston: Twayne, 1982.

Hatch, Connie. "The Desublimation of Romance." In "Sexuality: Re/Positions," ed. Sylvia Kolbowski. Special issue, *Wedge*, no. 6 (Winter 1984): 20–23.

Hegel, G. W. F. *Faith and Knowledge*. Translated by Walter Cerf and H. S. Harris. Albany: State University of New York Press, 1977.

———. *Glauben und Wissen, oder Die Reflexionsphilosophie der Subjectivität in der Vollständigkeit ihrer Formen, als Kantische, Jacobische, und Fichtesche Philosophie*. In *Jenaer Kritische Schriften*, ed. Hartmut Buchner and Otto Pöggeler, in *Gesammelte Werke*, 4:313–414. Hamburg: Felix Meiner Verlag, 1968.

———. *Grundlinien der Philosophie des Rechts oder Naturrecht und Staatswissenschaft im Grundrisse.* Vol. 7 of *Werke.* Frankfurt am Main: Suhrkamp Verlag, 1970.

———. *Hegel's Philosophy of Right.* Translated by T. M. Knox. Oxford: Clarendon Press, 1942.

———. *Phänomenologie des Geistes.* Edited by Wolfgang Bonsiepen and Reinhard Heede. Vol. 9 of *Gesammelte Werke.* Hamburg: Felix Meiner Verlag, 1980.

———. *The Phenomenology of Mind.* Translated by J. B. Baillie. London: George Allen and Unwin; New York: Macmillan, 1931.

———. *Phenomenology of Spirit.* Translated by A. V. Miller. Oxford and New York: Oxford University Press, 1977.

———. *The Philosophy of History.* Translated by J. Sibree. New York: Dover, 1956.

Hendrickson, Paul. *Looking for the Light: The Hidden Life and Art of Marion Post Wolcott.* New York: Alfred A. Knopf, 1992.

Herschel, Sir John. "Note on the Art of Photography, or The Application of the Chemical Rays of Light to the Purpose of Pictorial Representation." *Proceedings of the Royal Society* 4 (March 14, 1839).

Hervey, Mary F. S. *Holbein's "Ambassadors": The Picture and the Men.* London: George Bell and Sons, 1900.

Hill, Paul, Angela Kelly, and John Tagg. *Three Perspectives on Photography.* London: Arts Council of Great Britain, 1979.

Honey, Maureen. *Creating Rosie the Riveter: Class, Gender, and Propaganda during World War II.* Amherst: University of Massachusetts Press, 1984.

Houlgate, Stephen. *Freedom, Truth, and History: An Introduction to Hegel's Philosophy.* London and New York: Routledge, 1991.

Hugunin, James R. "Disputing Grounds." *Views* 13, no. 4, and 14, no. 1 (Winter 1993).

Hunt, Lynn. "History beyond Social Theory." In *The States of "Theory": History, Art, and Critical Discourses,* ed. David Carroll. New York: Columbia University Press, 1990.

Hunter, Ian. *Culture and Government: The Emergence of Literary Education.* London: Macmillan, 1988.

Hurley, F. Jack. *Marion Post Wolcott: A Photographic Journey.* Albuquerque: University of New Mexico Press, 1989.

———. *Portrait of a Decade: Roy Stryker and the Development of Documentary Photography in the Thirties.* Baton Rouge: Louisiana State University Press, 1972.

Jaeschke, Walter. "Politik, Kultur, und Philosophie in Preussen." In *Kunsterfahrung und Kulturpolitik im Berlin Hegels,* ed. Otto Pöggeler and Annemarie Gethmann-Siefert, 29–48. Hegel-Studien, vol. 22. Bonn: Bouvier Verlag Herbert Grundman, 1983.

————. *Reason in Religion: The Foundation of Hegel's Philosophy of Religion.* Translated by J. Michael Stewart and Peter C. Hodgson. Berkeley, Los Angeles, and Oxford: University of California Press, 1990.

Jameson, Fredric. *Postmodernism, or The Cultural Logic of Late Capitalism.* Durham, N.C.: Duke University Press, 1991.

Johnson, Charles S. *Growing Up in the Black Belt: Negro Youth in the Rural South.* Washington, D.C.: American Council on Education, 1941.

————. *Shadow of the Plantation.* Chicago: University of Chicago Press, 1934.

Johnson, Charles S., Edwin R. Embree, and W. W. Alexander. *The Collapse of Cotton Tenancy: Summary of Field Studies and Statistical Surveys, 1933–35.* Chapel Hill: University of North Carolina Press, 1935.

Kant, Immanuel. *The Critique of Judgement.* Translated by James Creed Meredith. Oxford: Clarendon Press, 1952.

Kaplan, Robert D. "The Coming Anarchy." *Atlantic Monthly,* February 1994, 44–76.

Keller, Ulrich. *The Highway as Habitat: A Roy Stryker Documentation, 1943–1955.* Santa Barbara, Calif.: University Art Museum, 1986.

Kinnamon, Keneth, and Michel Fabre, eds. *Conversations with Richard Wright.* Jackson: University Press of Mississippi, 1993.

Kirby, John B. *Black Americans in the Roosevelt Era: Liberalism and Race.* Knoxville: University of Tennessee Press, 1980.

Kirstein, Lincoln. "Photographs of America: Walker Evans." In Walker Evans, *American Photographs.* New York: Museum of Modern Art, 1938.

Klemm, Gustav Friedrich. *Allgemeine Cultur-Geschichte der Menschheit.* Leipzig: B. G. Teubner, 1843–52.

————. *Allgemeine Culturwissenschaft.* Leipzig: Romberg, 1854–55.

Kristeva, Julia. *Black Sun: Depression and Melancholia.* Translated by Leon S. Roudiez. New York: Columbia University Press, 1989.

————. *Julia Kristeva: Interviews.* Edited by Ross Mitchell Guberman. New York: Columbia University Press, 1996.

Kroeber, A. L., and Clyde Kluckhohn. *Culture: A Critical Review of Concepts and Definitions.* Papers of the Peabody Museum of American Archaeology and Ethnology, Harvard University, vol. 42, no. 1. Cambridge, Mass.: The Museum, 1952.

Lacan, Jacques. "Desire and the Interpretation of Desire in *Hamlet.*" *Yale French Studies,* nos. 55–56 (1977): 11–52.

————. *The Four Fundamental Concepts of Psycho-Analysis.* Edited by Jacques-Alain Miller. Translated by Alan Sheridan. Harmondsworth, U.K.: Penguin Books, 1979.

———. *Le séminaire*. Book 11, *Les quatre concepts fondamentaux de la psychanalyse, 1964*. Text established by Jacques-Alain Miller. Paris: Editions du Seuil, 1973.

Laclau, Ernesto, and Chantal Mouffe. *Hegemony and Socialist Strategy: Towards a Radical Democratic Politics*. London and New York: Verso, 1985.

Lange, Dorothea, and Paul Schuster Taylor. *An American Exodus: A Record of Human Erosion*. New York: Reynal and Hitchcock, 1939.

———. *An American Exodus: A Record of Human Erosion in the Thirties*. New Haven, Conn., and London: Yale University Press, 1969.

Lasch, Christopher. *The Agony of the American Left: One Hundred Years of Radicalism*. Harmondsworth, U.K.: Penguin Books, 1973.

Lebensztejn, Jean-Claude. *Zigzag*. Paris: Flammarion, 1981.

Lecercle, Jean-Jacques. *The Violence of Language*. London and New York: Routledge, 1990.

Lemann, Nicholas. *The Promised Land: The Great Black Migration and How It Changed America*. New York: Alfred A. Knopf, 1991.

Lenin, V. I. *Selected Works of V. I. Lenin*. Vol. 2. Moscow: Foreign Languages Publishing House, 1952.

———. *The State and Revolution*. Peking: Foreign Languages Press, 1965.

———. "Writings on the Commune." In Karl Marx and V. I. Lenin, *Civil War in France: The Paris Commune*, 89–129. New York: International Publishers, 1988.

Leuchtenburg, William E. *Franklin D. Roosevelt and the New Deal, 1932–1940*. New York: Harper and Row, 1963.

Lévi-Strauss, Claude. *The Savage Mind*. Chicago: University of Chicago Press, 1966.

Levy, Michael. *National Gallery Catalogues: The German School*. London: National Gallery Publications Department, 1959.

Lorentz, Pare. "Dorothea Lange: Camera with a Purpose." In *U.S. Camera Annual 1941*, ed. T. J. Mahoney, vol. 1, *America*. New York: Duell, Sloan and Pearce, 1941.

Lübbe, Hermann. "Deutscher Idealismus als Philosophie Preussischer Kulturpolitik." In *Kunsterfahrung und Kulturpolitik im Berlin Hegels*, ed. Otto Pöggeler and Annemarie Gethmann-Siefert, 3–27. Hegel-Studien, vol. 22. Bonn: Bouvier Verlag Herbert Grundman, 1983.

Luckenbill, Dan. *The Pachuco Era*. Catalog of an exhibit at the University Research Library, Department of Special Collections, September–October 1990. Los Angeles: University of California, Los Angeles, 1990.

Lyotard, Jean-François. *The Differend: Phrases in Dispute*. Translated by Georges Van Den Abbeele. Minneapolis: University of Minnesota Press, 1988.

————. *The Inhuman: Reflections on Time.* Translated by Geoffrey Bennington and Rachel Bowlby. Stanford, Calif.: Stanford University Press, 1991.

————. *Postmodern Fables.* Translated by Georges Van Den Abbeele. Minneapolis and London: University of Minnesota Press, 1997.

MacCabe, Colin. "Realism and the Cinema: Some Notes on Brechtian Theses." *Screen* 15, no. 2 (Summer 1974).

————. *Tracking the Signifier. Theoretical Essays: Film, Linguistics, Literature.* Minneapolis: University of Minnesota Press, 1985.

MacLeish, Archibald. *Land of the Free.* New York: Harcourt, Brace, 1938.

————. "The Soundtrack-and-Picture Form: A New Direction." In *New Directions in Prose and Poetry*, vol. 3. Norfolk, Conn.: New Directions, 1938.

————. "Unemployed Arts: WPA's Four Arts Projects. Their Origins, Their Operation." *Fortune*, May 1937, 108–17.

Madrid-Barela, Arturo. "In Search of the Authentic Pachuco: An Interpretive Essay." *Aztlán* 4, no. 1 (Spring 1973): 31–60.

Maharidge, Dale, and Michael Williamson. *And Their Children after Them: The Legacy of "Let Us Now Praise Famous Men": James Agee, Walker Evans, and the Rise and Fall of Cotton in the South.* New York: Pantheon Books, 1989.

Marx, Karl. *Capital: A Critique of Political Economy.* Vol. 1. Translated by Ben Fowkes. New York: Vintage Books, 1977.

————. "The Civil War in France." In Karl Marx and V. I. Lenin, *Civil War in France: The Paris Commune.* New York: International Publishers, 1988.

————. "The Eighteenth Brumaire of Louis Bonaparte." In Karl Marx and Frederick Engels, *Collected Works*, vol. 11. London: Lawrence and Wishart, 1979.

Matuszewski, Boleslas. *Boleslaw Matuszewski I Jego Pionierska Mysl Filowa: Dokumenty i wstepne kometarze.* Warsaw: Filmoteka Polska, 1980.

————. *Une nouvelle source de l'histoire (Création d'un dépot de cinématographie historique).* Paris: Imprimerie Noizetie, 1898.

Mazón, Mauricio. *The Zoot-Suit Riots: The Psychology of Symbolic Annihilation.* Austin: University of Texas Press, 1984.

McCausland, Elizabeth. "Photographic Books." In *The Complete Photographer*, ed. Willard D. Morgan, 8, no. 43 (November 20, 1942): 2783–94. Chicago: National Educational Alliance, 1942.

McCoy, Donald R. *Coming of Age: The United States during the 1920s and 1930s.* Harmondsworth, U.K.: Penguin Books, 1973.

McElvaine, Robert S. *The Great Depression: America, 1929–1941.* New York: Times Books, 1993.

McKay, Claude. *Harlem: Negro Metropolis*. New York: E. P. Dutton, 1940.

McLennan, Gregor, David Held, and Stuart Hall, eds. *The Idea of the Modern State*. Milton Keynes, U.K., and Philadelphia: Open University Press, 1984.

Mellow, James R. *Walker Evans*. New York: Basic Books, 1999.

Meltzer, Milton. *Dorothea Lange: A Photographer's Life*. New York: Farrar Straus Giroux, 1978.

Mercer, Kobena. "Black Hair/Style Politics." *New Formations*, no. 3 (Winter 1987): 33–54.

Milkman, Ruth. "Redefining 'Women's Work': The Sexual Division of Labor in the Auto Industry during World War II." *Feminist Studies* 8 (Summer 1982): 337–72.

Miller, Francis Trevelyan, editor in chief. *The Photographic History of the Civil War*. 10 vols. New York: Review of Reviews, 1911.

Miller, Jacques-Alain. "Le despotisme de l'Utile: La machine panoptique de Jeremy Bentham." *Ornicar? Bulletin périodique du Champ freudien* 3 (May 1975).

Milligan, Harry. "The Manchester Photographic Survey Record." *Manchester Review* 7 (Autumn 1958): 193–204.

Mitchell, Timothy. "The World as Exhibition." *Comparative Studies in Society and History* 31, no. 2 (1989).

Montoya, José. *Pachuco Art: A Historical Update*. Sacramento, Calif.: Royal Chicano Air Force, 1977.

Moore, Jack B. "The Voice in *12 Million Black Voices*." *Mississippi Quarterly* 42, no. 4 (Fall 1989): 415–24.

Moore, Joan W. *Homeboys: Gangs, Drugs, and Prison in the Barrios of Los Angeles*. Philadelphia: Temple University Press, 1978.

Mora, Gilles, and John T. Hill. *Walker Evans: The Hungry Eye*. New York: Harry N. Abrams, 1993.

Morris, Lloyd. *Incredible New York: High Life and Low Life of the Last Hundred Years*. New York: Random House, 1951.

Natanson, Nicholas. *The Black Image in the New Deal: The Politics of FSA Photography*. Knoxville: University of Tennessee Press, 1992.

Newhall, Beaumont. "Documentary Approach to Photography." *Parnassus* 10, no. 3 (March 1938).

Nichols, Bill. "Documentary Film and the Modernist Avant-Garde." *Critical Inquiry* 27, no. 4 (Summer 2001).

O'Doherty, Brian. "Inside the White Cube: Notes on Gallery Space. Part I." *Artforum* 14, no. 7 (March 1976): 24–30.

———. "Inside the White Cube: Part II. The Eye and the Spectator." *Artforum* 14, no. 8 (April 1976): 26–34.

————. "Inside the White Cube: Part III. Context as Content." *Artforum* 15, no. 3 (November 1976): 38–44.

Owens, Craig. "Photography *en abyme*." *October*, no. 5 (Summer 1978).

Palmer, Robert. *Deep Blues*. New York: Viking, 1981.

Park, R. E., and R. D. McKenzie, eds. *The City*. Chicago: University of Chicago Press, 1967.

Partridge, Elizabeth, ed. *Dorothea Lange: A Visual Life*. Washington and London: Smithsonian Institution Press, 1994.

Patterson, James T. *Congressional Conservatism and the New Deal*. Lexington: University Press of Kentucky, 1967.

Paz, Octavio. "The *Pachuco* and Other Extremes." In *The Labyrinth of Solitude: Life and Thought in Mexico*, trans. Lysander Kemp, 9–28. New York: Grove Press, 1961.

Penrose, Antony, ed. *Lee Miller's War: Photographer and Correspondent with the Allies in Europe, 1944–45*. Boston: Bulfinch Press, 1992.

————. *The Lives of Lee Miller*. New York: Holt, Rinehart, and Winston, 1985.

Pinkard, Terry. *Hegel: A Biography*. Cambridge: Cambridge University Press, 2000.

Plattner, Steven W. *Roy Stryker, U.S.A., 1943–1950: The Standard Oil (New Jersey) Photography Project*. Austin: University of Texas Press, 1983.

Porter, David L. *Congress and the Waning of the New Deal*. Port Washington, N.Y.: Kennikat, 1979.

Pugin, A., and A. W. Pugin. *Examples of Gothic Architecture: Selected from Various Ancient Edifices in England*. 3 vols. London: H. G. Bohn, 1850.

Quick, Paddy. "Rosie the Riveter: Myths and Realities." *Radical America* 9, nos. 4–5 (July–August 1975): 115–31.

Rabinowitz, Paula. *They Must Be Represented: The Politics of Documentary*. London and New York: Verso, 1994.

Radosh, Ronald. "The Myth of the New Deal." In *A New History of Leviathan: Essays on the Rise of the American Corporate State*, ed. Ronald Radosh and Murray Rothbard, 146–87. New York: E. P. Dutton, 1972.

Rathbone, Belinda. *Walker Evans: A Biography*. Boston and New York: Houghton Mifflin, 1995.

Raymond, Margaret Thomsen. "Girl with a Camera, Margaret Bourke-White." In *Topflight: Famous American Women*, ed. Anne Stoddard. New York: Thomas Nelson and Sons, 1946.

Readings, Bill. "The Deconstruction of Politics." In *Reading De Man Reading*, ed. Lindsay Waters and Wlad Godzich. Minneapolis: University of Minnesota Press, 1989.

———. *Introducing Lyotard: Art and Politics.* London and New York: Routledge, 1991.

Rees, A. L., and Frances Borzello, eds. *The New Art History: An Anthology.* London: Camden Press, 1985.

Reilly, John M. "Reconstruction of Genre as Entry into Conscious History." *Black American Literature Forum* 13 (Spring 1979).

———. "Richard Wright Preaches the Nation." *Black American Literature Forum* 16 (Fall 1982).

Reilly, Rosa. "Why Margaret Bourke-White Is at the Top." *Popular Photography,* July 1937.

Robbe-Grillet, Alain. *Ghosts in the Mirror: A Romanesque.* Translated by Jo Levy. New York: Grove Weidenfeld, 1988.

Rosenheim, Jeff L. "'The Cruel Radiance of What Is': Walker Evans and the South." In Maria Morris Hambourg, Jeff L. Rosenheim, Douglas Eklund, and Mia Fineman, *Walker Evans.* New York: Metropolitan Museum of Art, 2000. Published in association with Princeton University Press.

Rosenheim, Jeff L., and Douglas Eklund. *Unclassified: A Walker Evans Anthology.* New York: Metropolitan Museum of Art; Zurich: Scalo, 2000.

Rosler, Martha. "The Bowery in Two Inadequate Descriptive Systems." In *Three Works.* Halifax: Press of the Nova Scotia College of Art and Design, 1981.

Ross, Kristin. *The Emergence of Social Space: Rimbaud and the Paris Commune.* Minneapolis: University of Minnesota Press, 1988.

Rosskam, Edwin. "Not Intended for Framing: The FSA Archive." *Afterimage* 18, no. 8 (March 1981): 9–11.

Rothstein, Arthur. "Direction in the Picture Story." In *The Complete Photographer,* ed. Willard D. Morgan, 4, no. 21 (April 10, 1942). Chicago: National Educators Alliance, 1943.

Rowe, Mike. *Chicago Breakdown.* London: Eddison Press, 1973.

Rupp, Leila. *Mobilizing Women for War: German and American Propaganda, 1939–1945.* Princeton, N.J.: Princeton University Press, 1978.

Sanchez-Tranquilino, Marcos. "*Mano a mano:* An Essay on the Representation of the Zoot Suit and Its Misrepresentation by Octavio Paz." *Journal* (Los Angeles Institute of Contemporary Art) (Winter 1987): 34–42.

Sanchez-Tranquilino, Marcos, and John Tagg. "The Pachuco's Flayed Hide: The Museum, Identity, and *Buenas Garras.*" In *Chicano Art: Resistance and Affirmation, 1965–1985,* ed. Richard Griswold del Castillo, Teresa McKenna, and Yvonne Yarbro-Bejarano, 97–108. Los Angeles: Wight Art Gallery, University of California, Los Angeles, 1991.

Schapiro, Meyer. "On Some Problems in the Semiotics of Visual Art: Field and Vehicle in Image-Signs." *Semiotica* 1, no. 3 (1969): 223–42.

Schlesinger, Arthur M., Jr. *The Age of Roosevelt.* 3 vols. Boston: Houghton Mifflin, 1957–60.

Schor, Naomi. "*Cartes Postales:* Representing Paris, 1900," *Critical Inquiry* 18, no. 2 (Winter 1992): 188–244.

Sebald, W. G. *The Emigrants.* Translated by Michael Hulse. New York: New Directions Books, 1997.

Sekaer, Peter. *American Pictures.* Andover, Mass.: Addison Gallery of American Art, Phillips Academy; New York: Howard Greenberg Gallery, 1999.

Sekula, Allan. "The Body and the Archive." *October,* no. 39 (Winter 1986).

———. "Dismantling Modernism, Reinventing Documentary (Notes on the Politics of Representation." In *Photography against the Grain: Essays and Photo Works, 1973–1983,* 53–75. Halifax: Press of the Nova Scotia College of Art and Design, 1984.

Silverman, Kaja. "Fassbinder and Lacan: A Reconsideration of Gaze, Look, and Image." *Camera Obscura,* no. 19 (January 1989): 55–84.

———. *Male Subjectivity at the Margins.* New York and London: Routledge, 1992.

———. *The Threshold of the Visible World.* New York and London: Routledge, 1996.

Sitkoff, Harvard. *A New Deal for Blacks: The Emergence of Civil Rights as a National Issue.* New York: Oxford University Press, 1978.

Solomon-Godeau, Abigail. "Reconstructing Documentary: Connie Hatch's Representational Resistance." In *Photography at the Dock: Essays on Photographic History, Institutions, and Practices,* 184–217. Minneapolis: University of Minnesota Press, 1991.

Spear, Allan H. *Black Chicago: The Making of a Negro Ghetto, 1890–1920.* Chicago: University of Chicago Press, 1967.

Stange, Maren. *Symbols of Ideal Life: Social Documentary Photography in America, 1890–1950.* Cambridge and New York: Cambridge University Press, 1989.

Stansell, Christine. *City of Women: Sex and Class in New York, 1789–1860.* Urbana and Chicago: University of Illinois Press, 1987.

Steichen, Edward. "The F.S.A. Photographers." In *U.S. Camera Annual 1939,* ed. T. J. Maloney. New York: William Morrow, 1938.

Stein, Sally. "Figures of the Future: Photography of the National Youth Administration." In Pete Daniel, Merry A. Foresta, Maren Stange, and Sally Stein, *Official Images: New Deal Photography,* 92–107. Washington, D.C.: Smithsonian Institution Press, 1987.

———. "Marion Post Wolcott: Thoughts on Some Lesser Known FSA Photographs." In *Marion Post Wolcott, FSA Photographs*, 3–10. Carmel, Calif.: Friends of Photography, 1983.

Stothard, Charles Alfred. *The Monumental Effigies of Great Britain, Selected from Our Cathedrals and Churches, for the Purpose of Bringing Together, and Preserving Correct Representations of the Best Historical Illustrations Extant, from the Norman Conquest to the Reign of Henry the Eighth*. London, 1817–33.

Stott, William. *Documentary Expression and Thirties America*. Oxford and New York: Oxford University Press, 1973.

Stryker, Roy E. "Documentary Photography." In *The Complete Photographer*, ed. Willard D. Morgan, 4, no. 21 (April 10, 1942). Chicago: National Educational Alliance, 1942.

———. "The FSA Collection of Photographs." In Roy E. Stryker and Nancy Wood, *In This Proud Land: America, 1935–1943, as Seen by the FSA Photographers*. London: Secker and Warburg, 1973.

———. Papers, 1932–64. Archives of American Art, Smithsonian Institution, Washington, D.C.

———. "Still Photography." NDA 4, Roy Emerson Stryker Papers, 1932–64. Archives of American Art, Smithsonian Institution, Washington, D.C. NDA 4.

Stryker, Roy Emerson, and Nancy Wood. *In This Proud Land: America, 1935–1943, as Seen by the FSA Photographers*. London: Secker and Warburg, 1973.

Swanberg, W. A. *Luce and His Empire*. New York: Charles Scribner's Sons, 1972.

Tagg, John. *The Burden of Representation: Essays on Photographies and Histories*. London: Macmillan, 1988.

———. "The Burden of Representation: Photography and the Growth of the State." *Ten: 8*, no. 14 (1984): 10–12.

———. *Grounds of Dispute: Art History, Cultural Politics, and the Discursive Field*. London: Macmillan; Minneapolis: University of Minnesota Press, 1992.

———. "Melancholy Realism: Walker Evans's Resistance to Meaning." *Narrative: The Journal of the Society for the Study of Narrative Literature* 11, no. 1 (January 2003): 3–77.

———. "Power and Photography—Part I: A Means of Surveillance. The Photograph as Evidence in Law." *Screen Education*, no. 36 (Autumn 1980): 17–55.

Talbot, William Henry Fox. *The Pencil of Nature*. New York: Da Capo Press, 1968.

Thompson, Jerry L. "Walker Evans: Some Notes on His Way of Working." In *Walker Evans at Work*. London: Thames and Hudson, 1983.

Trachtenberg, Alan. Foreword to Erskine Caldwell and Margaret Bourke-White, *You Have Seen Their Faces*. Repr., Athens: University of Georgia Press, 1995.

————. "From Image to Story: Reading the File." In *Documenting America, 1935–1943*, ed. Carl Fleischhauer and Beverly W. Brannan, 43–73. Berkeley, Los Angeles, and London: University of California Press, 1988.

————. "Introduction: Photographs as Symbolic History." In National Archives and Records Service, *The American Image: Photographs from the National Archives, 1860–1960*. New York: Pantheon Books, 1979.

————. *Reading American Photographs: Images as History, Mathew Brady to Walker Evans*. New York: Hill and Wang, 1989.

True, Frederick William. "The United States National Museum." In *The Smithsonian Institution, 1846–1896: The History of Its First Half Century*, ed. George Brown Goode. Washington, D.C.: De Vinne Press, 1897.

Turner, Ralph H., and Samuel J. Surace. "Zoot-Suiters and Mexicans." In *Racism in California: A Reader in the History of Oppression*, ed. Roger Daniels and Spencer C. Olm, 210–19. New York: Macmillan, 1972.

U.S. Senate, *Hearings before a Subcommittee of the Committee on Education and Labor, U.S. Senate, 75th Congress, Pursuant to Senate Resolution 266 (74th Congress), A Resolution to Investigate Violations of the Right of Free Speech and Assembly and Interference with the Right of Labor to Organize and Bargain Collectively*. 75 parts. Washington, D.C.: Government Printing Office, 1936–41.

Vanderbilt, Paul. "Reorganization Reports." Paul Vanderbilt Papers. Archives of American Art, Smithsonian Institution, Washington, D.C.

Wainwright, Loudon. *The Great American Magazine: An Inside Story of "Life."* New York: Alfred A. Knopf, 1986.

Weatherford, Doris. *American Women and World War II*. New York: Facts on File, 1990.

Weinstein, James. *Ambiguous Legacy: The Left in American Politics*. New York: New Viewpoints, 1975.

Weldon Johnson, James. *Black Manhattan*. New York: Alfred A. Knopf, 1930.

Williams, Raymond. *Culture and Society, 1780–1950*. London: Chatto and Windus, 1958.

————. *Keywords: A Vocabulary of Culture and Society*. New York: Oxford University Press, 1985.

————. *Politics and Letters: Interviews with New Left Review*. London: Verso, 1981.

Williams, William Carlos. "Sermon with a Camera." *New Republic*, October 12, 1938.

Woofter, T. J., Jr. *Landlord and Tenant on the Cotton Plantation*. New York: New American Studies, 1969.

Works Progress Administration, Federal Writers Program. *Georgia: The WPA Guide to Its Towns and Countryside*. Columbia: University of South Carolina Press, 1990. Originally published in the American Guide Series. Athens: University of Georgia Press, 1940.

Wright, Richard. "How 'Bigger' Was Born." Introduction to *Native Son*, xii–xiii. New York: Harper and Row, 1940. Originally published in the *Saturday Review of Literature*, June 1, 1940.

———. *Lawd Today*. New York: Walker, 1963.

———. *12 Million Black Voices: A Folk History of the Negro in the United States*. Photo-direction [*sic*] by Edwin Rosskam. New York: Viking, 1941.

Wynn, Neil A. *The Afro-American and the Second World War*. New York: Holmes and Meier, 1976.

Wyss, Beat. *Hegel's Art History and the Critique of Modernity*. Translated by Caroline Dobson Saltzwedel. Cambridge: Cambridge University Press, 1999.

Žižek, Slavoj. *Did Somebody Say Totalitarianism? Five Interventions in the (Mis)Use of a Notion*. London and New York: Verso, 2001.

———. *Tarrying with the Negative: Kant, Hegel, and the Critique of Ideology*. Durham, N.C.: Duke University Press, 1993.

Index

actualist cinema, 62

Adams, Ansel, 153

address: mode of (structure of), xxxii, xxxiii, 55, 68, 74, 90, 92, 99

Adelung, Johann Christoph, 41

advertising, 96, 104, 119, 120, 122, 124, 153, 154, 164

Advertising and Selling, 169

Agamben, Giorgio, 176, 328n258

Agee, James, 171, 172, 173, 319n192. *See also Let Us Now Praise Famous Men*

Agriculture, Department of, 89, 132, 140, 156

Altenstein, Karl Sigmund Franz vom Stein zum, 45, 46, 47

Althusser, Louis, 7, 11, 17, 22, 240, 269–70n10

American Association of Advertising Agencies, 99

American Federation of Labor (AFL), 117

American Photographs (Evans), 131, 140, 141, 142, 143, 144, 145, 152, 153, 154, 155, 156, 157, 159, 176, 310n109

Antal, Frederick, 7

anthropology, xxxiii, 40, 48

Anzaldúa, Gloria, 203

Apian, Peter, 290n13

apparatus, 3, 5, 21, 23, 246, 247, 254, 257, 259. *See also* Ideological State Apparatuses; State, the: state apparatus(es)

appeal, rhetoric of, 68, 90 92. *See also* rhetoric

Arago, François, xvi, 12

archive, xxviii, xxxi, xxxiv, 3, 6, 14, 15, 17, 18, 52, 54, 62, 136, 156, 159, 210, 212, 217, 218, 220, 222, 224, 225, 235

art history, xv, xxvi, xxx, xxxiv, xxxv, xxxviii, 7, 8, 9, 10, 11, 180, 196, 209, 210, 235, 236, 240, 243, 245, 247, 248, 256, 257, 258, 259, 260, 262; New Art History, xxx, 7, 8, 9, 10, 211; social history of art, xxxiv, 7, 8, 10, 210, 236, 245

Artists' Union, 88

John Tagg has taught at universities in Britain and the United States and has directed programs in art history and critical theory for more than thirty years. He is professor of art history and comparative literature at Binghamton University and J. Clawson Mills Fellow in the Department of Photographs at the Metropolitan Museum of Art in New York. He is author of *The Burden of Representation: Essays on Photographies and Histories* (Minnesota, 1993) and *Grounds of Dispute: Art History, Cultural Politics, and the Discursive Field* (Minnesota, 1992).

www.ingramcontent.com/pod-product-compliance
Lightning Source LLC
Chambersburg PA
CBHW072129170526

45158CB00004BA/1300